THE
ANZALDÚAN
THEORY
HANDBOOK

THE ANZALDÚAN THEORY HANDBOOK

AnaLouise Keating

Duke University Press   Durham and London   2022

© 2022 Duke University Press. All rights reserved
Printed in the United States of America on acid-free paper ∞
Typeset in Whitman and Trade Gothic
by Westchester Publishing Services
Cover design by Aimee C. Harrison
Text design by Courtney Leigh Richardson

Library of Congress Cataloging-in-Publication Data
Names: Keating, AnaLouise, [date] author.
Title: The Anzaldúan theory handbook / AnaLouise Keating.
Description: Durham : Duke University Press, 2022. | Includes
bibliographical references and index.
Identifiers: LCCN 2022003201 (print)
LCCN 2022003202 (ebook)
ISBN 9781478016281 (hardcover)
ISBN 9781478018926 (paperback)
ISBN 9781478023555 (ebook)
Subjects: LCSH: Anzaldúa, Gloria. | Anzaldúa, Gloria—Criticism
and interpretation. | Anzaldúa, Gloria—Philosophy. | BISAC: SOCIAL
SCIENCE / Ethnic Studies / American / Hispanic American Studies |
SOCIAL SCIENCE / Feminism & Feminist Theory
Classification: LCC PS3551. N95 Z73 2022 (print) | LCC PS3551. N95
(ebook) | DDC 818/.5409—dc23/eng/20220419
LC record available at https://lccn.loc.gov/2022003201
LC ebook record available at https://lccn.loc.gov/2022003202

COVER ART: Drawing by Aimee C. Harrison inspired by
Gloria Anzaldúa's glifo of a left hand, "Spiritual Activism:
Acts of Vision," first published in *The Gloria Anzaldúa Reader*.

para Gloria, Tildie, y todas almas afines

Contents

Giving Thanks

We receive information from ancestors inhabiting other worlds.
—Gloria Anzaldúa, *Light in the Dark*

This book has been over a decade in the making and has been touched by so many people (both human and more-than-human). How can I possibly mention everyone, given the many subtle influences over the years? Where do I even begin?

With Gloria Evangelina Anzaldúa, of course, who developed the theories explored in this book, who devoted her life to her writing, who boldly shared her ideas with the world, who risked the personal constantly, and who intentionally allowed *her* back to serve as a bridge for so many (*even to this day*). Thank you, Gloria! Thank you for your bold brilliance, your self-confidence, your deep love of writing. Thank you for believing in me, even when I didn't believe in myself. I am so very grateful that you trusted me to read your unpublished work decades ago; your confidence in me, back in the earliest days of my career, has made all the difference. You taught me to trust myself. Your mentorship over the years has shaped me; your friendship sustains me. This book is part of my repayment to you, a token and offering of gratitude.

I thank everyone involved in preserving Anzaldúa's manuscripts for the world. And again, I start with Anzaldúa herself: Thank you, Gloria, for having the foresight to carefully organize, annotate, and save your work—even your earliest fragments and drafts, your intimate writing notas, and so much more. Thank you for your packrat habits. I am so grateful to Hilda Anzaldúa for ongoing support: thank you for your pride in Gloria's accomplishments and your work to ensure their longevity. Thank you to the entire Anzaldúa family, with special thanks to Miranda Garza and Nelda Cantu. I give thanks to Irene Reti, Kit Quan, Christian Kelleher, and the Anzaldúa family for their work to preserve Gloria's work for future generations. I owe so much gratitude to Carla O. Alvarez and the staff at the Nettie Lee Benson Latin American Collection for assistance in helping me access Anzaldúa's archival materials and for all the ongoing work on behalf of this collection. Thanks to Stuart Bernstein for helping the Gloria E. Anzaldúa Literary Trust support Anzaldúa's legacy and for offering such sound advice and wise counsel.

I give thanks to my writing companions and colleagues over the years: conversations along the way with Kristin Alder, Kakali Bhattacharya, Suzanne Bost, Jessica Camp, Norma Cantú, Randy P. Conner, Betsy Dahms, Gabriel Hartley, David Hatfield Sparks, Robyn Henderson-Espinoza, Sara Ishii, Irene Lara, Mariana Ortega, Jessica Sadr, Sonia Saldívar-Hull, Becky Thompson, Ricardo Vivancos-Pérez, Carla Wilson, and Kelli Zaytoun have been invaluable. Special, extra, immense thanks to Suzanne Bost and Kelli Zaytoun for your prompt replies to my queries, for your feedback on various chapter drafts, for our archival excursions and conversations, and for your friendship. This book is better because of your feedback. Suzanne: You read the entire manuscript more than once and offered such generous, thoughtful insights and suggestions. Thank you for asking such great questions and for encouraging me to include more of myself in the book. Thank you, as well, to the anonymous readers of earlier versions of this manuscript: your suggestions greatly improved the finished product. I'm grateful to my graduate students in my Anzaldúa seminars for their interest in and curiosity about Anzaldúa and her theories. Seeing their passion has fed my own.

As usual, the people at Duke University Press have been a joy to work with. I greatly appreciate Gisela Fosado's excitement about this project, patience with this book's lengthy gestation, and useful advice; thanks also to Alejandra Mejía, Jessica Ryan, and everyone else at the press. I also very much appreciate Lisa Sinclair's careful copyediting and Brian Ostrander's attention to detail. (I realize that this project was challenging to edit, given our stylistic idiosyncrasies.) Thanks to the American Learned Society for a $5,000 grant, which helped to offset archival research costs.

I thank my family for all their support. Thank you, Tom and Joann Keating, for giving me such a solid foundation; thank you, Eddy Lynton and Jamitrice KreChelle Keating-Lynton, for your patience, understanding, encouragement, generosity, and all-around support. I'm a very lucky person! Over the years, Gloria has been a presence in our lives, and you have had to share me—first with Gloria, the flesh-and-blood person, and now with her writings and legacy. In my obsession with finishing this book (and many others, over the years), I've been an absent presence, at times. I lack the words to fully express my immense gratitude. Thanks to St. Expedite for jolting me out of the doldrums and hastening completion of this project and others (*Hodie! Hodie! Hodie!*). Thanks to the stone people, to the planets and stars, for support. As always, I am so grateful to the orishas, espíritus, and ancestors for guiding me, whispering words of encouragement that nourish my body/heart/mind/spirit and inspire my vision.

WRITING (ABOUT) ANZALDÚA, INTRODUCING THIS BOOK

In rewriting narratives of identity, nationalism, ethnicity, race, class, gender, sexuality, and aesthetics, I attempt to show (and not just tell) how transformation happens. My job is not just to interpret or describe realities but to create them through language and action, symbols and images. My task is to guide readers and give them the space to co-create, often against the grain of culture, family, and ego injunctions, against external and internal censorship, against the dictates of genes. From infancy our cultures induct us into the semi-trance state of ordinary consciousness, into being in agreement with the people around us, into believing that this is the way things are. It is extremely difficult to shift out of this trance.—Gloria Anzaldúa, *Light in the Dark*

This book offers an in-depth investigation of the theories and philosophy developed by Gloria Evangelina Anzaldúa (1942–2004). A versatile author, Anzaldúa published in a variety of genres: prose, poetry, short stories, hybrid autobiographical narratives, interviews, children's books, monographs, and multigenre edited collections. In addition to her published writings, Anzaldúa produced an enormous amount of unpublished material, including both partial and finished drafts of fiction, poetry, narrative, theory, and much more. As will become evident in what follows, this unpublished material is an overwhelmingly rich source of data with which we can more fully understand, work with, and apply Anzaldúa's philosophy. (*And, as you'll see, "overwhelming" could be the operative word here: Anzaldúa's prolific, generative writing has bequeathed to us a startling, almost endless, abundance of material and ideas with which to work.*) Because her philosophy intentionally and effectively challenges what, in the above epigraph, she calls "the semi-trance state of ordinary consciousness"—the status-quo reality in which we're immersed—it offers vital tools with which we can transform the world. Anzaldúa invites us to enter her intimate philosophical space and, through this invitation, emboldens us to draw on imagination and other alternative ways of thinking (*and feeling*) in order to "co-create" with her. As explained later in more detail, this deep-seated challenge can make Anzaldúa's work uniquely compelling.

As one of the first openly lesbian Chicana authors, Anzaldúa played a major role in exposing (*and transforming*) status-quo definitions of Chicana/o, queer, and female identities. And as editor or co-editor of three groundbreaking multicultural, multigenre feminist anthologies, she played an equally crucial role in shaping western (*especially US*) definitions of feminism, challenging limited approaches to multiculturalism, and developing inclusive movements for social justice. Although she worked outside the formal university system (except for occasional teaching engagements, academic conference "speaking gigs," and several stints in graduate school), Anzaldúa significantly (*and permanently*) impacted many academic fields, including but not limited to American studies, Chicana/o studies, composition studies, cultural studies, ethnic studies, literary studies, LGBTQ studies, and women's and gender studies. She has also permanently impacted feminist and queer theory (*though too often her contributions to the latter are downplayed*), and I predict that her impact on disability studies, esoteric studies, religious studies, and philosophy will continue to grow throughout this century. Her writings have been translated into many languages and excerpted in hundreds of anthologies.[1] And, as the development of the Society for the Study of Gloria Anzaldúa demonstrates, her words speak to a wide range of people located inside, outside, and straddling the academy: intellectuals, artists, educators, healers, social justice activists, and others from a wide range of social and geographic locations find Anzaldúa's work to be inspiring and transformational. Through the pages, across the years, within the metaphors, Anzaldúa's words find their way into the bodies, hearts, and minds of many. (*Although this last statement might sound a bit corny, it attests to the feedback I've consistently received, as people from many locations marvel at the impact of Anzaldúa's words on their psyches, spirits, and/or lives. It also corresponds beautifully to my opening epigraph, in which Anzaldúa asserts that her task is to give readers "the space to co-create"; I contend that this space begins within the individual, expanding [us] out into the world.)*

I have written this book for these people, and for Anzaldúa herself. I want her work to become even better known; I want readers to recognize, access, and apply the breadth of her theories, to more fully appreciate the generative potential of her words, and to become personally and collectively empowered through (*and by*) the process. For years, I've wondered why her sophisticated theories and powerful writing were not more fully studied and better known. Sure, many people (especially in ethnic, women's, and feminist studies) are aware of her work, but many in other academic disciplines are not. My goal with this book is to help Anzaldúa's work become even more widely respected, available, applied, and in other ways used. I want to give her work a hand, so to speak. (*Indeed, this desire inspired my book's title:* The Anzaldúan Theory Handbook.)

More specifically, I have five interrelated goals: (1) to offer an in-depth, expansive genealogical understanding of Anzaldúa's theories and the contextual/biographical dimensions of her work; (2) to encourage a more extensive engagement with a wide range of Anzaldúa's published and unpublished writings and to provide readers with additional tools to facilitate this engagement; (3) to explore (*and build on*) Anzaldúa's dialogic method, so that we might more fully appreciate, work with, and apply it; (4) to share what I've learned with others, so that they (*you*) might take the work even further; and, thus, (5) to develop and showcase an innovative approach to decolonial wisdom traditions and "doing" theory. I aspire to broaden and deepen Anzaldúan scholarship, shifting the conversation in new directions while underscoring the visionary yet pragmatic social justice dimensions of her work. And, because Anzaldúa brought innovation, imagination, and spirit into her philosophical worldview and theory creation, I have tried to do the same. I offer an investigation that, like Anzaldúa herself, challenges the academic status quo and "the semi-trance state of ordinary consciousness."

While some of Anzaldúa's theories (particularly those of the borderlands, the new mestiza, and mestiza consciousness, as presented in *Borderlands/La Frontera*) have received much well-deserved scholarly attention over the years, and other theories (like conocimiento, nepantla, and spiritual activism) have received increased attention in the twenty-first century, still other theories (like autohistoria and autohistoria-teoría, nos/otras, new tribalism, geographies of selves, and El Mundo Zurdo) have received less attention, although scholarly interest in them continues to grow.[2] The over-emphasis on select theories is not surprising, given that they're easily accessible in Anzaldúa's published work while other theories are most fully articulated in unpublished writings. (*That said, I can't help but wonder: How might Anzaldúa's use of Spanish to name many of her theories have hindered some scholars—especially those unfamiliar with Spanish—in engaging deeply with her work? Does the provocative nature of some theories inhibit theorists' explorations, leading them to pay most attention to those that seem "safer"?*) However, as I demonstrate in what follows, these lesser-studied theories are crucial for those readers hoping to understand the development of Anzaldúa's thinking, the complexity of her work, and its relevance for contemporary life. By investigating those dimensions of Anzaldúa's theories, writings, and methods that have received less critical attention and by exploring the interconnections between these overlooked concepts and Anzaldúa's better-known theories, this book opens additional areas of investigation, offers new entry into Anzaldúa's thought, and models additional ways to "do" Anzaldúan theory.

Key to this in-depth investigation has been my years-long engagement with Anzaldúa's archives, especially her enormous (*overwhelming*) collection of manuscript drafts and writing notes.[3] Indeed, as I demonstrate in the following chapters, Anzaldúa's stunning collection is her most complex, contradictory, and open-ended text (*or, perhaps, texts*)—filled with intimate, unexpected glimpses into Anzaldúa's worlds. As Suzanne Bost notes, this unfinished archival text challenges and, at times, upends scholars' most cherished ideas about Anzaldúa and her work. (*I'm so excited for you to accompany me on this deep dive into Anzaldúa's archives!*) For over half a decade, I've immersed myself in Anzaldúa's manuscripts in order to track her writing process, understand her complex theory-creation method, trace the synergistic development of key theories, and more fully comprehend her overarching philosophical framework. In the following pages, I share my discoveries with you. When I drafted my proposal for this project, I planned to showcase my own thinking, to offer analyses and applications of Anzaldúa's theories, creating a conventional academic book (*a "monograph" on Anzaldúa*). However, the more deeply I dove into her theories, the less closely I followed my original plan. Anzaldúa's manuscripts upended my project, inviting (*compelling!*) me to change tracks, to focus more closely on the theories themselves, rather than on my personal insights, analyses, and applications.

And yet, I could not remove myself entirely from this study: not only would the adoption of an objective voice be duplicitous (*because we're all, by virtue of our time in these human bodies, subjective, partial, and biased*), but Anzaldúa herself would have strongly critiqued this pseudo-objectivity (*and haunted my dreams*). Since the early 1990s, she has encouraged me to put myself into my writing, to include my voice and perspective (*not in a Look-at-me! Look-at-what-I-can-do! kind of way but rather in a dialogic, co-creative approach*) as I explore and interact with her work. And so, to honor Anzaldúa's guidance while foregrounding *her* work, I've used parentheses and italics to earmark the most subjective (*opinionated, and/or provocative*) statements. Spending so much time over the years with Anzaldúa and her work has enriched my own scholarship and emboldened my voice. With her guidance, I've learned to dive deeply into my inner wisdom, encountering there what she theorized as el cenote.[4] She has created the path, inviting and encouraging me to dive deeply and, through this deep-diving excavation, to risk the personal in startling ways.

Risking the Personal

I've designed this book to generate new dialogues and conversations that will enrich Anzaldúan scholarship (*and the experiences of other Anzaldúa readers*) in at least three interrelated ways: First, I foreground the personal, defined broadly to include both individually and culturally specific elements, both psychic and physical experiences. Throughout her career, in theory and practice, Anzaldúa emphasized the importance of incorporating the personal into the written word. And when I say "the personal," I mean the intimate personal, the shameful personal, the details about ourselves that we tend to hide—even from ourselves. Anzaldúa's use of the personal goes so far beyond that conventional feminist slogan ("the personal is the political") that I developed a theory, "risking the personal," to understand and describe it. As I explained in my introduction to Anzaldúa's edited collection of interviews, *Interviews/Entrevistas*, throughout her work (and in conversation), Anzaldúa

> draws extensively on her own life—her early menstruation; her campesino background; her childhood in the Rio Grande Valley of South

Texas; her experiences as a brown-skinned, Spanish-speaking girl in a dominant culture that values light-skinned, English-speaking boys; and her sexual and spiritual desires, to mention only a few of the many private issues woven into her words. And you'll find this same willingness to risk the personal—to disclose intimate details, beliefs, and emotions—taken to a further extreme throughout the interviews collected in this volume. The risks are real, as Anzaldúa exposes intimate details about her life, her beliefs, and her desires. ("Risking" 2)

When I first wrote these words I believed that Anzaldúa's main purpose in risking the personal was to make profound connections with readers. By diving so deeply into her own life, and by sharing her deepest, most secret insights and desires with others, she invites us into her worlds, so that we might connect deeply with her: "By incorporating her own life into her work, Anzaldúa transforms herself into a bridge and creates potential identifications with readers from diverse backgrounds. She models a process of self-disclosure which invites (and sometimes compels) us to take new risks as we reflect on our own experiences, penetrate the privacy of our own lives" (2).

After having spent two more decades with Anzaldúa and her work, exploring her theory-making process in all its messy chaotic detail, I now believe that risking the personal is even more complex and thoughtful than I'd previously assumed. In part, this shift comes simply from the extra time I've spent with Anzaldúa and her manuscripts. But also, after deeply exploring her theories of el cenote, conocimiento, and nepantla, I recognize the philosophical framework (including, especially, what I've named her metaphysics of radical interconnectedness) that undergirds this method. More specifically, Anzaldúa's metaphysics of radical interconnectedness posits that each individual (*both human and more-than-human*) is interrelated with all existence: personhood does not stop with our skin, our individual self-enclosed identity, our simple life (birth date, history, and so on). Rather, we are each a walking representation/expression of spirit, linked at psychic subterranean levels with all others (*and "other" here exceeds and precedes the human*). This interrelatedness ensures that, when we dive deeply (*and boldly*) into our own psyches to access new insights, we discover/receive insights that resonate powerfully with others.

Risking the personal is multidimensional and key to Anzaldúa's method of knowledge creation for herself, as well as her readers. By diving so very deeply into her own life, and by engaging dialogically with everything (*and everyone*) she encountered, Anzaldúa opened herself to the cosmos and enacted theory-building conversations. As I explain in chapter 1, risking the personal is not about self-elevation, solipsistic navel-gazing, or confessional self-expression. It is, rather, a vehicle for intimate engagement with readers. Intense excavation into the most personal dimensions of her life is part of Anzaldúa's method: diving deeply into her own psyche, and beyond, into el cenote, she arrives at insights and creates knowledge that profoundly impacts our lives.

This book honors Anzaldúa's emphasis on the personal in other ways as well: in addition to exploring her theories of autohistoria and autohistoria-teoría (which, as explained later in more detail, are intimately concerned with the personal), I draw on biographical events in Anzaldúa's life, my own extensive interactions with Anzaldúa, and my experiences editing her work to complicate and deepen this investigation of Anzaldúan theory and to offer new insights into her writing and theorizing process. (*And here, I guess you could say, I, too, risk the personal—both my own personal and Anzaldúa's, as I showcase some of our weirdest, least rational experiences and beliefs. As a very private person, I find these risks quite challenging.*)

This book foregrounds Anzaldúa's unpublished writings, which are incredibly extensive (*and often highly—indeed, almost unbelievably—personal*). A perfectionist, Anzaldúa produced multiple drafts of each published piece and left a vast range of unpublished material—including both partial and completed (but never published) projects.[5] These unpublished manuscripts offer intimate entry into Anzaldúa's mind, illuminating her philosophy and method. I've drawn on this material, putting it into dialogue with her published work to offer new insights into her process; to model an archival research method with important implications for Anzaldúan studies (and for other archival studies—particularly those focused on women-of-colors[6] authors); and to uncover additional dimensions of her theories (including, for instance, the shift from the Medusa state to the Coatlicue state; the interrelationships among her epistemological theories of la facultad, new mestiza consciousness, nepantla, and conocimiento; and the origins of her theory of spiritual activism). I have spent almost two decades immersed in Anzaldúa's unpublished writings, and in this book I share much (*but not all*) of what I've learned. I want others to benefit from my efforts, to learn from my mistakes, and in other ways to build on what I offer. (*And throughout the following chapters, I provide suggestions for ways to do so.*)

I showcase the rich multiplicity, the wild diversity, and the generative potential in Anzaldúa's work. I want this book to increase scholarly
and activist engagement with Anzaldúa's theories; open new directions
in Anzaldúan scholarship; model additional forms that critical thinking,
literary analysis, and theorizing can take; and transform our approach
to scholarship. In short, I've written the book that I wanted to read years
ago: a book that takes risks, that dives deeply into Anzaldúa's intimate beliefs (including the metaphysical, psychic, and esoteric), that looks at Anzaldúa's intense, highly political engagement with spirit, that acknowledges
Anzaldúa's provocative perspectives on identity—and that does this work,
and more, with intellectual humility. I wanted a book that could help me
make sense of Anzaldúa's torturously recursive writing process, a book I
could share with my students and others—with anyone interested in learning more about Anzaldúa, her theories, and/or themselves. I wanted an
accessible book—a book that didn't rely on overly elite theoretical language
(*though, as I discuss in chapter 2 and as Anzaldúa notes in "haciendo caras,"
there's a place and a time for "high" theory*). I wanted a book with legs, a
book that would inspire us to do additional work. A profound, practical,
energizing book.

Mapping This Book's Trajectory: An Overview

This book is divided into three parts. Part I, "Prelude to Theorizing: Contexts and Methods," includes three chapters offering a framework with
which to more fully understand the origins, depth, and breadth of Anzaldúan theories. No one writes in a vacuum. Our bodies, our surroundings,
all the minutia of our lives, and so much more subtly (*and not so subtly*)
shape whatever we produce. This obvious fact is doubly (*or TRIPLY*) true
in the case of Anzaldúa, who risked the personal—constantly and in startling ways. She dove deeply into the stuff of her own life, metaphorically
ripping open her heart to and for her writing.[7] To more fully understand
the development of Anzaldúa's theories and unique perspectives, we must
understand her life—at least, in part. (*And here I emphasize the partiality of
our understanding. To presume we could ever understand the totality of another's life [or even our own] is hubris.*) Chapter 1, "Risking the Personal, Redux:
A Biographical-Intellectual Sketch," offers a biographical overview to assist
readers in situating the theories in the life and the life in the theories, expanding your appreciation for both. As the title suggests, this exploration

of Anzaldúa's life focuses especially on her thought; although intimate, it's not exhaustive. It's a sketch: neither a portrait, nor a mural.

Writing was central to Anzaldúa; it was her destiny and vocation. As she asserts in her unpublished writing notas, "I write . . . to create a new reality. I write because it's my calling, my task to do in the world. I write. It is a ritual, a habit, a propensity bred in my bones. . . . I write because I like to think on paper. I write because I like to think, and to track my thoughts. I write because I want to leave a discernable mark on the world" (Writing Notas G). Chapter 2, "Writing as Ritual, Habit, Mission, Partner, and Joy: Anzaldúa's Writing Process," dives deeply into Anzaldúa's relationship to writing, focusing especially on its intuitive, collective, creative, metaphysical dimensions. Like many authors, Anzaldúa did not proceed in linear fashion, from fully developed idea to logically organized outline to completed essay. She generated her ideas as she wrote, and the writing process was, itself, a co-creator of the theories—a co-author of sorts. As she explains in a 1991 interview, "I discover what I'm trying to say as the writing progresses" (*Interviews* 174). Anzaldúa often began a new project (whether story, essay, or poem) with a question, a personal experience, an urgent need, an intuitive hunch, or an emotional gesture; conducting what I call "oracular research," she worked through these seedling ideas as she wrote and revised, and she did so in ways only partially under her conscious control. Through this radically recursive process, the words took on lives of their own, morphing in ways that often (*perhaps almost always*) surprised Anzaldúa herself. In short, she learned as she wrote; she developed her ideas as she revised. And for Anzaldúa, revision was endless. In chapter 2, I draw from my analyses of her manuscripts and her published discussions of writing, as well as my experiences working with her, to offer an overview of her writing process. (*Anzaldúa's process both mirrors and has shaped my own, especially concerning this book, which has truly taken on a life of its own, growing into a format quite different from what I set out to produce.*)

Anzaldúa's creative process emerged from and was anchored in her relational worldview—her metaphysics of radical interconnectedness. Whether writing poetry, short stories, narratives, essays, or other prose, she did so within a dialogic framework that was multilayered, recursive, and relational. Anzaldúan theory emerged in conversation with Anzaldúa's life, shaped by her physical circumstances, events, and contexts at that time, or what I call *situational engines*: factors, forces, and environments that initiated and/or directed (but did not entirely control) the theory's development. Chapter 3, "How the Theories Emerged: Haciendo teorías con Gloria," explores these situational engines, as well as Anzaldúa's complex relationship to theory and the act of theorizing (both inside and outside higher education). Each Anzaldúan theory was shaped by the specific contexts and events of her life at that particular time: the profound drive to be a writer; the urge to create; the need to earn a living; the struggles (*and joys*) of embodied existence (*including very early, extremely painful menstruation; short stature; dark skin; insomnia; type 1 diabetes and its cascading impacts; and much more*); the friends and people around her; the ideas Anzaldúa encountered in books, school, trees, water, and the beyond-human world; intellectual trends of the day; external local, national, and international political events; invitations to write and/or speak on a specific topic; funding opportunities; and so on.

With background and context firmly established, part II, "The Theories Themselves," focuses on eighteen key Anzaldúan theories. Like many scholars, I first read Anzaldúan theory as though each arrived into the world fully developed and thus as somewhat static. However, this assumption (*and approach*) is too limited (*and limiting*). After having spent so much time working with Anzaldúa—both in person and in spirit—I've realized that each theory emerged slowly over time, taking unexpected shifts, breaks, detours, and departures. To share what I've learned through my multiyear analysis, part II consists of one lengthy chapter (chapter 4), broken into eighteen subchapters, each offering an overview and genealogy of an Anzaldúan theory: autohistoria and autohistoria-teoría, borderlands, el cenote, the Coatlicue state, conocimiento, the Coyolxauhqui process, desconocimiento(s), la facultad, geographies of selves, El Mundo Zurdo, la naguala, nepantla, nepantleras, new mestiza, new mestiza consciousness, new tribalism, nos/otras, and spiritual activism. Each entry includes several sections: carefully selected opening quotations, a (*relatively*) succinct definition, the theory's story (origins and development), related Anzaldúan theories, questions to explore in future research, and key manuscripts that scholars might find useful when investigating the theory.

From these investigations, we move even more deeply into Anzaldúa's unpublished materials in part III, "Excavating the Future: The Archives and Beyond." As the title to this section might suggest, I invite you to approach Anzaldúa's archives in the tradition of Sankofa (the Akan word and principle reminding us that when we go backward, to retrieve the wisdom of the past, we can move forward more effectively, creating better anchored, more brilliant futures). The final chapters look back, to explore Anzaldúa's archives; they offer insights about this archival material that can assist us in creating the future of Anzaldúan studies—a future firmly rooted in Anzaldúa's own work. (*Here, too, we follow Anzaldúa's serpentine pattern and process.*)

As if she knew that she'd become a well-known author, Anzaldúa began saving her papers and manuscript drafts in the 1970s and carefully (*some might say obsessively*) preserved material related to her creative process throughout the remainder of her life. And, because she devoted her life to her writing and was a perfectionist with her craft, she produced many drafts of each published piece and left an enormous amount of unpublished material that includes both partial and completed projects. Her archive, the Gloria Evangelina Anzaldúa Papers, located at the Nettie Lee Benson Latin American Collection, University of Texas, Austin, is enormous: It consists of hundreds of boxes which if stacked in a line would take up more than 125 feet; the boxes are packed with documents spanning Anzaldúa's life—from birth certificates to obituaries, and beyond. Anzaldúa saved a startlingly wide array of materials: fiction, poetry, and essay manuscripts; an entire play in poetic verse; multiple versions of her pre-*Borderlands* autobiography; early drafts of *Borderlands* with unexpected, highly significant authorial *and* editorial revisions; thousands of pages of writing/research notas; letters, emails, and other correspondence; candle affirmations; Tarot, I Ching, channeled, and astrology readings; favorite books filled with marginalia; drawings, glifos, and doodles; audio and video recordings of writing workshops, meditations, and speaking gigs; and much more. In short, the archive is an enormous, untapped resource filled with secrets and potential insights.

However, at least in part because of Anzaldúa's recursive, complex creative process, it's incredibly challenging to make our way through the material. Even the finding aid (*over one hundred pages in length!*) can seem daunting. Anzaldúa's archives defy linear, chronological organization; they overwhelm us, causing us to overlook hidden treasures. In part III, I offer information, tools, and guidance that make these materials more accessible for readers. I also share fascinating insights to deepen our appreciation for Anzaldúa's contributions while expanding our understanding of her work. Chapter 5 focuses on the archive and chapter 6 on the material within the archive.

Drawing on my experiences as part of the team assembling Anzaldúa's materials after her death, as well as my experiences as her "writing comadre" and editor, chapter 5, "The Gloria Evangelina Anzaldúa Papers: Creation Story, Treasure Map, and More," serves as an origin story. In it, I retell the archives' biography, from emergence to current status. Chapter 6, "Anzaldúa's Archival Manuscripts: Overview, Insights, Annotations," offers brief annotations of Anzaldúa's prose manuscripts. Perhaps only the most avid scholars and biggest fans will read this chapter from start to finish (*but what stories it can tell, if you take the time to do so!*). I envision this chapter more as a tool (*or perhaps an entire toolbox*) for scholars and other Anzaldúa readers who'd like to get a more solid sense of Anzaldúa's range (*the incredibly diverse variety of topics she explored*), depth (*for instance, the many manuscripts on a single topic*), and influences (*naguala, poststructuralism, graduate school, and so on*). I have aspired to offer a chapter that can streamline your research (*and maximize your time at the archive*) while also increasing your appreciation for Anzaldúa and her work.

And, finally, the book concludes with a brief postscript in which I offer some suggestions for how to work with Anzaldúa and her theories.

As this brief summary of the book's contents suggests, while in some ways *The Anzaldúan Theory Handbook* functions more like a conventional monograph than a handbook, in other ways it does not. (*Just look at chapter 6! Or the very long chapter 4! Or all these italicized statements!*). But how could a monograph on Anzaldúan theories be conventional, given the unconventionality of the theories themselves—made even more unconventional by Anzaldúa's radical faith in her readers' creative inner wisdom?

PART I

PRELUDE TO
THEORIZING:
CONTEXTS AND
METHODS

1. RISKING THE PERSONAL, REDUX

A Biographical-Intellectual Sketch

What gave me strength to resist that pull of class and cultural injunctions was the fact that I was a freak. Or rather, that the world had made me a freak. That freakishness was the source of my stubbornness. It was what taught me to be angry, to be rebellious, to refuse. I'd listen to the wind howl, and wonder if it was *la Llorona's* wail. I'd hear the coyotes howling, hear *los perros ladrando*. The patient endurance of cactus. The deep rooted mesquites. These sounds always took me back to when I was four or five years old.—Anzaldúa, "Autohistoria de la artista as a Young Girl"

Born on September 26, 1942, in South Texas to Urbano and Amelia Anzaldúa, sixth-generation Mexican American rancher-farmers, Gloria Evangelina Anzaldúa was intimately acquainted with difference—or what, in the above epigraph, she describes as "freakishness." She had a number of salient differences from the dominating cultural norms—differences of ancestry, class, language, and embodiment (*especially her body*). Anzaldúa's physical differences began with her emergence into this world: she was born with a rare hormonal condition that marked her infancy and triggered puberty at the age of six, when she grew to her adult height of four feet eleven inches and began experiencing inexpressibly painful monthly menses. As she recalls in "Autohistoria de la artista as a Young Girl,"

Other children do not double over with lightning stabs. They do not have 106 degree fevers that turn their curly hair straight. They do not live with a dull persistent pain, do not wash bloody rags, gagging on the menstrual odors, hanging them on shrubs in secret, hiding them from brothers, uncles, cousins. At age six, other children do not have budding rose tits under tight muslin girdles, wear a rag pinned to their panties, they do not refuse to take communal showers *cúbrete, escóndelo*. They do not shoot up to tower, skinny and hunched, with faint blue veins, ears you can see light through. No wonder these ordinary children guessed something was "wrong" with her.

As this passage suggests, Anzaldúa's early sense of difference was complex and impossible to fully articulate: her physiological differences were visual to others but also hidden; the intense physical pain she experienced each month, coupled with these marked differences, estranged her from her own body at a very early age.

These physical differences were compounded by Anzaldúa's experiences as a young Spanish-speaking Chicana in South Texas's segregated education system, where she was treated as inferior because of her Mexican heritage. Indeed, this negative treatment began with the young Anzaldúa's first day in school, in 1948. Because the name listed by the state was different from her actual name, the young Gloria did not respond when the Anglo teacher called roll for attendance; she was punished and deeply shamed for this unintentional silence.[1] From kindergarten through high school, Anzaldúa was marked as different from her peers. An eager learner, she worked diligently in school and excelled in her coursework; in high school she was separated from her Chicanx peers and placed in accelerated classes where she was typically the only Chicana. As she explains in an interview, "That segregation, even more, cut me away from friends because the white kids didn't want anything to do with me and the teachers weren't used to having such a bright Chicana" (*Interviews* 23).

Anzaldúa's radical, multilayered sense of difference and alienation profoundly shaped her philosophy, politics, and career by fostering both a deep empathy for other outsiders and the desire to create a more equitable, radically inclusive world—seen in theories like El Mundo Zurdo, nos/otras, and las nepantleras. (*I attribute her generous inclusiveness, at least in part, to these early personal experiences of alienation and rejection for not fitting into the various norms. She understood, viscerally, the injustice and pain of this ar-*

bitrary exclusion, and she worked to alter the restrictive norms while creating expansive concepts of community.) Anzaldúa attributed her desire to write, teach, and philosophize to her experiences of alienation. As she states in "On the Process of Writing *Borderlands/La Frontera*," "These feelings of being an outsider, an alien, generated in me the impetus to explain things to myself and others. Communicating feelings often makes me feel like a tea kettle letting off steam. While writing and speaking act as a safety valve, they are also political acts that spring from the impulse to subvert, resist, educate, and make changes" (187).

With the South Texas landscape (*what she often refers to as "the monte" and translates as "woods, mountains, countryside"*) and its many more-than-human occupants, Anzaldúa experienced an intimacy and acceptance that she did not find at school (*or, perhaps, even with her own body*). This intimacy offered models for dialogic engagement with her surroundings that would greatly impact her theory-making process. Boundaries blurred, and she was viscerally aware of the sentience in trees, mesquite, lagoon, and more. Her early story, "El paisano is a bird of good omen," offers insight into Anzaldúa's intuitive interconnections with the more-than-human world. These dialogic encounters were also facilitated through her deeply empathic nature. Even as a very young child, the boundaries between herself (*her physical body*) and the outer world became permeable (*Interviews* 25–26). Through her time outdoors, in the monte, she developed a deep sense of relational selfhood and groundedness with the South Texas land that nurtured her writing and taught her the transformational impact of words: "I also belong to a landscape essential to my survival, one that is carved into my very bones. I was a thin sun-baked child playing in the *monte* who believed in the magic power of words. A word once spoken affected the world, could change things" ("Autohistoria"). These early experiences deeply impacted her animist metaphysics and, thus, her theoretical framework. It was also here, in the monte, where Anzaldúa first encountered her nagual ("Autohistoria"), a spirit guide who remained with her throughout her life, entering into her work most prominently via her later theory of la naguala.

From her family (*especially her grandmothers and father*), Anzaldúa inherited a love of stories that confirmed her experiences with multiple, overlapping realities filled with shape-shifters, naguales, La Llorona, and all sorts of spirits. As she recounts in various interviews, her father encouraged her love of reading and underscored the importance of school, including a college education. Anzaldúa was a voracious reader, often consuming multiple books in a single day. Reading brought escape from her current situations, from her feelings of alienation, isolation, and weirdness; and, perhaps more importantly, books gave her access to a world of ideas and new perspectives that she used to help make sense of her life. As she recalls in "Autohistoria de la artista as a Young Girl,"

> As soon as I can read, I begin to devour the school library shelf by shelf. The search for knowledge dominates my childhood. At a very early age I want to be a philosopher/artist/writer, to have access to knowledge, *y sabiduría*. Knowledge will tell me who I am and why I'm in pain, and how best to deal with it. I get the poet-philosopher idea from reading Nietzsche, and strategies for coping with pain from *The Meditations of Marcus Aurelius*. From *Jane Eyre* I learn about human dignity, and from books on horses I learn endurance to oppression. When I shut my eyes I see a whipped and spur-raked horse valiantly withstanding its human tormentors.

This love of learning and search for healing wisdom traditions animated Anzaldúa's life, motivating her interest in education, ideas, philosophy, survival, and transformation. Through reading, Anzaldúa entered other worlds, acquired additional knowledge, and encountered others like herself. Characters like Jane Eyre, who affirmed Anzaldúa's uniqueness, were especially important. The books she "devoured" changed her, nourishing her lifelong confidence in the power of language to impact and shape reality at the most intimate of levels. In "Mujeres que tienen lengua" Anzaldúa associated her voracious reading with her later decision to be a writer: "I may have started to write to escape from a world I couldn't control, into one that I could manipulate." As she became intimately aware of the imagination's world-building power, she worked to harness it in order to create new knowledge, develop more inclusive communities, and enact additional ways to effect progressive social change.

Anzaldúa's love of reading intensified after her father's death in June 1958, when she was fifteen years old. The death was violent and completely unexpected: his aorta burst as he was driving, causing the truck to veer off the road and crash. This startling event entirely disrupted Anzaldúa's life and shattered her worldview, increasing her responsibilities at home and impacting family dynamics. (As the oldest child, Anzaldúa took on additional work and tried diligently to support her mother.) This apparently senseless event compelled her to question her family's beliefs and those of organized religion—especially assumptions concerning stark epistemological-ontological divisions like those between good and evil or between heaven and hell.[2] Anzaldúa narrates this life-changing event in her early autohistoria, "People Should Not Die in June in South Texas," which concludes with a bleak rejection of monotheistic religion and conventional beliefs.

Anzaldúa began keeping a formal journal in October 1961, when she was in high school. Even in this early journal, we see her desire to read and think, to do what she calls "brainwork," to become a philosopher, to be well-known for her writing. Or, as she states in her entry of November 14, 1961, "I told myself to keep in mind my purpose in living—To become a *great* writer—to ward off inactivity and in difference [*sic*] towards a new day." The early journals functioned as a record of her inner life (especially her intellectual life) and a confidant with whom she shared intimate details and mundane occurrences. She often used lists to organize her thinking and emotions; enumerate and examine her values; track the intentions, goals, and progress of her various writing projects; and brainstorm ideas for specific pieces. She recorded insights from her imaginal journeys and conversations with her soul ("Antigua"), poetry fragments and initial drafts, short story ideas, messages from her nagual, daimon, and other inner guides;[3] notes from numerology and other spiritual/magickal technologies; quotations and insights gleaned from her extensive, wide-ranging reading; and much more. Journaling was a vital part of Anzaldúa's life and a key participant in her creative production from the 1960s onward; typically, she filled at least one notebook each year until around the 1990s when she partially transitioned into writing notas. (*I mark the beginning of Anzaldúa's philosophical and literary careers with these early journals; they offered her the private space necessary to freely explore her thoughts, to unleash her imagination, to grapple with her emotions and fears, to plant the seeds that grew roots, branches, and leaves.*)

As discussed earlier, despite the ongoing discrimination she experienced in school, Anzaldúa excelled and enjoyed learning.[4] Because she believed that education offered an effective vehicle to enact progressive social change (and give young Mexican American children better educational experiences than her own), she obtained her teaching certificate in college and, after graduating, worked in the Texas public school system, where she taught students from preschool through high school while battling the same racist system she had experienced. During summers she attended graduate school at the University of Texas, Austin, earning a master's degree in English and Education. Discouraged by the Texas public school system's entrenched racism, Anzaldúa left the state for Indiana, where she worked from May 1973 to September 1974 as a liaison between the Indiana public school system and migrant farm workers' children, advising teachers and administrators on curriculum and pedagogies while checking in on the children themselves.

Even as she supported herself through this education-related work, Anzaldúa pursued her interest in writing. By the early 1970s Anzaldúa aspired to make a unique, lasting contribution to the world through her literary work, writing in her journal on September 21, 1973,

> In 39 yrs. The lang. will be different. If this is so, how can my writing last as long, or longer. A new literary/media invention in a verbal/visual form? A new invention, one that will adapt to change. One tries to out guess the lang. changes. Write something and leave out "the"? Revise the spelling? Write in short form? Simplify? What??

As this passage suggests, she approached the question of enduring fame through aesthetics, seeking an innovative style with which to convey her innovative thoughts. In spring 1974, Anzaldúa enrolled in a creative writing course at Indiana University where she received a boost to her confidence through the encouragement of her instructor, Mrs. Hemley. As she notes in an entry on February 11, 1974, "She gave me encouragement. She said I had a rare *intelligence*, had a lot of potential *talent*, and that I was very *creative*." Hemley also introduced Anzaldúa to Julio Cortázar's work, stating that Anzaldúa's writing resembled his: "Mrs. Hemley (get this!) said that I was the best writer, the one with the most potential [in the class.] . . . I felt so good. Now, I'm going to have to justify her belief in me."

Although Anzaldúa took the position in Indiana in order to make a positive difference in the lives of young migrant children, she again found the system too rigid. After a year at the job, she decided that she could be more effective in making social change with a doctoral degree: "The most receptive minds are in the universities, or so I'm told. With a doctorate I'll be able to teach Chicanos and Chicanas there. *Ando toda tníliada* [*sic*], as Chicana and female of course the university will give me a T.A.ship" ("Autohistoria"). And so, Anzaldúa resigned from her job, withdrew her savings, and in fall 1974 enrolled in the PhD program in Comparative Literature at the

University of Texas, Austin. However, the economic possibilities fell short of her expectations; she did not receive a teaching assistantship or other support, and she became even more dissatisfied with organized education: "But I end up painting rooms and sweeping halls for my rent. I'm tired of fighting. There's something wrong with this system that has no room for me" ("Autohistoria"). It's worth noting the quiet confidence in this statement. Though beaten down by discriminatory experiences in graduate school and dogged by financial insecurity, Anzaldúa was sufficiently sure of her own powers and value that she did not internalize the treatment she received but instead turned the mirror toward the systemic issues.[5] (*This quiet yet very solid confidence occurs elsewhere in Anzaldúa's life: it runs like an underground river throughout Anzaldúa's unpublished self-reflective writings; it turns outward, expressed in her confidence in her writing comadres' ability to offer useful feedback on her writing, and inward, woven into her theories of la facultad, el cenote, and conocimiento.*)

Graduate School (1970s)

Despite continued economic challenges, Anzaldúa's three years in Austin were a time of great intellectual, personal, political, and psychic growth. An avid student of ideas, she loved exploring new concepts, philosophies, and worldviews. As she notes in a journal entry on June 24, 1974, "I would like to be a professional college student. I love to learn. I love to read."

Through her friendships (*especially her friendship with Randy Conner*) Anzaldúa was introduced to feminism and feminist theory, which gave her additional tools with which to expose, examine, and challenge the status-quo stories (or what Anzaldúa called "consensual reality") that supported socially unjust systems. As she states years later in her 1996 writing notas, "Unconsciously accepted viewpoints as natural, as reality, need to be questioned in order to create a just social order. Feminism is the most promising active political movement working for change in the world" (107.13). Anzaldúa continued to read voraciously, exploring Mesoamerican history and myth, esoteric knowledge traditions, astrology, European literature, contemporary theory, and much more.[6] As this list suggests, she did not assume that feminism, Marxism, and other political theories offered the only approach to effecting radical change. In addition, she sought avenues to effect metaphysical, deep structural change. As part of these ontological explorations she experimented with "mushrooms, peyote and LSD" at least in part to "get a more accurate reading of the nature of reality" ("Cono-cimientos").[7] Anzaldúa read a wide range of esoteric literature, including parapsychology, alchemy, and eastern philosophy, and implemented what she read in her own life: she meditated, experimented with astral travel, practiced self-reflection exercises designed to cultivate "feeling-tones," and adopted other nonordinary practices.[8] Anzaldúa discussed these experiences in her journals and interviews, later translating them into fiction and poetry. Although taking a full load of courses, she continued her political activist work, participating in various social justice movements such as the Chicano movement, farm workers', anti-war, civil rights, and women's rights movements. She also devoted much time to her creative writing, producing short stories, a novella, and poetry. In at least one course, she was able to negotiate with her professor, who allowed her to produce a short story rather than the more conventional academic project.

Despite her important friendships, Anzaldúa also experienced insomnia, great loneliness, and erasure, leading to what she later described as her "unconscious suicide attempt due to isolation and invisibility in graduate school" ("On My Method"). In part, these feelings of estrangement were due to her isolation as one of only a very few Chicanas in her doctoral program; moreover, the curriculum was overwhelmingly Eurocentric, and this cultural erasure further marginalized her. Other events impacted her as well. In November 1974 Anzaldúa was mugged while leaving campus. Although she chased down the thief and testified against him in court, the mugger's violent threats of revenge, combined with the physical assault of the mugging itself, intensified her insomnia and further eroded her sense of security. The mugging also initiated her into new levels of psychic experiences. As Anzaldúa explains in her conversation with Christine Weiland, "That mugging opened me up because it was a violation of my spirit, an invasion" (*Interviews* 103). In the months and years following this event, Anzaldúa experienced additional metaphysical openings, including a vastation and a series of vibrational encounters with spirits, as well as dreams and/or travels to other realms that "showed [her] the existence of other worlds"[9] (*Interviews* 104). She describes these experiences in her unpublished early autohistorias, her Prieta stories, and *Light in the Dark/Luz en lo Oscuro*. (*I mention these events here because they permanently marked Anzaldúa's life and work, inviting her to broaden and deepen her philosophical explorations. They assured her that reality is much larger than we have assumed, that the line*

between human and more-than-human worlds can be blurred. Perhaps most im-
portantly, they affirmed her early experiences, the folklore she learned as a child,
and offered her a vital source of potential agency that could be accessed through
self-reflection, thought, and imagination. I believe that Anzaldúa recognized the
possibilities: regardless of our external situations [our bank account, our ap-
pearance, our age, etc.], we can tap tremendous inner power which connects us
with a much larger outer world and opens us to possibilities for transformation.
These possibilities—and this relational, multidimensional worldview—offer a
compelling alternative to the Cartesian Eurocentric worldview that Anzaldúa
and many others encountered in western literature and education.)

By the mid-1970s, then, Anzaldúa had embraced (*or, perhaps, "co-created" would be a more accurate term*) an expansive metaphysical system analogous to (*if not in some ways identical to*) an animist philosophy. While she believed in the radical potential of each human being, she avoided conventional forms of hyper-individualism, instead situating us in extremely relational terms. As she notes in an October 1975 journal entry, "People are like ants and wasps, and termites. They lead two lives. The individual me. And the one where the individual is a component, a cluster of cells of the huge organism." This "huge organism" is the entire world—or, perhaps, the cosmos itself. Anzaldúa's time in Austin greatly increased her confidence in both her ability to write and her holistic worldview, seen in her newfound ability to articulate—in fiction and theory—the animism she experienced as a child. We see this animist worldview in these October 1975 journal notes for her story about Andrea:

> [S]he looks at the tree. It is alive and conscious. She looks at the squirrel. The squirrel is part of the tree's consciousness. Then down at the pieces of gravel under her feet. Each is a tiny piece of the same consciousness of that of the tree and the squirrel . . . a single live animal, a single organism—not just this park [but] the whole world, the entire universe one single animal. She walks through the park the microbes in her body enjoying the breeze, sensing her senses, thinking her thoughts.

Everything is both radically diverse and intimately interconnected, sharing (*or possibly creating*) a complex sentience. This metaphysics of interconnectedness becomes an important component in Anzaldúa's theory-making method and in the theories themselves.

Dedication to the Craft

Throughout her doctoral studies, Anzaldúa worked diligently on her fiction and poetry. By fall 1977, she had decided that art—because it offers revolutionary, innovative perspectives and intimately impacts each person—was the most effective pathway toward radical social change. She resolved to devote her life to her writing. She paused her doctoral studies, packed her belongings into her car, and drove to California, where she immersed herself in the San Francisco literary scene.[10] As she recalls in conversation with Weiland, "It was a time of great change in my life because I moved from Austin, tore up my Mastercharge and BankAmericard, and gave up the idea of becoming a university professor. . . . I just threw everything out. I was going to be a writer full time, committed" (*Interviews* 101). And, for the rest of her life, Anzaldúa prioritized the writing over all else—devoting her life to it, supporting herself economically through it, and denying herself many other pleasures in service to it.

Anzaldúa's commitment to writing was wholehearted. She focused on several book-length projects; joined the Feminist Writers' Guild; developed and led the El Mundo Surdo Reading Series and El Mundo Surdo writing workshops; taught creative writing courses at San Francisco State; and in other ways fostered her creativity.[11] She also continued battling with physical issues, including a painful fall down a cliff in May 1979, a severe infection, and a hysterectomy in March 1980. Anzaldúa describes this latter experience in an unpublished autohistoria, "La Cascabel," in which she vividly recalls her out-of-body near-death experience. These out-of-body experiences invited her to pay even more attention to the worldview and values of her home cultures; they demonstrated "that the soul exists . . . that there was something of value in the spirituality of my culture."

In 1979, Anzaldúa received a scholarship to attend a workshop retreat led by Merlin Stone, the author of *When God Was a Woman* and a leading feminist intellectual. The other organizers viewed Anzaldúa as inferior due to this scholarship status (*and perhaps for other reasons as well*). Because she had so frequently experienced tokenization and erasure as a queer, working-class/poor Chicana, Anzaldúa recognized this second-class treatment and, after conversation with Stone, determined to edit a collection of writings by feminist women of color. She initiated work on the project, but after about six months realized that the job was too much for one person (*especially given her ongoing health-related struggles, described earlier*).

And so she invited Cherríe Moraga to join with her on this project, and together they created the well-known multigenre collection *This Bridge Called My Back: Writings by Radical Women of Color* (1981). The editors were intentional in their use of the phrase "women of color," presenting it as a form of alliance-building and an intervention into the overly simplistic black/white racial binaries of that time.[12] Using poems, essays, personal narratives, and letters, *This Bridge* introduced intersectionality into US feminist thought almost a decade before the term made its way into legal studies and other areas of academic thought. *This Bridge*'s final sections, "Speaking in Tongues: The Third World Woman Writer" and "El Mundo Zurdo: The Vision," affirm Anzaldúa's long-standing interest in effecting transformation through art-making and spiritual activism.[13] These sections also offer a blueprint of sorts for Anzaldúa's future career as well as an early manifesto for queer theory. At a time when many activists emphasized separatism, joining primarily (if not exclusively) with others in their particular identity-based groups, Anzaldúa offered an alternative: "Third World women, lesbians, feminists, and feminist-oriented men of all colors are banding and bonding together to right that balance. Only together can we be a force. I see us as a network of kindred spirits, a kind of family" ("La Prieta" 209).

This emphasis on multiplicity and radical inclusiveness is a hallmark of Anzaldúa's work. Whereas many (*if not most*) twentieth-century feminist theorists prioritized or focused exclusively on gender, Anzaldúa insisted that gender be examined relationally, in dialogue with other identity components like culture, race/ethnicity, class, geography, health, sexuality, and religion/spirituality. Importantly, Anzaldúa defined identity broadly, to include dimensions typically omitted from conventional articulations. (*For Anzaldúa these dimensions are ontological as well as physically embodied.*) She insisted on an expansive feminism that does not automatically center sexism but instead flexibly addresses a wide range of social justice issues while challenging *all* normative social identity categories.

East Coast Years

Seeking fresh inspiration and new alliances, Anzaldúa left San Francisco in 1981, moving to the East Coast with only a partial plan. As she describes it in "Esperando la serpiente con plumas (Waiting for the Feathered Serpent)," "In need of a new rite, one that discar[ds] oppression like an old coat, I move from San Francisco to the East Coast. Del mar pacifico a la mar atlante. I carry with me $230, a few raggedy clothes, my books, my portable altar of crystal, candle, I Ching, divination stones, Tarot, and incense. I stay with friends, sleep in the bed of people I barely know—thirteen beds in thirty days." Anzaldúa lived on the East Coast for the next four years—in Cambridge, Massachusetts (house-sitting for friends); in New Haven, Connecticut; and in Brooklyn, New York. She continued to focus on her writing and supported herself through small speaking engagements and writing workshops, her income supplemented with financial gifts from her family in South Texas.[14] *This Bridge* met an important need in US feminist thought, and Anzaldúa was frequently invited to do readings and speak on related topics at conferences and universities. The pay for these "gigs"[15] was small, and Anzaldúa lived frugally, often postponing dental work, doctors' visits, and whatever else stood in the way of her writing. Always a multitasker, she threw herself into numerous writing projects during her East Coast years, including her autohistoria, "La serpiente que se come su cola: The Death Rites of Passage of a Chicana Lesbian," which exists in three unpublished drafts; *Night Face*, a poetry collection she submitted to several literary contests; a book-length prose poem; and more. Each summer, from 1982 through 1986, she taught creative writing at the Women's Voices Summer Writing Workshop for Oakes College, University of California, Santa Cruz; and from 1984 to 1986 she worked on and off as a lecturer in the Adult Degree Program, Vermont College of Norwich University, where she taught creative writing, literature, and feminist studies.

As Anzaldúa continued to hone her writing skills, she also studied esoteric wisdom traditions, yoga (*especially kundalini and kriya yoga*), and related topics. Perhaps through these studies she aspired to generate additional spirit-driven agency and power. This passage from "La serpiente que se come su cola" offers unique insights into Anzaldúa's situation, aspirations, and worldview at that time:

> She wanted to erect a permanent bridge to that Source and to daily cross that bridge. She wanted to renew her burnt out soul, her exhausted crippled body. Her body was the bridge, the link between the external world and the inner one. She wanted to make that bridge a channel for the descent of the spirit. She wanted to re-connect her bonds of kinship with all life. She wanted a bridge of communication

to the non-human world. Her people had made the mistake of using human sacrifice to connect. She wanted to get to that place when she spend [*sic*] time alone, when no other voices vied with hers to be heard and when the static in her head ended, she could hear her own soul speak.

The "she" here is Anzaldúa herself. Throughout this manuscript Anzaldúa uses third person to narrate her own experiences. This third-person narration marks an important shift in Anzaldúa's practice of autohistoria-teoría, allowing her both to detach from the personal but also (*and simultaneously*) to dive more deeply into the hidden dimensions of herself where she encounters el cenote's treasures.[16] By detaching slightly from the experiences, she carefully shapes them in order to speak even more profoundly to readers while facilitating her personal excavation. In this passage (*and elsewhere in the manuscript*), Anzaldúa enacts shadow work: she uses meditation, self-reflection, writing, and other spiritual technologies to access nonrational wisdom and insights. She does so, at least in part, because she's become entirely depleted—her soul "burnt out," her body "exhausted," her intimate interconnections with spirit (*which for Anzaldúa infused and shaped* EVERYTHING) frayed. Rather than reject the body, she approaches it as a bridge between the inner and outer worlds, between material and nonmaterial dimensions of reality.

This interest in the psyche and soul work was not spiritual bypassing for Anzaldúa; rather, it represents her long-standing desire to bring occult traditions into dialogue with political activism in order to create new alliances and tactics for social change.[17] She believed the current political tactics and organizing to be insufficient and exclusionary—incapable of effecting radical transformation. As she put it in a 1983 biographical statement, she was "involved in fusing spiritual disciplines with political activism and in creating bridges between various 'worlds,' including those of women, third world people, and gay people."[18] Titles of Anzaldúa's talks during these years further document her intertwined interests in spirituality and politics, women-of-color writers, "bridging differences," and Chicana feminists and Chicana identity. Portions of these talks in various forms made their way into *Borderlands*, and the ideas and energies with which she grappled appear in later writings as well. (*These interests, though they morphed in different ways, were deeply embedded in all of Anzaldúa's work.*)

California Return, *Borderlands*' Emergence

In 1985, and after much careful deliberation, Anzaldúa returned to the West Coast, moving in August to the San Francisco Bay Area where she rented a studio apartment in Oakland. The following spring she relocated to Santa Cruz, where she spent the remainder of her life, first renting an apartment on Walti Street and then, in 1991, purchasing a house near West Cliff Drive, on Lighthouse Point and about two blocks from the Pacific Ocean.[19] This house and landscape were important to her later projects and figure prominently in *Light in the Dark*. In early 1986, Anzaldúa sent *Borderlands*, a slim poetry manuscript of approximately one hundred pages, to Spinsters/Aunt Lute Books, and on April 14, 1986, she received a letter from the editor, Joan Pinkvoss, expressing interest in publishing her book.[20] Anzaldúa then worked diligently to produce an introduction for the volume. Originally, she conceived this prose section to be a single essay composed of four parts. To develop this essay, she wrote new material and drew on unpublished writings (journals and manuscripts) and talks. But in typical Anzaldúan fashion, the words proliferated and the ideas expanded until the manuscript became the iconic *Borderlands/La Frontera: The New Mestiza* (1987).[21] With its code-switching, multigenre, feminist lens, *Borderlands* arrived in the world exactly on time. It was well-received by progressive academics and scholars, especially those interested in Chicana, multicultural, queer, and/or feminist thought. *Borderlands*' positive reception elevated Anzaldúa's status, increasing her reputation as a leading Chicana lesbian author and opening additional speaking and writing opportunities for her. *Borderlands* also builds on Anzaldúa's earlier queer manifesto in *This Bridge Called My Back*, offering another early articulation of queer theory—several years before the term made its way into academic classrooms and scholarship.[22]

In spring 1988 Anzaldúa was the Distinguished Visiting Professor in Women's Studies at the University of California, Santa Cruz, where she taught "Women of Color in the U.S.—Third World Feminism Theory & Literature," and "Historias," a creative writing seminar. In both courses, she aspired to make recent works and ideas by women of colors[23] more accessible to the UCSC community. "People have a sense of white feminism," she explained in a 1988 interview with the school newspaper, "but not Third World feminism" ("Chicana Writer"). Frustrated with the lack of available texts by women-of-colors authors, she began editing her second collection,

Making Face, Making Soul/Haciendo Caras: Creative and Critical Perspectives by Women of Color. As she explains in her introduction,

> I got tired of hearing students say that *Bridge* was required in two or three of their women's studies courses; tired of being a resource for teachers and students who asked me what texts by women-of-color they should read or teach and where they could get these writings. I had grown frustrated that the same few women-of-color were asked to read or lecture in universities and classrooms, or to submit work to anthologies and quarterlies. . . . Repeatedly tokenizing the same half dozen mujeres was stymieing our literary/political movement. Drained of our energy, we few tokens had little left to deploy into the development of our own literary and political movements.
>
> The urge to anthologize, to bring more voices to the foreground, grew stronger. ("haciendo caras," xvi)

This pragmatic, context-related approach is a recurring trait throughout Anzaldúa's life: she sees a need—experiences this need viscerally, in ways that negatively impact her life as well as the lives of others—and sets out to address the need, doing so in ways that elevate the collective, rather than just herself.[24]

Graduate School, Redux (Late 1980s/Early 1990s)

During her early post-*Borderlands* years, Anzaldúa also aspired to develop an interdisciplinary Chicana literary theory that could build, but in more focused fashion, on the work initiated in *Borderlands*. To further enhance her knowledge and engage more deeply with a community of thinkers, she decided to complete her doctoral degree and in 1988 applied to the History of Consciousness Doctoral Program at ucsc.[25] Incredibly (*to her and perhaps to most readers*), her application to this program was denied; however, the admissions committee immediately gave her materials to their colleagues in American Literature, who unanimously accepted Anzaldúa into their PhD program, offering her a small stipend and a teaching assistantship; and in fall 1988, Anzaldúa enrolled. (*I call attention to Anzaldúa's [non]admissions experience to remind us that even when she had achieved a measure of success, Anzaldúa still experienced profound rejection—even from those who in some ways might have celebrated and/or used her work. While we can't know for sure, it seems useful to consider how this rejection might have impacted her time at*

UCSC, *her relationship with academic theory, and the stressors with which she struggled. This experience also demonstrates Anzaldúa's flexibility: her overriding goal here was to achieve her doctoral degree; when her first avenue to that degree was blocked but another opened immediately, she seized the opportunity.*) In "Barred Witness: Literary/Artistic Creations and Class Identities" Anzaldúa reflects on her decision to return to graduate school for a second time, despite the painful experiences it evokes:

> I have been in and around and on the fringes of universities for the past twenty-six years—as student, as teacher, and for the second time now I find myself *entremedias,* in between, occupying that strange space of having been first a lecturer and now a graduate student. From this position I can see clearly that the university for me is often a haven, a refuge, sometimes a prison and a hell. *Es una Área de conflicto y enfrentamiento en donde el racismo cobra vida.* Often my isolation (especially if I am teaching) is more intense than when I'm in the "real world" outside the University. I'm participating in a racist institution by even being in the university.

And yet, Anzaldúa intentionally sought this liminal academic space, knowingly entering this painful, uncomfortable site: "What 'moves' me to frequent institutions of higher learning, to constantly come up against the Other? The allure of learning and knowledge—heady stuff and ultimately exciting. The obstacles I face and the frustrations leave me no choice but to keep on struggling—which for me means to keep on writing—and make 'furtherances' in my own self-creation." As this statement suggests, university life and the academic world more generally functioned, for Anzaldúa, as another (*or as several*) borderlands, additional nepantlas forcing her to immerse herself in multiple systems of difference where she could cultivate new knowledge and creative projects.

During her UCSC graduate school years Anzaldúa grappled extensively with the most current western theories at that time, focusing especially on what was sometimes called "high theory": she took courses with Donna Haraway, Teresa de Lauretis, José Davíd Saldívar, and other well-known scholars, and explored poststructuralist, postcolonialist, and psychoanalytic theories. As her term papers, dissertation prospectus, and chapter drafts indicate, she dove deeply into these theoretical perspectives. She did not automatically dismiss them as too narrow, elite, and biased but instead viewed them as resources (*limited though they might be*) for her own knowledge production; she aspired to learn them thoroughly, to take what was useful and leave the rest. Perhaps we could say that Anzaldúa (*at least somewhat*) loved theory; as she puts it in "Poet is Critic," "I need theoretical visions to survive, I need theories." Not surprisingly, though, Anzaldúa did not fully succumb to the lure of theory or become entirely directed by the highly acclaimed theories of that time (*though future work with her manuscripts will help us to understand in what ways, if any, the theories shaped her—for instance: did she sometimes defer to them?*). Even as she sometimes adopted the theoretical language of the day, Anzaldúa read with a discerning eye, noting that many of these supposedly new theories, with their emphasis on fragmentation and intersubjectivity, explored (*and, too often, seemed unthinkingly to celebrate*) themes that she and many other women of colors and marginalized peoples had experienced intimately (*and painfully*) for their entire lives. Despite their limitations, these theories offered Anzaldúa perspectives and tools with transformational potential. The point was to *change* reality, not just to comprehend it more fully. As she writes in "Notes for Lloronas Dissertation," "I want to use theory to help change things and not simply to make sense in its own terms to explain or justify what already exists."

Anzaldúa's key interests at this time included questions of representation and theory production. In addition to bringing voice to marginalized perspectives, such as her own, she aspired to create new theories, as well as innovative methods, genres, and writing techniques that worked with and, simultaneously, transformed personal experience—what she eventually named autohistoria-teoría.[26] Building on aspirations articulated in *Borderlands*, Anzaldúa had become even more convinced of writing's metaphysical and ontological functions: "I believe very strongly that intellectual work coupled with the work of the imagination can actually bring about changes in reality, even to the point of creating new realities. This faith is very precious to me. Against the odds, public and private, I have become a do-it-yourselfer, one who attempts, through her poetic artistic journey, to build a bridge to the other side of consciousness" ("Autohistoria"). Importantly, Anzaldúa's goal was not simply to become better versed in the existing theories of her day. It was, rather, to glean from these theories whatever could usefully facilitate her own theory creation and intellectual-aesthetic growth. (*Here, I use "intellectual-aesthetic" to signal the importance of Anzaldúa's art-making: she nurtured her imagination in partnership with rational thought and discursive reasoning.*)

By late 1990 Anzaldúa had finished her coursework, passed her qualifying exams, and finalized her dissertation topic: an extended revisionist
exploration of La Llorona, a figure with whom she'd been intensely engaged for decades, if not her entire life.[27] Her goal in revisiting this historic-
mythic figure was to rewrite La Llorona's story more generously, in ways
that could resonate more fully with her own life and the lives of others.
As she states in "La Llorona y la víbora que se mete por allá" (93.19), a
1989 paper written for a course taught by Teresa de Lauretis, "I want to
help *la llorona* by writing her story differently, by 'rewriting' it. Her ghostly
body, wandering and wailing is my vehicle for carrying symbolic identity
and for changing the concept of identity as well. For me as a writer she is
my necessary monster, a *musa bruja* whose utterances decode, and hopefully destroy, the denigrating cultural roles assigned us." As we know from
Borderlands, Anzaldúa's interest in La Llorona ran deep. Until encountering Coyolxauhqui in the early 1990s, La Llorona was Anzaldúa's principal
mythic representation of personal and collective trauma, "contain[ing] the
symbolic product or synthesis of the lived experiences of all mestizas. . . .
La llorona is a scream that punctures a hole in space, a bloodcurdling wail
that keeps alive the trauma of the past, a trauma frozen in time, eternal, a
trauma of separation and death" ("La Llorona y la víbora").[28]

As Anzaldúa's various dissertation titles imply, her project focused on
trauma, identity, writing, reading, and knowledge production.[29] She used
storytelling, psychoanalytic and postmodernist theories, and her own
shadow work to explore La Llorona's historical meanings and to offer alternative perspectives: "For me, la llorona symbolizes alienation: estrangement from self, estrangement from others (especially men) and from
groups, estrangement from social environment, rebellion against cultural
norms and in time estrangement from institutions of higher learning and
from bodies of knowledge" (93.4). Anzaldúa conceived her dissertation
project to be interdisciplinary, including explorations of folklore, myth,
and history related to La Llorona, as well as a qualitative dimension—as
evidenced by the extensive research she preserved for her archives. However, as Anzaldúa noted, La Llorona has her limitations—especially the
male-driven nature of her stories in which she seems to react to Cortés's
actions rather than act autonomously. (*And although Anzaldúa doesn't point
it out, her work on La Llorona seems primarily laden with pain and grief; it's as
if Anzaldúa's Llorona functions cathartically, clearing the way for fresh growth
and insights.*)

Perhaps not surprisingly, given that identity includes embodiment and physical bodies are typically located in geographic place, space became another key concept and motivator in the Lloronas dissertation, as evidenced especially (but not exclusively) in the chapter on "Chicana Space."[30] Here Anzaldúa brought her experiential wisdom from the Mexico-US and metaphoric borderlands into dialogue with recent theoretical developments in geography and cultural studies to explore inner space, territorial space, imaginal space, psychic space, and more. However, as she forced western spatial metaphors and theories to do such extensive work, she realized their profound limitations and sought alternatives, thus opening space for nepantla's emergence in the 1990s. (*Sorry about that bad pun; I couldn't help myself.*) As explained in chapter 4, nepantla made its way slowly into Anzaldúa's work, starting with the fiction; it does not appear in the Lloronas dissertation itself. (*This absence is notable and striking: What does it indicate about nepantla's functions in Anzaldúa's later work? How might nepantla have assisted her later theory creations—possibly serving as midwife of sorts?*) Anzaldúa worked diligently on the dissertation and, in typical Anzaldúan fashion, expanded it considerably (*and, some might say, uncontrollably*). By August 1, 1990, the table of contents had grown to seventeen chapters, divided into two volumes: "Volume One—Writing and Representation" and "Volume Two—Llorona: Noche y su nidada" (108.6). (*The dissertation director in me was shocked and somewhat outraged to see this sprawling, enormous table of contents with enough topics and material for several books. "How did no one reel her back?" I wondered. "It's no surprise she didn't finish this dissertation; it became so unwieldy and huge as to be impossible to complete," I complained to my Anzaldúa-scholar friends. I can't help but believe that the enormity of the task contributed to Anzaldúa's depression.*) Although Anzaldúa eventually "ditched" this project, she produced thousands of pages, and her time at UCSC increased her confidence in her identity as a theorist, fortifying her own theory creation for the rest of her life.[31]

While it could be tempting to assume that Anzaldúa, author of the highly acclaimed *Borderlands* and co-editor of the iconic *This Bridge Called My Back*, was confident of her brilliance and moved boldly through these academic spaces, this is not the case. Her drafts and writing notes indicate that she experienced grave self-doubts and extreme stress throughout her UCSC graduate school years. "Barred Witness: Literary/Artistic Creations and Class Identities," a dissertation chapter, offers invaluable insights into Anzaldúa's mindset during this time. In it, she outlines the physical costs and deeply internalized misgivings that contribute to her "post-traumatic stress disorder":

> La musa Bruja whispers, "Watch it, you're heading for overload" when I'm trying to do it all. The stress spreads, metastasize like a cancer in hidden sites in the brain or emotional tissues. It can take root in the very bone. The pressure points in my life, I feel as if I can't hold stress taking a big chunk of my well being despite my stately nerves. My living environment is dangerous to my health—high crime rate, violence against women. Attending graduate school is high up there in stress. . . . We . . . victims of post-traumatic stress disorder suffer from chronic depression, suicidal tendencies, inability to feel or identify feelings. At risk as oppressed class subject. . . . Heavy workload, demands made on me by others, uncomfortable surroundings, traveling and making presentations.

Although Anzaldúa does not mention it here, her perfectionism and a desire to exceed readers' expectations (*expectations that were already quite high, due to* Borderlands' *positive reception*) weighed heavily on her, creating another underlying stressor. As she acknowledges elsewhere in the same draft, "I push myself to a point of agony with excessive demands on myself. At what costs? Episodes of severe depression; near panic states may result from measuring personal worth and self-esteem by success and productivity." Not surprisingly, this perfectionism, in turn, led to writing blocks: "Harboring attitudes of perfectionism is a sure way to be blocked."

To be sure, Anzaldúa did not view herself as a passive victim. She self-reflected deeply and worked continually to make necessary adjustments in response to the stress and its underlying conditions. As she puts it in "Barred Witness," "I change and changed the way in which I was allowing these situations to affect me." However, I cannot help but wonder if part of her coping strategy involved intentionally distancing herself from the dissertation, which had become increasingly unwieldy (*to say the least!*), especially after she was diagnosed with diabetes in 1992.

Diabetes; or, The Body Rebels (Again)

Diabetes changed Anzaldúa's life, bringing additional uncertainty, challenges, and pain. As she wrote in "SIC: Spiritual Identity Crisis," "Living in this body is like living on a fault line / I never know when the ground beneath my feet will open up. / At the mercy of my own flawed biology." As "sic" and her writing notas demonstrate, Anzaldúa took her typical introspective, analytical curiosity into her body and the disease, examining it (and her experiences with it) from every angle imaginable. She studied diabetes thoroughly—researching causes, demographics, dietary recommendations, cures, experimental advances, alternative medicine, side effects, and so on. She monitored her food intake, her blood sugar levels, her sleep, and her moods—working endlessly to balance her health. She realized that the diabetes had probably been lurking in her body for years and was awakened through increased stress in her life (*I'm looking at you, graduate school*).

The diabetes demanded huge chunks of Anzaldúa's attention and time: extensive research to explore possible treatments and cures; lengthy searches for health insurance and medical providers on her specific plan;[32] and long waiting periods at various specialists. Even grocery shopping consumed more of Anzaldúa's precious hours, as she carefully read each label to select the healthiest versions of each item. (*I accompanied her on some of these shopping trips: she read the contents of each product as carefully as she would read the latest scholarly book.*) And, of course, she paid constant, close attention to diet, exercise, and blood sugar levels—coordinating them each day, modifying her schedule as much as possible to achieve balance. As this passage from "sic" suggests, Anzaldúa was meticulous in her self-observations and paid great attention to her self-care: "Plan the meals, shop for food, always reading the labels for sugar and fat grams, cook the food. Eating certain foods in measured spoonfuls at regular intervals 365 days a year. So tempting to eat forbidden food only I'll pay the price later—the food will make my blood sugars rise. Always got to stay with the 'balancing act,' the holy triangle of diet, exercise and insulin. I checked my blood glucose to find out if I'm out of balance only I already know. My body tells me so." And to complicate her life even further, the diabetes triggered a cascade of secondary conditions, including neuropathy (numbness in her feet), Hashimoto's disease, yeast infections, blurred vision, increased insomnia, paralyzing depression, hypothyroidism, and more.[33] The diabetes also threw Anzaldúa into extreme introspection and self-questioning as she struggled to make sense of it all.

But even as Anzaldúa worked tirelessly to understand and manage the diabetes, she could not take a break from her speaking engagements and other economic endeavors. As a self-employed writer, she had no steady source of income to rely on. Although her books sold fairly well, the royalties were not sufficient to support her, nor did they offer the consistency to ensure economic security, and Anzaldúa continued to rely heavily on speaking engagements, which typically involved a public lecture and one or two additional events with students and/or faculty.[34] The preparation for these gigs was time-consuming and exhausting; it included multiple conversations with event organizers, payment negotiations, travel plans, meetings with students, book signings after the event, and much more.

Anzaldúa aspired to create talks that met the needs of each specific audience. She questioned the organizers to learn about the prospective audience and their needs; she talked with students and others at the events; and in other ways she worked to develop carefully designed presentations that could meet people's needs. Because the topics so often involved power dynamics and systemic identity-related issues, these gigs put psychic and physical strains on Anzaldúa. As she frankly asserts in "Barred Witness,"

> I feel drained by the demands made upon me beyond those specified by my gig agreement. Often as I am on display, as I put myself on display I feel stronging [sic] that a part of me, the activist the public speaker belongs to them, the readers, listeners, as to me. I feel that I am public property. Most of the time it feels right, this is part of the work I do in the world. At other times I feel that every one wants a piece of me, a piece of my flesh, and they take and they take.

She found it challenging to negotiate travel arrangements, lodging needs, and stipends. Event planners in social justice fields (e.g., women's studies, ethnic studies, etc.) expected Anzaldúa to charge as little as possible for her time (*because, after all, the academy did not fully support their economic needs*), not understanding that the gigs were crucial to her livelihood and a costly strain on her health. They sometimes expressed (*or implied*) resentment at Anzaldúa's fees, and this resentment subtly impacted her or influenced decisions to not ask for what she truly needed (*such as direct flights or first-class airline tickets to accommodate her health*). Although this work was very taxing, Anzaldúa usually enjoyed it and found it to be a meaningful part of her vocation. As she explains to Jamie Evans, doing gigs was part of her life's task: "As a bridge and a messenger I open myself up, listen to hear what these people are experiencing and what they're saying. I have messages I want to impart to other people" (*Interviews* 197).

Even as Anzaldúa struggled to manage the diabetes while supporting herself through speaking engagements, she continued to write—as often and as much as she could possibly manage. As her projects and writing notes from the early to mid-1990s indicate, she focused significant attention on imagination, art, and transformation, producing two bilingual children's books, many short story drafts, and an expansive study of border arte.[35] Around this time, Anzaldúa initiated a new process for idea generation that in many ways resembled her earlier journaling but focused a bit less on her reactions to external events and people, producing what she called "writing notas." These notas became a key component in her writing process. (*I cannot overemphasize their importance to Anzaldúa's later projects and their potential value to scholars; they're a huge, incredible goldmine of brilliant ideas and material.*) Typically handwritten, they include her journeys into el cenote; freewrites where she explores a variety of ideas, emotions, fears, and physical states of being; and prewriting stream-of-consciousness material about specific topics. Anzaldúa seems often to have written nonstop, "coughing out" onto paper insights from her psyche. Later, she'd go through the handwritten notas, sometimes keying material into drafts and computer files and other times making additional comments. In November 1996 Anzaldúa initiated a more organized approach to these notas, lettering them alphabetically (Writing Notas A, B, and so on). There are thousands of pages of handwritten notas, covering a wide range of topics, including (but not limited to) random notes on and quotations from whatever she was reading; fleeting thoughts, ideas, inspirations, and questions; long-term project outlines and drafts; and recurring topics like writing, depression, self, subjectivity, identity, and ethics. Anzaldúa used the notas for philosophical reflection, self-reflection, and shadow work—deep dives into both the personal and collective cenote.[36]

The Mature Philosophy's Slow Emergence

In the mid-1990s, at the invitation of the directors of Movimiento de Arte y Cultura Latino Americana (MACLA)'s Center for Latino Arts and Villa Montalvo's Artist Residency Program, Anzaldúa developed a proposal for a Latina/Chicana artist residency focusing on the concept of nepantla. The result, "Entre Américas: El Taller Nepantla," brought together Anzaldúa and four other artists from the United States and Mexico in fall 1995.[37] This invitation allowed Anzaldúa to focus intensively on the relationship between nepantla, creativity, art, and identity. As the "lead artist," Anzaldúa initiated the framework and assisted each artist in exploring their creative process in relation to nepantla ("Taller Nepantla"). Manuscripts related to this workshop indicate that Anzaldúa was at a pivotal point in her idea generation and theory creation. Focusing primarily on artists-activists (*or what might later be called artivists*), she describes nepantla as a journey of sorts, composed of "stages and levels":

> It begins when the artist/activist receives a call to art. She then decides to become an artist. The artist, as shaman—seer, visionary, healer, undergoes a physical or pyschic breakdown, a falling apart. I call this stage Coyolxauhqui after the Aztec moon goddess who was dismembered by her brother, Huitzilopochli. It is like the *negrido* stage in alchemy. . . . Several stages follow. One of these stages is the Coatlicue state which I have described in *Borderlands/La frontera*. The "compostura" (composing, construction) stage is the last one—that of putting the pieces of Coyolxauhqui back together. When things and one's life is put back together one's consciousness has been reforged and one becomes aware of things one had not been aware of before. One sees things in a new light, with a new mestiza consciousness. ("Taller Nepantla")

Here we see Anzaldúa simultaneously looking backward, toward her early research on alchemy and key ideas from *Borderlands*, and forward, with an early articulation of the Coyolxauhqui process, so important to her later theory of conocimiento. Elsewhere in this document she refers to "entering into the serpent" (a key concept in *Borderlands*) and explores the energy of shifting (another crucial component in conocimiento). Because art, for Anzaldúa, included a mandate to transform (rather than simply represent) reality, these writing notes and drafts also indicate her deepening, extremely rich explorations of how imagination, fiction, and alternate states of being/thinking impact and alter consensual reality.

As Anzaldúa delved even more deeply into the imaginal, her vision continued expanding (*even as she also returned to additional versions of her earlier goal*), and she aspired to create a comprehensive philosophy. As she writes in a 1996 manuscript, "Re-configuring Fronteras: New Navigations of Nepantla and the Cracks between Worlds," "I am trying to create a whole philosophy, applying it broadly, not just to artistic, compositional processes

[but] also to the construction of identity and reality and the production of knowledge, and not just applying it to internal journeys but to ways of being out in the world. Not just by developing ways of coping but of learning new facultades to do this work." Here we see the breadth of Anzaldúa's vision, as well as its decolonial potential: she aspired to develop a philosophy encompassing identity, epistemology, ontology, metaphysics, and ethics. This philosophy would be practical, accessible, and transformative. Crucial to these aspirations were Anzaldúa's deepening explorations of nepantla and Coyolxauhqui.[38] As implied by the above excerpts, the former concept offered her a broader framework with which to think through her identity, epistemology, and ontology; and the latter concept offered her an autonomous approach to consider wounding, healing, and transformation as an ongoing process.

Despite her struggles with diabetes and the havoc it wreaked on her body, psyche, and mind, Anzaldúa continued multitasking and setting high expectations for herself. The following excerpt from her 1997 journal illustrates the breadth, complexity, and optimism of Anzaldúa's multitasking. As she sets out on her six-week residency at Hedgebrook she gives herself many goals:

> Revise & rewrite 24 short stories and work on an essay (memoir). . . . The other enormous task I've set for myself is to challenge the roots of commonly held beliefs, values and assumptions and encourage transformation. I think that fiction is a subtle, even sneaky, way to do this. I'm relying on the subtext of each story to carry this mechanism. In addition I plan to key in 90 pages of handwritten material—this will be one of the ways of entering into the stories and the essay. I'd like to live up to Hedgebrook's permaculture philosophy: growth happens by letting go rather than imposing or controlling.

Here we see Anzaldúa aspiring to revise twenty-four short stories, develop her autohistoria-teoría, and transcribe ninety handwritten pages of notas, while—at a larger scale—continuing to hone her transgressive, transformational philosophy. (*Her Sagittarius Ascendant speaks loudly in these aspirations.*)

Hedgebrook was not the only writing retreat that Anzaldúa attended during this decade. In the mid- and late 1990s she applied for and was accepted into several artist residencies, where she revised her fiction and personal essays; completed her collection of interviews; and worked on additional projects. Arguably Anzaldúa spent the majority of her time (*and if not of her time, certainly of her passion*) on her Prieta stories, which she viewed as autohistoria and planned to publish as a book. With these stories, she hoped to exceed *Borderlands*, to produce a book that spoke powerfully to a wide, diverse audience. As she confesses in 1999, "I don't want Borderlands [*sic*] to be my magnum opus. I want to achieve something greater. I'm trying to learn the structure of myth in order to create stories that will appeal to everyone" (Writing Notas H). Her quest to produce these stories deepened her interest in ontology, as can be seen in her writing notas from this time:

> By pondering and reinterpreting cultural myths, I can explore human processes, stages of life, and learn to see myself and others and our life issues in different ways. I try to correlate psychotherapy, shamanism, science and philosophy, spirituality to come up with patterns that inform the needs of human beings and reveal the Creative Life Force and Intelligence that permeates all living things by putting a 21st Century face on ancient myths. How people relate to this Creative Intelligence. Myths that speak to our conditions. I use affirmations, repetition of thoughts in the form of words to establish the belief system I want. (Writing Notas H)

This passage also points to Anzaldúa's desire to build a new paradigm, one more in sync with twenty-first-century needs as well as her animist-inflected metaphysics.

In 1997 three scholars in curriculum studies, Marla Morris, Mary Aswell Doll, and William E. Pinar, invited Anzaldúa to contribute a short piece to their edited collection, *How We Work*, in which writers from a variety of academic disciplines "describe some of their working methods, offering hints and presenting personal quirks and reflections." Although Anzaldúa was selective in the projects she took on, this one appealed to her greatly. It was, after all, on the topic of her first love, writing; Anzaldúa agreed to participate, creating a tight schedule in which she would draft, revise, edit, and submit the essay in four months. (*When I came across Anzaldúa's notes with this optimistic timeline, I laughed out loud. She was far too meticulous and careful to write an entire essay in only four months. Moreover, I knew that the essay she eventually produced was "Putting Coyolxauhqui Together"—a long, sprawling piece that eventually made its way into* Light in the Dark *and required an agonizing amount of time to complete.*) Not surprisingly, the piece had a timeline of its own, demanding considerably more than Anzaldúa had assumed.[39] Indeed, the fact that Anzaldúa tried out at least eleven different titles before landing on the final one, "Putting Coyolxauhqui Together: A Creative Process," hints at her struggles with this piece. (*Also not surprisingly, the "final" version Anzaldúa submitted to the editors was more than twice their requested length; thus, she also spent much additional time revising and tightening.*) However, this project also allowed Anzaldúa to reflect deeply on her own writing/thinking process and use this reflection to further develop her philosophy. As she returned to her previous work on nepantla while studying Coyolxauhqui's story and energy as they expressed themselves in her life, she deepened the former, proposing "the nepantla mind," and transformed the latter into an early articulation of the Coyolxauhqui process. These theories became increasing important in the final years of Anzaldúa's life, playing vital roles in the formulation of conocimiento and the trajectory of *Light in the Dark*.

The Final Years

The last four years of Anzaldúa's life were filled with writing projects, including a large (*unwieldy*) co-edited collection, several landmark essays, and a dissertation/book.[40] During these final years Anzaldúa's health became more precarious, and her duties as a homeowner increased.[41] Shortly after we finished *Interviews/Entrevistas* in late 1999, Anzaldúa began working with me on a co-edited, multigenre collection tentatively titled "This Bridge Twenty Years Later." We had two key aspirations for this project: (1) to assess the progress made among feminists and other progressive social justice thinkers/actors since the 1981 publication of *This Bridge Called My Back*; and (2) to propose a more intentional engagement with various politics of spirit, or what Anzaldúa and I called spiritual activism.[42] (*"Spiritual activism" is Anzaldúa's term; I enthusiastically adopted it in 1998 when she first mentioned it to me, and I've flowed with it ever since. Spiritual activism, as theory-praxis, has become foundational to my life and life's work. I will be forever grateful to Anzaldúa for bringing spiritual activism into academic thought.*) Eventually titled *this bridge we call home: radical visions for transformation*, this multiyear project gave Anzaldúa an opportunity to return to and reflect on women-of-colors theorizing, El Mundo Zurdo, inclusive alliance-making, transformation, and other key topics from earlier points in her career. It also gave her the (*forced*) opportunity to draft another chapter for her next book, and she set out to produce the "sister essay" to "Putting Coyolxauhqui Together," or what she informally called her "conocimiento essay."[43]

In this piece, eventually titled "now let us shift. . . . the path of conocimiento. . . . inner work, public acts," Anzaldúa pulled together the many strands of her philosophy and reflected deeply on her life—including her struggles with diabetes—to offer a systemic philosophy of change that, she hoped, could function as a new paradigm for the twenty-first century and beyond. The manuscript drafts from this project are extensive and offer valuable insights into Anzaldúa's life and worldview at the time. Look for instance at this passage from an early draft: "**Change** Diabetes. Knocked you off your feet, derailed your train. You don't know what's happening. You lose the ground beneath your feet, your reference point. How do you react? Do you try to reconstruct yourself, pull the pieces back together the way they were?" (49.4). Anzaldúa used self-reflective questions such as these for guidance. Drawing on writing notas, transpersonal psychology, philosophies of consciousness, shadow work, ritual, and her own experiences (especially those surrounding *This Bridge Called My Back* and her struggles with diabetes), Anzaldúa delved deeply (*and painfully*) into the dynamics of change (*especially the demands for change that arise when we're confronted with unexpected obstacles*).

These drafts depict Anzaldúa in dialogue with reality, focusing especially on the conflictual conversations that occur when we encounter unanticipated conflicts, challenges, and delays. This passage, from a draft titled "Conocimientos, Now Let Us Shift: Inner Work and Public Acts," beautifully illustrates her dialogic process while offering valuable insights into her worldview:

> Obstacles occur at the outer level (when [*sic*] you sense that someone or something has harmed you, has ruined it all. You feel confused, disappointed, betrayed. Obstacles at the inner level come from your need to protect yourself from being touched. You don't like the way reality is now and you want it to go away. When it doesn't you numb yourself, deaden yourself in order to escape it.
>
> Descono**l51**cimientos. [*sic*][44] But the reality will not go away until it has taught you what you need to know. It will keep returning with new forms, names, manifestations until you learn about what and where you are separating yourself from reality, where you are pull-

ing back, closing down, retreating. What do you do when things are unbearable?

Anzaldúa's point was not that we must simply accept reality "as is," so to speak. Rather, she explored the social constraints creating this reality and proposed tactics to transform them, as well as ourselves. Especially significant here is the relational quality to this analysis. For Anzaldúa, reality was not some backdrop on which humans live out our lives, imposing our will on the world. Rather, reality (and everything/everyone in it) participates with us in a multidimensional co-creative learning process filled with human and more-than-human actors.

As Anzaldúa drafted, redrafted, and revised this piece, her emphasis shifted from nepantla to conocimiento and she explored strategies, epistemologies, and ontologies that can assist us in working with nepantla states to effect progressive transformation, to build a more equitable world— one that acknowledges and co-creates with nature's sentience.[45] Anzaldúa worked for almost two years on this piece, expanding it far beyond her original vision. It's as if she enacted the dialogue with reality that she called for and, in the process, transformed reality itself.[46] During this time (2000– 2002), Anzaldúa was also drafting a new preface for the third edition of *This Bridge Called My Back*, writing a preface for *this bridge we call home*, working with me to offer feedback to *bridge* contributors, and revising her Prieta stories.

In addition to these various writing projects, Anzaldúa also decided to finish her doctoral degree, and in September 2001 she began meeting regularly with several doctoral students in the area, "las comadritas," exchanging chapter drafts and offering support for each other during the final stages of dissertating. Rather than return to her 1990s Lloronas dissertation, Anzaldúa took a somewhat different direction, pulling from "now let us shift" and other more recent work that reflected her current interests.[47] This decision seems more like a shift than a radical change, as seen in the document titled "Lloronas book_Rewriting Reality," which blends the old with the new. As her letters, notes, and computer drafts from the time indicate, she envisioned the dissertation as a publishable book.[48]

Shortly after the 9/11 terrorist attacks on the United States, Anzaldúa was invited to contribute a short testimonio to Clara Lomas and Claire Joysmith's edited collection, *Testimonios Latinos in the U.S. 11 September—11 October 2001*. Already glued to the news, Anzaldúa dove even more deeply into the investigative reporting and firsthand accounts of the US bombings of Afghanistan. In typical Anzaldúan fashion, she expanded the piece beyond the editors' word count and insisted on revising it past their deadlines. At one point, she decided that it needed more work and withdrew it, but the editors and her writing comadres persuaded her to allow its publication. During these final years, Anzaldúa was also revising "Geography of Selves" and drafting "Flights of Imagination" (two chapters for *Light in the Dark*), beginning an essay on disability and spirituality, and responding to interview questions on intersections between Chicanas/os and Native peoples.[49]

Don't let this long list of projects fool you: even as Anzaldúa wanted to spend all her time writing, her body and her house made many demands on her, slowly dragging her down and greatly interfering with her work. She experienced profound depression and additional difficulties with the diabetes, often further complicated by her insomnia. As she wrote in an email to me on January 16, 2004,

> still struggling to control my BGs (blood glucose [levels]) which have been out of control for the last few weeks. my habit of staying up two days in a row & then crashing is a sure fire cure for insomnia, but it wrecks my blood sugar control. my sleeping schedule, & most of my life, is dysfunctional. i've always felt like an alien from another planet or another realm. my writing dates do help keep me somewhat on track.

Anzaldúa seems to have cut back on her writing during the final six months of her life, though she continued trying to work, trying to manage the diabetes, trying to complete the dissertation which (*not surprisingly*) had expanded behind her conscious control. (*After having spent so long looking through the drafts to this project, I cannot help but wonder whether it played a role in hastening her death.*) The fact that she missed her self-imposed deadlines to finish the dissertation further diminished her spirits. (*And there were other challenges as well, perhaps to be revealed later.*)

For these reasons and others, in May 2004 (*around the 15th of the month, but we don't know the exact date*), Anzaldúa released her body and departed from this timeline, though her work lives on, her theories continue to grow, and her philosophy expands, as you'll see in the chapters, sections, and years to come.

Postscript and Reminder to Readers

Although I've tried to dive deeply into Anzaldúa's life, I have omitted much material; I've kept the scope relatively narrow as I've tried to focus on the events in life that functioned as situational engines for the theories. I focused especially on the inner, outer, and liminal events that impacted her theory-making and worked with her to create and shape the theories themselves. Put differently, I showcased the events in Anzaldúa's inner and outer life that functioned as theory co-creators, and I located these events by paying special attention to what Anzaldúa herself explored in her autohistorias, interviews, writing notes, and conversations. As you'll see in more detail (and complexity) when you peruse chapter 6, she created several semi-autobiographical pieces—or what she called "autohistorias"—which she sometimes expanded into autohistorias-teorías. These texts provided much of the information included here. Especially useful were the following unpublished manuscripts and their many iterations: "Esperando la serpiente con plumas (Waiting for the Feathered Serpent)" and "La serpiente que se come su cola: The Death Rites of Passage of a Chicana Lesbian," "Autobiography," and "Autohistoria de la artista as a Young Girl."[50] I also drew considerably on conversations that I had with Gloria over the years; whenever I stayed with her in Santa Cruz, we'd take daily walks, talking about ideas, familia, and more. Gloria loved to reminisce about her life. I'd just ask a simple question, and off she'd go—sharing stories and memorias.

But what I've offered is incomplete. Omitting information about her vital interactions with familia and friends, this intellectual sketch could inaccurately lead you to believe that Anzaldúa lived an isolated life. *This is not the case.* She crafted a life of solitude, not isolation. Her family was an important source of support throughout her life and continuing today; she had powerful, strong friendships that endured and strengthened over the decades (some continuing even to this day). And, of course, Anzaldúa's interior life (including the imaginal) was far richer than any words could possibly convey.

2. WRITING AS RITUAL, HABIT, MISSION, PARTNER, AND JOY

Anzaldúa's Writing Process

I write because it's my calling, my task to do in the world. I write. It is a ritual, a habit, a propensity bred in my bones. It is what I do. I write because I like to think on paper. I write because I like to think, and to track my thoughts. I write because I want to leave a discernable mark on the world.—Anzaldúa, Writing Notas G

What was her particular mission in writing? Her particular joy in writing? Her particular strength in writing? Her personal vision? The world behind her work makes its presence known to her, wants her to know it on its own terms. It wants to be attended to. —Anzaldúa, "Nepantla: In/Between and Shifting"

For me, every phase of writing happens at the same time, there is no set sequence. Simultaneously I use the "additive" method. Fleshing out a skeletal frame and adding and adding much like a whale or a flamingo I take in large quantities of "water" and eject it through a filtering (revisioning) system, keeping the images and passages that are necessary to the text I'm writing. The "subtracting" method.—Anzaldúa, "The Writing Subject: Racial Ethnic/Others inside Enemy Territory"

Writing was Gloria Anzaldúa's vocation—the work she was called to do in the world. Indeed, as these epigraphs suggest, Anzaldúa believed that she was born to write. Writing was "bred in [her] bones"; she had no choice in the matter. Writing was her obsession, her passion, her nemesis, her joy, as well as the source of her livelihood. From her teen years onward, she aspired to be an author-philosopher, to create work that would powerfully live on after her death. She wrote to think, to reflect, to create transformative knowledge for herself, her readers, and the world. From 1974, when she took her first creative writing class at Indiana University, until the end of her life she committed herself to the writing. She reaffirmed this commitment in September 1977 when she left Austin, Texas, and moved to California, resolving never again to take on a full-time conventional job but instead to devote herself to her writing (*to sacrifice her life to the words, to the work of la musa bruja*). For the remainder of her life, Anzaldúa supported herself through part-time gigs, adjunct teaching, writing workshops, and speaking engagements. And all throughout this time, she honed her craft through research, self-reflection, and constant practice.

Not surprisingly, given this strong passion for writing, Anzaldúa often wrote about her writing process, from her initial inspirations and brainstorming to crafting, revising, editing, and reading. Key published pieces include "Speaking in Tongues: A Letter to Third World Women Writers," "Tlilli, Tlapalli: The Path of the Red and Black Ink" (chapter 6 in *Borderlands*), "To(o) Queer the Writer: *Loca, escritora y chicana*"; and chapters 2 and 5 in *Light in the Dark* (ESPECIALLY chapter 5, "*Putting Coyolxauhqui Together*"). But the actual amount of material that Anzaldúa produced on the topic is much greater than this list suggests, thanks to her lengthy writing process (*as well as her perfectionist tendencies and constant revisions*). Anzaldúa generated many drafts for each published piece—some with important, previously unseen clues into her process. Moreover (*and more copiously*), she wrote many never-published essays and dissertation chapters focused on writing. Especially important here are the following: "Poetry & Magick: A Practicum for Developing Literary + Psychic Skills" (1976–81), "Autohistoria de la artista as a Young Girl" (1990); several chapters from the 1990s dissertation ("*Autohistorias-teorías—Mujeres que cuentan vidas*: Personal & Collective Narratives That Challenge Genre Conventions," "Barred Witness: Literary/Artistic Creations and Class Identities," "The Writing Subject: Racial Ethnic/Others inside Enemy Territory," "THE POET IS CRITIC/THE POET IS THEORIST: Speaking in Tongues, Queridas mujeres escritorias de color Carta Two"); and a writing guide, which she worked on from the 1980s until her death. Additionally, Anzaldúa's writing notes (discussed in chapter 1) contain thousands of self-reflections, observations, and analyses on the topic. In the following pages, I draw on these many texts as well as my intimate knowledge of Anzaldúa (as co-editor, editor, writing comadre, researcher, and friend) to explore her complex relationship to writing and her relational, recursive creative process.

Writing served many functions in Anzaldúa's life. She wrote for survival, resistance, and transformation; for knowledge production (at multiple levels ranging from self-knowledge to the creation of new collective knowledge); and for social change. She wrote to bear witness. She wrote to create community. She wrote to challenge, expose, exorcise, and heal the erasure she experienced due to gender, race, class, sexuality, physical appearance, and other social biases and constraints. She wrote to redefine herself and the world—to change herself and her readers. These writing-related functions intertwined throughout her work, from beginning to end. In a 1996 unpublished poem, "What is Writing," Anzaldúa describes writing as excavation, illumination, slow and steady transformation: like dripping water that, drop by steady slow drop, can hollow out stone; or, like small shoots of grass that patiently, over time, create tiny fissures and cracks in rocks as they grow, so writing subtly effects large change. But this transformative process is painful: it's "an addiction to an activity / which causes anxiety and interference with your life." Writing demands a stripping-away of the self-enclosed ego as writer surrenders to the work's wisdom: "throwing away yourself / and letting the work take you"; writing also transforms this surrendered self: "and in the end giving back your self."

As this poem suggests, for Anzaldúa, writing was radically, painfully dialogic. Writing demanded a relational dance between herself (*the many pieces of herself, from inner nagual and ancestral roots to emotions, experiences, and desires*), language (*multiple languages*), the emergent draft and theories, and the world itself (*which "makes its presence known to her, wants her to know it on its own terms"*), and (*of course*) her readers. Not surprisingly, given this cacophonous constellation of conversation partners, Anzaldúa defines writing as "a different kind of intelligence / greater than writer and reader combined / that worms its way through the molds and masks / and spills onto the page" (Writing Notas A). This intelligence does not automatically emerge in some beautiful first draft (*though it might be whispering softly to us*), but rather it painfully drags itself into existence through the revision process, through painstaking, patient work. As this unpublished poem suggests, then, for Anzaldúa writing was participatory; the texts she "produced" were not products so much as they were co-creations with

Anzaldúa herself: each project, each text was agentic and helped to birth it-self into being (*always in conversation with the larger outer and inner worlds*).

Anzaldúa was a meticulous writer with extremely high standards. How she agonized over her words! (*How. She. AGONIZED. Over. Her. Words.*) She wrote many drafts for each piece and typically refused to release her work into the world until she felt that it met her strict requirements—regardless of an editor's demands or a publisher's deadlines. Indeed, our 2002 edited collection, *this bridge we call home: radical visions for transformation*, was published a year after the contracted date because Gloria did not feel that her contribution for the volume ("now let us shift") met her expectations. As will become abundantly clear in what follows, despite her celebration of writing Anzaldúa struggled greatly with it during many parts of her pro-cess. Writing took on enormous epistemological, ontological, and ethical weight—at least in part because she delved so deeply into her individual and collective psyche and worked to recover and rebuild its hidden (*sub-merged, lost, abandoned, repressed*) parts. Thus in "Ethnic Autohistorias" she likens writing to "an act of exorcism," and in an interview she describes it as "making soul," a "struggle" in which "a piece of experience is worked on, is connected to the soul, connected to making soul. It's where the spir-itual, psychic component of writing comes in. . . . You have to destroy, tear down, in order to put together and rebuild. That's why writing has saved our lives, because it makes sense out of this chaos. But the process is pain-ful" (*Interviews* 222). For Anzaldúa, this pain was so extreme that it felt like dying: "[I]t doesn't get easier after the first draft, or should I say the first 'death.' The completion of a draft, of a particular piece, is a struggle to the death" ("Plunging into El Cenote"). And yet, Anzaldúa was also in love with writing, describing herself as

> married—to the writing. She gave to it her energy, her higest inspri-ations [*sic*] and aspirations. To draw flower and song—poetry—from her insides and to whittle into shape, texture, color, to wring poetry out of it was her passion and her obsession. She was possessed by la Musa Bruja. La Musa was her altar and she slept, ate and made love on it. She was a priestess of La Musa Bruja, a prisoner of her temple. ("La serpiente")

As this brief excerpt suggests, Anzaldúa gave herself over to the writing.

It would require an entire book focused exclusively on the topic to thor-oughly explore Anzaldúa's complex relationship to writing. (*Even the above passage from "Esperando" invites further analysis: consider the possibilities that open when we consider Anzaldúa as both priestess and prisoner of la musa bruja.*) We would need to dive deeply into her unpublished manuscripts to understand how she defined it, the many nuanced functions she believed writing could serve, her investigations into individual/collective representation, her theories about how writing could challenge, expose, and transform consensual reality. We would need to investigate, in great detail, the many challenges she experienced as she developed her skills and honed her craft. These challenges could be divided roughly into two types: (1) the broad, systemic challenges that Anzaldúa, along with many women-of-colors authors/philosophers, experienced; and (2) the unique constellation of challenges (physical, social, intellectual, psychic) that emerged from Anzaldúa's specific embodied location. In the first category, we'd explore how the Anglo-dominant education system punished Spanish-speaking children, making their relationship to writing unnecessarily traumatic; the fact that she, like so many others, was shamed by her teacher for not knowing English; the larger cultural scripts that gave defeatist messages to women of colors and other marginalized groups, insisting that they were "not supposed to make art or theory"[1] but were instead to be the objects, not the subjects (*never the subjects*), of discourse;[2] the lack of mentorship to assist with the many steps involved in publication;[3] the tokenization; the financial insecurity; the many larger sociocultural stressors, or what Anzaldúa calls her "post-traumatic stress disorder . . . chronic depression, suicidal tendencies, [and] inability to feel or identify feelings" and its destructive physical impact: "The stress spreads, metastasize like a cancer in hidden sites in the brain or emotional tissues. It can take root in the very bone" ("Barred Witness").

And that's not all! This book would also explore how Anzaldúa's unique constellation of personal challenges further complicated her relationship to writing/theorizing. We'd need at least one chapter focused entirely on embodiment: how her body (both the physical conditions and her relationship to them) impacted her writing; how the early menses marked her as different from family, friends, and peers, and how this difference shaped her perspectives; how her horrific monthly periods complicated her relationship with her body; how these complications made their way into her work; how her periodic but lifelong struggles with insomnia impacted her writing; how her hysterectomy led to a near-death experience and how this NDE impacted her metaphysics; and how her 1992 diagnosis of type

1 diabetes completely upended her writing schedule, further complicated her already complex relationship with embodiment, and in other ways disrupted and shifted her life and work.[4]

After tracing these and other physical challenges, this book would demand an entire chapter (*or more!*) devoted to Anzaldúa's perfectionism, tracing its roots and exploring how it shaped her relationship to writing and theorizing while preventing her from publishing her work more quickly and more frequently.[5] Here we'd investigate how Anzaldúa's drive to demonstrate excellence in the face of a world that questioned her ability to do so further fueled her perfectionist tendencies, elevating her decisions about what constituted "good enough" to publish. Relatedly, this chapter would speculate on the pressure Anzaldúa must have felt to produce a follow-up to *Borderlands*—given its iconic status and scholars' various reactions to it. Importantly, these chapters would not focus exclusively on the challenges Anzaldúa experienced but would, in each instance, investigate how she worked with these challenges, almost turning them on their heads, using them productively to inspire her work.[6] (*I've briefly mentioned many challenges Anzaldúa experienced to remind us that her productiveness and range are even more amazing given the severity of obstacles she encountered.*)

But this is not that book. I focus here on Anzaldúa's process (*by which I mean the actual steps she enacted as she wrote*) and its dialogic knowledge production (*that is, the ways she did not use writing exclusively for self-expression; rather, she always approached writing as conversation with the larger inner and outer worlds—with other human and nonhuman beings, the imaginal, history, myth, and much more*). In the following sections, I explore Anzaldúa's writing process in more depth, offering first an overview and then a step-by-step summary.

Anzaldúa's Recursive Writing Process: The Bare-Bones Overview

I met Gloria Anzaldúa in 1991 at the University of Arizona and was fortunate to become one of her "writing comadres"—the term Anzaldúa used to describe her peer review partners and friends.[7] A few days after first meeting her, she asked me to read and offer feedback on an unpublished short story draft. I was shocked! Who was I, a nobody at the earliest stages of my career (*a career which, at that time, I was somewhat ashamed of, due to the non-elite university where I worked as well as my religiously conservative family's deep suspicion of graduate education and my career choice*)? Anzaldúa didn't treat me as an awestruck fan or student, but rather as a fellow writer—a colleague with valuable insights to offer.[8] I was thrilled beyond what any words could convey. There I was, stumbling through the first days of my academic career, and yet Gloria Anzaldúa (*the* Cloria Anzaldúa, *creator of the three most influential books I'd ever read* [This Bridge Called My Back, Borderlands/La Frontera, *and* Making Face, Making Soul]) asked *me* for feedback and seriously considered my comments. I was struck by Anzaldúa's humility, by her willingness to share her unfinished writings with others, and by the painstakingly partial state of the manuscript itself. To be sure, it was a captivating story (good plot line, great characterization, interesting ideas, powerful metaphors, captivating dialogue, etc.); however, the draft was uneven and needed more work (*the prose did not sing; it stuttered, stumbled, and paused*). Because I'd assumed that Anzaldúa's words flowed effortlessly from her keyboard and pen, I was startled to realize the extent of her revision process. I'm not alone in this type of Anzaldúan encounter. If you look through her archival materials, you'll see that she regularly shared unfinished drafts with others. Because she always wrote with audience in mind and aspired to impact her readers, she involved readers at almost every step of the way: she wanted to know how her words impacted us; she used our feedback as she revised, with the goal of effective, expansive, transformational communication.

Anzaldúa typically worked on multiple projects simultaneously; wrote numerous drafts of each piece; made extensive revisions on each draft; drew connections among various projects; and incorporated peer critiques from her writing comadres, editors, and others. During the late 1970s and early 1980s, for example, she was working on at least nine different projects: Her copious journals, "La Prieta," "Speaking in Tongues," "Esperando la serpiente con plumas" (her autohistoria, of which she produced three drafts), a manuscript titled "Poetry & Magick," a treatise on El Mundo Zurdo, a book-length dramatic poem (*La Chingada*), short stories ("La boda," "Sabas Q," etc.), a poetry collection (*Night Face*), and *This Bridge Called My Back*. These projects were at various stages of completion, and Anzaldúa typically moved among several during the same week—and often within the same writing period. Not surprisingly, then, she would sometimes take ideas, images, or even passages from one piece and include them in others. The intersections between "La Prieta," "Speaking in Tongues," and *This Bridge Called My Back* beautifully illustrate this movement.[9] Anzaldúa's writerly multitasking continued throughout her career. In the late 1990s and early 2000s, for example, she was completing *Interviews/Entrevistas*; co-editing *this bridge we call home*; drafting "now let us shift," "(un)natural bridges," and "counsels from the firing . . . past, present, future"; teaching a creative writing course; working on "SIC" ("Spiritual Identity Crisis"); giving lectures; and drafting chapters that, she hoped, would make their way into the dissertation and other publications. This multiplicity and movement further enhanced the dialogic quality of Anzaldúa's process: the ideas flowed from one manuscript to another and then back again, altered by each tiny shift and larger move. Questions she grappled with in one piece could be answered, expanded, and/or changed in others. In short, Anzaldúa's process was deeply dialogic and recursive. (*"Recursive" only somewhat conveys the spiraling, intricately interwoven nature of her process.*) As explained later in more detail, Anzaldúa produced her work through multilayered, ongoing self-reflective conversations with inner and outer worlds: imaginal figures, contemporary ideas, other writers, other parts of herself, and other pieces of her own writing. This winding, sprawling movement makes it challenging (*and inevitably limited and flawed*) to delineate her writing process as a series of steps. (*And yet, here we go . . .*)

In a draft of what eventually became "Putting Coyolxauhqui Together: A Creative Process" (chapter 5 in *Light in the Dark* and Anzaldúa's most sustained attempt to describe her writing process from beginning to end), Anzaldúa divided her method into nine stages:

1. Dream, envision and conceptualize the total "story"; take notes; imaging sections/scenes, beginning, middle, and end; broad outline; free write
2. Research; take notes; key in everything; free write; print draft
3. Organize, add, delete sections (3 to 6 pre-drafts); free write
4. Gestate for several days
5. First draft, use imaging process let the story develop on its own, occasionally looking at outline and notes; free write
6. Read through; revise; free write
7. Revision, revise and rewrite (10–30 drafts). Too much detail confuses, bores. What does reader need, how does she want to react? Write to the reader's expectations but also against her expectations. Comadres read the story
8. Gestate, lie fallow

9. Edit; rewrite; proofread; tidy up (two to four drafts); send out and go public. And to the marketplace.

This list is striking for several reasons, including its recursivity, multiple gestation periods, and frequent freewrites (*in five out of the nine stages!*). Perhaps most importantly (*and surprisingly?*), the fact that Anzaldúa did not produce her first draft until midway through this long list indicates that her method consisted of two distinct yet intimately intertwined stages: in the first (consisting of items 1 through 4 in her above list), she generated (*and channeled*) ideas; and in the second (items 5 through 9), she struggled to convey these ideas powerfully with eloquent words.

Anzaldúa confirms this twofold method in an unpublished early draft, "How I get myself to the writing," in which she divides her process into two: (1) the "original creative out-pouring on the page"; and (2) "the serious work of organizing, editing, revising, [and] typing." While she enjoyed the first stage tremendously, she approached the second with wariness (*and possibly, at times, with dread*): "The original creative out-pouring on the page is easy for me—I can do it anywhere, anytime[,] standing in bank lines standing in swaying subway trains. But the rest is another matter." And again in *Light in the Dark*, she reiterates this twofold process: "Writing is not only the physical act of drafting and revising but also involves feeding the muse books on mythology and Aztec nagualismo (shamanism), reading voraciously in all disciplines, and taking notes. Writing also involves envisioning and conceptualizing the work, and dreaming the story into a virtual reality" (102). In what follows, I explore Anzaldúa's complex process in more detail. As I do so, it's important to remember that these divisions are somewhat arbitrary. As Anzaldúa notes, "The different stages in embodying the story are neither clearly demarcated nor sequential nor linear; they overlap, shift back and forth, take place simultaneously" (*Light* 102).

The Call and Oracular Research: Inspiration, Idea Generation (Summoning the Muse)

Generally, Anzaldúa's projects began with an invitation of some sort—an opening gesture that summoned the project into being. This call could be outer, inner, or (most likely) some combination of the two: an invitation to speak at a conference or university; the opportunity to contribute a piece to an edited book collection or journal; an assignment for a specific course;

a major project for a degree; the inner drive to express some insight or semi-felt intuition about a specific experience or to solve an intellectual, emotional, and/or personal problem; the desire to connect with others or to share what she'd learned.[10] After answering the call in the affirmative, Anzaldúa gathered and generated ideas, enacting what I describe as "oracular research." Idea generation occurred through self-reflective dialogues with inner and outer worlds initiated through a wide variety of activities: meditation, freewrites, walking, dreaming, visualization, imaginal journeys, reading, time in nature, metaphysical technologies, freewrites (*Look! I wrote "freewrites" twice: They were that important to Anzaldúa's process, as her journals and writing notas attest*), and more.

I describe this phase as "oracular research" to underscore its transpersonal, nonrational, sacred components, as well as the animist metaphysical framework through which Anzaldúa wrote. We find signs of Anzaldúa's oracular research throughout her work, perhaps nowhere more openly (*and bravely*) than in the early autohistoria "Esperando la serpiente con plumas," in which, in a section titled "How I Wrote This Book," she states,

> Who do I consult? Myself. I am my own oracle, seer, prophet. The "authorities" I go to are my Creative Consciousness or Higher Self, what the ancient Hawaiians call Aumakua; I go to my Inner Self, the Unihipili. And the organizing principle of this act—I couldn't have done it without my Conscious Self—the Uhane and its right and left hemispheres of the brain. the other "experts" I consult are the *I Ching*, the Tarot, numerology, and the astrological Sabian symbols— any and all tools I can get my hands on to facilitate the channeling of information from the Sourse [*sic*]==my soul my Creative Consciousness, what others call the Muse or Goddess or God.

As these passages suggest, Anzaldúa employed a wide range of metaphysical, scientific technologies from western, eastern, and Indigenous wisdom traditions. Despite this diversity of worldviews, they all offered Anzaldúa portals and/or engines to assist her in thinking more holistically (*as evidenced by her reference 'to both right and left brain hemispheres*) and connected more closely with the larger cosmic force animating herself and all existence. Importantly, this larger force both is and is not Anzaldúa herself: it's neither a wholly external divine force, nor synonymous with her inner intuitive nature. Rather, it is all this and more. As she states in a biographical statement, "To help me get messages from Self to self, I use the I Ching, the Tarot, playing cards, and the astrological Sabian symbols as intermediary tools" ("Faculty Self-Description"). These various metaphysical technologies functioned as windows and doorways offering Anzaldúa access into the more-than-human wisdom and knowledge from the cosmos.[11]

Anzaldúa's oracular research thus functioned as intentional alignment—that is, as carefully orchestrated attempts to connect herself (*her inner world*) with sacred wisdom (*both inner and outer*). Whether she consulted the I Ching, Tarot, the planets (via astrology), numbers (numerology), or a pendulum, Anzaldúa asked these technologies to assist her in gaining wisdom from the larger cosmic forces to which she was indebted and to which she had committed herself. (*As my use of the word "asked" implies, the technologies are living entities who function in partnership with humans; they must be approached with respect—asked, not commanded.*) She sought both profound insights and practical guidance about writing projects and other dimensions of her life. For example, on May 10, 1982, she consulted the I Ching, asking, "What would be the best topic/focus of my reading at Old Wives [Bookstore] in June?" and received "51. The arousing shock & thunder" and "47. Oppression Exhaustion/Adversity" in reply (61.18). On October 22, 2001, as she developed her foreword to the third edition of *This Bridge Called My Back*, she consulted the I Ching, asking, "What should I focus on in the TBCMB foreword?" and then used the I Ching's reply ("59. Dissolving Rigidity") as she wrote (52.3). Importantly, these oracular replies were not linear commands but rather conversational notes with which Anzaldúa engaged, using intuition and other guides to interpret them. We see these interactions in her journals, writing notas, and research files, where she recorded her discoveries and messages.

Anzaldúa's oracular research also entailed a type of "awake dreaming" in which she tapped into (and often entered) the imaginal—complex, nonspatial, nontemporal dimensions of reality that exist alongside and within our own more conventional, three-dimensional world.[12] Her 1997 essay draft, "The Writing Habit: How I Work—Process and Stages," offers useful insights into these oracular dreams. For Anzaldúa, "dreaming" entailed "voluntary immersion in [the] imaginal world, into el cenote, a reservoir where these stories and histories are stored. It is an archive where I taste a forgotten knowledge triggered by an order or some trivial incident and suddenly out pours ancestral information stored beyond the files of personal memory, information stored as iconic imagery somewhere in the sea of unconscious, an ocean of uncanny signs. It is a subliminal dive deep down in my cenote. Either I find a way in or it finds a way out." As explained in more detail in chapter 4, Anzaldúa's theory of el cenote represents an individual/collective source of transpersonal guidance and archetypal meaning that can be accessed through self-reflection and intentional openness to unexpected insights. El cenote offers "roadmaps to guide us" and, as such, assists with our "soul work" (49.2).

Although Anzaldúa describes her deep dives into the imaginal as "voluntary," it would be inaccurate to assume that she entirely controlled them. While she exercised intentionality and used rational thought, she relied extensively on la facultad and engaged with the images themselves as agentic beings. She did not create them but, rather, they appeared *to* her. Nor did she try to control them; instead, she opened herself to their wisdom. (*To be even more direct: the images were not entirely products of her imagination, psyche, or mind; they had lives of their own, beyond hers.*) As she explains in the same draft, "As I pay attention to the image, try to decipher its meaning, I get a presentiment, a feeling that stays with me, that worries me, haunts me and which speaks a secret language, one shared with the spirits of trees, sea, wind, and animals. It is like sensing a supernatural presense [sic] in things" ("Writing Habit"). Here we see that Anzaldúa approached the imaginal with respectful intentionality and relied on intuitive, nonrational epistemologies to communicate with them. In short, Anzaldúa established complex, reciprocal relationships with the images, respecting their guidance on how to proceed. As she notes in a later draft of this essay, "An image is a sign post that points you in a direction. By paying attention to an image you honor it, thus reclaiming whatever it represents. An image is a means of direct conocimiento without an intermediary. When you let the image take you wherever it needs to go you learn what the image teaches."

At what could seem like a more pedestrian level, Anzaldúa's oracular research included gathering information from conventional sources (*publications, human authorities, and so on*). Anzaldúa was a voracious reader (*and note-taker*); she did extensive research on specific topics she planned to explore, reading many books, articles, and online material. She regularly looked through her earlier journals, writing notas, and paper drafts to locate additional information and material on a specific topic. As she researched and took notes, she remained open to oracular guidance, trusting la facultad and synchronicity to guide her.

Pre-drafts: Freewrites

Interwoven with this research stage, and as part of her idea generation, Anzaldúa produced a series of "pre-drafts"—pages of intuitively guided material too disjointed to be considered an actual draft. She summarizes this part of her process in "How I get myself to the writing":

> Sitting at my couch. Picking up paper and pencil. Identifying the topic/area I want to write on. Not entertaining preconceived ideas about it. Going into meditation (it only takes a few deep breaths) and the ideas start to surface—the form of images. I put pen to paper. When the words-images stop flowing, I close my eyes and go into meditation. A few seconds or minutes later the flow begins again. That is exactly how I wrote this essay. I play this movie before I go to sleep (once or twice during the day). Next day this "movie" is acted out by me.

This passage also indicates how intention functioned in Anzaldúa's process: She uses imagination with careful forethought to create movies in her mind, in which she visualizes her writing process stage by stage (the meditation, the inspirational freewriting, and so on). She replays this movie several times throughout the day in order to implant in herself a successful writing period. (*Indeed, one could say that this intentional seeding is a critical dimension of Anzaldúa's organic writing.*)

During her pre-drafting phase, Anzaldúa again used a combination of ritual, intuitive guidance, additional freewrites, and rational thought to further develop (*and discover*) the project's direction. Here, in second person voice, she describes one of the many forms that her rituals might take:

> You light copal incense, hoping the scent and the ritual will coax you into the writing. You stare at the fluttering flame of the Virgen de Guadalupe novena candle and invoke the memory de tus muertos, your dead, tus mamagrandes y tu papá who persevered and persisted and who walk between realities. You brew some chai tea, find music to accompany your visionary scape, to shift consciousness from beta toward alpha. Tex-Mex? Ambient? Enigma? Lourdes Pérez? The cavernous cello sounds of Yo-Yo Ma playing the Bach suites it is. You do a five-minute meditation observing your mind streaming, say your writer's prayer, and begin to compose. At this point, your task is to re-

member, translate into language the images arising from your body, the sea, the theater of dreams—allowing them to surface at will and capturing them in your net of words. (*Light* 102)

Note how Anzaldúa prepares herself for the writing by opening avenues for communication. She enacts ritual to summon energies and guides; she creates a comfortable, inspiring environment in which to write; she meditates and seeks further guidance; and then (*only then*) she begins to write. Note also her view of this process as a form of reception in which she works to capture wisdom from other realms (including her own body). As with the first stage, these freewrites involved immersion into el cenote:

> You conjure up el cenote, throw yourself in and swim among images and memories of other writing times. You freewrite five to six pages at warp speed. You do not focus on form. You don't consider technical problems yet. You keep the critical, editing voice at bay. You go from tightly focused writing to brief pauses where you allow your attention to dart here and there. Keying in the words, you're scribe, medium channeling the story, and conductor orchestrating the process. (*Light* 104)

By writing nonstop (*and keeping the critical voice at bay*), Anzaldúa allowed inspiration to flow without censorship or other forms of analysis. The point here was to access multiple modes of knowing and produce an abundance of images and insights, regardless of whether they would make their way into a draft. The first pre-draft was quite rough, lacking transitions, logical organization, and other conventional writing elements. But this rough quality was also a strength; its loose, disorganized form allowed additional insights to emerge.

Drafting, Revising

After completing four to six pre-drafts, Anzaldúa developed her first draft—a somewhat organized version of the most recent pre-draft. As with the previous stages, she relied heavily on la facultad, but here she also employed additional analytical thinking as she searched for patterns, reading through the most recent pre-draft with curiosity and openness. Anzaldúa believed that the organization would rise organically from the material itself: she was "not aiming for a linear, logical structure of ideas, but instead for an architectural body that supports and allows access to its innards" (*Light* 106). She looked for recurring patterns that constellated into a meta-pattern of sorts, offering a larger framework to guide the essay's structure and creation. She rearranged, deleted, and inserted material, "search[ing] the field of bones for una seña of the root metaphor, the umbilicus to which all elements of la historia connect, a literary equivalent to chaos theory's strange attractor, . . . an image-pattern that will point to a framework which could contain the organized whole" (*Light* 101). When Anzaldúa located this "conducting thread," she used it as "temporary" framework for the first draft and created a short outline of the project's tentative structure, placing it at the top of the first page. In future drafts, she revised by loosely reorganizing material according to this outline. Once again, imagination and "dreaming" played key roles. As Anzaldúa moved through her day, doing little chores around the house, preparing meals, taking meditative walks, and so on, she stayed in relationship with the piece and receptive to further insights.

As she wrote and revised, Anzaldúa did so (*always!*) with her audience in mind (*multiple audiences, including herself*). She asked questions concerning the degree of details to include, focusing especially on her readers' needs: "Too much detail confuses, bores. What does the reader need, how does she want to react?" (*Light* 208). While Anzaldúa was no control freak, trying to manage every specific detail about readers' reactions, she did strive to challenge her readers to shift and grow—despite the discomfort that can arise when our preconceptions are challenged. She aspired to "[w]rite to the reader's expectations but also against her expectations" (*Light* 208). The point was not simply to share ideas but to impact readers physically and emotionally. Thus in "Nepantla: In/Between and Shifting" Anzaldúa articulates her desire to "transfer an emotional experience to the reader."[13]

And here, after the first draft, the revisions began. Typically, Anzaldúa printed the draft and carefully edited it by hand. She read each draft multiple times, making extensive changes that involved some or all of the following actions: rearranging individual words, entire sentences, and paragraphs; adding or deleting large chunks of material; copying and repeating especially significant phrases; and inserting material from other writing notas and/or works in progress. Throughout her drafting and revision process, Anzaldúa focused simultaneously on content and form. She wanted the words to move in readers' bodies and transform them, from the inside out, and she revised repeatedly in order to achieve this impact. She revised for cadence, musicality, nuanced meaning, and metaphoric complexity. We see this thoughtful attention to her revision process in Writing Notas J, in a section titled "Revision Guide-lines for Prose":

> My advice is to scrutinize each sentence and ask: What exactly am I trying to say? What concrete words, images, metaphors will make it clearer? Can I use fewer and prettier and shorter words? Don't let the language dictate what you should think nor let it construct your sentences, nor let it conceal your meaning. Let meaning choose the words. Think of the concrete object, then hunt for the exact words that describe what you are visualizing: First get your meaning through pictures or sensations then choose the phrases that will best convey the meaning. Then focus on what impressions your words may make on the reader. Lifeless, dead, vague phraseology. Name things by calling up mental pictures of them. What are your real aims in writing this piece? What are your declared aims?

(*We could develop an entire writing workshop with this advice as guidance!*) Note how Anzaldúa mixes aesthetics with self-reflection. The point is not simply to create beautiful images and passages but rather to use language effectively in order to communicate—to make change in herself and her readers—to bring us new knowledge, to shake up our worlds. As she goes on to observe later in the same section, "There's a political purpose to writing—that is to push the world in a certain direction, and to change others' ideas of reality, and what reality to strive for."

At the micro level, Anzaldúa's revisions were meticulous, time-consuming, and multifaceted. (*I have so much agonizing firsthand experience with this meticulous revision process; although the revisions were usually worth the time spent, it could be frustrating for those of us waiting on Gloria to complete a joint project; her constant reworking of the same material, making [what seemed like] micro changes, was frustrating to behold. The "final" products, though, were well worth the wait.*) As she narrowed her focus to paragraph- and sentence-level edits, Anzaldúa carefully examined each sentence's structure, word choice, rhythm, and so on. As she explained in an email near the end of her life, she carefully worked with "every subject, then every paragraph, then every sentence, then every word."[14]

Anzaldúa repeated her multilayered revision process numerous times; at various points she would share the manuscript with one or more of her writing comadres. Typically, she requested both specific and general comments which she then selectively incorporated into future revisions. She included these questions either in a separate message or at the top of the draft itself (*which is very convenient for researchers!*). After giving a draft to her writing comadre(s), Anzaldúa would work on another of her many projects while allowing the piece shared with the comadres to "gestate" in her mind/soul. This recursive process repeated several to many times. At some point along the way, Anzaldúa moved on to proofreading and editing the draft, after which she would either send it out for publication or put it away, to be worked on at a later date—although as her extensive archives indicates, this "later date" did not necessarily arrive. Perhaps not surprisingly, at times, even after she published a piece, Anzaldúa would return to it, making additional edits and revisions.[15]

Postscript: On Writing about Anzaldúa's (Writing/Theorizing/Creative) Process

This chapter was one of the most challenging for me to produce and, in fact, I tried mightily to resist its call. I had hoped that by focusing on Anzaldúa's theory-making process I could sidestep (*by which I mean: entirely avoid*) an exploration of her writing process. I knew from my years of working with Gloria that her process was torturous, tedious, and at times toxic. I feared that immersing myself in it would taint my own process and further delay completion of this book. (*I experienced something similar while editing* Light in the Dark.) And, indeed, producing this chapter was challenging (*that's an understatement!*). Although she wrote often about writing, the discussions themselves were circular, recursive, and at times confusing. The challenge was complex: How could I possibly tease apart Anzaldúa's organic, holistic process? And, once teased apart, how could this circular, at times nonrational, process be put into words? (*Language and reading are linear. Sure, metaphors take us into complex multidimensionality, but in the act of reading the words march across the page, one by one, building up, accumulating their meaning.*)

However, to borrow Anzaldúa's phrase: Vale la peña. (*And also: Wow!*) I am so grateful to have been compelled to explore this topic and write this chapter. (*Shout out to la musa bruja y La Gloria for insisting that I do, for the constant nagging.*) I learned so much about Anzaldúa's writing process (*even after so many years of working with Anzaldúa and writing about her work!*). When I recognized that the freewrites were so important to her writing process, it helped me greatly to understand her work (including her archives) more fully. I could make more sense of the vast journals and thousands of pages of writing notas, viewing them as part of her oracular research—a complex dialogue between herself, her life, and reality itself. With the birth of the archive, the process continues, drawing readers further into Anzaldúa's oracular research.

3. HOW THE THEORIES EMERGED

Haciendo teorías con Gloria

The poet, the critic, and the theorist in me are the same person and she is engaged in the task of producing meanings.—Anzaldúa, "Poet is Critic"

Theory, then, is a set of knowledges. Some of these knowledges have been kept from us—entry into some professions and academia denied us. Because we are not allowed to enter discourse, because we are often disqualified and excluded from it, because what passes for theory these days is forbidden territory for us, it is vital that we occupy theorizing space, that we not allow whitemen [sic] and women solely to occupy it. By bringing in our own approaches and methodologies, we transform that theorizing space.—Anzaldúa, "haciendo caras"

Anzaldúa offers one of her most succinct yet comprehensive analyses of western theory in "haciendo caras, una entrada," the introduction to her 1990 edited collection, *Making Face, Making Soul/Haciendo Caras: Creative and Critical Perspectives by Women of Color.* Created in part as an intervention into elite academic theory during the time when Anzaldúa herself was immersed in poststructuralist thought while taking graduate courses at the University of California, Santa Cruz, *Making Face, Making Soul* offers a compendium of theory by women of colors, curated by Anzaldúa to illustrate the many ways that she and other women of colors theorize. Her goal, at least in part, was to challenge the reigning intellectual stereotypes of that day—stereotypes that associated philosophy and theory (especially academic "high theory") with white-raced men.[1] An avid reader, longtime student, and self-taught philosopher, Anzaldúa was very aware of these stereotypes and had been negatively impacted by them throughout her education and academic career. Not only was she typically one of very few women of colors in school, but the vast majority of work she had been exposed to was by white men and (though less frequently) white women. Moreover, her innovative theorizing in the recently published *Borderlands/ La Frontera* had been downplayed, criticized, or entirely overlooked. In the late twentieth century, theory was generally defined as a product of Enlightenment thought, an abstract way of thinking and writing that severs mind from body, relies primarily on rationality, employs elite language, and analyzes reality by *detaching* it from everyday life.

But for Anzaldúa, theory can and should be deeply embedded in daily existence: we theorize through our embodied engagements with the world and use this theorizing to more effectively navigate through and transform it. (*And, as you'll see, transformation is key to Anzaldúan theory.*) Thus in "haciendo caras" she offers an expansive definition that democratizes theory, presenting it as commonplace: "Theory originally meant a mental viewing, an idea or mental plan of the way to do something, and a formulation of apparent relationships or underlying principles of certain observed phenomena which had been verified to some degree" (xxv). Here, theory is not an artificially elevated form of knowledge production engaged in by the select (*highly elite*) few. Rather, theorizing (whether explicit or implicit) is vital for us all. Like her dialogic writing process, Anzaldúa's approach to theory-making is deeply relational and, thus, radically inclusive. By virtue of our existence on this planet, we are in relationship with the world and all its inhabitants; as we move through it, we interpret our experiences, making theory as we do. However, the academy has not recognized this breadth but has, instead, defined theory narrowly, as the abstract intellectual products of an elite group of people.

Not surprisingly, Anzaldúa took issue with this theoretical elitism and its destructive effects. Thus in an unpublished manuscript, "Re-conocimientos and Producing Knowledge," she contrasts her approach with the conventional theorizing mainstream academics do and asserts that she and other women of colors make theory "to save our lives and this is where our theory is different—it is connected to survival, life and death experience." Similarly, in "Violent Space, *Nepantla* Stage," Anzaldúa asserts that academic theory typically functions as "[i]ntellectual violence and mind mugging" that negatively impacts marginalized people: "In the academy—their identities are constantly contested, unde[r]mined and trashed by the upholders of dominant culture who use theory to police and terrori[z]e, to manipulate and control, people's lives and identities." At times, this theoretical violence included appropriation and outright theft, a topic Anzaldúa briefly explores in "Violent Space, *Nepantla* Stage," as she acknowledges the self-doubt she experiences when sharing her "unpublished work [with] white professors and even friends." (*In short, when theory is defined narrowly and enacted in these brutal ways, our identities are negated, our minds are mugged—our ideas stolen and our self-confidence shaken, if not destroyed.*) For Anzaldúa and other women of colors at that time (*and, too often, still today*), conventional academic theory did not serve them or other nondominant groups well.

Anzaldúa offers an extensive analysis of elite theory in "The Poet as Critic, The Poet as Theorist," a chapter from her 1990s UCSC dissertation. Describing the theories she was exposed to in graduate school as a "private club in which 'high' and white theorists (both male and female) speak only to one another and intentionally or unintentionally close ranks against us, the outsiders," she analyzes their destructive impact. When we work diligently to comprehend and master these theories, the theories (*and their elite worldview*) master (*and colonize*) us: as we "learn the Western European patriarchal male way of writing theory," we experience a "colonization of the mind"; our ancestral/home epistemologies and ontologies are negated—"taken over by that other's order." We are not the intended audience for "high" theory. If we simply read and ingest it, adopting it without questioning the values, framework, and positionality it represents, we lose (*temporarily or forever*) our self-confidence and, thus, "stunt" our intellectual growth. When we assimilate the elite theories, they assimilate us, telling us what and how to think; this theoretical colonization is insidious and subtly compels us to doubt our own thoughts, identities, and perspectives, making us internally fragmented and split—divided from ourselves. Indeed, such theory can function like "a loaded gun put in the services of domination to continue a system of oppression" ("Poet is Critic").

Anzaldúa's point, though, was not to entirely dismiss conventional academic theorizing but rather to engage with it more intentionally, in healthier, transformative ways. And so, in typical Anzaldúan (*post-oppositional*) fashion, she enacts a twofold move in which she defines theory more expansively and, simultaneously, offers an alternative approach to theory-making. As she explains,

> I like theory. For me the issue is not whether to be pro-theory or anti-theory—because everything is derived from theory, or derives theory. The issue is the privileging of a certain kind of theory. In academic departments a new hierarchy has been set up. Among the genres theory is posited as the "superior" kind of writing and autobiography as the lowest, with poetry and fiction somewhere in the middle. I take issue with "high" theory's separation between theory and practice. There is no separation. Theory is a practice, theory affects the people who live by that particular theory, though the "practice" of the particular theory remains invisible. ("Poet as Critic")

Defining theory more broadly, she makes visible these invisible practices and enacts a different approach that replaces the more typical "colonization of the mind" (described earlier) with what she calls "a cultivation of the mind" in which we work *with* academic theory to glean useful lessons and techniques that we can employ. Put differently: we do not simply memorize and reproduce academic theory but, instead, we use theory (*and perhaps our experiences in formal school more generally*) as tools to intentionally foster our intellectual development; through this cultivation, we create our own theories that validate our lives while transforming social structures and perhaps reality itself. This empowering approach begins with an attitude of alignment with ancestral traditions and inner guides: "[I]f our rhythms are already established, firm and grounded, then we are able to integrate that other Western European theorist's way. Then we won't be swamped, lose ourselves, lose our emotional bodies, our intellectual bodies." By thus appropriating "high" theory and redefining the theory-making process, Anzaldúa can insist on its usefulness.

Like the act of writing more generally, the act of creating theory (*which, for Anzaldúa, was inextricably intertwined with and part of the writing process itself*) served a variety of interrelated purposes, including survival, resistance, knowledge production, and social transformation. She theorized to ensure her own survival—to concretize and share her own experiences, using them to formulate new theoretical perspectives that could assist in creating a world in which she and others like her could thrive.[2] She created theories that challenge consensual reality (*or what I call our status-quo stories*), exploring the limitations in our existing worldviews and offering more expansive and equitable visions.[3] Indeed, Anzaldúa returned to graduate school in 1988 at least in part to share (*and thus normalize*) her expansive understanding of theory and, in the process, to valorize her own existence as well as the existence of other outsiders while (*and by*) creating new theories and methods: "Those of us who live and work in the dangerous fields of academe would like to learn new ways of writing and presenting our ideas, to legitimize who we are, what we are, what we do, where we do it, and what that means for anthropological feminism" ("Violent Space"). During the 1980s and 1990s, incorporating personal experiences into one's academic work (unless one was an anthropologist) was typically critiqued as inferior: "Deriving theory from personal experience and the use of personal narrative to theorize is often considered low theory by academicians." Anzaldúa intentionally challenged this convention; her theories emerge relationally from the personal—which she uses in sophisticated, complex ways. But the point was not simply self-expression or increased personal or cultural representation. Her aspirations were even larger than these important goals. She wanted to create new theories and new forms of theorizing that could change reality itself on multiple levels: "I advocate the use [of] theory to help change things and not simply to make sense in its own terms to explain or justify what already exists" ("Poet is Critic").

Making Theories

Like her writing process more generally, Anzaldúa's theory-making method was grounded both in her own body and in her animist, relational, holistic worldview. Anzaldúa offers an insightful discussion of her method in "Poet as Critic," in which she underscores the physical, embodied materiality of her approach. Distinguishing her theory-making from conventional academic methods, she locates its origins and presence both in her "specific racial and cultural background" and in the particularities of her body and life, in her "own sweat, tears and blood experiences." This specific embodiment makes "[i]ts theoretical presence . . . different. It embodies, remains close to the body and the five senses." She takes this embodiment with her as she develops theories that invite readers into her life: "Step into my skin, mujer, and journey with me and La Llorona through this landscape." In this dissertation chapter draft, Anzaldúa recreates her theory-making process by retracing how she developed her theory of "blank spots." (*As I explain in chapter 4, blank spots is an early version of what later becomes her theory of deconocimientos.*) She draws on memory and self-reflection, using earlier personal events in her life to more robustly analyze and address present-day contemporary situations. Importantly, Anzaldúa revisits these events as fully as possible, immersing herself deeply in them by using imagination, visualization, emotion, and other types of nonrational thought to relive and reflect on a specific incident from her life. As she explains, "This is how I 'do' theory. When I re-experience an event, a series of tiny explosions of association—poetic association, not logical ones—interlock as pieces of my life unfold in my mind's eye. Bits of knowledge gained from others and from books are attached to these experiences." Anzaldúa's deep dive into the embodied personal leads her into transpersonal avenues of knowledge creation; as she relives scenes from her life, she works with the emotions that these deep dives unleash, viewing them almost like little bridges or translational devices leading her into images and, eventually, into words: "I rouse up feelings from my emotional body to summon forth the metaphors. The metaphors attract other metaphors. Then I find a symbol to carry these experiences—or the symbol finds me." Instincts also play a role in this process, as does rational thought: "The instincts organize and structure the writing. And, lastly, I let my critical faculties look over the whole thing." Not surprisingly, Anzaldúa does not sharply distinguish between this method for her theory creation or the creation of poetry or fiction: "This is how I write theory, how I write a poem, a story, a book review, a critical piece. . . . I derive theory through the act of writing."

Anzaldúa's theory-making is ontological as well. As will become even more evident in the following chapter, each theory emerged from and grew through a complex series of conversations—some inward, some outward, some an intertwined, complicated mixture of the two. The people, places, events, necessities, ideas, and spirits that Anzaldúa encountered functioned as conversational partners: dynamic situational engines that fueled the theory's development. I define these conversational partners broadly, to include consensus reality; life contingencies; the imaginal; language; readers; and, of course, Anzaldúa's personal and collective history. These partners *participate* in Anzaldúa's method. She situates herself in relation to them and works with them; these relationships generate new ideas. I describe fellow participants as "situational engines" to underscore their temporal, spatial, and energetic dimensions. In what follows, I touch on several key conversational partners who appear consistently in Anzaldúa's theory production.

Positing a spirit-infused world, Anzaldúa moved through her days with a receptive openness to everyone/everything she encountered. She was in constant dialogue with her surroundings. The outer world was not an empty canvas on which she expressed her emotions or thoughts. Nor was it a useful resource that she mined for images. Rather, the world around her talked *with* (not to) her, and together they co-created new knowledge— messages that Anzaldúa translated and shared in her work. These messages represent a synergistic blend of Anzaldúa and her external environments. Look for instance at the first paragraph of *Light in the Dark*'s final chapter, in which she recounts her daily walks across Lighthouse Field, the small national park located near her home in Santa Cruz, California. This paragraph beautifully, succinctly depicts Anzaldúa's dialogic theory-making process. She sets off on her daily walk with an open, receptive attitude. She embarks on a knowledge co-creation journey, ready to learn from the world around her. As a "glistening black" snake crosses her path, its sinuous movement invites her into a fully embodied, holistic epistemological shift—into an "intellect of heart and gut." She moves through the field attentively, open to messages she might receive; she articulates this receptivity with great intentionality. She underscores (*and perhaps activates*) this participatory relationship by initiating an exchange between herself and spirit: "You stop in the middle of the field and, under your breath, ask the spirits—animals, plants, y tus muertos—to help you string together a bridge of words." Anzaldúa uses ritual (she casts an offering) and prayer to further deepen the reciprocal relationship between herself and a spirit-infused world, situate her life experiences within it, and dedicate her writing to exploring and revealing its power and wisdom. By thus opening herself to the possibility of participatory knowledge creation, Anzaldúa moved through her life with intentional awareness and receptivity, confident that she could converse with and learn from everything (*everyone*) she encountered. She gleaned messages everywhere. (*By "messages," I don't mean already existing packaged insights that Anzaldúa collected as if reading Post-it notes stuck to trees. Rather, each message was itself created through mutual engagement of all participants.*) The insights did not preexist—either in Anzaldúa or in that which she encountered—but instead emerged through the encounter itself, as a conversation of sorts.

Not surprisingly, given the fact that Anzaldúa's philosophical motivation for theory creation was driven (*at least in part*) by her desire to expose, challenge, and transform consensual reality, a key conversational partner in every theory was, inevitably, some aspect of the status-quo stories— those dimensions of human life and our world that have become so normalized as to be taken entirely for granted. (*As I explain in* Transformation Now!, *status-quo stories reflect a paralyzed, static worldview: "It is what it is," say those who don't believe that change is possible: "That's just how things are."*) These status-quo stories include unquestioned systemic power hierarchies; social identity categories and scripts; ontological beliefs (e.g., the Enlightenment-based mechanistic, materialist worldview); epistemological norms (e.g., the elevation of rational thought and objectivity over intuition, emotion, and subjectivity); ethical mandates (e.g., survival of the fittest); and so on. These unquestioned narratives about reality prevent growth. Anzaldúa aspired to create theories that produce new knowledges and invite readers to perceive reality differently—theories that reshape reality itself (not just consensual reality but ontological reality) in the service of social justice. Anzaldúan theories work to challenge the status quo and create a more equitable world—one built on a different metaphysical framework. Thus in *Light in the Dark* she explores how we might "change or reinvent reality" (44) and calls for new ways of reading and theorizing.

These dialogues with consensual reality are foundational to all Anzaldúan theories. With new mestiza consciousness, la facultad, and conocimiento, for example, Anzaldúa offers alternatives to western culture's over-validation of rational thought and empirical analysis. With conocimiento, she posits a spirit-infused world that contrasts greatly with the Newtonian scientific world (but resonates with quantum physics). With nos/otras, new tribalism, and nepantlera, she intervenes in status-quo stories about subjectivity, personhood, and hyper-individualism.

It is, of course, a commonplace to assert that Anzaldúa brought herself and her life into her work. However, she did not simply use life events as background, framework, or some other narrative device. Rather, she engaged with specific events as meaning-shaping partners. Here I refer both to collective historic events like the 1989 Loma Prieta earthquake in Northern California and the 2001 attack on New York City and the Pentagon, as well as to personal events like her early menstruation; childhood encounters with her nagual; graduate studies at UCSC; the diabetes diagnosis; the Villa Montalvo Latina artists' retreat; and specific speaking engagements, writing invitations, and teaching gigs. These and other life markers impacted, shaped, and guided Anzaldúa's theories in concrete, participatory ways. Take, for example, her speaking engagements. Due to the many constraints on her time, as well as her preferred style, she did not present formal papers that she had written out in advance. Instead, she created her talks in conversation with her audience. Typically, the conversation began soon after the invitation itself, as Anzaldúa asked questions like these: What is the topic you want me to explore? Can you tell me about the students and audience? What are you hoping to accomplish? She jotted down notes from these conversations and used this information to guide her research and brainstorming sessions. She researched related topics, produced pages of writing notas, dug through previous writing notas and other materials, and selected key concepts for place markers or anchors from which to spin her ideas.[4] Through these conversations, the theories grew. As she observes in a section of Writing Notas D titled "Gig," "I try out my story and stories with those I come into contact [with]. I expand, flesh out, adjust my stories as a result of 'discovering' other things about it as I tell it anew or as I monitor reactions of my listeners." Anzaldúa approached these conversations with an attitude of trial-and-error: How do the words and concepts "land"? What's the audience reaction? What questions do they offer? How can communication be improved? She, too, discovered new insights through these multilayered interactions.

CONVERSATIONAL PARTNER #4: SISTER THEORIES

Anzaldúa's theories themselves often served as dynamic conversational partners, both with each other and with Anzaldúa herself. At times, she brought several distinct theories together, putting them into dialogue with each other and with a specific topic (like transformation, knowledge, or space). Thus, for example, nepantla, conocimiento, and spiritual activism emerged in complicated conversation from her explorations of creativity, knowledge production, and transformation from the early 1990s onward. Her theories of nos/otras, new tribalism, and geographies of selves co-emerged in dialogue together as Anzaldúa investigated issues related to Latinx identity formation in keynotes and essays during the late 1990s and early twenty-first century. Her theories of El Mundo Zurdo and the borderlands illustrate another form this conversational co-creation could take. In a 1988 interview, Anzaldúa located the origins of borderlands in *This Bridge Called My Back*—more specifically, emerging from El Mundo Zurdo, or what she refers to as the "left-handed world." As the interviewer explains, "Anzaldúa's idea of balancing between worlds developed from her writing in *This Bridge Called My Back*, when she started writing about what she calls the 'left-handed' world. But, she says, the 'left-handed' metaphor wasn't big enough to contain all that she wanted, so she changed to 'borderlands,' drawing on her idea of balancing between worlds on a tightrope. 'It's all a progression,' she says. 'There's a progression in the fiction, the poetry, and the essay writing. They're all aspects of the same ideas, but they unravel differently and it's coming out in different stages'" ("Politics of a Poet").

CONVERSATIONAL PARTNER #5: READERS

As with her approach to writing more generally, Anzaldúa theorized with readers in mind. She wanted to communicate effectively and was deeply interested in how her theories were interpreted and received. Unlike most academic theorists and intellectuals, who typically write for a relatively small audience of insiders (*either others in a specific field or academic scholars and students more generally*), Anzaldúa writes for a broader group of people, including those beyond the academy. As she asserts in "Poet as Critic," "Though it is the 'in thing' and 'trendy' to write 'high,' in-house theory which only a small group of academics understand, the theory we produce must include a different audience, non-academic audiences as well." This broad scope is not surprising, given Anzaldúa's theoretical aspirations. After all, if we write theory to change the world, we want those who live in the world to have easy access to the theories.

Anzaldúa produced theories that were deeply invitational in their dialogic potential. She did not want simply to insert her views into readers' minds. Rather, she invites us to theorize *with* her, to create theory in dialogue, communion, conversation. As she explains in "Poet as Critic," "The writings are to be experienced, to be felt. They are to be assimilated by your emotional body, and to be processed by it while the intellect does its work on it. I don't believe in interpreting the material, opening up your skulls and feeding it to you. Using your own experiences and associations, I want you to interpret and translate the material for yourself. This is, of course, hard for us to do. We've been taught to distrust any thing that originates in ourself. We're used to some external authority telling us how to do things." Note the holistic nature of this invitation. Anzaldúa wants her readers to interact with her images and words, to bring our own embodied experiences (*including the reading experience itself*) to them. It is important to note Anzaldúa's confidence in her readers. She trusts that we each hold tremendous inner wisdom; she encourages us to defy the external directives that discourage intellectual autonomy and look within.

Even as she wrote for a broad beyond-academic audience, Anzaldúa also wanted to engage academic readers, including students, professors, and other scholars. The archival material indicates her keen interest in this audience's reception to her work: in addition to collecting and preserving a large amount of scholarship about her work, she also commented on the scholarship in writing notes.[5] (*Indeed, I can personally attest to the depth of Anzaldúa's curiosity; she asked me to send her copies of articles and book chapters on her work whenever I encountered them.*) While Anzaldúa had little or no desire to control how scholars defined or used her theories, she sometimes responded to misinterpretations or limited understandings by developing additional theories that clarified her goals. (*"Speaking across the Divide" illustrates this engagement.*) Not surprisingly, given the many ways *Borderlands* was taken up and used, several later theories emerged in conversation with readers' reception to this iconic book. As I explore in more depth in the next chapter, the shifts from borderlands to nepantla and from new mestiza consciousness to conocimiento, as well as the creation of new tribalism, illustrate this audience-derived conversational engine. As she explains in her early nepantla manuscripts, "When a term gets taken over (misappropriated), I find another one" ("Reconfiguring Fronteras," "Nepantla: The Crack between Worlds"). (*Here we see Anzaldúa's post-oppositionality. Rather than struggle to maintain control of a theory's interpretation, she moves on and reconceives the theories themselves.*)

And on to the Theories Themselves . . .

Not surprisingly, given this complex creative process, disentangling Anzaldúa's theories can be challenging (*to say the least*). To assist others in more fully grasping the breadth and depth of Anzaldúan theory, in chapter 4, I excavate and explore eighteen key Anzaldúan theories. I encountered four main challenges in my theoretical excavation process: First, the theories were still under development and thus shifting in various ways during the last decade of Anzaldúa's life. Second, and closely related, Anzaldúa herself uses overlapping, sometimes contradictory terms (because she, too, was still figuring them out) which cannot be organized in linear chronological fashion. Look for instance at the following passage from "*Autohistorias-teorías—Mujeres que cuentan vidas:* Personal & Collective Narratives That Challenge Genre Conventions," in which she moves among terms from one sentence to the next: "Writing *autohistoria-teorías* is an act of recovery and retrieval or re-invention of that self, body, culture, history and heritage which has been ripped off or stolen. To write *autohistoteoría* is to attempt to reconstitute a culture, a language, a people, for it is in the telling and re-telling that we construct culture." Third, and closely related, Anzaldúa sometimes offers different definitions for these terms, even within the same text. And fourth, Anzaldúa's challenge to conventional western forms of thinking further complicates (*though also enriches*) our explorations.

PART II

THE THEORIES THEMSELVES

Existing language is based on the old concepts; we need a language to speak about the new situations, the new realities. There's no such thing as pure categories anymore. My concepts of nos/otras and the new tribalism are about disrupting categories. Categories contain, imprison, limit, and keep us from growing. We have to disrupt those categories and invent new ones.—Anzaldúa, *Interviews*

All of my work, including fiction and poetry, are healing trabajos. If you look at my central themes, metaphors, and symbols, such as nepantla, the Coyolxauhqui imperative, the Coatlicue state, the serpent, el mundo zurdo, nos/otras, the path of conocimiento you'll see that they all deal with the process of healing.—Anzaldúa, "Speaking across the Divide"

Part II offers brief overviews and genealogies of key Anzaldúan theories: autohistoria and autohistoria-teoría, borderlands, el cenote, the Coatlicue state, conocimiento, the Coyolxauhqui process, desconocimiento, la facultad, geographies of selves, El Mundo Zurdo, la naguala, nepantla, nepantleras, new mestiza, new mestiza consciousness, new tribalism, nos/otras, and spiritual activism. Each entry consists of several sections, described in more detail below: several opening quotations, a succinct definition, the theory's story (origins, development, and speculation on where Anzaldúa might have further developed it), related Anzaldúan theories, questions for future research, and key manuscripts that scholars might find useful when investigating the theory.

OPENING QUOTATION(S): I begin each entry with Anzaldúa's words, both to situate the theory and to foreground Anzaldúa herself. I chose quotations that called out to me, distinctively reflecting key elements of the theory, pointing to chronological shifts over time while also showcasing Anzaldúa's unique voice.

DEFINITION: This portion is especially designed for those new to Anzaldúa or the specific Anzaldúan theory. With these definitions, I offer a succinct (or fairly succinct) entry into the theory, opening a small door or window as it were. However, succinctness is relative here; the theories are too complex, intertwined, and shifting to be easily conveyed in a few words. As you read and work with these definitions, please remember the impossibility of this definitional task, keeping in mind that the definitions are more invitational than exhaustive. Ideally, as you work with the theories you'll adopt a version of the intellectual humility that Anzaldúa generally employed.

THE THEORY'S STORY (ORIGINS AND DEVELOPMENT): Each theory has its own story (multiple origins and various strands of growth), which I share here in short genealogical explorations. While some theories (like new mestiza consciousness and borderlands) seem to have arrived almost fully developed, other theories (like autohistoria-teoría, nepantla, and conocimiento), grew incrementally over the years. And still others (like nos/otras) had extremely long gestation periods and were in earlier stages of incremental growth at the time of Anzaldúa's passing. But reader beware! Anzaldúa's recursive writing process, coupled with the entanglement of various theories, creates challenges to these genealogical investigations. Anzaldúa regularly drew from early manuscripts as she composed, copying and pasting from one document into another (and another and another and another, which at times might hit the researcher as an endless spiraling cycle). This recursivity creates challenges when trying to pinpoint chronological shifts. These challenges are further compounded by the fact that Anzaldúa did not always put dates on her drafts. Even when she did date them, it's not always clear whether the dates refer to the revisions or to the actual composition. (For more on this challenge, see part III.)

To determine a theory's chronology, I used the following data: manuscripts, writing notes, publications, interviews, emails, and other forms of communication, as well as Anzaldúa's comments about the theories themselves. Working with Anzaldúa's recollections was tricky! While she offers insight into many of her theories' origins and development, these insights (though always useful) sometimes contradict other evidence, thus adding more complexity. Look for instance at the different creation stories she offers for la facultad. In a 2003 email conversation, she states that she did not develop this theory "until [she] wrote Borderlands" ("Disability & Identity" 300); however, her manuscripts tell a different story, suggesting that she developed her theory of la facultad about five years earlier as she wrote *Borderlands'* precursors, "Esperando la serpiente con plumas" and "La serpiente que se come su cola."

Because Anzaldúan theories are living entities, I conclude this section with speculations on possible directions in which Anzaldúa might have taken the theory, had she lived longer. For inspiration, I looked at her writing notes, manuscript drafts, and life events, as well as my journals and notes on our conversations about her work. Drawing on the chaotic array of material I've explored for this book, as well as my knowledge gained from working with Anzaldúa and ongoing writing-related rituals I use for my current work with her, I share my speculations with you.

RELATED THEORIES: As mentioned previously, Anzaldúa's theories are intertwined and emerge in dialogue with each other, creating harmonies of sorts. To assist scholars in tracing these interconnections, I've included a list of other Anzaldúan theories related to the theory under investigation.

FUTURE DIRECTIONS: This brief section contains a list of the questions that occurred to me over the years as I worked on this project and dove into Anzaldúa's theories. I offer them as possible avenues for further exploration; I hope that they'll resonate with readers—perhaps resonate so deeply as to invite further exploration. This section was motivated by my desire to pay it forward.

USEFUL TEXTS: To facilitate additional investigations, I've also compiled a list of key manuscripts in which Anzaldúa develops or in other ways engages with the theory. Because her writing process was so recursive, these lists are not exhaustive; they are, however, as expansive and in-depth as I could provide while remaining within the scope of this project. Whenever possible, I have also included some of the key writing notas in which she explores/creates the theory, but because her writing notas are so enormous and diverse, this list (even more so than the manuscripts mentioned) is not exhaustive.

How to Read Part II

You can read the following chapter from start to finish, working your way alphabetically from autohistoria y autohistoria-teoría to spiritual activism. Or you can take a topical approach, reading theories in constellations: For epistemology, you might look at la facultad, new mestiza consciousness, and conocimiento (in this specific order, if you're striving for chronological understanding). For collective identity formation and alliance-building, you might look at El Mundo Zurdo, nos/otras, new tribalism, and geographies of selves—four theories that emerged in conversation with each other. For an even broader investigation of identity, you'd need to add new mestiza and nepantlera into this mix. For creativity, you might read la facultad, autohistoria y autohistoria-teoría, el cenote, the Coyolxauhqui process, nepantla, and conocimiento. For ethics, I'd recommend spiritual activism as the jumping-off point, and then use your intuition to guide you. (If you, like me, view Anzaldúa's radical coalition-building as part of her ethics, be sure to include nos/otras and new tribalism in this topical study.) And, of course, you can dip in and out, follow your own intuition, or use these entries as a resource while you work on your own projects.

As will be very evident in what follows (regardless of where you begin), Anzaldúan theories take on lives of their own. They emerge from Anzaldúa's resistance to the status quo, her desire to write and make change, and the specific conditions of her life at particular times—the events she's been invited to speak at and/or the projects she's writing about.

4. EIGHTEEN ANZALDÚAN THEORIES

Autohistoria y Autohistoria-teoría

I introduce the neologism *autohistoria* to create a new genre.—"Notes for Lloronas Dissertation" (1989–90)

To write *autohistorias-teorías* is to participate in two or more literary genres, registers, separate temporalities, historical periods, some belonging to the dominant culture and some to the colonized. It is to write *en un estilo mestisaje*, that is, code switching in construction, perspective, and language. It allows the undervoice, the subtext and secret messages to specific readers to be heard. A different perception of reality operates. One that incorporates spiritual space so that there is a triple or quadruple vision/consciousness corresponding to [the] overlapping worlds of [the] narrator, the Borderland places in which the mestiza constructs a new identity. Frames exist within frames, which in turn exist within other frames. Characteristic "moves" in *autohistorias-teorías* from close-up to long shots and back to zoom-in for middle shots makes them self-reflective, meta-discursive in approach.—*"Autohistorias-teorías— Mujeres que cuentan vidas"* (1988–91)

There's a difference between talking *with* images/stories and talking *about* them. In this text I attempt to talk *with* images/stories, to engage with creative and spiritual processes and their ritualistic aspects. In enacting the relationship between certain

images and concepts and my own experience and psyche, I fuse personal narrative with theoretical discourse, autobiographical vignettes with theoretical prose. I create a hybrid genre, a new discursive mode, which I call "autohistoria" and "autohistoria-teoría." Conectando experiencias personales con realidades sociales results in autohistoria, and theorizing about this activity results in autohistoria-teoría. It's a way of inventing and making knowledge, meaning, and identity through self-inscriptions.
—*Light in the Dark/Luz en lo Oscuro* (2004/2012)

DEFINITION

"Autohistoria" and "autohistoria-teoría" are Anzaldúa's terms for two closely intertwined polyvocal, transformational literary genres and methods that blend personal and cultural biography with memoir, fiction, history, myth, and poetry, as well as other forms of storytelling and knowledge production. These mixtures occur in a variety of context-specific ways, leading to a variety of innovative forms. Although Anzaldúa developed this theory and method to describe her own autobiographically inflected practice and products, as well as those of other women-of-colors authors, by the late 1990s she had expanded and deepened this complex theory-method to foreground the ontological dimensions while emphasizing self-(re)invention's complex relationship with truth, reality, and social justice. A key characteristic is the blurring of boundaries—whether between genres, methods, realities, and/or identities. The difference between autohistoria and autohistoria-teoría is one of focus and degree: while the former primarily examines the individual and the personal, the latter complicates, deepens, expands. Because these theories are so intertwined and overlapping, I discuss them together while highlighting and in other ways teasing apart their nuanced distinctions.

Deeply infused with the search for personal and cultural meaning, or what Anzaldúa describes in her post-*Borderlands* work as "putting Coyolxauhqui together," both autohistoria and autohistoria-teoría are informed by reflective self-awareness employed in the service of social justice work. This intentional emphasis on social justice as an essential, foundational component distinguishes Anzaldúa's theories from mainstream autobiographical theories. Autohistoria focuses on the author's personal life story; however, as the autohistorian tells her own life story, she simultaneously (*but not monolithically*) tells the life stories of others as well. Unlike conventional autobiography, then, which often functions as self-expression or self-narration in which the individual author offers an intimate story of their life, autohistoria presents the self in relation to communal dimensions, creating a personal-collective selfhood interwoven into a complex hybrid subjectivity. Not surprisingly, given autohistoria's emphasis on exposing and changing the status quo, the autohistorian typically highlights the most transformational moments and episodes in their life. As Anzaldúa notes in "Plunging into El Cenote," "Autohistorias usually focus on significant transformative people and events in our lives. The events may be physical, imaginative, daydreams, images, scenarios from altered (inbetween) states of consciousness." Autohistorias can take a variety of forms, including fiction, prose narrative, poetry, visual narrative, journal, and more. Importantly, autohistorians do not remain bound by the existing genre conventions. As Anzaldúa notes, "The artistic business of translating bits of personal history and experience into 'authentic' autobiography or 'fictionalized' literary autobiography, memoir, or testimonial calls on traditional genre techniques as well as made-up techniques as one writes" ("Plunging").

The distinction between autohistoria and autohistoria-teoría is one of degree—the amounts and types of personal/autobiographical material we use, where this use leads us, how its guidance invites us to transform (ourselves, the work we produce, and reality itself), and the amount of theoretical self-reflection and application we bring into this process. As Anzaldúa explains in "Autohistorias-teorías—Mujeres que cuentan vidas: Personal & Collective Narratives That Challenge Genre Conventions," an unpublished essay that she first drafted while in graduate school during the late 1980s and early 1990s, "When the events and experiences depicted let the reader experience theory through . . . coding philosophical, political and psychoanalytic theories, and the emphasis is on the theories just as much (or more than) on the acts of the writing subject, the autohistoria becomes autohistoria-teoría. . . . In the autohistorias-teoría [sic] the self-reflective theorizing and analysis takes precedence over the anecdotal, personal narrative. It theorizes about the autobiographical essay and its process in an attempt to determine or explore identity and other issues." Autohistoria/autohistoria-teoría is multilayered in temporal, epistemological, and ontological dimensions; it combines the author's personal story (internal, intangible emotions and thoughts as well as external events and interactions) with their familial/cultural story (present-day story as well as ancestral history and roots), and then encodes both with information from the imaginal. To capture this complexity, the author roves through time—diving deeply into her personal, ancestral, and cultural pasts, relying on memory, spirit guides, and imagination. Put differently, the autohistorian enacts multidimensional self-reflection: "The *autohistoria/autohistorias-teoría* [*sic*] is a coherent story pieced together from the remembered fragments." This "piecing together" is a complex, recursive method involving self-reflection, imagination, analysis, and intuition. Often, it also entails research (*including oracular research*)[1] and other forms of investigation, ranging from conventional academic study to shamanic journeys in which we move within and beyond the physical body to access the imaginal. Typically, the autohistorian also looks at the creative process itself, reflecting on its methods and discoveries in order to develop additional theories and perspectives.

Anzaldúa's essay "*Autohistorias-teorías—Mujeres que cuentan vidas*" offers the most comprehensive discussion of this theory and points to her expansive aspirations for it, as seen in section titles like these: "The Theory in the Story," "Retrieval and Re-invention," "Revising Reality and Reality as Fiction," "Narrative Is an Infrastructure Where Reality Is Re-worked," and "Representation or Reality?" As this list indicates, Anzaldúa assigns to autohistoria-teoría a variety of epistemological, ontological, and literary functions that include decolonial, transformational work. She envisions autohistoria-teoría as a profound meaning-making process that challenges and often expands previous understandings of the authorial "I"; the presumed boundaries between fiction and truth; the nature of reality itself; how stories and narratives contain and create theory while reinventing reality; and how we produce autohistoria-teoría by self-reflection, reinvention, and transpersonal excavation.

As this list also demonstrates, autohistoria and autohistoria-teoría move beyond representation to include (re)creation of reality. In so doing, they challenge typical assumptions about literary representation (e.g., that literature re-presents an already existing reality) and promise that writing can alter reality—including the concrete, three-dimensional physical world in which we live. As Anzaldúa explains elsewhere in the same essay, autohistoria-teoría challenges the assumption "that writing is the representation of something which is already there in reality (or in the writer's head) before she sets to work." As Anzaldúa's parenthetical remark indicates, autohistoria-teoría's ontological challenge is epistemological as well—writing autohistoria gives the author new information: "Pictures, scenarios, representations are created, or at least assembled anew, out of raw experience and not nothing, and that something comes with its own plot *during* the act of writing and not before. . . . [T]he writing subject also 'speaks' (creates) the categories of culture."

Importantly, "fiction," as Anzaldúa defines and uses it here, does not represent lies, falsehoods, or misconceptions. Rather, fictionalized elements function as doorways inviting both writer and readers into additional, previously unrecognized dimensions of reality (*including, at times, our own lives*). As Anzaldúa states in a section of writing notes titled "Autohistoria," "Fiction is not an unreality, but a different reality—the movement of imagination" (Writing Notas L). Fictionalizing our stories activates imagination; this activation, when approached with integrity and the desire to create new knowledge, gives access into the imaginal, opening the way for additional wisdom and information about reality—information that cannot be accessed via rational thought. When we live deeply and intimately with these insights, honoring them through ritual and conversing with them (via the images in our mind), we acquire even more insights that we convey to readers, using rational thought, logical language, and the other accoutrements of western thought (*along with intuition, emotion, and other nonrational venues*). This complex epistemological "fiction" is an important component to Anzaldúa's theory.

Autohistoria-teoría can also function as method in which the author employs self-reflection, relational thinking, transpersonal excavation, and imagination to produce new knowledge—including innovative aesthetic forms. As the writer intentionally revisits earlier events in their life, seeking clarity, they discover and create new insights. The goal is not to move backward along some linear timeline in order to recover accurate factual truth about events that occurred in the past. Indeed, in autohistoria-teoría there is no single goal; rather, there are multiple goals that unfold through the writing process itself: as the autohistorian writes, she might access emotional insight offering closure and/or more complex understanding of events embodied in our tissue, lingering at a cellular level, though we typically repress it. As Anzaldúa explains in "*Autohistorias-teorías—Mujeres que cuentan vidas*,"

> I think that writing *autohistorias* evokes the memory of a trauma retroactively by means of association. It recalls the scene of trauma (an instance of racism or rape, for example) and releases anger, fear

or sexual excitement. Though the writer has little defense, memory does not catch her unarmed—she has a weapon, the pen. Often, instead of repressing the recollection, she highlights it, brings it to center stage, replays it, examines it from front to back and scrutinizes it in the act of not only recording it but of writing it with a myriad of choices and poetic license.

As her speculative tone suggests, Anzaldúa in this passage both describes and enacts the teoría and method that accompanies this genre. (*This passage also points to the autohistoria's healing potential.*)

As a method, autohistoria-teoría also includes deep-diving self-reflection in which we confront hidden truths about ourselves, encountering what Anzaldúa sometimes calls the "Shadow Beast." While in some ways Anzaldúa's entire oeuvre could be said to illustrate, enact, and create this method, chapter 5 of *Light in the Dark/Luz en lo Oscuro* offers the most extensive exploration and demonstration of it.

AUTOHISTORIA Y AUTOHISTORIA-TEORÍA'S STORY (ORIGINS AND DEVELOPMENT)

Anzaldúa's interest in creating innovative autobiographical formats and theories is long-standing, as evident in her early unpublished book-length autobiographies and her early published essay, "La Prieta"; her writing workshops and classes (conducted from the early 1980s until the time of her death); her numerous unpublished papers on the topic; her UCSC dissertation in the early 1990s; her interviews; and more. Anzaldúa used the term "autohistoria" to describe one of her own literary genres prior to her UCSC coursework and had been thinking about the autobiographical and the inclusion of the personal, historical, and cultural—especially for Chicanas and other women of colors—for her entire writerly life. Indeed, one could argue that she was feeling her way toward this complex theory in her early book manuscripts, "Esperando la serpiente con plumas (Waiting for the Feathered Serpent)" and "La serpiente que se come su cola: The Death Rites of Passage of a Chicana Lesbian" (1982)—seen especially, perhaps, in her attempts to negotiate between first- and third-person voice.[2]

Although Anzaldúa's interest in self-writing spans almost her entire life, she did not begin articulating autohistoria-teoría as a theory (per se) until 1988, when she reentered graduate school and began work on a doctoral degree in literature; she was still exploring and shaping this theory at the time of her death. Prior to landing on the term "autohistoria," Anzaldúa cycled through several other possibilities, including "auto canto," "auto canción," and "autoretratos." Arguably, she selected "autohistoria" because this word, unlike the others, includes the word "historia" and thus simultaneously underscores the importance of both story and history—that is, the fictional and collective dimensions: two crucial elements in this theory. Unlike mainstream western autobiography, autohistoria is never conceived of, enacted as, or interpreted to be the story of an entirely unique, self-enclosed individual; autohistoria and autohistoria-teoría always intentionally, overtly include communal, collective components.

Anzaldúa's doctoral studies at UCSC were instrumental in the theories' development. During her coursework and dissertation research she engaged deeply with recent scholarship on cultural and literary representation—especially so-called minority discourse focusing on marginalized groups (women, lesbians, women of color, etc.). Anzaldúa's manuscripts from these years indicate that she was deeply immersed in such dialogues—questioning scholars' assertions, analyzing their self-positioning, and in other ways talking with them. And, of course, she had contributed importantly to these representational issues through landmark publications like *This Bridge Called My Back* and *Borderlands/La Frontera*. She was conversant with scholarly analyses of her work, and it's likely that this awareness might have impacted her writing on these theories (and others).

Anzaldúa offers the first formal articulation of autohistoria-teoría in a 1988 class paper, "Ethnic Autohistoria-teorías," in which she explores conventional forms of autobiography and offers her own theory. She planned to expand this paper into the dissertation's main focus, as indicated by her 1990 letter and prospectus on her qualifying exam, titled "Self-Representation and Identity in Contemporary Ethnic/Other Autobiography." She explains that she developed her theory because neither the existing genre forms and conventions nor recent literary and cultural theory could adequately describe ("contain") the hybrid, synergistic mixture that she found in "autobiography, memoir, fictitious narratives, and personal and theoretical essays by some racial ethnic/Others" (*"Autohistorias-teorías—Mujeres que cuentan vidas"*). As she considered the characteristics making these texts distinct, she focused on two key relationships: those between the personal and the collective and those between fact and fiction.

She was trying to articulate how representation can work, how one can simultaneously express one's personal stories but also connect with (yet not impose or interfere with) others' stories.

When she shifted her focus away from the dissertation in the mid-1990s, Anzaldúa seems also to have put less energy into the theory itself; she returned to it briefly when drafting "Putting Coyolxauhqui Together" and considered including it in her twenty-first-century dissertation but decided that the chapter "*Autohistorias-teorías—Mujeres que cuentan vidas*" needed too much work to meet her compressed timeline.[3] Her computer folders indicate that she planned to continue revising the chapter and to include it in her next book. It's likely that she would have delved into imagination's role in the process, especially given her emphasis on the fictive elements, her elevation of fiction into ontological dimensions, her interest in Henri Corbin's imaginal, and (*especially*) her work on the Prieta stories.

RELATED THEORIES

- el cenote
- Coatlicue state
- conocimiento
- Coyolxauhqui process
- desconocimiento

FUTURE DIRECTIONS

- What are the differences between autohistoria and autohistoria-teoría?
- What can careful analysis of the many drafts of "Ethnic Autohistorias-teorías: Writing the History of the Subject" teach us about Anzaldúa's development of these theories?
- What can a close analysis of Anzaldúa's Prieta stories (which she sometimes referred to as "autohistorias") teach us about her *theory* of autohistoria?
- What can an analysis of "Putting Coyolxauhqui Together" (chapter 5 of *Light in the Dark*) teach us about Anzaldúa's method and about autohistoria-teoría as a method for others?
- What are these theories' ontological implications? How might we apply them to speculative realism, speculative fiction, and other literary genres?

- In what ways can these theories function performatively—that is, how can they help to bring about the realities they (we) envision?
- What's the relationship between writing autohistoria, identity development, and transformation?
- How can we use these autohistorias-teorías to create theory?
- How is Anzaldúa innovating theory?
- Although Anzaldúa seems to speak with factual/literal authenticity, we should always interrogate her words more deeply. In her 1994 writing notas (107.6) she writes: "Seduction. / Hide the personal when I profess to be writing personally." What are the implications of this self-advice, to hide the personal, when we read her autohistorias? (What, for instance, might Anzaldúa be hiding?)
- What came first, autohistoria or autohistoria-teoría, or did Anzaldúa develop them simultaneously—in dialogue?
- How might the distinction between autohistoria and autohistoria-teoría be helpful—to Anzaldúa, to writers, to scholars?
- How did Anzaldúa's doctoral work (especially the theories she read and her UCSC instructors' engagement with her work) impact the development of autohistoria and autohistoria-teoría?
- In Writing Notas L, Anzaldúa describes her Prieta stories as "autohistoria of the imagination." Applying this theory to Anzaldúa's work more generally—what might we learn? How might this description assist us as we interpret her writing?
- In "*Autohistorias-teorías—Mujeres que cuentan vidas*: Personal & Collective Narratives That Challenge Genre Conventions" Anzaldúa credits her knowledge of testimonio to Jorge Luis Borges, writing, "It was from Jorge Luis Borges that I learned that fiction, theory, and autobiography could be combined in the same work." What similarities and differences can we see between her theory of autohistoria-teoría and Latin American testimonio?[4]
- In chapter 3 of *Light in the Dark*, Anzaldúa defines "visual narrative" as "autohistorias" (62). How might we apply autohistoria and autohistoria-teoría to art, altar-making, and other visual products?

- What's the relationship between conocimiento and autohistoria-teoría? Do we use conocimiento when enacting autohistoria-teoría? Do we use autohistoria-teoría as we explore our conocimientos?

USEFUL TEXTS

- "Autohistoria de la artista as a Young Girl"
- "Autohistorias as Process Writing"
- "*Autohistorias-teorías—Mujeres que cuentan vidas*: Personal & Collective Narratives That Challenge Genre Conventions"
- "Autroretratos de la artista as a Young Girl"
- "Autohisto-teorías: Theorizing Self-Representations"
- "Barred Witness: Literary/Artistic Creations and Class Identities"
- *Borderlands/La Frontera*
- "Esperando la serpiente con plumas (Waiting for the Feathered Serpent)"
- *Interviews/Entrevistas*
- *Light in the Dark/Luz en lo Oscuro*
- "Lloronas—Women Who Wail: Ethnic/Other Explorations of (Self)-Representation and Identity and the Production of Writing and Knowledge"
- "Nepantla: Theories of Composition and Art"
- "On My Method and Ways of Ordering and Structuring"
- "Plunging into El Cenote: Creative Nonfiction"
- "Poet is Critic, Poet is Theorist"
- "La Prieta"
- "Proving Ground: Theorizing Ethnic Art-Making"
- "Putting Coyolxauhqui Together: A Creative Process" (multiple drafts)
- "Rampas de entrada, An Introduction"
- "Re-reading, Re-vision, Re-writing: The Art of Self-Editing"
- "Self-Representation and Identity in Contemporary Ethnic/Other Autobiography"
- "La serpiente que se come su cola: The Death Rites of Passage of a Chicana Lesbian"
- Writing Notes 108.6, 107.5, 108.7
- Writing Notes H, J, K, L, M

Borderlands

The U.S.-Mexican border *es una herida abierta* where the Third World grates against the first and bleeds. And before a scab forms it hemorrhages again, the lifeblood of two worlds merging to form a third country—a border culture. Borders are set up to define the places that are safe and unsafe, to distinguish *us* from *them*. A border is a dividing line, a narrow strip along a steep edge. A borderland is a vague and undetermined place created by the emotional residue of an unnatural boundary. It is in a constant state of transition.—*Borderlands/La Frontera* (1987)

I think of the borderlands as Jorge Luis Borges's Aleph, the one spot on earth containing all other places within it. It's like el árbol de la vida which crosses all dimensions—the sky, spiritual space, the earth, and the underworld. It's also like el cenote, the Mayan well—un ombligo (an umbilical cord) connecting us to the earth and to concrete reality. All people in nepantla—Natives, immigrants, colored, white, queers, heterosexuals, from this side of the border, del otro lado—are personas del lugar, local people, and relate to the border and to the nepantla states in different ways.—*Light in the Dark/Luz en lo Oscuro* (2004/2012)

DEFINITION

From its inception, Anzaldúa's theory of the borderlands (and her use of the term "borderlands" to describe it) has had a twofold meaning, referring both to the national/geographic region between the United States and Mexico and to the juxtaposition of other physical and nonphysical boundaries related to consciousness, identity, culture, and reality. Anzaldúa's first published description of this theory in the preface to *Borderlands/La Frontera: The New Mestiza* illustrates this range of meanings: "The actual physical borderland that I'm dealing with in this book is the Texas-U.S. Southwest/Mexican border. The psychological borderlands, the sexual borderlands and the spiritual borderlands are not particular to the Southwest. In fact, the Borderlands are physically present wherever two or more cultures edge each other, where people of different races occupy the same territory, where under, lower, middle and upper classes touch, where the space between two individuals shrinks with intimacy" (n.p.). Observe the breadth and depth in this definition, as well as Anzaldúa's shift from lower to upper case "B." This shift is intentional; as Anzaldúa explained in an interview the year after *Borderlands*' publication, "I use a small 'b' when I mean the literal space, the borderlands. When I use a capital 'B,' I'm talking about psychological or sexual or spiritual space" (qtd. in Baldwin). Five years later she reiterates: "[W]hen I capitalize it, it means that it's not the actual Borderlands, the Southwest or the Canada-U.S. border, but that it's an emotional Borderlands that can be found anywhere where there's different kinds of people coming together and occupying the same space or where there are spaces that are sort of hemmed in by these larger groups of people."[5] However, Anzaldúa was not always consistent with this distinction; nor were her copyeditors and publishers. These blurred boundaries between "borderlands" and "Borderlands" (*while ironically appropriate to the theory itself*) make it vital to consider context and think broadly when analyzing or using this theory.

While a border implies a stark division between one space and another, borderlands indicates the blurring of these boundaried locations. As Anzaldúa explains in *Borderlands*, "Borders are set up to define the places that are safe and unsafe, to distinguish *us* from *them*. A border is a dividing line, a narrow strip along a steep edge. A borderland is a vague and undetermined place created by the emotional residue of an unnatural boundary. It is in a constant state of transition" (25). As this passage implies, Anzaldúa uses her theory of the borderlands to challenge power dynamics and arbitrary divisions, suggesting that no aspect of reality can be neatly divided into entirely separate parts.

Anzaldúa associates the borderlands with outsiders—those pushed to the margins of conventional worlds. As she explained shortly after *Borderlands'* publication,

> The Borderlands is a metaphor and it means many things. It's a metaphor for the colonization of space and its people, like the Southwest, which has been taken away from the Indians and the Chicanos. It is also a metaphor for the space that women and men of color have been forced to make in between the cultures they lived in. . . . In my own culture, I am pushed to the margins because of my sexual preference and my feminist views. The Borderlands is the interface between the different worlds, the different cultures. Wherever two or three worlds come together, there's this little space that we squeeze people into who don't belong. To carry the metaphor further, the Borderlands is representative of the female body, how it has been entered, violated, taken over, just like the physical land. (qtd. in Baldwin)

Anzaldúa's theory of the borderlands also represents her early attempt to develop a holistic epistemology with which she could articulate her own experiences as well as those of other bridge people.

Anzaldúa herself described her theory of the borderlands as a "bridge idea"—a concept enabling her to connect distinct topics synergistically, in order to create new meanings. Thus in "Re-configuring Fronteras" she describes this theory as a "generative idea, one that I've continued to test, apply, and elaborate." In this unpublished essay, she associates the theory's origins with "Chicana culture" and then charts its development "into neighboring disciplines such as composition and geography," suggesting that it could also "be applied interdisciplinarily."

BORDERLANDS' STORY (ORIGINS AND DEVELOPMENT)

Anzaldúa offers several origin stories for this theory. In a 1988 interview, she associates its birth with *This Bridge Called My Back*, in her theory of El Mundo Zurdo (the left-handed world)—especially the attempt to balance among multiple worlds: "The mixture of bloods and affinities, rather than confusing or unbalancing me, has forced me to achieve a kind of equilibrium. Both cultures deny me a place in their universe. Between them and among others, I build my own universe, El Mundo Zurdo. I belong to myself and not to any one people. I walk the tightrope with ease and grace. I span abysses." However, this metaphor could not fully represent the complexity of the balance that she sought to achieve, and so she developed the metaphor of the borderlands ("Politics of a Poet").

Before articulating the theory in prose, Anzaldúa developed it through poetry, culminating in her 1985 collection of poems titled simply "Borderlands." As an analysis of the poems included in this unpublished manuscript indicates, Anzaldúa conceived of the borderlands expansively, to include the Texas-Mexico border, psychic and imaginal borderlands, internal divisions, and more. In the following two years, Anzaldúa further developed this theory as she revised "Borderlands," adding a lengthy introductory essay and reorganizing the original poems. With these revisions, she expands both the geographic and the metaphoric theoretical dimensions.

Eventually, however, the word "borderlands" became too limited to accurately convey the range and depth of meanings to which Anzaldúa aspired, and in the 1990s she began shifting away from the term and replacing it with "nepantla." After *Borderlands*' publication, when Anzaldúa realized that the theory was often interpreted too narrowly and identified exclusively with the Texas/Mexico geographic location, she sought other ways to articulate the complexity to which this theory aspired. As she explains in a 1991 interview, "I find people using metaphors such as 'Borderlands' in a more limited sense than I had meant it, so to expand on the psychic and emotional borderlands I'm now using 'nepantla.' With nepantla the connection to the spirit world is more pronounced as is the connection to the world after death, to psychic spaces. It has a more spiritual, psychic, supernatural, and indigenous resonance" (*Interviews* 176). Anzaldúa's shift from borderlands to nepantla was further encouraged by expansions in her own thinking. As she learned more about readers' reception to the theory, she made additional connections and applications to other dimensions that she had not considered while developing the theory in the 1980s. As she explained in an interview later published in *DisClosure*,

> [W]hat I have found, from talking to women . . . [is] that there are many other Borderlands that I hadn't conceived of that they apply the metaphor of the Borderlands to their situation and it could be like a relationship between say a white woman and a black woman who are lovers and their emotional physical life kind of becomes a Borderlands.
>
> When a term or metaphor gets taken over I find another one. In exploring and reinterpreting the Nahuatl concept of Nepantla since *Borderlands* came out, I have continued to cross worlds and theorize that crossing. Nepantla is an in-between state, neither/nor, that uncertain terrain one crosses when moving from one place to another, when traveling from the present identity to a new identity. Nepantla can be seen in the dream state, in the transition between worlds, as well as in the transitions across borders of class, race, or sexual identity.

As this statement might suggest, Anzaldúa herself blurred the boundaries between borderlands and nepantla, using the terms in different ways. While in some manuscripts she uses "nepantla" as almost a replacement for borderlands, in others, she does not. Especially in writings from the early 1990s, Anzaldúa seems undecided about whether to further expand borderlands' meaning (associating it with aesthetics and the imaginal), or to replace borderlands with nepantla, mentioning "borderlands" less frequently as the years progressed.

By the late 1990s, Anzaldúa had shifted almost entirely from "borderlands" to "nepantla" until, by the twenty-first century, she seems to have left the former term almost entirely behind. This shift is most evident in *Light in the Dark*, where she refers to "borderlands" only six times, and these references all occur in chapter 3, a revised version of her 1991 essay on border arte. Given that she refers to nepantla over one hundred times in the same book, we could logically assume that Anzaldúa had retired her theory of the borderlands, so to speak. However, given her dialogic theory-making process (*as well as shifts in nationalism and the politics of the Mexico-US border*), it's likely that, had she lived longer, Anzaldúa would have returned to this theory, innovating it in startling, useful ways.

RELATED THEORIES

- conocimiento
- la facultad
- geographies of selves
- nepantla
- nepantlera
- new mestiza
- new mestiza consciousness

FUTURE DIRECTIONS

- What is the relationship between the development of borderlands, the new mestiza, and new mestiza consciousness?
- What can close analysis of the *Borderlands* drafts teach us about how mestiza consciousness and borderlands theory inform each other?
- What can an analysis of the manuscripts teach us about the development of Anzaldúa's theory of the Borderlands as exceeding the geographical borderlands?
- Anzaldúa sometimes claimed that *Borderlands* emerged from her earlier autobiographical work (especially "Esperando" and "La serpiente"). What can an analysis of these early manuscripts teach us about her theory of the borderlands?
- What can an analysis of Anzaldúa's discussions of crossing borders teach us about her theory of the borderlands, and how might we use this analysis to build on her borderlands theory?
- What does an analysis of Anzaldúa's essay drafts from the early 1990s teach us about her shift from borderlands to nepantla?
- In what ways, if any, did Anzaldúa's exploration of art and conversations with visual artists impact her borderlands theory?

- How might Anzaldúa have returned to, revised, and in other ways worked with this theory in the twenty-first century, as various forms of nationalism increase and more overt hostility against immigrants of color expands?
- What's the relationship between Anzaldúa's borderlands theory and geographies of selves?

USEFUL TEXTS

- "*El arte de la frontera*: The Border as *Nepantla*, Place and *Pueblo*"
- "Barred Witness: Literary/Artistic Creations and Class Identities"
- "Border Arte"
- "Borderlands" (1985 poetry manuscript)
- *Borderlands/La Frontera: The New Mestiza*
- "The Borderlands/La Frontera" (1986 manuscript draft)
- *DisClosure* interview draft
- "En estilo mestizaje—In the Writing I Cross Genres, I Cross Borders"
- *Interviews/Entrevistas*
- "Nepantla: The Crack between Worlds"
- "Nepantla: The Creative Process"
- "Nepantla: In/Between and Shifting: Theories of Composition and Art"
- "Nepantla: Theories of Composition and Art"
- "New Mestiza Nation"
- "Nos/otros: 'Us' vs. 'Them,' (Des)Conocimientos y compromisos"
- "Notes—CONOCIMIENTO"
- "Re-configuring Fronteras: New Navigations of Nepantla and the Cracks between Worlds"
- "Taller Nepantla: Letter of Proposal for the *Nepantla* Project"
- Writing Notas C, G

El Cenote

Fishing objects long forgotten, or objects from a past life or the Collective Life out of the deep well was a necessary act. This was the only way to feed consciousness.
—"Esperando la serpiente con plumas" (1982)

To remember one must go into el cenote in oneself to catch the fleeting, fleeing images of events and feelings stored within the tissues of the body.—"Ethnic Autohistorias-teorías" (1989)

El cenote, the well of inspiration, the source of our guiding voices, contains our depth consciousness, a greater knowledge that comes up/out in creative work and in moments of conocimiento. Their sources come from the generation of ancestors that live within us and permeate every cell in our bodies (as Hawaiians and other traditional cultures believe). Other sources are the higher centers within that we are not aware of because we are separated or exiled from them. We are in touch with only a small corner of the entirety of our inner universe.—"Self-in-Community" (2003)

DEFINITION

In geography, a cenote is a sinkhole or collapsed cave that opens into a deep underground reservoir of water. Found throughout the Yucatán, cenotes are often beautiful sites, surrounded by trees and lush vegetation. For precolonial Maya, cenotes were sacred sites, locations for rituals—including the sacrifice of precious belongings and sometimes even human lives. With el cenote, Anzaldúa draws on this history to develop a theory of profound inspiration with transpersonal, transhistorical implications. She associates el cenote with creativity, the unconscious, the imagination, the imaginal, and other writing-related concepts: it is the "well of images and sounds" ("Woman Who Writes"); "the dream pool" (Writing Notas 107.8); "the site of imagination, the creative reservoir where earth, female, and water energies merge" ("Border Arte"); "a reservoir or filing cabinet in your mind that stores memories, dreams, fantasies, accumulated bits of information and pieces of lived experience" (Writing Notas D); "primal imaginative soup" (Writing Notas D); a "psychic fourth dimension" ("Nepantla: In/Between and Shifting"); "the river in which my life flows" (Writing Notas E); "uncharted territories of inner space" (Writing Notas 108.1); "a creative womb" (Writing Notas F); and "un ombligo (an umbilical cord) that connects us to the earth and to concrete reality" (Light 57). As these descriptions suggest, el cenote represents a profound, expansive source of creativity that manifests at individual and collective levels. It is both our personal storehouse of discoverable memories and our entry into the transpersonal, communal source of creative images and insights that exceed the personal and, perhaps, the human itself, offering those of us who dare to dive deep into its Source "the message from the god" (Writing Notas D). El cenote connects us to the imaginal; it's Anzaldúa's "symbol for the imaginal realm and for accessing the imagination or letting the imagination access [her]" ("Writing Habit").

We can access el cenote in a variety of ways, ranging from simple recognition to elaborate ritual. We tap into el cenote by acknowledging its reality and throwing ourselves into its depths, by "going deep, listening, capturing images, words" (Writing Notas 107.10). This deep-diving work occurs through self-reflection, meditation, active engagement with the imaginal world and culturally specific mythic figures ("Nepantla: In/Between and Shifting"), and dialogic encounters with the outer world such as those Anzaldúa describes in *Light in the Dark*. Regardless of the approach we take, tapping into el cenote demands receptivity—the willingness to release our overreliance on rational thought and our desire to fully control our process. As Anzaldúa explained to the participants of her El Cenote writing workshop, "You dig into your cenote, tap your well, and from the unconscious out will come the image and the words[;] all you have to do is be receptive" (Writing Notas D). And yet, "be[ing] receptive" is not easy.

Not surprisingly, given el cenote's historic association with sacrifice, accessing el cenote comes with a cost. Because diving into this well requires that we release total control, we inevitably open ourselves to the unknown. Thus Anzaldúa reflects on her own deep dives into el cenote, asking herself in her writing notas if she's willing to dive into "the black pit, [the] cave in el cenote," where she'll be forced "to accept [her] own irrationality . . . & confront the monster, human frailty" (Writing Notas D). Surrendering into el cenote demands a sacrifice. As Anzaldúa states in a 1988 *Trivia* interview, "[W]hen you do an art, of any kind, there's certain sacrifices that you have to . . . go through. Things you have to give up."

El cenote in Anzaldúan thought both represents and feeds artistic creation, knowledge production, and other forms of transformation. A key component in Anzaldúa's dialogic creative process, el cenote is part of the inward reflection that balances the outward reception; they are two actions of one larger creative act, together sharpening our skills and inviting us to access additional dimensions of reality.

EL CENOTE'S STORY (ORIGINS AND DEVELOPMENT)

This theory is at least partially born from Anzaldúa's attempts to understand how creativity and the creative process occurred in herself and others. Anzaldúa drew from geography, Mayan tradition, Jungian shadow work, magic, and her own imaginal journeys to investigate and articulate el ce-note; importantly, she began doing so before arriving at the term itself. The image of a watery, deep, transpersonal source of potential inspiration and expanded consciousness was with her from the late 1970s, if not earlier. In the early 1980s, she used the metaphor of a well to represent this collective unconscious source of profound creativity and growth. As she writes near the opening of "Esperando la serpiente con plumas," "Fishing objects long forgotten, or objects from a past life or the Collective Life out of the deep well was a necessary act. . . . Evolution. Consciousness." Similarly, in her 1982 essay, "Altares: On the Process of Feminist Image Making," she uses the image of a well to symbolize "connection with that creative force gen-erating life deep in our psyches."

In the late 1980s Anzaldúa first employed the term "el cenote" to de-scribe this deep reservoir of images, using it as the name of a writing workshop, "El Cenote Writing Workshop," that she initiated and led in fall 1987 in Oakland, California. As she asserts in a letter advertising this work-shop, "I see our creative self and the creative act as a *cenote*, an immense circular hole full of water with trees growing out of the sides and overhang-ing the brink. *El cenote* is a well or water reservoir in caves; it is a place of pilgrimage, a sacred place. I hope that together and separately we can take daily trips to that place" (9.2). By this time, then, Anzaldúa viewed el ce-note as a tremendous source of inspiration and divine power with depths that exceed rational knowledge. As she recalls, "I named my writing work-shop . . . El Cenote to indicate the rich imaginal reservoir that the writer can access. The underground rivers, we only see the small arms of them where they rise up and burst through the skin of the earth" ("La Prieta is Dreaming"). She used guided meditations to assist workshop attendees in accessing this inner transpersonal source: "You dig into your cenote, tap your well, and from the unconscious out will come the image and the words all [sic] you have to do is be receptive. To get the students to be re-ceptive I would lead them in a guided meditation that would allow them to shift out of the rational, logical mind and allow the imagining mind to come forth" (Writing Notas D).

Although Anzaldúa never devoted entire manuscripts to el cenote (as she does to other theories, like autohistoria-teoría, nepantla, El Mundo Zurdo, the Coyolxauhqui process, and conocimiento), she frequently men-tioned it in discussions of writing, artists, creativity, and imagination. As the years progressed she described el cenote in increasingly expansive terms. In the late 1980s and early 1990s, when she investigated memoir and developed her theory of autohistoria-teoría, she often associated el cenote with personal memories and culturally specific traditions. Thus in her 1990 bildungsroman, "Autohistoria de la artista," she describes her process for reanimating memories as entering "a place she calls *el cenote*. In her imagination she descends into the sinkhole the waterhole. In *el cenote* memories collide, conflict, converge, condense and negotiate relationships between past, present and future."[6]

In the mid-1990s Anzaldúa described el cenote as both culturally specific and transcultural: "El cenote represents memories and experiences—the collective memory of the race, of the culture—and your personal history" (*Interviews* 240). By 1996 she had expanded the definition even further: "My tradition comes from a cenote, a pool formed by the water of many rivers: the indigenous Mexican, the Chicano, the Euro-American, the cultures of color, the Spanish and Latino and these create a creature of mestisaje a cultural syncretism" (Writing Notas 107.13), and in her twenty-first-century *Light in the Dark*, she moved beyond the human to embrace the cosmos: "We are connected to el cenote via the individual and collective árbol de la vida, and our images and ensueños emerge from that connection, from the self-in-community (inner, spiritual, nature / animals, racial / ethnic, communities of interest, neighborhood, city, nation, planet, galaxy, and the unknown universes)" (5).

In some of her final writings Anzaldúa put el cenote into dialogue with shamanism, astrology, and la naguala. In "Self-in-Community," for example, she describes el cenote as "a realm accessed by the watcher, la naguala, an inner presence with an artistic, aesthetic eyes [*sic*]." Again associating el cenote with "the imaginal realm" and its "several levels," she suggests that we access el cenote through our bodies, and associates it with "archetypal stories." Had she lived longer Anzaldúa would have further explored el cenote's relationship to creativity and embodiment as she reflected on her changing relationship with her own diabetic body and expanded her theory-praxis of spiritual activism. It's also likely that she might have worked more closely with her own cenote experiences, exploring various ways to access el cenote and to use its rich imagery and profound wisdom as part of our progressive social change work.

- B/borderlands
- Coatlicue state
- conocimiento
- Coyolxauhqui process
- la facultad
- la naguala
- nepantla
- nepantlera

FUTURE DIRECTIONS

- In her early work (late 1970s and early 1980s) Anzaldúa associated the source of inspiration with "the Well" and "the Windmill"—images used throughout her short story "El paisano is a bird of good omen." How might we bring el cenote into our interpretations?
- What's the relationship between el cenote and sacrifice—especially when considered as part of the artistic process and/or Anzaldúa's embodied writing? How might we see this implied relationship throughout Anzaldúa's work (for instance, in some of the poetry in *Borderlands*)?
- Surrender plays a role in both the Coatlicue state and el cenote. What might we learn about Anzaldúa's theories of subjectivity (and about subjectivity more generally) when we put these theories into dialogue with personhood?
- How might Anzaldúa have used el cenote in her theory of creativity?
- How can el cenote function as a decolonizing inspiration and force?
- Writing Notas L indicates that Anzaldúa was thinking in rich ways about el cenote and its functions, including its potential connections with la naguala. How might we further extend (and enact) these connections?
- What's the relationship between el cenote and the imaginal? How can we use visualization to access el cenote and in other ways awaken our creativity?

- "Altares: On the Process of Feminist Image Making"
- "Autohistoria de la artista as a Young Girl"
- "*Autohistorias-teorías—Mujeres que cuentan vidas*: Personal & Collective Narratives That Challenge Genre Conventions"
- El Cenote Communication (9.2)
- "Esperando la serpiente con plumas"
- *Interviews/Entrevistas*
- "Lectures on Themes and Theories"
- *Light in the Dark/Luz en lo Oscuro*
- "Nepantla: Gateways and Thresholds"
- "Nepantla: The Creative Process"
- "Nepantla: In/Between and Shifting"
- "Nepantla: Theories of Composition and Art"
- "Plunging into El Cenote"
- "Putting Coyolxauhqui Together"
- "Self-in-Community"
- "The Woman Who Writes: The Writing Subject Plunging into El Cenote"
- Writing Notas D, E, F, L

The Coatlicue State

There is another quality to the mirror and that is the act of seeing. Seeing and being seen. Subject and object, I and she. The eye pins down the object of its gaze, scrutinizes it, judges it. A glance can freeze us in place; it can "possess" us. It can erect a barrier against the world. But in a glance also lies awareness, knowledge. These seemingly contradictory aspects—the act of being seen, held immobilized by a glance, and "seeing through" an experience—are symbolized by the underground aspects of Coatlicue, Cihuacoatl, and Tlazolteotl which cluster in what I call the Coatlicue state.—*Borderlands/La Frontera* (1987)

The Nahuatl world and the Coatlicue state are different stages of the same terrain. When you come out of the Coatlicue state you come out of nepantla, this birthing stage where you feel like you're reconfiguring your identity and don't know where you are. You used to be this person but now maybe you're different in some way. You're changing worlds and cultures and maybe classes, sexual preferences. So you go through this birthing of nepantla. When you're in the midst of the Coatlicue state—the cave, the dark—you're hibernating or hiding, you're gestating and giving birth to yourself. You're in a womb state. When you come out of that womb state you pass through the birth canal, the passageway I call nepantla.—*Interviews/Entrevistas* (1994)

DEFINITION

Though often overlooked or downplayed, the Coatlicue state is an important component in Anzaldúa's complex onto-epistemology, as well as a theory unto itself. With the Coatlicue state Anzaldúa focuses on the relationship between knowledge, ignorance, oppression, and transformation. The Coatlicue state represents the resistance to new knowledge, the intense inner struggles and negative states that this resistance provokes, and the promise (though not guarantee) of new insights. The Coatlicue state's struggles take a variety of forms but often entail the juxtaposition and transmutation of contrary internal and external forces as well as embodied manifestations (especially addictions and profound depression) in the knower.

Because this theory—like Anzaldúa's theory of the Coyolxauhqui process—grows from her engagement with a mythic figure, it's useful to begin by summarizing the version of Coatlicue's story with which Anzaldúa was most familiar. According to Aztec teachings, Coatlicue, whose name means "Serpent Skirts," is an autochthonous earth goddess of life and death and mother of the gods. In Aztec renditions of her story, Coatlicue is a truly terrifying figure; as Anzaldúa explains in *Borderlands*, she has a horrific appearance, with a skirt of writhing serpents, a necklace of human skulls, and serpent-like claws for hands and feet. She is headless, with "two spurts of blood gush[ing] up, transfiguring into enormous twin rattlesnakes facing each other." Importantly, Coatlicue's decapitation results in new life. As Anzaldúa works with this mythic figure, she underscores Coatlicue's complexity, viewing her as more than the grotesque, horrific face shown to the world; Coatlicue—and Coatlicue's estate—offer an array of possible meanings and outcomes. Just as Coatlicue rules over both life and death, so her estate offers complex, complementary, transformational possibilities: "Our greatest disappointments and painful experiences—if we can make meaning out of them—can lead us toward becoming more of who we are. Or they can remain meaningless. The *Coatlicue* state can be a way station or it can be a way of life" (68).

Anzaldúa offers her most extensive discussion of this theory in *Borderlands'* central prose chapter, "*La herencia de Coatlicue*/The Coatlicue State," in which she draws on her own experiences (especially her physical and emotional challenges) to describe it as complex resistance to new knowledge. Near the chapter's opening she explains that when she began menstruating at a very young age she felt that "[h]er body had betrayed her" (43). As this use of third person pronouns suggests, the Coatlicue state represents disembodied double consciousness and self-alienation: To gain distance from her physical, emotional, and psychic pain, Anzaldúa tried to separate herself from her body and identify only with the mind, with what she calls "the conscious I." This self-division (a self-division replicated by Cartesian epistemology's mind/body dichotomy) signals entry into the Coatlicue state, and Anzaldúa explains that each time she attempts to ignore physical or psychic information she experiences extreme conflict that leads to depression, paralysis, and despair. Resolution cannot occur until she acknowledges and begins to explore these previously suppressed physical, emotional, and/or psychic states—an exploration that takes place by connecting with, rather than rejecting, her physical body. Anzaldúa associates the Coatlicue state with repression, depression, disembodiment, and the resistance to acknowledging new insights (often painful insights about ourselves). The Coatlicue state also represents the underground shadow work (confrontations with sorrow and pain) typically necessary (indeed, typically vital) as we move toward greater insights. Despite Coatlicue's horrific visage, the Coatlicue state also represents an optimistic story of how change can happen, how addiction can be useful, how we can reconcile with our embodiment and, through this reconciliation, obtain new insights and "make soul."

Anzaldúa applies the Coatlicue state to various situations, including creativity, the writing process (especially writing blocks), health crises, and external and internalized racism. As she explains in *Borderlands*, psychic conflicts are analogous to those she experiences as a Chicana: the opposing Mexican, Indian, and Anglo worldviews she internalized lead to self-division, cultural confusion, and shame. By sitting with this internalized hatred, she learns to examine it more closely and recognize its projected nature. The Coatlicue state gives us a way to make sense of the obstacles we might experience—obstacles that, at the time we're experiencing them, seem completely meaningless and totally overwhelming. Because it offers a framework to comprehend apparently senseless obstacles and pain, the Coatlicue state can deeply resonate with those who have been oppressed, whose worldviews and belief systems have been denied, suppressed, or in other ways dismissed by the dominating culture.

Anzaldúa's earliest reference to Coatlicue occurs in a poem from the late 1970s. Titled "La Coatlicue," this poem describes Coatlicue as the cosmic source of all existence: "[A]ll being springs from her / animal, vegetal, piedra" (223.2). However, Anzaldúa did not engage theoretically with Coatlicue (*as* Coatlicue) until she was drafting and revising *Borderlands* for publication. Instead, her revisionist mythmaking focused on Medusa. For Anzaldúa and many other mid-twentieth-century feminists, the Greek myth of Medusa—a beautiful woman raped/seduced by Poseidon in Athena's temple, punished by Athena for the rape, transformed into a monster whose visage turned anyone viewing her to stone, and eventually beheaded (*and thus silenced*) by Perseus—represented many forms of disempowerment women experienced in patriarchal cultures.

Analysis of the 1986 and early 1987 *Borderlands* manuscripts indicates that the Coatlicue state grew from Anzaldúa's earlier theory of "the Medusa state"—a term she regularly used in the late 1970s and early 1980s to describe her struggles with depression, writing blocks, and the resistance to new insights. She expands on her theory of the Medusa state in her drafts of *Borderlands*—both as the poem "Encountering the Medusa" (included in "Borderlands," the poetry manuscript) and as a section of the prose portion, titled "The Medusa State." Indeed, the three earliest versions of chapter 4 are titled "The Medusa State"; these drafts range in length from three pages in the earliest version (written ca. October 1986) to ten pages in the third version as Anzaldúa develops her theory of the Medusa state. In these drafts Medusa functions as a complex, highly personal archetype—what Anzaldúa, borrowing from James Hillman, describes as a "person inhabiting my psyche." She associates Medusa with "paralysis," with her early onset menstruation and the accompanying shame, what she describes in the second draft as "Medusa . . . the shamed exposed self," and with shamanic journeying: "The Medusa state is part of the journey along with dismemberment, death, descent into hell and resurrection—the shaman's journey." As late as November 1986, Anzaldúa was still using the term "Medusa state" to describe what becomes in the published volume the Coatlicue state: "My resistance, my refusal to know some truth about myself brings on that paralysis, depression. I wallow in its depth, sinking deeper and deeper. When I reach bottom, something forces me to push up, walk toward the mirror, confronting the Medusa that wears my face." In early 1987, either Anzaldúa or her editor suggested that "Medusa" be replaced with "Coatlicue"—a figure with whom Anzaldúa was already familiar and had occasionally referenced. From that time forward, Anzaldúa named her theory "the Coatlicue state" rather than "the Medusa state."

During the late 1980s and early 1990s, Anzaldúa continued working with this theory. Not surprisingly, given the Coatlicue state's close ties to depression, in her graduate work at UCSC, she put the Coatlicue state into dialogue with psychoanalytic theory and melancholia. However, after 1992, when Anzaldúa encountered Coyolxauhqui, she referred to the Coatlicue state less often as her attention shifted from mother to daughter, from Coatlicue to Coyolxauhqui and the complex Coyolxauhqui process. In 1995 she associates the Coatlicue state with desconocimientos ("Nepantla: The Creative Process"), and in the following years she expanded this association as she drafted "now let us shift" for *this bridge we call home*, struggled to manage her diabetes, and theorized conocimiento. In 2000 she used the Coatlicue state to name and describe conocimiento's third stage: "The Coatlicue state, desconocimiento and the cost of knowing" ("Conocimientos"). Applying the Coatlicue state to her personal struggles with diabetes, she deepened and expanded the theory, associating it even more intimately with embodied knowledge. Importantly, she charts how insights can emerge from the body, activated (in part) by the trauma itself. Had Anzaldúa lived longer, it's likely that she would have taken this analysis even further, exploring the ways we can use our embodied existence to transform desconocimientos into insights.

RELATED THEORIES

- el cenote
- conocimiento
- Coyolxauhqui process
- desconocimiento
- nepantla
- new mestiza consciousness

FUTURE DIRECTIONS

- What do investigations of Anzaldúa's early theory of the Medusa state teach us about the Coatlicue state?

- What else can we learn about the Coatlicue state by examining *Borderlands'* early drafts?
- How did the Coatlicue state change after Anzaldúa put it into dialogue with nepantla in the mid-1990s?
- Relatedly, how might Anzaldúa's dialogue between the Coatlicue state and nepantla have impacted the latter's development?
- When we read the stories of Coatlicue and Coyolxauhqui in dialogue, how might this dialogic reading impact our understanding and use of the Coatlicue state?
- What is the relationship between the Coyolxauhqui process and the Coatlicue state? How can we work with them as we analyze and develop consciousness?
- How might Coatlicue be related to Llorona?
- How might the Coatlicue state function as a critique of radical individualism and the Cartesian isolated thinker? (See for instance Anzaldúa's discussion of the Coatlicue state as conocimiento's third stage in *Light in the Dark*: "You look around, hoping some person or thing will alleviate the pain. Pero virgen santísima, you've purposely cut yourself off from those who could help—you've no desire to reconnect with community" [130].)
- What does an analysis of the many drafts of "now let us shift" indicate about how Anzaldúa altered the concept from its earlier versions? (Was the Coatlicue state the third stage of conocimiento's path from the beginning, or did Anzaldúa reorganize the stages? Is it in the earliest versions of conocimiento's journey?)
- How does analysis of the Coatlicue state enable us to more fully understand her theory of desconocimientos?

USEFUL TEXTS

- "Borderlands"
- *Borderlands/La Frontera*
- "Coming into Play: An Interview with Gloria Anzaldúa"
- "Encountering the Medusa"
- "Exploring Cultural Legacies: Using Myths to Construct Stories of Modern Realities"
- "The Hauntings of Llorona"
- "How I've Survived"
- "Nepantla: The Creative Process"

- *Interviews/Entrevistas*
- *Light in the Dark/Luz en lo Oscuro*
- "Noche y su nidada/Night and Her Nest"
- "Nonfiction Drafts"
- "now let us shift" (in multiple drafts and versions)
- "Speaking across the Divide"
- "Spiritual Mestisaje"
- Writing Notas H, J, L

Conocimiento

To activate the conocimiento and communication we need the hand.—"New Mestiza Nation" (1992)

[Conocimiento is] my term for an over-arching theory of consciousness, of how the mind works. It's an epistemology that tries to encompass all of the dimensions of life, both inner: mental, emotional, instinctive, imaginal, spiritual, bodily realms, as well as outer: social, political, lived experiences. I guess it's a pretty ambitious project—and me not even a trained philosopher! I've been working on this idea for years. It's hard to explain it in a few words because it has so many layers and encompasses many fields and territories.—*Interviews/Entrevistas* (1998)

The model of el mundo zurdo has expanded to the model of conocimiento by incorporating the soul and spirit with nepantla and consciousness/awareness acting as the bridge between political activism and spiritual activism.—"Chapter Annotations" (2004)

DEFINITION

Arguably Anzaldúa's most comprehensive theory, conocimiento represents a holistic, activist-inflected epistemology, ontology, metaphysics, and ethics designed to effect change on multiple levels. The culmination of Anzaldúa's philosophy, conocimiento offers a bold expansion of the epistemology she developed during the 1980s, which consists of la facultad, the Coatlicue state, and new mestiza consciousness. With conocimiento, Anzaldúa fleshes out the transformational elements of these earlier theories, focusing especially on their intuitive, psychic, nondichotomous, transformational potential. Conocimiento deepens and expands Anzaldúa's *Borderlands* theories of new mestiza consciousness and la facultad in several ways: like new mestiza consciousness, conocimiento represents a nonbinary, connectionist mode of thinking that can assist with alliance-making; like la facultad, conocimiento often unfolds within oppressive contexts and entails a deepening of embodied perception that brings access to nonordinary realities. But with conocimiento, Anzaldúa includes additional ontological and metaphysical dimensions that were implied by but underdeveloped in her earlier epistemology.

An intensely personal, fully embodied onto-epistemological process that gathers information from physical and nonphysical contexts, conocimiento is profoundly relational, enabling those who employ it to make connections between apparently disparate events, persons, experiences, and realities; these connections, in turn, lead to new knowledge expressed through transformational action, innovative art, and much more. Conocimiento is a holistic, relational, recursive seven-stage process—a pattern, form, or journey—that occurs when social justice activist/thinkers create new knowledge, ways of living, communities, artworks, identities, and so on.

Conocimiento's role as Anzaldúa's overarching philosophy, coupled with its complexity and inclusion of several other Anzaldúan theories, makes it challenging to comprehensively define. This challenge is further complicated by Anzaldúa's depiction of conocimiento as seven recursive stages. The English language and the use of a numbering system invites us to view conocimiento in linear terms; however, conocimiento is nonlinear: its stages do not necessarily occur sequentially (although sometimes they do). Anzaldúa names conocimiento's seven stages as follows:

1. el arrebato. . . . rupture, fragmentation. . . . an ending, a beginning
2. nepantla. . . . torn between ways
3. the Coatlicue state. . . . desconocimiento and the cost of knowing
4. the call. . . . el compromiso. . . . the crossing and conversion
5. putting Coyolxauhqui together. . . . new personal and collective "stories"
6. the blow-up. . . . a clash of realities
7. shifting realities. . . . acting out the vision or spiritual activism

Conocimiento typically begins with "el arrebato"—a rupture in our sense of reality or daily lives: we experience an event, are exposed to an idea, or have some encounter that thoroughly disrupts us at a foundational level— shaking and possibly even uprooting our identity, beliefs, worldview, etc. This disruption throws us into the second stage, "nepantla": a painful, chaotic, liminal space-time in which we're "torn between ways"; we don't know what to do, where to go, what to believe. Overwhelmed by pain and/or confusion, we're immersed in uncertainty which can lead (or force) us into the third stage, the Coatlicue state—a depressive period in which we deny our incipient awareness. Unwilling to acknowledge the implications of el arrebato's foundational shift, we use addictions and other distractions to ignore it, enacting a willed ignorance, or what Anzaldúa calls "desconocimiento." However, conocimiento's potential new knowledge does not go away; it lies dormant, buried deeply within our body and psyche, the repressed insights/emotions stored in our tissue and our subconscious. We might remain in this frozen denial forever. Or, we might not. Perhaps something shifts us into the fourth stage as we recognize and answer "the call," which can come from within or from without (or both, intertwined): we encounter a message in nature, we experience a new insight, we grapple with shifts in our health. In short, we experience a "conversion" of sorts: something shifts; we acquire (or receive) new insights or perspectives that invite us to cross over. We accept the invitation and cross that bridge. Enacting the fifth stage, we determine to rewrite our individual and collective narratives. Like Coyolxauhqui, we gather the fragments of our lives (our selves) and rewrite our story—revise our understanding of reality. In the sixth stage, we apply this new story and live according to this new version of reality; we implement our new truths.

But conocimiento, like life itself, is not a linear journey of forward-moving growth and improvement; instead, conocimiento proceeds through twists, turns, and apparent reversals. Taking our new story into the world provokes resistance and obstacles, underscored by Anzaldúa's name for this sixth stage: "the blow-up"—a harsh encounter where worldviews clash. This collision can send us spinning into another phase—maybe we sink into the Coatlicue state (*again!*) for a while, and for sure we experience more nepantla—again torn between ways, in deep pain, feeling a type of freefall perhaps. The clash can be so extreme that it functions like an arrebato—ripping the ground away from beneath our feet yet again (*throwing us "back" into another first stage*). But if we stay with the conflict, we will (*again!*) hear the call. If we follow this call, we return to the insights gained in previous stages (*especially stage 5*) and we work to implement our new vision: we enact "spiritual activism," Anzaldúa's name for the seventh stage, though one could argue that the entire journey is spiritual activism's unfolding enactment (*and in some places Anzaldúa herself seems to use "spiritual activism" and "conocimiento" interchangeably*).

Both theory and method, conocimiento offers a framework and map to guide us as we move through our lives and the world, as well as the tools (methods) we can apply to make sense of our journey; to inspire and guide our growth; to create new knowledge that alters physical reality; and to articulate this knowledge production. Anzaldúa applied conocimiento to a variety of contexts, ranging from the creative process and knowledge production to coalition-building among activist groups (feminists, Latinx, and more). As she explains in 1999, "In part, conocimiento is a theory of composition, of how a work of art gets composed, of how a field (like anthropology or literature or physics) is put together and maintained, of how reality itself is constructed, and of how identity is constructed" (*Interviews* 177). Anzaldúa refers to both "conocimiento" and "conocimientos" in ways that can seem confusing at times, but the distinction is important to note: Although it might seem counterintuitive, "conocimientos" (plural) indicates the insights produced by conocimiento, while "conocimiento" indicates the overarching philosophy.

CONOCIMIENTO'S STORY (ORIGINS AND DEVELOPMENT)

Anzaldúa began working with conocimiento in the early 1990s, using it as an epistemological term and place marker for the complex theory of consciousness she aspired to create but did not have an opportunity to develop until the end of the decade. By late 1998 she viewed conocimiento as her "over-arching theory of consciousness" and further expanded its ontological dimensions, associating it with inner "instinctive, imaginal, spiritual, bodily realms, as well as outer: social, political, lived experiences" (*Interviews* 177); and in 1999, a watershed year, Anzaldúa drafted her essay on conocimiento for *this bridge we call home*. By this point she had determined to use conocimiento as the scaffolding (and dialogic partner) on which to reconfigure and further develop earlier theories like El Mundo Zurdo, la facultad, the Coatlicue state, and new mestiza consciousness, as well as later theories like new tribalism and nos/otras.

Anzaldúa first mentioned conocimiento in 1991, at which point she associated it with postcolonialism and described it as an activist epistemology that critiques and intervenes in consensual reality. As she explained to Inés Hernández-Ávila, she planned to discuss conocimiento in her dissertation/book in progress at that time: "I reflect on the five hundred years of resistance, of reclaiming America, intellectuals, artistas, escritoras cultivating a certain kind of awareness—esa facultad of looking and seeing through all the lies, the veils, and the hidden stuff. The tongue has always been the symbol of speech, the symbol of communication, and I use it in my theory of conocimiento: using the eyes for seeing and the tongue for communicating, writing, and speaking of what is seen. La mano, the hand, is the active member of the body, the part of the body that does things" (*Interviews* 182–83).[7] As this description indicates, from its inception Anzaldúa used conocimiento to join inward reflection with outward actions: "Con los ojos y la lengua en la mano: You tie in the sensitive, conscious political awareness with the act of writing and activism" (*Interviews* 183). Two years later, in an interview with Jamie Evans, she expanded this theme to emphasize radical listening. She associates conocimiento with holistic alliance-making that links inward reflection with outward action, and explains that, whereas previously she used the "model of the bridge, drawbridge, sandbar, or island" to describe alliance-making, she is now using the "model" of conocimiento:

> "Conocimiento" is the Spanish word for collesento, getting to know each other by really listening, with the outer ear and the inner ear. Really looking at each other and seeing with our eyes and communicating to each other la boca, orally, or with a pen. And always, always putting ourselves out on the line by raising our hands. The hand is the symbol for activist work, for doing. . . . You want to put your voice out; you want to raise your hand and make yourself heard. Because it's not enough to see and to understand. You have to do, you have to go out there and do. . . . Con la mano. With the hand. Activism. For me, writing is a form of activism—because of the things I've been talking about where I put forth my messages as a bridge. (*Interviews* 206)

For Anzaldúa, conocimiento's listening is a radical communal act that requires the willingness to open ourselves to our internal and external others in profound ways.

Although in these passages and elsewhere during the early to mid-1990s Anzaldúa refers to conocimiento as a "theory" and "model," during these years it functions primarily as a placeholder for such. In interviews and writing notes she uses "conocimiento" as a synonym for knowledge—e.g., "culturally forbidden conocimiento," "counterknowledge (contra-conocimiento)" (108.3)—rather than as a full-blown theory. Her writing notes indicate that she's living into the theory but has not yet developed it as such. Conocimiento, as complex onto-epistemology with seven recursive stages, emerged viscerally from Anzaldúa's experiences as she reflected deeply on the internal and external events of her life. Everything she encountered (from diabetes to inspired writing sessions, from speaking engagements to profound writing blocks, from meditation to walks by the Pacific Ocean, and much more) served as synergistic theory engines, assisting her in conocimiento's creation.

It's not until the mid-1990s, as Anzaldúa investigates and delineates her theory of the creative process, that conocimiento slowly unfolds into language, emerging especially during her work with nepantla. In writing notas, the Villa Montalvo material, and unpublished manuscripts from this time, she describes nepantla in ontological and epistemological terms that resonate with what, a few years later, she will incorporate into conocimiento. In notas from 1994, for example, she explores artists' creativity, describing their challenge to consensual reality. Associating artists with "[e]l concept de nepantla [that] questions the notion of reality . . . [and] the traditional ways of experienc[ing] the world," she describes a dialogic epistemology that resonates strongly with what will soon become conocimiento: "By listening to the environment and our inner cenotes, we cultivate an intense empathy with the world, an openness to other dimensions and realities of existence than the familiar and everyday. Aware that significant portions of experience escape verbal formulation and fail to account for or identify certain segments of reality, unnameable categories and the culturally forbidden, we attempt to shift the frame of reference, produce our own counterknowledge (contra-conocimiento) and art and write the theories" (108.3). This description bears many similarities to her description of conocimiento's journey in *Light in the Dark*. Note also her use of the word "contra-conocimiento" to scope out the theory itself. And a year later, in her notes for Villa Montalvo, Anzaldúa outlines a ten-stage theory of the creative process that resonates with what, in less than five years, becomes conocimiento's seven stages:

1. la llamando the call
2. commitment [to] the work, a piece of writing
3. facultad—trancing
4. switching modes, accessing el cenote—completing elaboration going deep
5. pondering el brinco, salto

6. Coyolxauhqui—ordering, confusion. Necessary chaos. State of anguish
7. composición
8. conocimiento
9. cambio
10. comunidad (107.10)

Here conocimiento is just one stage (*the eighth*) in this ten-stage process, rather than the entire process itself. (*It's also important to note that Anzaldúa drew very heavily on her own writing process as she analyzed these stages of the creative process.*)[8]

When Anzaldúa began co-editing *this bridge we call home* in 1999, she determined that her contribution to the volume would continue this investigation, and for the next two years she worked intensively on it. The number of manuscript drafts she produced are almost overwhelming and merit close study.[9] Through the lengthy process of drafting and revising this essay, which she referred to as her "cono essay" and envisioned also as a chapter in her dissertation, she deepened and expanded conocimiento, transforming it from an epistemology into an entire philosophy with epistemological, ontological, ethical, and aesthetic implications. As an early draft title, "Creative Acts of Vision: Viviendo nepantla con conocimiento," suggests, Anzaldúa began by focusing on nepantla, rather than conocimiento, and set out to explore how we can navigate nepantla with conocimiento/awareness. But in her self-reflection, shadow work, research, and revision process, she shifted her emphasis from nepantla to conocimiento. Conocimiento developed along with the essay, and Anzaldúa expanded its implications in many ways. To mention only a few: she took conocimiento beyond the individual to include cultural, historical, and nonhuman dimensions; developed conocimiento (like nepantla before it) into a series of stages (however, with conocimiento, the stages became extremely recursive); and associated conocimiento with intense self-reflection and shadow work, as well as the imaginal and a type of panpsychic consciousness.

Despite conocimiento's epistemological dimensions, Anzaldúa rarely associates it with her earlier theory of new mestiza consciousness. As the above narrative suggests, the theory owes its lineage more closely to nepantla (*which, to be fair, has ancestral connections to mestiza consciousness*). However, in *Light in the Dark*'s final chapter, she does associate the two, locating new mestiza consciousness in conocimiento's fifth stage "*putting Coyol-*

xauhqui together . . . new personal and collective 'stories,' thus implying that it was no longer entirely sufficient for her needs.[10]

Although conocimiento seems to culminate in *Light in the Dark*, Anzaldúa's writing notas and computer files from the early twenty-first century indicate that she planned to further develop this onto-ethico-epistemology in several ways. First, she had put conocimiento into further dialogue with spiritual tools and technologies. In Writing Notas J, she draws on recent scientific investigations to explore "delocalized consciousness in space and time," and she references eastern energetics as she investigates the Sanskrit seven-chakra system, insisting that "[t]he mind is not localized in the brain. Each of the seven chakras is a thinking center. The heart has its own mode of perception. The gut (the gastro-intestinal system) also has its own mode of perception." While these ideas partially appear in *Light in the Dark*, it's likely that Anzaldúa would have continued working with conocimiento's implications for energetics and embodiment (both physical and subtle bodies). Second, quite possibly, she would also have used conocimiento to analyze and in other ways address external events. In her 2001 writing notas, for example, she speculates on possible applications, asking "Could I apply the seven stages of conocimiento to nations?" (108.7). And third, she would have continued investigating associations among queer theory, la facultad, and conocimiento, shaping them into additional theories like "queer conocimiento" and "inner conocimiento," and including them in a later book.

RELATED THEORIES

- el cenote
- Coatlicue state
- Coyolxauhqui process
- desconocimiento
- la facultad
- El Mundo Zurdo
- la naguala
- nepantla
- nepantlera
- new mestiza
- new mestiza consciousness
- new tribalism
- nos/otras
- spiritual activism

- In the mid-1990s Anzaldúa describes nepantla as a path with multiple stages, several of which resonate powerfully with what she will later delineate as conocimiento's stages. When and why does the shift from nepantla to conocimiento occur? What are the implications of this shift for both theories?
- Relatedly, what does an analysis of nepantla's stages and those of conocimiento teach us about these theories?
- In the 1997 manuscript "Nepantla: In/Between and Shifting," Anzaldúa writes, "The significance of the forbidden fruit—by eating [this fruit a] person becomes the initiator of her own life." This passage resonates powerfully with conocimiento's journey, as described in *Light in the Dark*. What might we learn about conocimiento and Anzaldúa's theorizing method by putting these two passages into dialogue?
- The archive includes two boxes filled with manuscript drafts of what eventually became "now let us shift," an essay that Anzaldúa informally called her "conocimiento" essay (and that became chapter 6 in *Light in the Dark*). What does close analysis of these many drafts teach us about conocimiento's development? How might the context of Anzaldúa's life (especially her health and her work projects) in the late 1990s and early 2000s have impacted conocimiento's development in these drafts?
- How did Anzaldúa arrive at conocimiento's seven stages? (Why seven, and why these specific seven?) What do the earlier iterations of these stages teach us about conocimiento and her thinking process?
- How does Anzaldúa herself cultivate and enact conocimiento?[11]
- How did Anzaldúa's use of conocimiento shape her work?
- What are conocimiento's methods, both as described and as enacted? What are the methods of conocimiento explored/demonstrated by Anzaldúa?
- What is the relationship between conocimiento and El Mundo Zurdo?
- What is the relationship between conocimiento and spiritual activism—not only in terms of the published chapter where spiritual activism is the seventh stage in conocimiento's recursive

path, but also in the various drafts? When did Anzaldúa incorporate spiritual activism? And/or, did conocimiento grow from spiritual activism, taking on a life of its own?

- In several manuscripts Anzaldúa associates conocimiento and consciousness with energy. (For instance, in Writing Notas M she states, "Consciousness/conocimiento is a kind of energy.") What are the implications of this association? How might we further develop and apply it? And in what ways, if any, might it apply to her much earlier discussions of a "yoga of the body" in *Interviews*?
- Anzaldúa frequently used the metaphor of the open hand holding a heart to describe conocimiento. What might this image tell us about the theory? How could we work with this image and Anzaldúa's discussions of it to further develop an ethics of conocimiento?
- How might conocimiento function as a philosophy and/or technology of change?

USEFUL TEXTS

- "Bridge, Drawbridge, Island, Sandbar"
- "Conocimientos: Creative Acts of Vision, Inner Works, Public Acts"
- "Conocimientos, Now Let Us Shift: Inner Work and Public Acts"
- "counsels from the firing . . . past, present, future"
- "The Cracks between the Worlds and Bridges to Span Them"
- "(Des)Conocimientos: Resisting New Forms of Domination/ Oppression"
- *Interviews/Entrevistas*
- *Light in the Dark/Luz en lo Oscuro*
- "Navigating Nepantla and the Cracks between the Worlds"
- "Nepantla: Creative Acts of Vision"
- "Nepantla: In/Between and Shifting"
- "Nos/otros 'Us' vs. 'Them,' (Des)Conocimientos y compromisos"
- "Re-configuring Fronteras: New Navigations of Nepantla and the Cracks Between Worlds"
- "Re-conocimientos and Producing Knowledge: The Postmodern Llorona"
- "Taller Nepantla"

- Writing Notas 107.9, 107.10, 108.3, 108.7
- Writing Notas H, I, J, K, L, M

The Coyolxauhqui Process

In my work I reenact the rupture, departure and passage from one world to another and all the states and stages on the way. I experience the psychic dismemberment symbolized by Coyolxauhqui. In the process of composing the text, both the text and I undergo un desmiembrimiento y luego una recompuesta pulling the text together and putting myself back together. It is a kind of death-rebirth cycle of the work and of the writer.—"Nepantla: Theories of Composition and Art" (1993)

Coyolxauhqui is my symbol for the necessary process of dismemberment and fragmentation, of seeing that self or discipline, differently. It is my symbol for reframing, that allows for putting the pieces together in a new way. It is an ongoing process of making and unmaking. There is never any resolution. This is also the process of healing.—"The Cracks and Holes between the Worlds" (2000)

The Coyolxauhqui imperative is to heal and achieve integration. When fragmentations occur you fall apart and feel as though you've been expelled from paradise. Coyolxauhqui is my symbol for the necessary process of dismemberment and fragmentation, of seeing that self or the situations you're embroiled in differently. Coyolxauhqui is also my symbol for reconstruction and reframing, one that allows for putting the pieces together in a new way.—*Light in the Dark/Luz en lo Oscuro* (2004, 2012)

DEFINITION

According to Aztec mythic history, Coyolxauhqui, also called "la diosa de la luna" (goddess of the moon), was Coatlicue's oldest daughter. After Coatlicue was impregnated by a ball of feathers, Coyolxauhqui encouraged her four hundred brothers and sisters to kill their mother. As they attacked her, the fetus, Huitzilopochtli, sprang fully grown and armed from Coatlicue, tore Coyolxauhqui into over a thousand pieces, flung her head into the sky and her body down the sacred mountain, and killed his other siblings. But as Anzaldúa knew, Coyolxauhqui greatly exceeds this story. Associating Coyolxauhqui with the fragmentation that occurs through oppression, colonialism, trauma (personal, ancestral, national, cultural, etc.), disembodiment, susto (soul loss), depression, physical illness, and other forms of wounding, Anzaldúa develops her theory of the Coyolxauhqui process. In her work, this complex process—which consists of three intertwined theories ("the Coyolxauhqui imperative," "the Coyolxauhqui principle," and "putting Coyolxauhqui together")—represents the urgent desire to move from fragmentation toward wholeness; the journey toward healing that occurs as we work to acknowledge, comprehend, and recover from these deep wounds; and the reassurance that healing, though always ongoing and never complete, will occur. (*This reassurance is especially important when we're immersed in the Coatlicue state which, as explained later, serves almost as incubator for the Coyolxauhqui process.*) Importantly, whatever wholeness we might achieve does not transcend, deny, or in other ways erase the wounds but instead incorporates and makes meaning from them. The Coyolxauhqui process, then, is also a meaning-making endeavor that uses painful situations and events to produce personal and collective knowledge. As discussed later, Coyolxauhqui's story enabled Anzaldúa to make sense of her own life while also offering a theory and framework for others. It is revolutionary in its potential.

The Coyolxauhqui process can be initiated through the Coyolxauhqui imperative—an urge, an inner compulsion, or a strong desire for healing and repair. As Anzaldúa asserts in *Light in the Dark*, "The Coyolxauhqui imperative is to heal and achieve integration" (16). This desire for wholeness is not a naive wish for return to some pristine Edenic situation but rather a desire to forge an innovative, holistic state of being that honors and works with, while also healing, the fragmented parts of our lives. At times, this desire exceeds conscious awareness and functions even when we're shattered—ripped asunder into multiple parts: "Yet while experiencing the many, I cohere as the one reconstituted and restructured by my own unconscious urge toward wholeness" (*Light* 50). This "unconscious urge" can express itself through that part of the Coyolxauhqui process that Anzaldúa calls "putting Coyolxauhqui together": we examine some component of our lives, sort through the fragments (acknowledging the pain, damage, and wounds), and selectively bring these shards together, integrating them into a new shape.

Just as Coyolxauhqui is both fragmented and whole, so this theory offers an approach to healing that acknowledges partiality and pain while making space for optimism, inspiration, and hope. Anzaldúa has built into this theory the recognition that healing is an ongoing, never-ending process; whatever reconstituted wholeness we might achieve will not be complete (if completion is defined as some type of pre-wound perfection or total cure) but rather represents temporary completion, coming together for this time but always also with the recognition that further change will occur.

Not surprisingly, given Coyolxauhqui's intimate relationship with Coatlicue (*who was, after all, her mother!*), Anzaldúa's theories of the Coatlicue state and the Coyolxauhqui process are closely related. While the Coatlicue state represents the resistance to change (*a resistance so paralyzing that it throws us into inertia*), the Coyolxauhqui process can be described as the lengthy (*possibly endless*) process of change itself. With the Coyolxauhqui process, we begin pulling the pieces together. The gestation in Coatlicue's womb has deeply energized and nourished us, so that we might initiate the slow, jagged transformational process. Thus in her theory-praxis of conocimiento Anzaldúa associates the Coatlicue state with conocimiento's third stage and the Coyolxauhqui process with the fifth. Just as Coatlicue gave birth to Coyolxauhqui, so the depths of despair we typically experience while in the Coatlicue state germinate the insights and healing that occur during the Coyolxauhqui process. To carry the analogy with these Mesoamerican gods even further, perhaps we could say that, just as Coyolxauhqui's journey involved killing her mother (and this murder in fact led to her own death), so the Coyolxauhqui process represents overcoming (*by moving through*) the Coatlicue state's paralysis. The close relationship between these two ancient deities reminds us how painful the creative process can be. (*Pain and artistic blocks are not "one and done"; they recur, in different ways, throughout the larger recursive process.*)

While the Coyolxauhqui process can take many forms and applications, Anzaldúa applies it most extensively and frequently to creativity. As she explains in "Speaking across the Divide," "The path of the artist, the creative impulse, what I call the Coyolxauhqui imperative, is basically an attempt to heal the wounds. It's a search for inner completeness." She often associated this imperative with cultural trauma and other individual/collective woundings, as well as her desire to write. She explores this association at length in *Light in the Dark*, especially chapter 5, appropriately titled "Putting Coyolxauhqui Together," and chapter 6, where it becomes the sixth stage in conocimiento's recursive process, "putting Coyolxauhqui together . . . new personal and collective 'stories.'"

THE COYOLXAUHQUI PROCESS'S STORY (ORIGINS AND DEVELOPMENT)

Although Anzaldúa did not engage with Coyolxauhqui and her story until 1992, Coyolxauhqui's key themes of fragmentation, dismemberment, wounding, healing, and loss were crucial to Anzaldúa decades before she

encountered Coyolxauhqui herself. As early as the 1982 "Esperando la serpiente con plumas," she described her goals for this book in words that
resonate with the Coyolxauhqui process: "[T]o put back together parts of
the flesh severed from us. To heal our deep, deep wounds. To return to
the things we allowed ourselves to be split from. To breathe in through
our open mouths, through all the orifices in our bodies, through our skins
breathe in the wind, the air, the fire, the water—all elements estranged
from us." Similarly, in interviews from this time period Anzaldúa again uses
the language of dismemberment and reconstitution to describe her own
self-healing process: "I need to accept all the pieces: The fucked-up Glorias
go with the compassionate, loving Glorias; they're all me. To say I'm going to
get rid of this Gloria or that Gloria is like chopping off an arm or leg" (*Interviews* 41). In her conversation with Christine Weiland she explains that her
spiritual training has taught her that her task in life is "to pick up the pieces
that were chopped off: reclaiming the body, sexuality, spirituality, anger. It's
leading me towards wholeness" (*Interviews* 127). In short, Coyolxauhqui
resonated with Anzaldúa viscerally and at the deepest levels for over a decade prior to her actual encounter with this shamanic mythic figure.

Anzaldúa learned about the Aztec moon goddess in 1992, and the following year began incorporating Coyolxauhqui into her theories of creativity, writing, and other healing modalities. She offered her first extended
discussion in the 1993 "Nepantla: Gateways and Thresholds" in which she
associates Coyolxauhqui with numerous aspects of the writing process:
the sacrifice entailed as we throw ourselves into our work; the memories
stored in the body that we excavate as we write; the re-traumatization that
can occur as we do this excavational writing; and the revision process that
feels like dismemberment. From this point through the mid-1990s, during a
time when she was deeply immersed in questions of creativity and art, Anzaldúa used Coyolxauhqui to describe various stages of the artistic process.
In manuscripts like "Taller Nepantla," she positions Coyolxauhqui early in
the creative journey, directly after the artist has received the call to her
art: "The artist, as shaman—seer, visionary, healer, undergoes a physical or
psychic breakdown, a falling apart. I call this stage Coyolxauhqui after the
Aztec moon goddess who was dismembered by her brother, Huitzilopochli
[*sic*]. It is like the negrido stage in alchemy." In the earliest stages of development Anzaldúa seems almost to conflate Coyolxauhqui with Coatlicue
and her state, associating both primarily with the pain and sacrifices she

and other artists experience while they create (*or try to create*), describing it in 1993 as "El sacrificio called on by the act of writing or making art, Coyolxauhqui, exile displacement, dismemberment" ("Nepantla: Gateways and Thresholds"). And in 1995 Anzaldúa associates Coyolxauhqui with the Coatlicue state: "Learning to cope with **Coatlicue** states of desconocimientos" ("Nepantla: The Creatiave [*sic*] Process," her bolding).

Unlike later years, when Coyolxauhqui becomes a culminating force (inspiring the drive to create the new story), here she represents an earlier stage: the artist's "physical or psychic breakdown, a falling apart." As Anzaldúa explains in the interview with Andrea Lunsford,

> One of the visuals I use [in talks] is Coyolxauhqui, the Aztec moon goddess and first sacrificial victim. Her brother threw her down the temple stairs and when she landed at the bottom she was dismembered. The act of writing for me is this kind of dismembering of everything I'm feeling—taking it apart to examine and then reconstituting or recomposing it again but in a new way. So I really have to get into the feeling—the anger, the anguish, the sadness, the frustration. I have to get into this heightened state which I access sometimes by being very quiet and doing some deep breathing, or by some little meditation, or by burning some incense, or by walking along the beach, or whatever gets me in there. I get all psyched up, and then I do the writing. I work four, five, six hours; and then I have to come off. It's like a withdrawal. I have to leave that anger, that sadness, that compassion, whatever it is I'm feeling. (*Interviews* 257)

Although Anzaldúa first associated the Coyolxauhqui process with writing, she soon realized its implications for the creative process more generally: "I started out just talking about writing and then I branched off into other art forms: into musical composition, choreographed dances, film, video—these arts all have elements in common. Even architecture and building construction have something in common with composition" (*Interviews* 269). As she delved even further into theorizing the Coyolxauhqui process, Anzaldúa expanded its applications to identity and ontology: "I started looking at how I create aspects of my identity. Identity is very much a fictive construction. . . . Then I took all of this knowledge a step further, to reality. I realized that if I can compose this text and if I can compose my identity, then I can also compose reality out there" (*Interviews* 269).

The Coyolxauhqui process achieves its fullest expression in *Light in the Dark*, in which Anzaldúa expands previous versions in several ways: First, she defines its scope more broadly, to include both the coming apart and the coming together, as well as the promise of healing. Second, she applies the Coyolxauhqui process to both personal and collective efforts: "The Coyolxauhqui process is currently working on each person and her or his culture as both attempt to become more inclusive, more whole" (89). And third, she applies it to a variety of contexts: art, creativity, and art-making (chapter 3); individual and collective identity (chapter 4); the writing process (chapter 5); our life's journey and the nepantlera's birth, development, and work (chapter 6). As this list as well as its leading role in the final two chapters suggests, the Coyolxauhqui process represents a culmination of sorts: Anzaldúa's attempt to share, in written form, a key healing lesson from her life. Had she lived longer, it's very likely that Anzaldúa would have applied this theory to onto-epistemological issues. Evidence from interviews and late manuscripts like "Self-in-Community" indicate that she would have continued working to develop her theory of "Coyolxauhqui consciousness," possibly putting it into dialogue with conocimiento.

RELATED THEORIES

- autohistoria-teoría
- el cenote
- Coatlicue state
- conocimiento
- la facultad
- new mestiza consciousness
- nepantla
- nepantlera
- spiritual activism

FUTURE DIRECTIONS

- Although Anzaldúa rarely acknowledges it, Coyolxauhqui's story revolves around the (attempted) murder of her mother. What are the implications of this matricide for Coyolxauhqui, Anzaldúa's theory of the Coyolxauhqui process, and her theory of the Coatlicue state?

- In Writing Notas H, Anzaldúa refers to "Coyolxauhqui energy": "I'm trying to make junctures with the scattered and broken pieces that is me. I'm calling a peace meeting, a junta of all the pieces and having Coyolxauhqui energy, the energy of my inner process, presiding over all the raging voices." How does this Coyolxauhqui energy infuse *Light in the Dark* and, perhaps, other Anzaldúan texts? How might we harness and work with it today?
- How might Anzaldúa have applied Coyolxauhqui to decoloniality—including the process of decolonizing reality?
- What's the relationship between Coyolxauhqui and depression? How might Coyolxauhqui offer ways to address, work with, and perhaps heal depression's paralysis?
- What's the relationship between the Coyolxauhqui process, auto-historia, and autohistoria-teoría?
- Given Coyolxauhqui's associations with the body's memory, how might we work with the Coyolxauhqui process as we explore healing personal and collective traumas?
- How might we develop Anzaldúa's theory of "Coyolxauhqui consciousness"?

USEFUL TEXTS

- "+notes-b"
- "Esperando la serpiente con plumas"
- "Exploring Cultural Legacies: Using Myths to Construct Stories of Modern Realities"
- "Geographies of Selves"
- "The Writing Habit: How I Work—Process and Stages"
- *Interviews/Entrevistas*
- *Light in the Dark/Luz en lo Oscuro*
- "Nepantla: Creative Acts of Vision"
- "Nepantla: Gateways and Thresholds"
- "Nepantla: Theories of Composition and Art"
- "Queer Conocimiento"
- "Speaking across the Divide"
- "Territories and Boundaries: Geographies of Latinidad"
- Writing Notas 107.12
- Writing Notas D, I, K, L, N

Desconocimiento(s)

What's really interesting to me is a kind of a paradox: There are groups of people who really want to work with other people and then there are other groups who want to separate and isolate out. One reason I'm doing this kind of work is that I've always been a mediator, I've always been a bridge. I think that ignorance is one of the enemies we have to combat—ignorance of power, ignorance about each other's histories, ignorance about other ways of living and other perspectives. Ignorance is a form of desconocimientos, an intentional kind of ignorance.—*Interviews/Entrevistas* (1993)

Desconocimiento. Not wanting or not able to understand because the mind refuses to take it in, the eye refuses to see, the ear to hear, an escape from understanding those who are different from oneself. An occultation of difference, a blocking off.
—Writing Notes 107.6 (1995)

The demons of today are not the seven deadly sins, but the small acts of ignorance, desconocimientos, frustrations, feelings of powerlessness, feeling betrayed, feeling poverty of spirit, of imagination, of dreams. The struggle, the fight is against ignorance and all the small desconocimientos that serve small comfort but are actually killers of the spirit. The energy suckers, those and that which takes our time and huge chunks of your psychic energy. Takes away your options so that you have little choice in what happens to you. Where someone else or something else is running you. You feel helpless, powerless, entrapped.—"Nos/otros 'Us' vs. 'Them,' (Des)Conocimientos y compromisos" (1999)

DEFINITION

One of Anzaldúa's lesser-developed theories, desconocimiento(s) is an important part of her epistemology; it represents a resistant relationship to new knowledge—an inability, reluctance, or refusal to recognize vital information (or what Anzaldúa describes below as "certain kinds of cono-cimientos") about ourselves, others, and/or the world. This refused knowledge is incipient, lurking at the edges of consciousness ready to break through at any moment; however, because it threatens us with unfamiliar, possibly dangerous, information about ourselves and our world, we push it down: "Like most people you fear the unknown and the knowledge that leads you out of the familiar and safe. You are in terror of certain kinds of conocimientos—they rip your mask off, lay bare all your sufferings, fears, and conflicts, expose your frailties, weaknesses, and vulnerabilities. To alleviate your discomfort and fear you turn your conocimientos (knowings) into desconocimientos (willed ignorance, a numbing of awareness), the shadow side of conocimiento. Not ready to face the truth about yourself, you shut out knowledge of what's causing you the conflict" ("+notes-b"). As Anzaldúa here suggests, desconocimientos represent painful, agonizing potential insights, often about ourselves; it's for good reason that we typically deny them! By describing desconocimientos as "willed ignorance," Anzaldúa underscores the subtle role intentionality can play in this (non) knowledge production: if ignorance is at least partially willed, we can use our will to confront, explore, and transform it. Like her use of both singular and plural forms of conocimiento (conocimiento/conocimientos), the singular/plural versions of this term refer to different components of the theory: desconocimiento (singular) is the entire process of not-knowing, while desconocimientos are the smaller shadows and potential insights that we intentionally or unintentionally repress.

Until acknowledged and explored, desconocimiento inhibits change; the refusal to know becomes a refusal to grow. When we remain trapped by our desconocimientos, we stunt our growth. Though the refusal to confront (and thus transform) these desconocimientos keeps us "safe," this safety comes with a price: it locks us into consensual reality and the status quo—we remain stagnant and frozen in place. We repeat the same gestures, circle endlessly around the same topics, and deepen the ruts in which we're trapped. We immerse ourselves in addictions, sadness, or other painful (non)actions in order to avoid painful insights about ourselves and/or the world. Anzaldúa associates this stagnation with the third stage in conocimiento's journey: "the Coatlicue state . . . desconocimiento and the cost of knowing" (Light 128). As we repress some truth about ourselves, the "weight of desconocimientos" drags us into the Coatlicue stage: "When stress is overwhelming, you shut down your feelings, plummet into depression and unremitting sorrow. Consciousness diminished, your body descends into itself, pulled by the weight, mass, and gravity of your desconocimientos. To escape emotional pain (most of it self-imposed), you indulge in addictions" (Light 129). As this passage suggests, like other components of Anzaldúa's philosophy, desconocimiento(s) is completely embodied: it occurs within our physical-psychic selves, and it plays itself out as we move through the physical-material world.

Importantly, Anzaldúa does not condemn desconocimiento but instead presents it as vital to knowledge production in at least two ways. First, like the Coatlicue state, desconocimiento offers the underground creation of new knowledge: "Yet you feel you're incubating some knowledge that could spring into life like a childhood monster if you paid it the slightest attention" (*Light* 129). Second, when acknowledged, desconocimiento works like a message indicating the need to alter what and how we think. In such instances, desconocimientos function productively, pushing us toward new insight and growth. When we recognize our desconocimientos and are willing to explore them, we grow. Thus, for example, in her 1999 writing notas, Anzaldúa reflects on her own knowledge creation process: "Blank spots, desconocimientos, a blind spot in my consciousness, something I've missed, so again and again I'm thrown in repeats of certain experiences that cause me discomfort. My soul-daemon throws them at me so I can look for the lesson and cultivate the skills to handle it in a new way, to look at the problem from a new perspective." Linking desconocimientos with her "soul-daemon," Anzaldúa situates them into a larger (*metaphysical*) framework that exceeds the individual and is part of an expansive sacred process.[12]

Desconocimientos occur in a variety of experiences and contexts, ranging from personal insights and identity development to group identity, coalition-building, and the writing process. Applied to shadow work and alliance-building, desconocimientos often result from a knower's (non)relationship to difference—from the refusal to acknowledge and explore that which seems alien, unusual, or strange. Thriving on sameness, desconocimiento is fueled by the denial of difference. As such, it often plays a crucial role in supporting (*normalizing, naturalizing*) systemic racism, sexism, and other forms of oppression (*as well as other status-quo story components*).

This theory can be challenging to analyze and discuss because Anzaldúa uses the word "desconocimiento" in several ways, applies it to different contexts, and distinguishes between the singular and plural versions of the term. Although at times she seems to use "desconocimiento" simply as a synonym for ignorance, at other times she uses it to represent her complex multilayered theory that explores the dynamics in willed ignorance. Moreover, Anzaldúa was still developing this theory, in dialogue with conocimiento, at the time of her death.

DESCONOCIMIENTO'S STORY (ORIGINS AND DEVELOPMENT)

Although Anzaldúa did not refer specifically to "desconocimientos" as such until 1993, she explored the concept of semi-willed ignorance in earlier work—especially in *Borderlands*, in which she discussed her own resistance to knowing and what she theorized as the Coatlicue state. She returned to her investigations of this state of not-knowing in the late 1980s and early 1990s, describing it as "blank spots" in her dissertation project, especially the chapter drafts titled "Barred Witness: Literary/Artistic Creations and Class Identities" and "The Poet is Critic, the Poet is Theorist."[13] In the latter, she explains that she coined this term as an alternative to the more commonly used (but "disablist") "blind spots." The product of conventional socialization, blank spots represent the learned ignorance and epistemological violence that erases the experiences and lives of nondominant people: "When a person is literally 'blanked out' because she is different racially or because she is a woman, a part of her is killed. The 'blanking out' is psychological murder."

Anzaldúa first used the term "desconocimientos" in a 1993 interview with Jamie Lee Evans, in which she applies it to separatism, alliance-building, and activists' reluctance or refusal to learn about each other's lives and beliefs. Naming herself a "mediator" and a "bridge," she describes ignorance as an impediment to building bridges and coalitions among differently situated people: "[I]gnorance is one of the enemies we have to combat—ignorance of power, ignorance about each other's histories, ignorance about other ways of living and other perspectives" (*Interviews* 197). In order to create productive alliances, we must be willing to transform our desconocimientos into mutual understanding.

During the mid-1990s Anzaldúa used the term desconocimiento not as a theory in itself (nor as a centered focus of her attention) but simply to describe parts of larger concepts—the willed ignorance that impedes alliance-building and knowledge production or the "tentative knowing" that occurs as part of a larger epistemological process. Thus, for example, she describes it as a necessary stage in her writing process: "I have to go into working out an idea with a tentative knowing, a desconocimiento, so that in the stage by stage process I will have come to a knowing, a conocimiento, of exactly what the idea answers" (Writing Notas 107.13). In 1995, Anzaldúa for the first time directly associates desconocimientos with Coatlicue: "Learning to cope with Coatlicue states of desconocimientos" ("Nepantla: The Creative Process").

Three events in the late 1990s and early 2000s inspired Anzaldúa to further develop desconocimientos *as* a theory: (1) her invitation to speak at the Urbana Latino conference; (2) her work co-editing *this bridge we call home* (especially the debates among contributors concerning the editors' radical inclusiveness); and (3) the 2001 terrorist attack in New York City and the subsequent invitation to contribute a piece reflecting on this event. Each event represented political situations loaded with power dynamics and questions of accountability, complicity, ignorance, and blame. As Anzaldúa developed her thinking in dialogue with these events, she incorporated her earlier dissertation work on "blank spots," along with her long-standing interest in Jungian shadow work. Just as acknowledgment and, eventually, acceptance of our shadows can assist our growth, so acknowledging desconocimientos produces new knowledge: "Desconocimiento Carl Jung described the shadow self as that part of yourself that you deny, that you cast onto the shadow of your psyche and being, and also unto others. Denying the shadow makes it stronger. You also deny positive aspects of yourself, the unlived qualities you want to allow but can't. You feel jealous of someone who expresses them because secretly you want to express them also" (Writing Notas J).

Desconocimiento arguably receives its most extensive treatment in Anzaldúa's theory of conocimiento. As she formulated and revised conocimiento's recursive journey, she explored desconocimientos' relationship to the Coatlicue state—especially the challenges involved in shifting from desconocimiento into conocimiento, the painful pleasure/comfort in remaining in desconocimiento, and the steep price paid for this ongoing resistance to knowing. As her 1999 writing notas indicate, Anzaldúa used her own experiences (including her struggles to live productively with diabetes) to explore and describe this painful epistemological-ethical state.

Thanks to this rich constellation of events, desconocimiento took on additional texture and weight. As Anzaldúa sought to understand how the fear of difference plays into and intensifies desconocimiento, she explored its relationship with complicity, accountability, and other forms of "forbidden knowledge." Had Anzaldúa lived longer, it's quite likely that she would have explored these relationships in more depth, possibly applying them to issues of internalized racism, whiteness, conflict resolution, and alliance-building. It's also likely that she would have put desconocimiento into dialogue with queer conocimiento, applying its "forbidden knowledge" to questions of clairsentience and other psychic powers. Given her holistic approach, it's also quite possible that she would have applied desconocimientos to nonpainful insights, to what she refers to above as "positive aspects of yourself, the unlived qualities you want to allow but can't."

- el cenote
- Coatlicue state
- conocimiento
- Coyolxauhqui process
- la facultad
- new tribalism
- nos/otras

FUTURE DIRECTIONS

- What is the developmental relationship between conocimiento and desconocimiento, and what might analyses of this relationship teach us about both theories? What, for example, are the implications of the fact that desconocimiento seems to have emerged *prior to* conocimiento?
- In "(Des)Conocimientos: Resisting New Forms of Domination/ Oppression," a 1996 essay examining nationalism's limitations, Anzaldúa associates desconocimientos with nationalism. How might we use this piece and her theory of desconocimiento more generally to investigate historical and contemporary nationalism?
- In Writing Notas J, Anzaldúa associates desconocimiento with consensual reality, suggesting that personal growth can occur by challenging desconocimientos. How might we apply this discussion to her theory of the path of conocimiento?
- Near the end of her life, Anzaldúa refers to the "small **desconocimientos** that serve small comfort but are actually killers of the spirit" ("+notes-b," her bold). What might these small acts be? How do they kill the spirit and in other ways numb us?
- How might desconocimiento function in dialogue with queer conocimiento?
- How might we apply Anzaldúa's theory of desconocimiento to critical whiteness studies, epistemologies of ignorance, and white fragility?
- What connections can we make between desconocimiento, the self's shadow, and creativity, or what Anzaldúa describes in Writing Notas L as "desconocimiento & your shadow & its connection

to creativity & healing. El cenote"? What might an analysis of her work teach us about the potentially synergistic relationship among these topics?

- How can excavating and in other ways working with desconocimientos lead to positive growth at individual and collective levels?

USEFUL TEXTS

- "+notes-b"
- "Barred Witness: Literary/Artistic Creations and Class Identities"
- "Conocimientos: Creative Acts of Vision, Inner Works, Public Acts"
- "Conocimientos, Now Let Us Shift: Inner Work and Public Acts"
- "(Des)Conocimientos: Resisting New Forms of Domination/ Oppression"
- *Interviews/Entrevistas*
- *Light in the Dark/Luz en lo Oscuro*
- "Nepantla: The Creative Process"
- "Nos/otros 'Us' vs. 'Them'"
- "The Poet as Critic, The Poet as Theorist"
- "Queer Conocimiento"
- "SIC: Spiritual Identity Crisis: A Series of Vignettes"
- Writing Notas 107.6, 107.7, 107.13, 108.7
- Writing Notas H, I, J

La Facultad

We possess a kind of instant "sensing[,]" a quick perception without conscious reasoning, a knowledge from within. An intense intuition. That "sensing" is mediated by the part of the brain that does not speak, that cannot verbalize, that communicates in symbols, metaphors, images. A faculty that perceives the emotions and intentions of others without need of verbal cues. That is attentive to looks, postures, gestures of disapproval and rejection. At stake in developing this sense is our survival—the queer, the creative, the different. And those who think differently. A kind of scanning of the environment in order to survive that sees patterns and cycles.—"Esperando la serpiente con plumas" (1982)

La facultad is the capacity to see in surface phenomena the meaning of deeper realities, to see the deep structure below the surface. It is an instant "sensing," a quick perception arrived at without conscious reasoning. It is an acute awareness mediated by the part of the psyche that does not speak, that communicates in images and symbols which are the faces of feelings, that is, behind which feelings reside/hide. The one possessing this sensitivity is excruciatingly alive to the world.—*Borderlands/La Frontera* (1987)

La facultad is a kind of soul consciousness, a capacity for self-knowledge, one that sees through, a double, triple, quadruple.—Writing Notas I (1999)

DEFINITION

La facultad is Anzaldúa's term for an intuitive, embodied epistemology that includes but goes beyond logical thought and empirical analysis. La facultad is a psychic sixth sense that exists as potential in all humans yet awakens in only a few. Typically, those in whom la facultad becomes activated are marked by difference: Existing on the outskirts of social norms, they don't entirely fit in with the dominating culture and consensual reality's standards. Viewed as threatening because they disrupt the status quo, they are threatened with violence. (*I use "threaten" twice to underscore the role projection can play in this violent, fear-based process.*) Sometimes, la facultad awakens as a mode of protection, enabling us to discern potential threats before physical or psychic violence ensues. As Anzaldúa writes in an early draft of *Borderlands*, la facultad represents "a kind of survival tactic people caught between the worlds unknowingly cultivate, though I think it's latent in everybody. We have faculties that we haven't used yet." Not surprisingly, given that it often awakens as part of survival, la facultad is deeply embodied. It emerges from within the body and it grows at least in part from the need to protect it. Thus in "Esperando," Anzaldúa describes la facultad as "the new faculty of listening to the body."

La facultad is similar, but not identical, to intuition. Like intuition, la facultad represents an inner knowing that exceeds rational thought, functions nonlinearly, and communicates at least partially through the body. But with la facultad, Anzaldúa incorporates an overt psychic component as well, a type of extrasensory perception or what she describes as "political and personal clairvoyance: the capacity to see in surface phenomena, the meaning of deeper realities and the essence of things" ("La serpiente"). Indeed, one could almost define la facultad as intuition's (r)evolutionary expansion. As Anzaldúa implies in her conversation with Christine Weiland, this perception originates in the body—through our embodied encounters—and opens us to additional material and nonmaterial dimensions of reality: "[W]hen you're up against the wall—when you have all these oppressions coming at you—you develop this extra faculty. You know the next person who's going to slap you or lock you away. Then you make use of faculties that belong to the other realm so that you already know the rapist when he's five blocks down the street" (*Interviews* 123).

As Anzaldúa's references to "deeper realities," "the essence of things," and "faculties that belong to the other realm" indicate, la facultad includes an important ontological component that complements, energizes, and shapes its epistemological dimensions. Indeed, Anzaldúa even seems to attribute la facultad's powers, in part, to its association with metaphysical dimensions. La facultad enables us to "see and hear into the soul" ("Esperando"), giving us "the capacity to see in surface phenomena the meaning of deeper realities, to see the deep structure below the surface" (*Borderlands* 60). Years later, in *Light in the Dark*, she associates la facultad with nepantleras, describing it as "a realm of consciousness reached only from an 'attached' mode (rather than a distant, separate, unattached, mode), enabling us to weave a kinship entre todas las gentes y cosas" (90).

Like conocimiento, la facultad can be challenging to interpret and discuss because Anzaldúa used the term in at least two fairly distinct ways: both as a synonym for "faculty" and as the embodied, nonordinary epistemology described earlier. For example, in her conversation with Inés Ávila-Hernández she refers to "facultades" as "skills, . . . learning how to cope with stress and oppression" (*Interviews* 180).

LA FACULTAD'S STORY (ORIGINS AND DEVELOPMENT)

Anzaldúa first referred to la facultad by name in her early 1981–82 autohistorias, "Esperando la serpiente con plumas" and "La serpiente que se come su cola." In these early manuscripts, la facultad represents her most fully developed epistemology. Drawing on personal experiences, she describes the transformational potential and emergent leadership qualities in herself and other forward-looking social justice advocates: politically progressive outsiders—"guerrilleras divinas, divine warriors, people of the purple ray, the highest vibrating color in the auric spectrum"—people who, because of their identities, practices, and/or beliefs, exist outside social norms. Existing on the outskirts of society, these divine warriors survived by developing "a new faculty" and new skills: "The darkskinned dyke and faggot is a mutation with the potentiality of developing a new faculty, hind sight, intuition. It [is] a technique we've had to develop in order to survive—like a butterfly (mariposa) with an extra wing on its left side. The butterfly has always been a symbol of spiritual rebirth. This technique is psychic or spiritual. It is a new strength" ("Esperando"). In formulating this description, Anzaldúa drew on Dane Rudhyar's *An Astrological Mandala: The Cycle of Transformations and its 360 Symbolic Phases*, as well as her personal experiences, to theorize la facultad as clairvoyance and other nonordinary physical-intellectual powers.

La facultad's epistemological centrality continues into the early drafts of *Borderlands'* prose section. However, as Anzaldúa revised the prose chapters she expanded her discussion of mestiza consciousness (which contains aspects of la facultad). Analysis of the various tables of contents reveals that when mestiza consciousness grew, la facultad shrank. As Anzaldúa developed and revised the prose introduction to *Borderlands*, she slowly integrated la facultad into mestiza consciousness. In the 1986 draft of *Borderlands'* prose section, which at that point consisted of four parts, "La Facultad" is the title (and topic) of part 3; however, in the published version, "la facultad" was reduced to a smaller section, and its most overtly clairvoyant/psychic characteristics were removed.

Although la facultad recedes after *Borderlands'* publication, it never entirely disappears. In fact, one could say that it lurks on the boundaries, buried within other theories, and deeply inspiring Anzaldúa's fiction. In the late 1980s and early 1990s Anzaldúa associated la facultad with the writing process and shamanic journeys. In her 1988 "The Poet as Critic," for example, she describes the "postmodern mestiza" author who code-switches, shifts among genres, etc.: "She is a modern shape-shifter (shaman) code switching, genre crossing; shifting from one ideology to another; shifting frames of reference, a splicing together [of] different cultures. . . . interweaving many different kinds of worlds and spheres together, all these spaces together developing a writing ability or faculty I call la facultad." In her 1995 Montalvo Workshop writing notas (107.10), Anzaldúa uses la facultad to describe that part of the creative process associated with perceptual shifts, or what she calls "switching modes" and "trancing": "The writer possesses la facultad, a developed sensitivity, a way of seeing and being that communes with inner essences beneath surface skins. The writer, like the shaman, goes back-and-forth, shifting between cognitive modes, from a rational state of awareness to an altered state, from poetic to logistic activities, going from one mode of consciousness to another, simultaneously dealing with antithetical elements, opposing and antagonistic" ("Nonfiction Drafts"). Here la facultad functions like a metaphysical-epistemological bridge, enabling the artist to move among inner and outer worlds. Through this movement, the artist learns to hold multiple divergent perspectives, synergistically transforming them into something new: "The result: not either/or but another kind of resolution" ("Nonfiction Drafts"). La facultad could be said to thrive in Anzaldúa's fiction, embodied by her protagonist, Prieta, who moves among worlds in stories like "Reading LP" and "Prieta and the Were-Jaguar").

Near the end of her life, Anzaldúa merged many of la facultad's most innovative qualities into her discussions of the imaginal and her philosophy of conocimiento. In *Light in the Dark* she associates la facultad with conocimiento's first stage, el arrebato, the event that shoves us into conocimiento's journey: "The urgency to know what you're experiencing awakens la facultad, the ability to shift attention and see through the surface of things and situations" (125). Elsewhere she associates la facultad with queer conocimiento and archetypal knowledge (Writing Notas M). Had she lived longer, it's very likely that she would have explored, in more depth, the relationship between la facultad and queer conocimiento, using la facultad's psychic components to nurture and grow queer conocimiento. Perhaps she would have explored la facultad's connections with El Mundo Zurdo and magic as well.

RELATED THEORIES

- Coatlicue state
- conocimiento
- El Mundo Zurdo
- la naguala
- new mestiza consciousness

FUTURE DIRECTIONS

- What can analysis of Anzaldúa's early autohistorias teach us about la facultad?
- What does close analysis of *Borderlands*' drafts teach us about the shift from la facultad to mestiza consciousness? How might la facultad shape and guide mestiza consciousness?
- Given the close association between la facultad's emergence and astrology (cf. Dane Rudhyar's *Sabian Symbols*), how might we use astrological insights with la facultad to enact change?

- What are the psychic implications of la facultad?
- How does la naguala enact la facultad, and how can we harness this work for progressive personal and social transformation?
- What might an analysis of Anzaldúa's short fiction (especially stories like "Prieta and the Were-Jaguar" and "Reading LP") teach us about la facultad?
- In her 1996 writing notas, Anzaldúa describes la facultad in ontological terms as she associates it with writing: "But all the while hidden in the background is the big pair of hands, the huge mind, the large eyes overseeing everything—if the writer doesn't obstruct it, hinder the big oversoul, la facultad, a kind of intuition. La facultad from the background, from the underground thrusts out its fingers, hands and pushes, propels the process of writing this way and that, moves the story in a particular direction" (107.13). In what ways, if any, do we see la facultad's ontological component in her later writings? How might *we* borrow from and build on this connection to develop new forms of writing, new writing practices, and, perhaps, new ontologies?
- What's the relationship between la facultad and queer conocimiento? How might Anzaldúa have woven la facultad into her theory of queer conocimiento?
- How might Anzaldúa have expanded on la facultad's embodied ways of knowing, in dialogue with "SIC"?

USEFUL TEXTS

- "+notes-b"
- *Borderlands/La Frontera*
- *Borderlands* manuscript drafts
- "Esperando la serpiente con plumas"
- *Interviews/Entrevistas*
- *Light in the Dark/Luz en lo Oscuro*
- "Nepantla: Creative Acts of Vision"
- "Noche y su nidada"
- "El paisano is a bird of good omen"
- "The Poet as Critic"
- Prieta stories
- "La serpiente que se come su cola"
- Writing Notas A, E, F, H, M, N

Geographies of Selves

What I have termed the bodily geography, or the geography of the body, how the body interacts with its environment & the objects around it.—Writing Notes 107.5 (1994)

Our bodies are geographies of selves made up of diverse, bordering, and overlapping "countries." Each of us is composed of information, each bears billions of bits of cultural knowledge, superimposing many different categories of experience. Like a map with river lines, highways, towns, lakes, and other outstanding features of places en donde pasan las cosas, we are "marked." Life's whip has left welts and thin silver scars on our backs; our genetic code has dug creases and tracks on our flesh. As our bodies interact with internal and external, real and virtual, past and present environments, people, and objects around us, we construct our identities. Identity, as consciously and unconsciously created, is always in process in the interaction of self with different communities and worlds. Who and what we are depends on a mix of our interaction with our alrededores/environments and new and old narratives of cultural identity. Identity is multi-layered, stretching in all directions, from past to present, vertically and horizontally, chronologically and spatially. Mass movements of people across neighborhoods, states, countries, continents and instant connection via satellites, Internet, and cell phones make us more aware of and linked to each other. Soon our consciousness/awareness will reach other planets, solar systems, galaxies. —"Geographies of Selves—Re-imagining Identities" (2004)

DEFINITION

One of Anzaldúa's least developed late theories, geographies of selves represents her attempt to conceptualize human identity as a radically embodied, relational, ongoing process shaped by numerous internal and external factors—including ancestral lineage, biology, the places we've lived, the people we've encountered, and much more. As the above epigraphs for this entry suggest, Anzaldúa worked to develop a framework broad enough to encompass the many variables and interactions that impact individual and collective identities—both internally and externally. We emerge from and are shaped by various specific landscapes, encounters, and terrains (defined broadly to include literal and metaphoric dimensions). She draws from her earlier theories of the Borderlands and new mestiza consciousness, as well as later theories like nos/otras and new tribalism, to represent selfhood as an always ongoing "process-in-the-making" (*Interviews* 239). Like her theory of the borderlands, geographies of selves acknowledges how borders and boundaries (both metaphoric and spatial) shape identity, sometimes in conflictual ways. And like her theory of new mestiza consciousness, her geographies of selves theory works with relational multiplicity and contradiction. But with geographies of selves, Anzaldúa expands these implications even further.

Geographies of selves also includes an intimate embodied component to reflect (*and address*) the various ways our identities are impacted by ancestry, physiology, environment, and more. Anzaldúa usefully demonstrates this breadth in her 1995 interview with Bentacor:

> [I]dentity is an arrangement or series of clusters, a kind of stacking or layering of selves, horizontal and vertical layers, the geography of selves made up of the different communities you inhabit. When I give my talks I use an overhead projector with a transparency of a little stick figure con un pie en un mundo y otro pie en otro mundo y todos estos mundos overlap: This is your race, your sexual orientation, here you're a Jew Chicana, here an academic, here an artist, there a blue collar worker. Where these spaces overlap is nepantla, the Borderlands. Identity is a process-in-the-making. You're not born a Chicana, you become a Chicana because of the culture that's caught in you. Then as you go to school you learn about other cultures because you meet kids from other races. By the time you get to grad school you've become acquainted with all these worlds. So you shift, cross the border from one to the other, and that's what I talk about in *Borderlands*. (*Interviews* 238–39)

Note the complexity in this description: by depicting identity as both "horizontal and vertical layers," Anzaldúa signals toward the sometimes conflictual multiplicity that impacts identity formation. Each person, in unique ways, negotiates the various influences that have shaped them— beginning with the specific body into which they are born. This theory gives us another way to mobilize and explore identity as an ongoing, dialogic process filled with multiple, sometimes startling, variables.

GEOGRAPHIES OF SELVES' STORY (ORIGINS AND DEVELOPMENT)

Unlike her theories of the borderlands, geographies of selves did not emerge almost fully developed; rather, it grew slowly and sporadically, and was still unfolding in 2004 at the time of Anzaldúa's death. We see this gradual development in the various ways Anzaldúa named it: "geography of self" (1994), "geography of selves" (1995), and, finally, "geographies of selves" (2004). As these incremental shifts from single to plural suggest, Anzaldúa's revisions involved expanding the theory to more fully encompass the multiplicity of our lives. Prior to developing this theory, Anzaldúa used the concept of way stations to articulate a relational, journey-based theory of identity to articulate the internal and external forces that shape and change us. In interviews and Lloronas dissertation chapter drafts, she describes the way station as those points in time and space when we have opportunities to change—sometimes drastically. As she writes in "ID—Subject to Shiftings: Disturbing Identities and Representations," "Identity is constantly changing and shifting, 'traveling,' as they say, running along now a straight track, now a curving one, now one that loops, backtracks then proceeds forward again. In fact there may be several tracks along which identity traverses, parallel tracks, criss-crossing tracks with identity the train, or trains, riding those tracks. The tracks span and web a tiny space or a continent. The way stations are signposts of identity constellating at specific points in life. When between way stations identity is discontinuous, forgotten." As this passage suggests, although her theory of the way station implies embodied movement through time and space, it focuses primarily on inner consciousness-based shifts. Geographies of selves enables her to flesh out this journey metaphor more fully (*pun intended*), incorporating the physical body and environment to present consciousness as completely embodied.

Anzaldúa first referred to a geography of self in her 1994 writing notes, using it to describe relational embodied identity. Here and for the next few years, her infrequent references are primarily descriptive, as indicated by the first epigraph to this entry, in which "geography" functions literally to describe embodied interactions with external surroundings. Although she does not reference Adrienne Rich's politics of location until the following year, it's likely that Anzaldúa was in dialogue with it, as suggested by this statement in her writing notes: "Adrienne Rich, in articulating the 'politics of location,' says: 'I need to understand how a place on the map is also a place in history within which as a woman, a Jew, a lesbian, a feminist I am created and trying to create. Begin, though, not with a continent or a country of a house, but with the geography closest in—the body'" (107.8). Whereas Rich here equates geography with the body, Anzaldúa uses the "geography of self" more broadly, to include landscape and embodied movement among various locations, and associates it especially with mestizas: "I see the mestiza as a geography of selves—of different bordering countries—who stands at the threshold of two or more worlds and negotiates the cracks between the worlds" ("Navigating Nepantla").

It was not until after Anzaldúa presented her keynote for the 1999 conference at the University of Illinois, Urbana-Champaign—"Territories and Boundaries: Geographies of Latinidad"—that she expanded this phrase (*and image*) into a theory. Given that the conference title and theme centered on geographical issues, this deepening is perhaps not surprising. While in her talk, "Nos/otros: Us vs. Them . . . El compromiso," Anzaldúa does not refer to the geography of selves, as she revises the transcript into a book chapter for the conference proceedings, she uses the theory to explore Raza identities, nationalism, sexism, transnationalism, and the possibilities of developing new coalitions. In the many drafts of this piece, we see Anzaldúa developing her theory as she investigates how we can best address intragroup conflict and enact successful alliance-building. Analysis of the drafts indicates that she developed this theory by bringing it into conversation with other identity-related theories that she was creating at that time, especially nos/otras and new tribalisms. By 2003, she had conceptualized geographies of self as exploring both "[t]he inner geography—identity and mental activity" and outer geographies, "[s]elf-in-communities: internal, external kinships," noting that "[w]e live in simultaneous 'countries'" ("Geographies of the Self"). In 2004 she took the theory even further: "The geography of our identity is vast, has many nations. Where you end and the world begins is not easy to distinguish. Like a river flooding its bank, cutting a new channel that winds in a new direction, we escape our skin, our present identity and forge a new one" ("Chapter Annotations"). Had Anzaldúa lived longer, she would have expanded on this larger vision, putting this theory into dialogue with planetary citizenship while, simultaneously, using it to critique the xenophobic debates over the US-Mexico border that intensified during Trump's presidency (2016–20).

RELATED THEORIES

- B/borderlands
- Coyolxauhqui process
- nepantla
- nepantleras
- new mestiza
- new tribalism
- nos/otras

- In several manuscripts (Writing Notes 107.8, "Nos/otros," and "Geographies of the Self") Anzaldúa references Adrienne Rich's discussion of "bodily geography." How can we put Anzaldúa's theory into dialogue with Rich's, and what are the theoretical implications of doing so? What new theories can we create?
- What can a close analysis of Anzaldúa's transcript for her talk at Urbana and the subsequent manuscripts she produced from this talk teach us about the development of this theory?
- What might analyses of this theory in dialogue with geography studies as a field of knowledge teach us about the theory (and possibly about the field itself)?
- Given Anzaldúa's long-standing interest in Henri Corbin, how might his theory of the imaginal have informed her theory of the geographies of selves, especially in her twenty-first-century versions which include the imagination?
- In "La Prieta is Dreaming" Anzaldúa describes Prieta as "a vast geography of selves"; how might we use this description as a lens to analyze the Prieta stories? And how might this analysis in turn help us to understand Anzaldúa's theory more deeply?
- In a 2003 draft of chapter 4 of *Light in the Dark*, Anzaldúa refers to an "inner geography" in a section titled "The Inner Geography—Identity and Mental Activity." What might this concept tell us about future directions for this theory?
- How might we take Anzaldúa's theory and apply it to later twenty-first-century discussions of immigration, borders, and/or nationalism?

USEFUL TEXTS

- "Geographies of the Self—Re-imagining Identity: Nos/otras (Us/Other) and the New Tribalism"
- "Geo of Selves—Old Notes"
- "Geographies of Selves—Re-imagining Identities: Nos/otras (Us/Other), Las nepantleras and the New Tribalism"
- "ID—Subject to Shiftings: Disturbing Identities and Representations"
- *Interviews/Entrevistas*

- *Light in the Dark/Luz en lo Oscuro*
- "Navigating Nepantla and the Cracks between the Worlds"
- "Nos/otros: Us vs. Them . . . El compromiso"
- "Nos/otros: 'Us' vs. 'Them,' (Des)Conocimientos y compromisos"
- "La Prieta is Dreaming/Genius Loci, the Spirit of the Place"
- Prieta stories
- "Reimaging Identities: The Geography of Our Many Selves"

El Mundo Zurdo

[S]he conceived of an equitable world with beauty and magic where the oppressed were no longer oppressed, where no one was oppressed and she called it El Mundo Zurdo for the left side, the side nearest the heart, the side associated with women. To her the rejection of the darkskinned by the whites and the queer and the female by all cultures made her a stranger, an "other." Exiled. And so she sought to connect with both these groups without being rejected by the one or the other. Only then could she and the darkskinned and the queer and female dispel their isolation, only then could she nourish her soul. She wished to connect with others without being swallowed, or assimilated. —"La serpiente que se come su cola" (1982)

The inner/outer work makes bridges between the life of the mind, the life of the body, and the life of the spirit. I call this connecting activity "el mundo zurdo." —"Spiritual Activism: Making Altares, Making Connections" (1996)

[H]umans and the universe are in a symbiotic relationship, . . . we live in a state of deep interconnectedness en un mundo zurdo (a left-handed world). We are not alone in our struggles, and never have been. Somos almas afines and this interconnectedness is an unvoiced category of identity. Though we've progressed in forging el mundo zurdo, especially its spiritual aspect, we must now more than ever open our minds to others' realities. —"counsels from the firings" (2001)

DEFINITION

One of Anzaldúa's earliest theories, El Mundo Zurdo (the left-handed world) represents a holistic, synergistic approach to difference and deviation. Typically, we define difference in binary-oppositional terms, as deviation from the norm (defined as a single, monolithic standard for all). With El Mundo Zurdo, Anzaldúa questions this imposed norm by redefining difference in relational terms. Thus in "La Prieta," her first published articulation of this theory, she calls for visionary alliances among those who have been marginalized and rejected due to their differences from mainstream culture: "We are the queer groups, the people that don't belong anywhere, not in the dominant world nor completely within our own respective cultures. Combined we cover so many oppressions. But the overwhelming oppression is the collective fact that we do not fit, and because we do not fit *we are a threat*. Not all of us have the same oppressions, but we empathize and identify with each other's oppressions" (208, her italics). Note her emphasis on difference as well as commonality: she calls on multiple groups and acknowledges differences in experiences while also pointing to a shared (though diverse) commonality. By so doing, she redefines difference relationally, using it as a unifying device that replaces sameness with nuanced understanding of relational difference: "We do not share the same ideology, nor do we derive similar solutions. Some of us are leftists, some of us practitioners of magic. Some of us are both. *But these different affinities are not opposed to each other.* In El Mundo Zurdo I with my own affinities and my people with theirs can live together and transform the planet" (208–9, my italics). Constituted through deviation and difference, El Mundo Zurdo might be the most queer of Anzaldúa's theories (*if "most queer" could even be measured!*). Indeed, even her preferred spelling of the term, "El Mundo Surdo" ("surdo" rather than "zurdo"), was itself queer in its resistance to the norm.

Like Anzaldúa's theories of conocimiento, nepantla, and spiritual activism, El Mundo Zurdo is expansive and can be applied to multiple dimensions of life and thought, including ontology, epistemology, identity, and social reform. Applied to ontology, El Mundo Zurdo represents nonordinary reality—or what Anzaldúa describes in Writing Notes L as "a separate reality . . . that participates [in] or enters everyday reality." Applied to epistemology, El Mundo Zurdo becomes the intuitive, nonrational ways of thinking that enable us to access this nonordinary dimension. Applied to social justice issues, El Mundo Zurdo offers a visionary, holistic approach to progressive societal change. Applied to identity, El Mundo Zurdo enables us to replace assumptions of sameness with relational commonalities. In her early poem, "The coming of el mundo surdo," for example, Anzaldúa defines herself in the framework of El Mundo Zurdo's relational difference: "Within my skin all races / sexes all trees grasses / cows and snails" (her spacing). Applied to alliance-building, El Mundo Zurdo invites us to create communities based on commonalities, where people from diverse backgrounds with diverse needs and concerns coexist and work together to bring about revolutionary change. These intentional, self-selected communities are composed of many different types of people united by two things: (1) their desire to challenge and transform status-quo stories ("[t]he rational, the patriarchal, and the heterosexual"); and (2) their experiences of alienation. These so-called deviances offer generative possibilities for future development and progressive change.

Although Anzaldúa does not use the language of methodology when discussing this theory, El Mundo Zurdo could also be described as a method enabling us to analyze data and investigate research problems innovatively. When we employ El Mundo Zurdo, we can discover new similarities and commonalities among differently situated people, elements, or groups. As we engage with its energy, we can draw unexpected connections among disparate items: "The inner/outer work makes bridges between the life of the mind, the life of the body, and the life of the spirit. I call this connecting activity 'el mundo zurdo'" ("Spiritual Activism").

EL MUNDO ZURDO'S STORY (ORIGINS AND DEVELOPMENT)

Anzaldúa offers her most extensive account of El Mundo Zurdo's origins in her 2002 preface to *This Bridge Called My Back*, in which she associates its birth with a guest lecture she gave at the University of Texas, Austin, for a class that her good friend, Randy Conner, was teaching: "[A] white gay male friend invited me to guest lecture his class. The idea of el mundo zurdo—the vision of a blood/spirit connection/alliance in which the colored, queer, poor, female, and physically challenged struggle together and form an international feminism—came to me to talk about in his class" ("Counsels"). However, the theory's origins are more complex than this recollection might suggest. Anzaldúa began developing El Mundo Zurdo in the late 1970s, in part through studying Sri Aurobindo's works, alchemy, and recent scholarship on the differences between left- and right-brain thinking. She journaled about El Mundo Surdo often and first wrote about it in her unpublished 1982 autohistoria "La serpiente que se come su cola," in which she associates the theory's development with her desire to combat social injustice while creating opportunities for radical inclusivity:

> Out of seeing the campesina break her back in bed under her man's hot breath, she conceived of an equitable world with beauty and magic where the oppressed were no longer oppressed, where no one

was oppressed and she called it El Mundo Zurdo for the left side, the side nearest the heart, the side associated with women.

To her the rejection of the darkskinned by the whites and the queer and the female by all cultures made her a stranger, an "other." Exiled. And so she sought to connect with both these groups without being rejected by the one or the other. Only then could she and the darkskinned and the queer and female could [sic] dispell [sic] their isolation, only then could she nourish her soul. She wished to connect with others without being swallowed, or assimilated.

Here we see El Mundo Zurdo's emergence from the various oppressions that Anzaldúa experienced, as well as others that she observed. She creates this theory as a visionary alternative that draws from political and spiritual teachings to offer an innovative synthesis: "She looked at the political ideologies and found them narrow, ignorant of the inner and spiritual demensions [sic] of the individual and the group. She looked at the spiritual philosophies, the new age awareness movement and found all but a few equally as narrow and despising of the political geography. The social movements . . . ignored the dance of the soul, the spiritual movements ignored the hierroglyphics [sic] of the body." As these passages suggest, Anzaldúa developed her theory of El Mundo Zurdo in the context of her spiritual-political vision.

Until 1980 or so, Anzaldúa intentionally spelled "Surdo" with an "S," rather than the conventional "Z." As she indicates in an edited draft of "La Prieta," she did so in order to pay homage to her home on the Texas-Mexican border: "I misspell 'zurdo' on purpose. The 's' is more natural to my Tejana Chicana tongue and I wish to distinguish the vision from its customary meaning of this word" (45.11). However, during the publication process for *This Bridge Called My Back*, the copyeditor standardized spelling on the page proofs, changing "Surdo" to "Zurdo." Recovering from an emergency hysterectomy, Anzaldúa did not read the page proofs until it was too late to correct the copyeditor's "corrections." At the time she was shocked and dismayed by this standardization; however, she came to accept it (*illustrating her ability to "pick her battles" and use her energy thoughtfully, focusing on the issues that seemed most vital*).

In the late 1970s and early 1980s Anzaldúa used literature, creativity, and art-making as vehicles to experiment with and embody this theory, working to physically materialize her visionary world. In 1978 she initiated two events that she named "El Mundo Surdo": a reading series at Small Press Traffic for Bob Gluck in San Francisco and a series of writing workshops. The reading series, while grounded in women-of-colors perspectives, was diverse and open to progressive people of any identity. Randy Conner, David Hatfield Sparks, Cherríe Moraga, and Anzaldúa herself were some of the many artists who performed. The El Mundo Surdo writing workshop met weekly and included meditation, visualization, chakra work, and other activities designed to activate authors' nonrational imaginative powers.

Anzaldúa's first published articulations of El Mundo Zurdo can be found in *This Bridge Called My Back: Writings by Radical Women of Color*, both in the title for the book's final section ("El Mundo Zurdo: The Vision") and in her own piece, "La Prieta," which opens this section. In both, she foregrounds the theory's visionary potential. As the title "El Mundo Zurdo: The Vision" suggests, this section includes contributions that focus on strategies to effect progressive change. Similarly, Anzaldúa concludes "La Prieta" with her vision of El Mundo Zurdo. After delineating her various experiences of rejection for not fitting into conventional social categories and identity politics, she redefines her so-called deviance as a vital tool for social justice work that begins with self-acceptance. As she embraces her own sense of difference, she achieves a dynamic balance empowering her to develop new forms of community: "The mixture of bloods and affinities, rather than confusing or unbalancing me, has forced me to achieve a kind of equilibrium. Both cultures deny me a place in their universe. Between them and among others, I build my own universe, El Mundo Zurdo. I belong to myself and not to any one people." "La Prieta" also contains the first published reference to El Mundo Zurdo as a "two-way movement" that synergistically intertwines inner and outer change: *The pull between what is and what should be*. I believe that by changing ourselves we change the world, that traveling El Mundo Zurdo path is the path of a two-way movement—a going deep into the self and an expanding out into the world, a simultaneous recreation of the self and a reconstruction of society" (her emphasis). This simultaneous movement signals El Mundo Zurdo's resonance with Anzaldúa's theory of spiritual activism.

Also during the early 1980s, Anzaldúa worked on a long essay tentatively titled "El Mundo Zurdo (the Left-Handed World): A Political-Spiritual Vision for the Third World and the Queer." Containing over seventy pages of material on spiritual technologies (I Ching, Tarot, astrology, etc.), paranormal experiences, alchemy, and meditation, this manuscript usefully underscores the metaphysical expansiveness that Anzaldúa incorporated into the theory. In the mid-1980s she drafted a short story collection titled *El Mundo Zurdo y otros cuentos*. These stories, about social outsiders, include paranormal events and in other ways affirm nonordinary realities and alternative epistemologies. As in her early poem, "The coming of el mundo surdo," she blurs boundaries among apparently distinct things, challenging conventional understandings of consensual reality.

During the late 1980s and early to mid-1990s, as Anzaldúa expanded her theory of nepantla, she mentioned El Mundo Zurdo less frequently. However, in the late 1990s several events encouraged her to return to this theory and develop it further: the republication of *This Bridge Called My Back* with Third Woman Press, the editing of *this bridge we call home*, and the development of her conocimiento philosophy—especially spiritual activism. As she writes in the notes to chapter 6 of *Light in the Dark*, "The model of el mundo zurdo has expanded to the model of conocimiento by incorporating the soul and spirit with nepantla and consciousness / awareness acting as the bridge between political activism and spiritual activism" (198). Had she lived longer, it's likely that Anzaldúa would have explored El Mundo Zurdo's ontological dimensions more deeply and developed connections between El Mundo Zurdo and the image/metaphor of the left hand, which she associates with spirit and alliance-making: "The left hand is not a fist pero una mano abierta raised with others in struggle, celebration, and song" (*Light* 153). Quite possibly she would have explored El Mundo Zurdo's bridging work with (*and into*) the imaginal as well.

RELATED THEORIES

- B/borderlands
- conocimiento
- la facultad
- la naguala
- nepantla
- nepantlera
- new tribalism
- nos/otras
- spiritual activism

- What can Anzaldúa's early unpublished autohistorias teach us about the origins, development, and definition of El Mundo Zurdo?
- What can Anzaldúa's alliance-making and her personal circle of friends teach us about El Mundo Zurdo?
- What can Anzaldúa's El Mundo Surdo reading series and writing workshops teach us about her theory?
- In her 1983 writing notes, Anzaldúa refers to El Mundo Zurdo as "the Great Cause" (107.3). What might this description indicate about her intention (*and more!*) with this theory? What can it tell us about her metaphysics at that time?
- In several essays Anzaldúa describes El Mundo Zurdo as a "connecting activity." What are the implications of this description? How can El Mundo Zurdo facilitate connections?
- What would a method of El Mundo Zurdo connectivity look like?
- How is El Mundo Zurdo an early queer theory?
- What contributions can an understanding of Anzaldúa's theory of El Mundo Zurdo make to twenty-first-century queer theory?
- Anzaldúa uses the image of "a hand with a heart in its palm" to describe El Mundo Zurdo in both *Light in the Dark* and her writing notes. What might this image teach us about the theory?
- How might we put Anzaldúa's theory of El Mundo Zurdo into dialogue with queer theory, queer methods, and other dimensions of queer studies scholarship?
- What can an analysis of the stories in *El Mundo Zurdo y otro cuentos* teach us about El Mundo Zurdo's ontological and psychic dimensions?
- How do Anzaldúa's Prieta stories illustrate and enact El Mundo Zurdo?
- What is the relationship between El Mundo Zurdo and spiritual activism?
- How can we use relational difference to generate social change?

USEFUL TEXTS

- "+notes-b"
- "The coming of el mundo surdo"

- "Conocimientos: Creative Acts of Vision, Inner Works, Public Acts"
- "counsels from the firing"
- "Esperando la serpiente con plumas"
- *Light in the Dark/Luz en lo Oscuro*
- "Notes on El Mundo Zurdo"
- "Poetry & Magick: A Practicum for Developing Literary + Psychic Skills"
- "La Prieta"
- "La serpiente que se come su cola"
- "Spiritual Activism"
- "Spiritual Activism: Making Altares, Making Connections"
- Writing Notas 107.3
- Writing Notas D, L

La Naguala

Often I gaze at my serpent staff to remind myself of the spirit of the body. Or I look at the portrait of my Nagual, my "animal self" to remind myself to treat my Unihipili (what the ancient Huna people of Hawaii refer to the inner self, the unconscious) with love and respect.—"On the Process of Feminist Image Making" (1982)

Inside us is a self-healing mechanism, the healer within that self-diagnoses and self-regenerates. I awaken this inner healer with imagery. The inner healer is part of the organizing principle—what we could call the soul, la naguala, inner spirit that guides us.—Writing Notas L (2002)

In putting images together into story (the story I tell about the images), I use imagistic thinking, employ an imaginal awareness. I'm guided by the spirit of the image. My naguala (daimon or guiding spirit) is an inner sensibility that directs my life—an image, an action, or an internal experience. My imagination and my naguala are connected—they are aspects of the same process, of creativity. Often my naguala draws to me things that are contrary to my will and purpose (compulsions, addictions, negativities), resulting in an anguished impasse. Overcoming these impasses becomes part of the process.—*Light in the Dark/Luz en lo Oscuro* (2004/2015)

DEFINITION

Derived from the Nahuatl word "nagual," or shape-shifter, la naguala has a number of interrelated meanings in Anzaldúa's work, including shaman, shape-shifter, guardian spirit, inner guide, witness, writing muse, daimon, spirit, and soul. Anzaldúa had a lifelong interest in and relationship with la naguala, initiated by childhood encounters with her own nagual, an experience she describes in interviews, fiction, and autohistorias. She associates la naguala with embodiment, the creative process, identity formation, divine guidance, intuition, and imagination (especially imagination's "shapeshifting power"). While her definition alters and expands throughout the years, Anzaldúa consistently identifies la naguala with psychic-spiritual powers that spring from and connect us with multiple dimensions of reality.

Emerging at least in part from the Mesoamerican philosophy and practice of nagualismo (shamanism), la naguala's philosophical foundation is a non-Cartesian ontology and epistemology that normalizes and naturalizes "shapeshifting (the ability to become an animal or thing) and traveling to other realities" (*Light* 32). Unlike Cartesian ontologies, which typically draw on Newtonian science to describe physical reality with a heft and a weight that make change relatively slow and ponderous, la naguala's shapeshifting ontology offers a different, quantum-like perspective in which physical reality itself is composed primarily of empty space through which we can pass when relying on naguala's spirit guidance to direct our embodied movements. Put differently, la naguala reconstitutes embodiment through these shifts.

Anzaldúa associates la naguala with a fluid consciousness, an internal/external guidance, or what she sometimes calls the "indweller," that includes but exceeds the individual human thinker. As she states in her 1999 writing notas, "The indweller is the consciousness attached to spirit. It is a presence that is always with us. It lights the path at our feet, it shows us the way, it succors and protects. Antigua mi diosa, the knower within" (Writing Notas H). Existing simultaneously in both internal and external worlds, naguala "shows us the way" when we appeal to its guidance and listen humbly to its directions. As inner guide, la naguala functions like a bridge between the individual and the cosmos, enabling us to access the cosmic by looking deeply within while, simultaneously, reading the external world for the soul's messages. (*And here we see an invaluable connection with risking the personal.*) La naguala calls us into this deep dive and assists us along our way: "I believe that there is order, that there is a force directing things, a personal/impersonal force I call the indweller or naguala" (Writing Notas J).

This ontological emphasis on spirit is crucial to la naguala's powers. Anzaldúa associates la naguala with spirit's presence in both our internal psyches and the outer world (in people, animals, landscape, ocean, and so on). This spirit is both singular and radically plural; it manifests itself in an endless variety of shapes and ways. As she states in Writing Notas B, "The naguala in us can cause transformation. The naguala within is the watcher who sees all. The naguala is our inner guide. The spirit is different forms (people, animals, objects) in different disguises but it is the same spirit. Spirit (the observer), mind (the process of observing) and the body (the observed) are the same thing." Anzaldúa associates la naguala with spirit and spirit with ontological origin, the metaphysical stuff of reality.

With its foundations in pre-Columbian philosophy and nonordinary reality, la naguala can be challenging to define, describe, and discuss in conventional western contexts. Even Anzaldúa struggled to fully articulate it, as demonstrated by the various ways she named it ("el nagual," "la nagual," "naguala," and "nagualismo") and her divergent descriptions of it. Indeed, Anzaldúa defines and describes la naguala in a startling variety of ways: as "El Diablo, . . . her shadow self" ("La serpiente"); the shape-shifting component of herself and other humans; an intellectual-imaginational faculty, or "imaginal consciousness" (*Light* 108); an alternative subjectivity or ability; a relationship between two or more things; and/or as an action—"the work of embodying consciousness" (*Light* 105). There are several reasons for this definitional challenge. To begin with, it exceeds Cartesian thought and thus often eludes or escapes perception, especially for those relying primarily on logico-empirical evidence. Although la naguala can be a lifelong presence within us, we typically move through life almost completely unaware of its presence—at best glimpsing it in fleeting, intangible ways. Moreover, its nonlinear, transtemporal qualities make it difficult to describe with written English's linear expression. And, of course, because Anzaldúa was still exploring and applying la naguala at the end of her life, she offers no conclusive definition or culminating statement but rather provides a variety of definitions and descriptions.

LA NAGUALA'S STORY (ORIGINS AND DEVELOPMENT)

Unlike some theories, such as la facultad, which seem almost fully developed from their first appearance, la naguala grows considerably over the trajectory of Anzaldúa's career. Anzaldúa referred to la naguala in a variety of manuscripts, beginning in the late 1970s, associating it with shape-shifting, altered consciousness, writing, and inspiration. She formulates la naguala in dialogue with her personal spiritual investigations, philosophical speculation, her autohistorias, both dissertation projects, her poetry, and her fiction. She had lived with la naguala since childhood, and the term and its functions called out to her in an increasingly strong voice as the years progressed. In her work she both articulates what she has already experienced and applies it to present and future work. She was still formulating this theory at the time of her death.

La naguala might be one of Anzaldúa's most personal theories; she developed it largely through dialogue with her own life—including her childhood encounters with the nonordinary, the stories she heard as a young girl, her spiritual practices, her out-of-body experiences, and her numerous health challenges. Anzaldúa narrates her childhood encounter with la naguala in an unpublished short story, where she describes it as a large black dog, and again in her 1982 autohistoria, "La serpiente que se come su cola," where it's "El Diablo, her nagual, her shadow self." In the 1982 autohistoria, "Esperando la serpiente con plumas," she associates her nagual with a Jungian-like shadow: "In San Francisco I confronted my Nagual, my shadow Self, my inner guide." For a short time during the late 1980s and early 1990s, Anzaldúa associated la nagual with identity-related shifts and transformations. In papers produced for her UCSC coursework and early dissertation chapters, she put la nagual into dialogue with phenomenology and other theories of embodied subjectivity. Thus, for example, in "La Llorona y la víbora que se mete por allá" she writes, "The physical body is the crossroads; the *nomos es un lugar pasajero*, it is a thoroughfare. For me *la Llorona* is the symbolic body, the nocturnal site of the ghostly body, the 'Other' body where myth, fantasy, utterance and reality converge. The 'body' is comprised of all four bodies, the physical, psychic, symbolic and ghostly. *La llorona*, the ghostly body carries the *nagual* possessing *la facultad*, the capacity for shape-changing and shape-shifting of identity." Although she would later explore this shape-shifting potential in her Prieta stories, Anzaldúa did not develop it in her theoretical writings at this time.

During the later 1990s Anzaldúa devoted considerable attention to her fiction where in some stories she depicts Prieta as a shape-shifter and in other stories as encountering were-animals—especially a were-jaguar. As she drafted and revised the stories, Anzaldúa reflected on her own creative process and inner voice, which she associated with her nagual. Writing Notas B, C, and D contain pages of speculation and exploration that reveal her thinking at this time. By 2000 Anzaldúa had further expanded la naguala's role as she continued exploring its ontological implications, investigating its connections with a multidimensional reality and the ways it might enable us to access deeper, more expansive dimensions. Thus in Writing Notas J she describes la naguala as a bridge between the individual and the cosmos: "I believe that there is order, that there is a force directing things, a personal/impersonal force I call the indweller or naguala." Again, we see that for Anzaldúa la naguala exceeds the self-enclosed individual. Though we can access la naguala's wisdom (and activate the naguala) through self-reflection and internal focus, la naguala cannot be reduced to the small ego.

In her final years, naguala called out to Anzaldúa in increasingly powerful and compelling ways, making itself heard through her body, her words, and her projects. As she experienced additional struggles with her health (e.g., managing the diabetes and regulating her blood sugar levels), she brought additional attention to questions of healing and wellness. Perhaps not surprisingly, given naguala's close ties with shamanism and shamanism's ties with healing, she deeply investigated la naguala's healing potential. She also explored la naguala in her fiction, often associating Prieta with shape-shifters, curanderas, and other naguala-inspired themes. Indeed, she underscored la nagual's centrality in her tentative titles for the book: "Bridges to la Naguala, Stories of la Prieta," "La Prieta and the Bridge to la Naguala," "La Prieta Bridges to la Naguala." Similarly, in her writing notes from these years we see Anzaldúa's explorations as she worked with la naguala. She used contemplation, imagination, self-reflection, and self-surrender to access la naguala's healing, transformative powers. At the time of her death, she was finalizing chapter 2 of *Light in the Dark*, "Flights of Imagining," in which she focuses on "the use of the imaginal in nagualismo, nature spirituality, appropriation of mexican [sic] indigenous cultural figures, symbols, practices, and shamanic journeying, as well as imaginal figures (archetypes) of the inner world" and other topics closely related to la naguala ("Chapter Annotations").

Given her late notes and her expansive discussions of la naguala in *Light in the Dark*, it's likely that Anzaldúa would have expanded its ontological and epistemological implications, as well as its potential contributions to a writing process and to healing more generally. The amount of material on la naguala found in some of Anzaldúa's final manuscripts (e.g., Writing Notas L, "+notes-b") indicates her enduring interest. Had she lived longer, it's quite likely that she would have further expanded her investigations, offering additional insights and instructions into how we might access la naguala to develop new knowledge and shift our embodiment and identities in additional ways. Possible areas of application include the writing process, embodiment, and health-related issues. Perhaps she would have deepened her analysis of la naguala's inner guidance and discussed how to more fully cultivate la naguala in our lives. In some of her final writing notes Anzaldúa seems to suggest that naguala is, potentially, a normal function of human life ("ordinary mode of being-in-the-world"), though a mode that we rarely enact. She also might have investigated naguala as method designed to access "information from the unconscious (naguals)."

RELATED THEORIES

- el cenote
- conocimiento
- Coyolxauhqui process
- la facultad
- El Mundo Zurdo
- nepantla
- nepantlera

FUTURE DIRECTIONS

- In her 1982 manuscript "Esperando la serpiente con plumas" Anzaldúa discusses her nagual in the section titled "Notes on El Mundo Zurdo." What might the implications of this association between la naguala and El Mundo Zurdo mean for both theories? How might we put them in dialogue?
- What relationships exist between La Llorona and la naguala in Anzaldúa's work?
- Where does la naguala appear in Anzaldúa's Prieta stories, and what can its presence teach us about the theory?
- How does Prieta function as a naguala, and what are the implications of this functioning?
- Anzaldúa also referred to the "daimon" in some of her writings. What's the relationship between the daimon and la naguala?
- What's the relationship between la naguala and el cenote? Does the former enable us to access the latter or perhaps serve as a channel of sorts?
- What's the relationship between la naguala and conocimiento?

- What's the relationship between la naguala and the imagination? See for instance Writing Notas L: "Coyolxauhqui . . . the process of the imagination in action, drives perception & knowledge to get information (from el cenote) and use it to create/construct spiritual fictional world. I call its witnessing presence naguala."
- How can we access our naguala and use la naguala's insights to reshape the external world?
- How might la naguala assist us in activating queer conocimiento?
- How can we, educators, activists, and scholars, enact la naguala?

USEFUL TEXTS

- "+notes-b"
- "Conocimientos: Creative Acts of Vision, Inner Works, Public Acts"
- "Esperando la serpiente con plumas"
- "Exploring Cultural Legacies: Using Myths to Construct Stories of Modern Realities"
- "ID—Subject to Shiftings: Disturbing Identities and Representations"
- *Light in the Dark/Luz en lo Oscuro*
- "La Llorona y la víbora que se mete por allá"
- "Notes on El Mundo Zurdo"
- "On the Process of Feminist Image Making"
- "Poetry & Magick"
- "Spirit Notes"
- Writing Notas 107.9, 108.5, 108.7
- Writing Notas B, C, D, G, H, J, K, L, M
- "Writing outside the Story"

Nepantla

Why did I come to this alien world *en nepantla, el lugar del aislamiento*, confronted I am afraid I will be forever alone, forever unlike others just like I was before *en el otro lugar. En Nepantla, el lugar entre medio.*—"En nepantla" (1991)

El concept de nepantla questions the notion of reality (reality is that which the consensus agrees to be real).—Writing Notas 108.3 (1994)

My talk focuses on my concept of nepantla, the liminal stages of transition which I use to describe how we create identity and art and how we practice spiritual activism. I am interested in how one can use the concept of nepantla to connect the inner life of the mind and spirit to [the] outer world of social action. It is a work of conocimiento. I want to bring a psychological/mythological dimension to identity formation, cultural transformation, and spiritual practice via the creative act.—"Nepantla: Creative Acts of Vision" (2002)

In nepantla we undergo the anguish of changing our perspectives and crossing a series of cruz calles, junctures, and thresholds, some leading to a different way of relating to people and surroundings and others to the creation of a new world.—*Light in the Dark/ Luz en lo Oscuro* (2004/2015)

DEFINITION

The Nahuatl word for "in the middle" or "in-between," "nepantla" is, arguably, the most complex theory in Anzaldúa's post-*Borderlands* work. The word and its meaning resonate deeply with Anzaldúa, signaling transition, uncertainty, ambivalence, and liminality. Thus she borrowed the term and allowed it to inspire and guide her as she developed a multidimensional theoretical framework to instigate and articulate the process of transformation and potential change that she applied to a wide range of topics, including identity, aesthetics, epistemology, ontology, metaphysics, and ethics. Anzaldúa's theory of nepantla represents both an elaboration of and an expansion beyond her earlier theories of the borderlands, the Coatlicue state, and new mestiza consciousness. Like the borderlands, nepantla represents liminal spaces that emerge when and/or where two or more worlds collide, leaving conflict and pain in their wake. Like the Coatlicue state, nepantla represents depressive conditions and uncertainty that might trigger anxiety, pain, and loss of control. And like new mestiza consciousness, nepantla represents an epistemology that contains, reflects, and transforms contradictions. But with nepantla, Anzaldúa foregrounds esoteric and Indigenous-inspired philosophies while expanding the ontological (spiritual, psychic, nonphysical) dimensions. As she explained in a 1991 interview, "With nepantla the connection to the spirit world is more pronounced as is the connection to the world after death, to psychic spaces. It has a more spiritual, psychic, supernatural, and indigenous resonance" (*Interviews* 176).

As Anzaldúa's reference to the supernatural suggests, nepantla offers a vehicle with which to challenge consensual reality. By opening space for non-Cartesian epistemologies and ontologies, nepantla invites us to bypass our overreliance on rational thought and gives us the tools (*gateways, as it were*) with which to do so. As such, nepantla is not a passive, neutral container for our ideas but rather it represents (*and embodies*) the energy of transformation. Nepantla includes the intention to change and grow. It invites change. When we use nepantla as a framework to investigate and work with identity, aesthetics, ethics, or any other dimension of life or thought, we bring this resonance into our investigations. Put differently, nepantla offers a spacious theoretical container in which contradictions can coexist and intermingle, allowing synergistic combinations to occur. Nepantla circumvents our overreliance on rational, logical thought, opening space for nonlinear, intuitive, imaginative insights. Instead of rejecting contradictions as illogical or unrealistic, with nepantla we embrace them. In nepantla, contradictory states or meanings don't just coexist, they energetically mingle and converse.

Although it can be tempting to romanticize nepantla by focusing exclusively on its potential to effect liberatory, progressive change, to do so overlooks the crucial roles uncertainty, difficulty, and pain typically play in its transformational process. Nepantla hurts. (*And often, nepantla hurts a* LOT!) Look for instance at Anzaldúa's use of nepantla to theorize identity (trans)formation. During nepantlas, individual and/or collective self-definitions shatter as apparently fixed identities—whether based on gender, nationality, ethnicity/race, sexuality, religious beliefs, worldview, and/or some combination of these categories and often others as well—begin breaking down. This loosening of familiar identity formations can be intensely painful, leading to isolation, alienation, and profound loneliness and self-distrust. Similar statements can be made about nepantla when applied to beliefs, worldviews, or any other aspect of life: When nepantla confronts us, we are alienated from our previous perspectives and challenged or forced to change. (*Or, of course, we can refuse the challenge, dig in our heels, and resist changing.*)

Nepantla is invitational and deeply democratic. Although our experiences, reactions, and engagements will vary widely, we all encounter the conditions to experience nepantla many times. Nepantla enters our lives and asks us to change. Sometimes, it intrudes—forcing us into chaotic, uncertain conditions and demanding that we change; but other times we can intentionally choose whether to engage with its transformative potential. We can refuse nepantla; we can retreat; we can hold onto our current worldviews by clinging to the status quo, burying ourselves in our descon-ocimientos, and/or losing ourselves in addiction (sinking into what Anz-aldúa sometimes calls the Coatlicue state). Or, we can embrace and move through nepantla, recognizing it as a temporary way station that shifts us toward a revitalized identity, vocation, belief system, and/or worldview. We can activate or work with nepantla through ritual transformation. Because nepantla originates outside of western thought and refers to recursive nonrational processes, it can be challenging for western-trained readers to comprehend without greatly oversimplifying. Moreover, nepantla's prolif-eration of meanings, dimensions, and applications makes it difficult, if not impossible, to succinctly define nepantla.

NEPANTLA'S STORY (ORIGINS AND DEVELOPMENT)

Anzaldúa's theory of nepantla grew from numerous dialogic encounters with life events, reader reception, creative projects, and other theories like the Coatlicue state, the borderlands, new mestiza consciousness, and con-ocimiento. Anzaldúa developed this theory through fiction, essay, lecture, and interview, applying it to identity formation, alienation, and epistemol-ogy. Her theory of nepantla grew in complexity and depth, doing more and more work as the years unfolded. By the mid-1990s it had become one of her most vibrant theories, branching off into additional directions, including las nepantleras, the nepantla body, the nepantla brain, and, most prominently, conocimiento.

Anzaldúa first used the term "nepantla" in her 1987 book, *Borderlands/La Frontera*, where it appears only once, to describe the internal sense of division and uncertainty—the "mental nepantlism, torn between ways"—experienced by Anzaldúa and other new mestizas (100). Although this brief description points to key traits that Anzaldúa later developed, she did not return to "nepantla" until the early 1990s, and seemed to do so at least in part because readers interpreted her borderlands theory too narrowly, defining it almost exclusively as the geographic location between Mexico and the United States. As she explained in a 1991 interview, "people were using 'Borderlands' in a more limited sense than I had meant it. So to elab-orate on the psychic and emotional borderlands I'm now using 'nepantla'" (*Interviews* 176).

During the early 1990s, Anzaldúa began developing nepantla by teas-ing apart borderlands' literal and metaphoric meanings. This work began with her 1991 speculative fiction short story, "En nepantla," in which the first-person, green-skinned narrator (Prieta) is compelled to leave home because "the Change was hard on [her] heels," and she no longer belonged. As she crosses to "the other side," where she hopes to find freedom, Prieta is stopped and dismembered by a "faceless Chalk" guarding the perimeters. This dismemberment represents a rebirth of sorts, and Prieta awakens with an altered sense of herself and the world: "I see a new piece of myself I never knew or had forgotten. . . . I feel alienated from this self that I do not recognize. The landscape shimmers then settles but not on the same bedrock. . . . Everything looks different." Here we see key themes that Anzaldúa developed in the following years as she theorized nepantla: transitions, identity shifts, epistemological and ontological alterations, coming apart/coming together (*Coyolxauhqui process!*), unequal power dynamics, pain, alienation, and psychic disorientation.

Around this time, as Anzaldúa began associating nepantla with art, creativity, and the creative process, the theory really took off. Invited to write about border art and border artists in relation to the Mesoamerican special exhibit at the Denver Museum of Natural History (renamed in 2000 as the Denver Museum of Nature & Science), Anzaldúa brought new attention to nepantla. In the early drafts "nepantla" functions almost entirely as a synonym for the border; however, as Anzaldúa continued working on this essay, she put nepantla into dialogue with a range of topics: border crossing, Mesoamerican myth, the "obstacles and dangers" border artists experience, and border art more generally. In so doing, she greatly expanded and deepened the theory. By the final drafts, she had clearly distinguished between borders and nepantla, using the former to represent geographic or other spatial locations of division and the latter to represent the psychological, epistemological, and psychic states evoked through this bifurcation. In addition to linking nepantla directly with art, she used the term to describe a portion of creative consciousness: "The *nepantla* state is the natural habitat of artists, most specifically for the Chicana/o and *mexicana/o* mestizo border artists who partake of the traditions of two or more worlds and who may be bi-national" ("*El arte de la frontera*"). The artist obtains new knowledge and perspectives which can then be translated into their work: "[E]l *dios murciélago*, the bat god with his big ears, fangs and protruding tongue representing the vampire bat associated with night, blood sacrifice and death. I make an instantaneous association of the bat man with the *nepantla* stage of border artists—the dark cave of creativity where they hang upside down, turning the self upside down in order to see from another point of view, one that brings a new state of understanding" ("*El arte de la frontera*"). Associating nepantla with "night, blood sacrifice and death," Anzaldúa here acknowledges nepantla's painful dimensions as well as its assistance in creative knowledge production. Like Prieta's experience of dismemberment in the short story "En nepantla," the production of a new mode of consciousness comes with a painful cost.

Throughout the mid- and late 1990s, Anzaldúa continued exploring relationships among nepantla, creativity, identity, and art. In 1995, she was invited to develop and collaborate on "Entre Américas: El Taller Nepantla," an artistic residency centering around the concept of nepantla that took place at Villa Montalvo, California. This invitation gave Anzaldúa a focused opportunity to explore nepantla. As the draft of her proposal for this workshop indicates, by this point she viewed nepantla as a complex, multilayered theory with states and stages that she applied to consciousness, the creative process, identity, and world-traveling. In this workshop and the many essay drafts that she produced for and from it, Anzaldúa reflected on her creative process, carefully dividing it into nuanced stages; she associated nepantla both with those painful shifts in consciousness that often accompany artistic production and with the artist's role as naguala, moving among multiple realities and worlds to gather new insights for her community.

During this period Anzaldúa also expanded previous definitions to describe nepantla as an action and faculty: "It is una facultad that accesses in between spaces, peripheral spaces and realities not senplaces [*sic*]. The ability to detect the 'nepantla spaces' requires the ability to shift. The shift is from rational, logical modes to what I have called 'entering into the serpent,' into the body which is the animal and spiritual part of us" ("Nepantla: The Creative Process"). By this point, nepantla had become foundational to Anzaldúa's developing philosophy, laying the groundwork for conocimiento. She had moved beyond simply analyzing nepantla's transitional stages of transformation to explore potential applications, suggesting how we might work with it—or, as she states in several manuscripts, how we might "navigate" nepantla states in order to intentionally facilitate creativity and transformation. In "Nepantla: In/Between and Shifting" (1997), for example, she uses nepantla to consolidate her developing aesthetic and organize her thoughts on writing and epistemology. Her writing notes from these years indicate her interest in expanding nepantla to theorize the "nepantla body" and the "nepantla brain."

In her final decade, Anzaldúa formulated nepantla into her process philosophy encompassing epistemology, ontology, and aesthetics. As she states in "Putting Coyolxauhqui Together,"

> Nepantla is your symbol for the transitional process, both conscious and unconscious, that bridges different kinds of activities by moving between and among different parts of the brain. The work of nepantla is a mysterious type of dreaming or perception which registers the workings of all states of consciousness. Shaman-like nepantla moves from rational to visionary states, from logistics to poetics, from focused to unfocused perception, from inner world to outer. Nepantla is the twilight landscape between the self and the world, between the imagery of the imagination and the harsh light of reality.

Here nepantla functions as a way of thinking, a mode of consciousness, and the ontological space where they occur. Importantly, because nepantla also acknowledges the pain and internal splitting that happen during transitions, this theory offered Anzaldúa a way to articulate holistic knowledge production without romanticization. As such she could subtly address misinterpretations of new mestiza consciousness that glorify the positive and downplay the pain.

In the following years Anzaldúa brought nepantla into dialogue with additional theories—especially conocimiento but also nagualismo, nos/otras, el cenote, and conocimiento. As I explained in "Re-envisioning Coyolxauhqui," nepantla includes an agentic quality in Anzaldúa's later work, functioning "as an actant, a strange collaborative endeavour: Nepantla works *with* Anzaldúa as she invents her theories of las nepantleras, nos/otras, new tribalism, geography of selves, spiritual activism, conocimiento, and the Coyolxauhqui imperative" (xxxv). Anzaldúa confirms nepantla's agentic quality in *Light in the Dark*, in which she states, "Nepantla concerns automatically infuse my writing: I don't have to *will* myself to deal with these particular points; these nepantlas inhabit me and inevitably surface in whatever I'm writing" (2).

Also during this time, Anzaldúa increasingly distinguished between nepantla and conocimiento as she developed her theory of the latter. We can track these alterations through analysis of the many drafts of "now let us shift" produced from 1999 to 2001. By 2000 she had deepened and somewhat organized the theory, as evidenced in "Nepantla: Creative Acts of Vision," a talk delivered at Psychology at the Threshold, the International

Archetypal Symposium hosted by the Pacifica Graduate Institute in Santa Barbara, California, where she described nepantla as "a work of cono-cimiento" enabling us to "connect the inner life of the mind and spirit to outer world of social action." Even as Anzaldúa shifted her attention to con-ocimiento, nepantla remained pivotal to her later philosophical thought; in *Light in the Dark*, for example, she refers to it more than one hundred times. Near the very end of her life, she further explored nepantla's onto-logical implications, as seen in writing notes for her 2003 Sonoma State University talk, in which she defines nepantla as "the point of contact y el lugar between ordinary and nonordinary realities (spirit realities)" and "the mid ground in a continuum that places spirituality at one end and soul at the opposite end."

Anzaldúa's unpublished late drafts and communication suggest that, had she lived longer, she would have continued these ontological explora-tions, perhaps linking them with investigations of nepantla's relationship to healing. It's also likely that she would have returned to the imaginal body, putting it into dialogue with the nepantla body. Given Anzaldúa's recursive process (rereading earlier writing notes, interviews, and essays, culling them for relevant passages and ideas), it's very likely that she would have theorized the nepantla body as a tool for healing and as an anchor of sorts, enabling the artist to be present and mindful—to herself, to her thoughts and feelings, and to the external world: "To make sense of this metamor-phic confusion, in order to take control of one's life, as a way of survival, as a way of inhabiting territory, to occupy one's body, to be present to oneself, give one access to oneself, to confront fears and to exorcise or cathercize, to change/transform consciousness, to make heal or make sacred what has been profaned/wounded, and as a way to reach/expand into other spaces/worlds" ("Nepantla: In/Between"). Perhaps she also would have explored how activating into this nepantla body functions in the writing process.

RELATED THEORIES

- B/borderlands
- el cenote
- Coatlicue state
- conocimiento
- Coyolxauhqui process
- desconocimiento

- la facultad
- geographies of selves
- nagual/nagualismo
- nepantlera
- new mestiza consciousness
- nos/otras

FUTURE DIRECTIONS

- How does an analysis of Anzaldúa's short stories enrich our understanding of her nepantla theory?
- What might a close analysis of Anzaldúa's "Border Arte" drafts and publications reveal about the development of nepantla and its divergence from her borderlands theory?
- Anzaldúa titled a 1995 manuscript "Nepantla: The Theory & Manifesto." How might nepantla function as a manifesto—for Anzaldúa and, potentially, for contemporary readers? How might nepantla energize activism?
- What can close analysis of Anzaldúa's Taller Nepantla workshop teach us about this theory, both in general but also as a theory of creativity and the creative process?
- How might Anzaldúa's friendships with artists (visual and written) have impacted her nepantla theory?
- What's the relationship between Anzaldúa's theories of nepantla and naguala? See, for instance, "Nepantla: In/Between and Shifting: Theories of Composition and Art," in which Anzaldúa describes the nepantla body in ways that resonate with her later theory of la naguala: "Undergoing a sudden healing or a spiritual awakening. One's perception is shaped by this experience of nepantla. One becomes aware that a nepantla body or imagining body dwells within one. One learns to read oneself, one's body as thoughts and images pass through it, one acquires a reading body when you shift attention [from] the everyday to some feeling, fantasy (fiction). The everyday reality 'disappears' or drops out of sight."
- What might the nepantla body teach us about embodied knowledge? What connections can we draw here between Anzaldúa's naguala and the nepantla body?

- In the late 1990s, as Anzaldúa revised the transcript from her 1993 *DisClosure* interview, she inserted a description of nepantla as process. What definitional shifts, if any, does this revision indicate? How might we view nepantla as a process philosophy?
- What might a close analysis of Anzaldúa's many drafts of "now let us shift" reveal about her philosophical move from nepantla to conocimiento? What might this shift teach us about both theories?
- In *Light in the Dark* and in various writing notas Anzaldúa refers to the nepantla body and the nepantla brain. What's the relationship between these concepts? How is the nepantla body or nepantla brain different from the physical body and conventional understandings of the brain? How might *we* build on what she has left us in order to further develop these theories?

USEFUL TEXTS

- "*El arte de la frontera:* The Border as Place, *Pueblo* and Image"
- "Conocimientos: Creative Acts of Vision, Inner Works, Public Acts"
- "En nepantla"
- *Light in the Dark/Luz en lo Oscuro*
- "Navigating Nepantla and the Cracks Between the Worlds"
- "Nepantla: The Crack between Worlds"
- "Nepantla: The Creative Process"
- "Nepantla: Gateways and Thresholds: Caminos y puertas"
- "Nepantla: In/Between and Shifting: Theories of Composition and Art"
- "Nepantla: Theories of Composition and Art"
- "Nepantla: The Theory & Manifesto"
- "sic: Spiritual Identity Crisis: A Series of Vignettes"
- "Taller Nepantla: Letter of Proposal for the *Nepantla* Project"
- "Violent Space, *Nepantla* Stage"
- "The Writing Habit: How I Work—Process and Stages"
- Writing Notas A, B, C, D, E, F, G, H, I, J, K, L, M, N
- "Yo vivo nepantla: In-Between States and Processes of Creating Identities and Other Realities"

Nepantlera

El concept de nepantla questions the notion of reality (reality is that which the consensus agrees to be real). Nosotras las artistas nepantleras create [a] strange new context by which to view the familiar world and see it in a new way. To see beyond the veils and distortions and to question and challenge the traditional ways of experienc[ing] the world is to see in a nepantlaish way. By listening to the environment and our inner cenotes, we cultivate an intense empathy with the world, an openness to other dimensions and realities of existence than the familiar and everyday.—Writing Notes 108.3 (1994)

Las nepantleras, like the ancient *chamanas*, move between the worlds. They can work from multiple locations, can circumvent polarizing binaries. They try not to get locked into one perspective or perception of things. They can see through our cultural conditioning and through our respective cultures' toxic ways of life. They try to overturn the destructive perceptions of the world that we've been taught by our various cultures. They change the stories about who we are and about our behavior. They point to the stick we beat ourselves with so we realize what we're doing and may choose to throw away the stick. They possess the gift of vision. *Nepantleras* think in terms of the planet, not just their own racial group, the US, or *norte américa*. They serve as agents of awakening, inspire and challenge others to deeper awareness.—"Speaking across the Divide" (2002)

DEFINITION

Anzaldúa invented the word "nepantlera" to articulate a specific type of mediator or agent of change who moves among multiple worlds and groups of people intentionally, to build bridges, create new alliances, and offer innovative perspectives that facilitate radical, progressive transformation. Drawing especially from her theories of nepantla, conocimiento, and spiritual activism, as well as her own experiences of art-making, alienation, and coalition-bridging, Anzaldúa developed her nepantlera theory to honor and encourage herself and anyone else called to take up this challenging, transformative work. Nepantleras are those who, for a variety of reasons, do not fit comfortably into consensual reality—whether because of their identity (sexuality/gender/ethnicity-race, etc.), beliefs, politics, interests, spirituality, appearance, abilities, aspirations, or some combination of these and other attributes as well. Although this inability to fit comfortably into the status quo leads to alienation and pain, nepantleras turn alienation into new insights and powerful tools for community-building and transformation.

Like nepantla, which represents liminality, painful transitions, and nonordinary realities, nepantleras are threshold people—mediators, "in-betweeners" (*Light* 148), who use their movement among multiple human, mundane, and nonordinary worlds to develop relational, "connectionist" theories and practices in the service of social justice. As the term's resonance with nepantla might suggest, nepantleras experience intense pain. Indeed, the experiences of nepantla through which nepantleras emerge are, by definition, painful. Moreover, the fact that nepantleras do not comfortably fit in with any single group can isolate them and trigger feelings of rejection and inadequacy. And their refusal to pick sides—to fully align themselves exclusively with one group or perspective—often leads to accusations of disloyalty or indecisiveness.

This liminal status and movement among multiple worlds serves a number of potentially transformative purposes. First, it enables nepantleras to recognize subtle commonalities (defined not as sameness but as similarities) shared by distinct peoples, worldviews, and beliefs. Second, this recognition, in turn, trains them to communicate effectively with a wide range of people. As Anzaldúa explains, "As intermediaries between various mundos, las nepantleras 'speak in tongues'—grasp the thoughts, emotions, languages, and perspectives associated with varying individual and cultural positions" (*Light* 3). Third, and closely related, they obtain a more nuanced understanding of differences. Whereas consensual reality defines difference hierarchically, as deviation from an elevated norm, nepantleras define difference relationally (*in El Mundo Zurdo ways*). By so doing, nepantleras build commonalities among divergent groups, creating a shared space for conversations and potential alliances to occur.

Nepantleras' inability or refusal to fit comfortably into the status quo enables them to see the limitations in social conventions and foundational yet flawed cultural beliefs. Rather than alter themselves to fit in with the existing system, nepantleras work to change the system itself. They use their outsider perspectives to more fully understand and profoundly challenge the status quo. They do so, in part, by calling attention to the fissures and cracks in the system. As Anzaldúa explains, nepantleras' "perspective[s] from the cracks" (*Light* 82) invite them to question "consensual reality" (our status-quo stories) and develop alternative perspectives (ideas, theories, actions, definitions, and beliefs) that partially reflect but also partially exceed existing worldviews.

While at times it can seem that nepantleras' bridge-building work is inevitable—a vocation they're fated to adopt—it is not. Doing the work of a nepantlera is a choice. Although nepantleras emerge through nepantla experiences, not everyone who experiences nepantla becomes a nepantlera. Unlike those who transition through nepantla experiences, nepantleras choose to remain in nepantla—betwixt and between multiple worlds. As Anzaldúa asserts, "To become nepantleras, we must *choose* to occupy intermediary spaces between the worlds, *choose* to move between the worlds like the ancient chamanas, *choose* to build bridges between the worlds, *choose* to speak from the cracks between the worlds, from las rendijas (rents). We must *choose* to see through the holes in reality, *choose* to perceive something from multiple angles" (*Light* 93, her italics). Choice is imperative here. It's this intentional work of moving among multiple worlds with the goals of creating new knowledge and building new forms of community that can especially distinguish the nepantlera from the new mestiza.

NEPANTLERA'S STORY (ORIGINS AND DEVELOPMENT)

Anzaldúa's nepantlera theory has multiple origins, including her personal experiences; her earlier discussions of queer people of colors as divine warriors, or "divinas guerrilleras," in "Esperando la serpiente con plumas"; her discussions of women-of-colors artists in "Speaking in Tongues: A Letter to Third World Women"; her well-known theory of the new mestiza in *Borderlands*; and, of course, her theory of nepantla. Situations and events that contributed to this theory include Anzaldúa's lifelong experiences of feeling like an outsider and her desire to depict this alienation in her art; her commitment to creating complex multicultural social justice groups and her involvement with social justice groups from the 1970s until her death; the 1990 National Women's Studies Association (NWSA) conference with its notorious division between white women and women of color; the 1995 Montalvo writing workshop where she focused intensively on the artist as shamanic world-traveler; her speaking engagement at the 1999 Geographies of Latinidad conference at the University of Illinois, Urbana-Champaign; and her work from 1999 to 2002 co-editing *this bridge we call home* and writing a new preface for the Third Woman Press edition of *This Bridge Called My Back: Writings by Radical Women of Color* (2002).

Prior to developing this theory, Anzaldúa occasionally used "nepantlero" and "nepantlera" as adjectives associated with artists and inspiration. She first used the word in her 1994 writing notas while considering how artists challenge consensual reality by offering different epistemologies. Defining nepantla as "el concepto [that] questions the notion of reality," she writes, "Nosotras las artistas nepantleras create strange new contexts by which to view the familiar world and see it in a new way. To see beyond the veils and distortions and to question and challenge the traditional ways of experienc[ing] the world is to see in a nepantlaish way." Drawing on her own experiences, she associates this innovative perceptual mode with the willingness to dwell in nepantla by carefully attending to our inner and outer worlds: "By listening to the environment and our inner cenotes, we cultivate an intense empathy with the world, an openness to other dimensions and realities of existence than the familiar and everyday." The following year, Anzaldúa again uses nepantlera as an adjective associated with innovative artistic production in her notes for the Villa Montalvo writing workshop:

> El aprendizaje, apprenticeship[.] Learn to acquire knowledge. Aprender a **soñar**, a usar *facultades nepantleras* como la abilidad de ver más allá del horizonte, de ver alrededor de las esquinas. Learning to access **el cenote**. El *cenote nepantlero* es una noria, un sinkhole profunds de la imaginacaión y la mente donde el presente, el pasado y el futuro y endonde los sueños, imagenes, símbolos, y memorieas, y en donde lo cotidiano y los soñiado viven en conjunto con el conciente y el subconciente, el terreno de las diosas ancestrales. ("Nepantla: The Creative Process," her italics and bold)

Here Anzaldúa uses "nepantlera" as an adjective describing nonrational epistemologies that enable us to see beyond our physical-material surroundings ("la abilidad de ver más allá del horizonte, de ver alrededor de las esquinas") and nonordinary realities ("El *cenote nepantlero*")—imaginal worlds that defy linear time and thus enable us to access our ancestors, our dreams, and ancient goddesses.

It's not until the later 1990s that Anzaldúa uses "nepantlera" as a noun and expands it into her theory of las nepantleras. Not surprisingly, she begins with artists. In her 1997 "Nepantla: In/Between and Shifting: Theories of Composition and Art" she refers to herself and the other artists who participated in the Montalvo workshop as "nepantleras": "Our exchanges are both personal and cultural. In working together we blur the boundaries between what is one's work and what is another's, the boundaries between literary work and visual art—we all enter nepantla. We have become nepantleras." Although Anzaldúa has not yet developed the theory, we see already the associations with multiplicity, movement among diverse worlds, and innovative insights. Note also the suggestion that one becomes (rather than is born) a nepantlera.

The theory's major expansion began in 1999 as Anzaldúa drafted "now let us shift. . . . the path of conocimiento. . . . inner work, public acts," her contribution to *this bridge we call home*. Drawing on both her experiences at the 1990 NWSA conference (where many women-of-colors participants walked out, fed up with the organization's ongoing racism) and her experiences co-editing *this bridge we call home* (where a fierce conflict erupted among contributors), she offered nepantleras as transformational mediators among divisive groups *and* as spiritual activists. Arguably, the theory attains its fullest expression in *Light in the Dark*, in which Anzaldúa explores it in chapters 4 and 6. "Nepantleras" appears in the title of chapter 4 ("Geographies of Selves—Reimagining Identities: Nos/Otras (Us/Other), las Nepantleras, and the New Tribalism"), in which Anzaldúa uses nepantleras to explore questions of nationalism and offer alternatives to nationalism and assimilation. Interestingly, Anzaldúa did not use the word "nepantlera" in the 1999 lecture that served as the basis for this chapter; however, through the revision process (and in dialogue with other projects, like "now let us shift") the concept of nepantleras becomes crucial to her argument in this chapter. Indeed, one could argue that introducing her theory of nepantleras—with their identity-blurring, world-traveling, shamanistic work—into her analysis of nation-building and assimilation greatly impacted Anzaldúa's critique of nationalism and cultural identity. Anzaldúa's notes for her final talk, delivered at Sonoma State University on May 12, 2003 (almost exactly one year before her passing), focus on nepantleras, suggesting that, had she lived longer, she would have continued developing this theory, deepening the ontological, metaphysical, imaginal, and psychic components. Quite possibly, she would have explored nepantleras as a type of twenty-first-century shaman. And just think, given her dialogic writing process, whereby she interacts with current events and uses this interaction to shape her theories, what she might have done with her nepantlera theory in the late 2010s and beyond.

- el cenote
- conocimiento
- geographies of selves
- El Mundo Zurdo
- la naguala
- nepantla
- new mestiza
- new mestiza consciousness
- new tribalism
- nos/otras
- spiritual activism

FUTURE DIRECTIONS

- What resonance do we find by putting Anzaldúa's "divine guerillas" ("Esperando") into dialogue with las nepantleras?
- What does las nepantleras' origin (at least in part) in Anzaldúa's theory of art teach us about her theory of las nepantleras?
- What can a close comparison of the similarities and differences between Anzaldúa's theories of new mestizas and nepantleras teach us about both theories and about her theory-making process?
- What work does las nepantleras do for Anzaldúa's other theories—especially geographies of selves, new tribalism, and nos/otras—given their synchronous emergence in manuscripts leading up to *Light in the Dark*?
- In what ways did nepantleras serve as an engine or fuel of sorts to transform "Geography of Selves" from the Urbana talk, with its focus on racial/cultural identities, to the more expansive focus in chapter 4 of *Light in the Dark*?
- Relatedly, how might las nepantleras have changed Anzaldúa's conception of la Raza from the 1999 Urbana talk to *Light in the Dark*, chapter 4?
- How does one become a nepantlera?
- How might Anzaldúa have continued developing her nepantleras theory in dialogue with her aesthetics?
- What can Anzaldúa's nepantleras teach us about post-oppositional spiritual activist work?

- "+notes-b"
- "counsels from the firing . . . past, present, future. Foreword to the third edition"
- "Esperando la serpiente con plumas"
- *Light in the Dark/Luz en lo Oscuro*
- "Navigating Nepantla and the Cracks Between the Worlds"
- "Nepantla: The Crack between Worlds"
- "Nepantla: The Creative Process"
- "Nepantla: In/Between and Shifting: Theories of Composition and Art"
- "Notes—preface"
- "now let us shift," especially draft 5
- "Re-configuring Fronteras"
- "Speaking across the Divide"
- Writing Notas 108.3, 108.7
- Writing Notas J, K, L, M, N

New Mestiza

Her *opus*, the inner work of integrating, of separating and a bringing together. And for this mestiza, this half-breed this mezcla de sangres, threads of a mixed cloth or hybrid her work was synthesis. She had yet to satisfactoryly [sic] undergo the *hierosgamos* [sic], the chemical wedding, the marriage of the yin and the yang, the white and the brown, of the azteca, maya coalhuilteca, Spanish, Moor, Arab-Berber, and Anglo-Saxon, she had yet to melt into an embrace purified of all opposition, she had yet to become incorruptible. The *coniunctio*, coitus with herself. The great work, that of becoming mestiza, a fusion of all the racial bloodes [sic] where they would flow in sync through the rivers of her body. She wanted to become a river that cannot be held back. Wanted more than anything to achieve that integration, become that serpent swallowing its own tail, the *urobouros*. Like the serpent she wanted a long life, body shedding life like a skin and resurrecting La serpiente que se come su cola.—"La serpiente que se come su cola" (1982)

But we Chicanos no longer feel that we need to beg entrance, that we need always to make the first overture—to translate to Anglos, Mexicans and Latinos, apology blurting out of our mouths with every step. Today we ask to be met halfway. This book is our invitation to you—from the new mestizas.—*Borderlands/La Frontera* (1987)

Mestisaje is not biological, the new mestiza is not a blood mestiza.—I failed to make this clear in *Borderlands*.—Writing Notas N (2003)

In conventional discourse, the word "mestizo" refers to a person of mixed Spanish and Indigenous racial ancestry. Drawing on her own experiences and self-definition as a mestiza, Anzaldúa takes this term and expands it, creating an innovative, flexible subjectivity. Her new mestiza represents a complex identity that can't be reduced to a single category or rigidly classified according to a specific set of traits. The product of two or more cultures ("culture" defined broadly to include but go beyond ethnicity/race), her new mestiza is a liminal figure who coexists in and moves among several worlds as she attempts to reconcile, rather than simplify, accept, or reject, the various worlds among which she moves. In so doing, she transforms them, creating something innovative. Anzaldúa's new mestiza represents at least three significant departures from conventional twentieth-century understandings of mestizo identity. First, she intentionally changed the gender, shifting from mestizo to mestiza. Second, she extended typical definitions of the mestizo as a member of a specific racial/ethnic group to encompass the experiences of others as well. And third, she associated her new mestiza with a specific mode of thought, what she named the new mestiza consciousness—a post-Enlightenment epistemology that synergistically embraces contradiction and relationality.[14]

Anzaldúa's new mestiza can be challenging to define given Anzaldúa's various uses of the term and the fact that she does not approach it as a theory. Nor does she offer a succinct definition. In fact, she only uses the term "new mestiza" three times in *Borderlands/La Frontera: The New Mestiza*: (1) in the book's title; (2) in the preface; and (3) in the final prose chapter. (*Given the large amount of scholarship on Anzaldúa's* new mestiza, *I was startled to find so few actual references to the term.*) Even in her later work, "mestiza" functions most often as an adjective modifying the new mode of consciousness offered in *Borderlands* and her later work. This definitional challenge is further compounded by the fact that Anzaldúa uses "new mestiza" in two distinct though overlapping ways: (1) to refer to herself (including her own racial, ethnic, and cultural identity) and other Chicanx; and (2) to refer to other people of various cultural backgrounds who, like her, do not fit into the various worlds they inhabit.

Anzaldúa provides her most extensive discussion of new mestizas in her 1992 essay "New Mestiza Nation," in which she carefully distinguishes between "mestiza," which she describes as "an old term," and her "new mestiza." While both terms represent complex identity mixtures, the latter "is more inclusive than a racial mestizaje" and thus more disruptive of consensual reality. As Anzaldúa explains, "The new mestiza is a category that threatens the hegemony of the neo-conservatives because it breaks down the labels and theories used to manipulate and control us. Punching holes in their categories, labels, and theories means punching holes in their walls." Also in this essay Anzaldúa offers one of her most succinct definitions of new mestizas and their work:

> The new mestizas have a connection with particular places, a connection to particular races, a connection to new notions of ethnicity, to a new tribalism that is devoid of any kind of romantic illusions. The new mestiza is a liminal subject who lives in borderlands between cultures, races, languages, and genders. In this state of in-betweenness the mestiza can mediate, translate, negotiate, and navigate these different locations. As mestizas, we are negotiating these worlds every day, understanding that multiculturalism is a way of seeing and interpreting the world, a methodology of resistance. (209)

Contradiction/multiplicity, liminality, movement, disruption, and transformation are key traits in Anzaldúa's new mestiza. The new mestiza draws from multiple cultural legacies and negotiates among a wide variety of worlds, ideas, perspectives, communities, and beliefs.

This ability to move among divergent worlds is key to the new mestiza's transformational powers. As Anzaldúa explains in "(Des)Conocimientos: Resisting New Forms of Domination/Oppression," "Because we live in intersections we are constantly operating in a negotiation's mode [sic]. Our activism, our cultural production, our very lives challenge identity and cultural categories." Anzaldúa's use of the word "negotiation" is instructive, for it hints at the complex communication skills new mestizas must enact. Because they partially inhabit various different worlds, they gain an intimate understanding of the limitations in the various perspectives and use this awareness while communicating among groups.

Although Anzaldúa's new mestiza is sometimes associated exclusively with those of mixed Indigenous and European heritage, and she acknowledges the etymological roots, Anzaldúa usually (though not always) defines her term more broadly. As she explains in "Spiritual Mestizaje," while both mestizaje and the new mestiza represent the "mingling of contradictory elements in the cauldron that is the body," the "mestisaje" that she refers to goes beyond racial/ethnic categories to include cultural legacies and other identity-related components:

> [M]estisaje is not just a mixture of bloodlines. I see it as a mixture of different cultures, different points of views, and different religions. In my own cultural sincretism of the indigenous with the Spanish there is La Virgen de Guadalupe, who was indigenous to Mexico, but also has elements of La Virgen María of Catholicism. My sincretism has greater portions of the indigenous shamanism than Christianity. I bring to it elements that have served me that I have picked up from other cultures and different spiritual practices, a lot of them from the East, such as Tibetan and Zen Buddhism, Sidha Yoga, the I-Ching, Taoism.

Once again we see Anzaldúa's insistence that the new mestiza cannot be conflated with biological identities.

NEW MESTIZA'S STORY (ORIGINS AND DEVELOPMENT)

The new mestiza makes its entry in *Borderlands/La Frontera: The New Mestiza* as Anzaldúa uses her life to develop a visionary mode of consciousness that addresses social injustice and challenges consensual reality. Significantly, however, this term does not appear in the early versions of the manuscript, nor is it part of the original title. As mentioned above, Anzaldúa only uses the phrase "new mestiza" three times in *Borderlands*—and one of these is in the title itself. As analysis of chapter drafts indicates, Anzaldúa developed the new mestiza only after articulating her theory of the B/borderlands. Indeed, we could say that the new mestiza emerges both from the borderlands and from *Borderlands*. In *Borderlands*, Anzaldúa's new mestiza is less a theory than it is her springboard with which to articulate a mode of consciousness (a subjectivity defined in action-based terms).

Prior to adopting the term "new mestiza," Anzaldúa defined "mestiza" in personal racial/cultural terms, referring to herself as a "mestiza." Typically, she did so to underscore her complex racial/ethnic/cultural heritage while foregrounding the Indigenous component—an ancestral connection that was generally ignored (*or disparaged*) among Mexican Americans during her childhood.[15] In her 1981–82 autohistoria, "Esperando la serpiente con plumas (Waiting for the Feathered Serpent)," for example, she associated

Esperando with her mestiza identity: "I want it to help me realize my Self more fully. To help me rediscover my ancestral spiritual traditions—the Coahuilteca, Aztec, Maya, Navajo, Basque Spanish, Sephardic Jew, and Moor. I want it to urge me to revele [sic] in my mestiza-ness." Again in "La serpiente que se come su cola: The Death Rites of Passage of a Chicana Lesbian" (1982) she describes herself as mestiza and underscores her Indigenous ancestry: "Which race stared out at her from the mirror? All of them. She was a mexicana, a mestiza, a hybrid, a mongrel. Una mezcla de sangres, una mezclilla [sic] rara. The different bloods often made of her body a battleground. She was a mestiza but the Indian permeated every cell in her body. All mestizos are part Indian and an Indian is an Indian is an Indian." And in *Borderlands*, Anzaldúa again self-identifies as a mestiza, describing herself as the product of "three cultures—white, Mexican, Indian," which she uses to develop "a new culture" that builds on but goes beyond these three (21–22). More specifically, Anzaldúa draws on this mestizaje to propose an innovative consciousness—a worldview, ethics, and social change technique: "The new *mestiza* copes by developing a tolerance for contradictions, a tolerance for ambiguity. She learns to be an Indian in Mexican culture, to be Mexican from an Anglo point of view. She learns to juggle cultures. She has a plural personality, she operates in a pluralistic mode—nothing is thrust out, the good the bad and the ugly, nothing rejected, nothing abandoned. Not only does she sustain contradictions, she turns the ambivalence into something else." In this, *Borderlands'* third and final reference to the new mestiza, Anzaldúa builds on her experiences of marginalization to propose an innovative, relational epistemology that embraces and transforms contradictions, which she variously calls "new mestiza consciousness" or "mestiza consciousness."

Given that Anzaldúa only referred to the new mestiza three times in *Borderlands*, readers' enthusiastic reactions to it might have surprised her, and after *Borderlands'* publication, she was frequently asked to discuss it. These invitations compelled her to articulate her definition of the new mestiza and distinguish more carefully between it and typical definitions of the mestiza. Not surprisingly, given her limited references to the new mestiza in *Borderlands* and the close association she makes between the new mestiza and her Chicana ancestry, readers often assumed that the new mestiza was almost if not entirely synonymous with Chicanas (or mixed-ethnic/racial people more generally). However, Anzaldúa herself defined the theory more broadly.

Even the same year as *Borderlands'* publication, she offers an expansive definition that goes beyond identity categories to include perception:

> The New Mestiza is us: lesbians, women of color, feminists—all who have crossed into some-one [*sic*] else's culture. . . . You become sort of a hybridized creature, with a little bit of this and a little bit of that. What happens in the consciousness of the person being grafted—different things are grafted onto her, different cultures, different ideas. Her consciousness starts operating in a different way. Something happens to the way she perceives the world and the way she thinks of herself. That new way is what I call the new Mestiza Consciousness. A new way of thinking and perceiving. . . . The New Mestiza cannot plead ignorance and cannot deny what she sees. She has to account for what she sees. She has to make some sense of it. She's not closed off to things. In part, this consciousness has been forced onto her and in part, she has chosen it. (qtd. in Irving 37)

In interviews, speaking engagements, and her later graduate studies, Anzaldúa adamantly insisted on this broader definition while acknowledging its unsettling implications. As she tells Ann Reuman, "One of the riskier things I did in *Borderlands* was to open up the concept of mestizaje, of the new mestiza and hybridity, to be nonexclusive, to be inclusive of white people and people from other communities" (Reuman 6).

Anzaldúa's return to graduate school in the late 1980s offered additional opportunities to develop this theory. As she immersed herself in poststructuralist and postmodernist thought, she brought her subjectivity as a new mestiza into dialogue with a variety of other theoretical perspectives and topics. Especially relevant here is her challenge to mainstream postmodern theory celebrating fragmented subjectivity as post-Enlightenment and new. (For Anzaldúa, this supposedly "new" theory, articulated by Anglo theorists, was not new at all but was, rather, employed by herself and other women of colors.) Also during these years Anzaldúa considered developing a "mestiza discourse"; drew on psychoanalytic theory to consider how the new mestiza challenges conventional understandings of identity; and emphasized the new mestiza's liminality. "1D—Subject to Shiftings: Disturbing Identities and Representations" is especially useful in documenting Anzaldúa's perspective at this time; the piece focuses on mestiza identity—definitions, the work it can do in offering social critique, and its potential innovations.

Because readers so often interpreted and applied her theory of the new mestiza more narrowly than she had expected, Anzaldúa moved away from the term. Writing notes and manuscripts from the early 1990s suggest her exploration of related terms like "naguales" and "shape-shifters." By 1994 or so, she had shifted her focus from "new mestiza" toward developing other theories to describe the innovative subjectivities she envisioned, including nos/otras, the new tribalism, and nepantleras. Given readers' confusion about the term and Anzaldúa's interest in challenging conventional social categories and consensual definitions of identity, it is perhaps unlikely that she would have returned to or further developed her theory of the new mestiza *as* the new mestiza. As she writes in a 2004 manuscript draft, "We must unchain identity from meanings that can no longer contain, to move beyond externalized forms of social identity and location such as family, race, gender, sexuality, class, religion, nationality. La nepantlera, artista/activista possessing consencia de mestiza, open to other viewpoints, able to shift fluidly and to operate in different worlds, offers an alternative self" ("Geographies of Selves"). In some ways, "new mestiza" is a term of Anzaldúa's past, one she continued to move away from as nepantlera took up more attention and time, as she viewed conflicts among social activists differently.

RELATED THEORIES

- autohistoria y autohistoria-teoría
- B/borderlands
- geographies of selves
- mestiza consciousness
- El Mundo Zurdo
- la naguala
- nepantla
- nepantlera
- new tribalism
- nos/otras

FUTURE DIRECTIONS

- What can analyses of Anzaldúa's early autohistorias teach us about her theory of the new mestiza?
- What can analyses of the early manuscripts of *Borderlands'* prose chapters teach us about the invention and development of Anzaldúa's new mestiza?

- In what ways, if any, does Anzaldúa's theory change through the various interviews and discussions of the theory that occurred shortly after *Borderlands'* publication?
- How did Anzaldúa's doctoral studies at UCSC impact her theory of the new mestiza?
- What can careful analyses of Anzaldúa's references to "mestiza" and "new mestiza" in *Borderlands* and her writings from the late 1980s and early 1990s teach us about her theory of the new mestiza?
- Anzaldúa tried to stay abreast of scholarship on her work; how might scholars' interpretations of her new mestiza have impacted her theory's development as well as her shift away from the theory, into her theories of nepantleras?
- What can comparison of Anzaldúa's discussions of the new mestiza in *Borderlands* and *Light in the Dark* tell us about the theory?
- What are the similarities and differences between Anzaldúa's theories of the new mestiza and las nepantleras?

USEFUL TEXTS

- "Barred Witness: Literary/Artistic Creations and Class Identities"
- "Begging to Differ, Dissenting Discourses: A Commentary"
- *Borderlands/La Frontera*
- "Chicana/Colored Creativities inside Enemy Territory: Speaking in Tongues, *Carta* Two"
- "(Des)Conocimientos: Resisting New Forms of Domination/ Oppression"
- "Esperando la serpiente con plumas (Waiting for the Feathered Serpent)"
- "Geographies of Selves—Reimagining Identities: Nos/Otras (Us/ Other), las Nepantleras and the New Tribalism"
- "ID—Subject to Shiftings: Disturbing Identities and Representations"
- "Nepantla: Gateways and Thresholds"
- "New Mestiza Nation: A Multicultural Movement"
- "Remolinos y conocimientos—Imagination and Global Community"
- "La serpiente que se come su cola: The Death Rites of Passage of a Chicana Lesbian"

- "Subjected to/by Others: The Post Modern Mestiz Sub-Ject"
- Writing Notas 107.12
- Writing Notas D, N

New Mestiza Consciousness

Separating the flesh (woman) from the spirit (man) and relegating woman below man also made female attributes like intuition, feelings, nurturing and other left-handed qualities inferior. The right-sided mode of seeing views things sequentially, linearly. It "differentiates," cuts into little pieces. Separates. It deals with physical Reality. It is selective in what it "sees" thereby rendering invisible what it considers irrelevant or unnecessary for physical survival and filters out what it fears or does not wish to see like psychic perceptions, memories of past lives, whole segments of dreams, intuitions, hunches. It keeps the "Other" world out. It sees the physical world as an object, as outside of and independent from us. It legitimized power over the "other" and those below her. The female soul was banished. It went underground. Along with her ousted into the infernal regions was the occult way of seeing.—"Esperando la serpiente con plumas" (1982)

The new *mestiza* copes by developing a tolerance for contradictions, a tolerance for ambiguity. She learns to be an Indian in Mexican culture, to be Mexican from an Anglo point of view. She learns to juggle cultures. She has a plural personality, she operates in a pluralistic mode—nothing is thrust out, the good the bad and the ugly, nothing rejected, nothing abandoned. Not only does she sustain contradictions, she turns the ambivalence into something else.—*Borderlands/La Frontera* (1987)

i think academics (& the rest of us) forget that the "new" theories rise up from the roots of the old ones. all our languages are based on binaries—more's the pity. it seems like i've (we've) been pushing for "an other way," the in-between way of nepantla, the inclusiveness of mestiza consciousness, or whatever you want to call it, for what seems like forever.—Email communication (2002)

DEFINITION

Arguably Anzaldúa's best-known theory, her new mestiza consciousness offers a post-Enlightenment epistemology and ethics that replaces the overemphasis on linear thought, the almost exclusive valorization of rationality, and the search for a unified monolithic truth with holistic, both/and ways of thinking and acting. Whereas Cartesian thought typically employs dichotomous, hierarchical frameworks and exclusionary categories, Anzaldúa's new mestiza consciousness takes a more expansive approach, offering "a more whole perspective, one that includes rather than excludes" (*Borderlands* 9). Importantly, new mestiza consciousness does not entirely reject logical thought and rationality; rather, it resituates them within a larger context that also incorporates intuitive, relational thinking, ambivalence, contradiction, and paradox. In this more generous framework, rationality becomes one mode of thought, among others, to be used in context-specific ways. Sometimes described as the "consciousness of the Borderlands" (*Borderlands* n.p.), new mestiza consciousness works with multiple, sometimes contrasting, positions and views. As Anzaldúa writes, it is "a consciousness that comes from inhabiting contradictory locations simultaneously" (Writing Notas I). As explained below, this ability to embrace contradiction is key to new mestiza consciousness's innovative, transformational powers.

Anzaldúa offers her most extensive discussion of new mestiza consciousness in *Borderlands/La Frontera*, in which she devotes the final prose chapter, "*La conciencia de la mestiza*/Towards a New Consciousness," to the topic. Although the name "new mestiza consciousness" could imply that this epistemology comes automatically (naturally) to mestizas, Anzaldúa depicts its development as a volitional process—a way of thinking that emerges in dialogue with specific situations and through intentional choice. This process is neither easy nor pain-free. Drawing on her own experiences of alienation in the various cultures with which she interacted, as well as her work with a variety of identity-related progressive social justice groups, Anzaldúa explains that the new mestiza learns to live with conflicting Indian, Mexican, and Anglo worldviews "by developing a tolerance for contradictions, a tolerance for ambiguity. She learns to juggle cultures. She has a plural personality, she operates in a pluralistic mode—nothing is thrust out, the good the bad and the ugly, nothing rejected, nothing abandoned. Not only does she sustain contradictions, she turns the ambivalence into something else" (79). This complex epistemological process entails intense emotional and psychic pain as Anzaldúa/the new mestiza trains herself to coexist with uncertainty while negotiating among and within contradictory standpoints.

Importantly this willingness to immerse oneself in ambiguity and paradox rather than simply rejecting or accepting them initiates new mestiza consciousness and is key to its ability to produce new knowledge. Indeed, Anzaldúa viewed this emphasis on embracing contradiction as the distinction between new mestiza consciousness and mainstream twentieth-century feminist epistemologies: "Second-wave feminism developed its own epistemology in the process of consciousness / I suggest that a mestiza consciousness, a consciousness that comes from inhabiting contradictory locations simultaneously, can be a productive location for knowledge production because it challenges dualism & is flexible & tolerant of ambiguity" (Writing Notes I). When this willing immersion in contradictions becomes a deeply ingrained approach, we generate the patient open-mindedness necessary for epistemological transformation to occur. By tolerating contradictions, new mestiza consciousness expands perception, enabling the thinker to observe previously ignored perspectives mindfully. This act of careful attention functions synergistically, bringing new creative energy to the mix: "This assembly is not one where severed or separated pieces merely come together. Nor is it a balancing of opposing powers. In attempting to work out a synthesis, the self has added a third element which is greater than the sum of its several parts. That third element is a new consciousness—a mestiza consciousness—and though it is a source of intense pain, its energy comes from continual creative motion that keeps breaking down the unitary aspect of each new paradigm" (*Borderlands* 79–80). By allowing contradictions to coexist (though juxtaposed to and clashing with each other), we open possibilities for new constellations to occur.

Not surprisingly, given its name, new mestiza consciousness sometimes evokes identity-related questions about appropriation and respectful borrowing: Is new mestiza consciousness restricted to those who are, themselves, mestizas—racially/ethnically mixed people? Or is new mestiza consciousness potentially enacted by others (and, if so, by who)? This confusion is not surprising, given that Anzaldúa herself uses "new mestiza" in two distinct though overlapping ways, sometimes using the term for her own racial, ethnic, and cultural identity but other times using it more broadly to refer to a "liminal subject who lives in borderlands between cultures, races, languages, and genders" ("New Mestiza Nation").

Despite this potential confusion and possible debate, Anzaldúa offers the term up for generous, expansive interpretation and application. She does not associate new mestiza consciousness (or the new mestiza) exclusively with a single ethnic- or gender-specific group. Although she attributes the origins of this theory to her own experiences *as* a Chicana-mestiza, she is adamant that new mestiza consciousness can be developed, nurtured, and employed by diverse people. As she suggests in an interview shortly after *Borderlands'* publication,

I have called that space the Borderlands, but I have also called it mestiza consciousness. If you are a woman of color, a faggot or a dyke, if you are in any way marked by your society as different, you are forced to develop certain inner senses. This happens to all who have to cross borders into different worlds, into different classes. The mestiza or border crosser has to become sensitive to a lot of different things in order to survive and as a result her consciousness expands. It's like being put into a crucible and fired. It tempers you. I write about these experiences of growth and expansion and opening up, which are experiences that lead toward evolution. (qtd. in Baldwin 3)

Here she indicates that new mestiza consciousness often emerges in those people who do not fit in with the social status quo—whether by virtue of race, ethnicity, sexuality, belief, or any other type of difference (including psychic difference, as indicated by her reference to "certain inner senses"). Similarly, in "New Mestiza Nation" Anzaldúa distinguishes between "mestiza," which she describes as "an old term," and her "new mestiza." While both terms represent complex identity mixtures, the latter "is more inclusive than a racial mestizaje" and thus more disruptive of consensual reality: "The new mestiza is a category that threatens the hegemony of the neo-conservatives because it breaks down the labels and theories used to manipulate and control us. Punching holes in their categories, labels, and theories means punching holes in their walls." Anzaldúa returns to this distinction near the end of her life: "Mestisaje is not biological, the new mestiza is not a blood mestiza.—I failed to make this clear in *Borderlands*" (Writing Notes N).

NEW MESTIZA CONSCIOUSNESS'S STORY (ORIGINS AND DEVELOPMENT)

New mestiza consciousness predates the term itself. Like many other feminists of the mid-twentieth century, Anzaldúa viewed western Enlightenment thought as too limited and sought alternatives to it. From the late 1970s onward, she believed that in order to enact progressive social change, it was crucial to develop a new, holistic mode of consciousness that synthesized the spiritual with the political. As she writes in "Notes on El Mundo Surdo Essay," "[M]y interest is in how to use spiritual strength & insight into personal & global problems." Throughout the early 1980s, in her autohistorias, El Mundo Zurdo manuscript, poetry, and fiction, she critiqued dichotomous thought and explored alternatives. In "Esperando la serpiente con plumas (Waiting for the Feathered Serpent)," for example, she analyzes western philosophy's binary-oppositional framework, its division of "the world into two opposing forces, the spiritual and the material," and its elevation of the former over the latter. This division creates a "hierarchical and dualistic paradigm," or what Anzaldúa calls a "holy caste" that facilitates multiple forms of oppression:

> This "holy caste" relegates "spirit" to man and flesh to woman. It denies non-human creatures like cats feelings, consciousness, awareness, and imagination. It is the same caste that justified the enslavement of Blacks, the extermination of the Indian. It is the same one that justifies the wholesale slaughter of animals for food consumption. By denying us "heathens" *being* or *soul* they could exploit us without compunction. The holy caste system gives license to one set of people to project their inner demons onto another group. . . . In this paradigm lies the root of sexism and racism, classism and homophobia.

Because "*[t]his paradigm is killing us*" (her emphasis), she worked to develop a holistic alternative, drawing on a wide array of esoteric and Indigenous teachings, as well as transpersonal thought. This list in "Notes on El Mundo Surdo Essay" illustrates the direction in which Anzaldúa was moving at that time:

> The consciousness movement__.
> Indigenous mysticism
> Active imagination → entering past lives
> lost parts of the Self
> Personal myth, inner guidance
> live in harmony with highest & truest selves
> attunement process
> Experience with the divine & nature
> Contact with the divine

As this stream-of-consciousness list suggests, Anzaldúa strove to create an innovative epistemology with individual and collective implications, one that merged the sacred with the mundane.

Anzaldúa first used the phrase "mestiza consciousness" in a letter to Randy Conner dated November 2, 1982, as she discussed her autohistoria book project, "La serpiente que se come su cola," which she described as "about the shaping of a mestiza consciousness (mine)." However, at this point the phrase is simply descriptive—another way she refers to her own thought process. Anzaldúa did not return to the phrase "new mestiza consciousness" until developing *Borderlands'* prose section in 1986. As an analysis of the manuscript drafts reveals, this theory emerged slowly as she teased out the description of her own consciousness, describing herself as a "mestiza lesbian."

Particularly important here is that mestiza consciousness emerged from la facultad: in the earliest drafts, Anzaldúa does not mention new mestiza consciousness but instead focuses on la facultad, which she describes in language very similar to that which she later used for new mestiza consciousness. Indeed, a careful analysis of the drafts leading to the published version demonstrates this shift. The theory coalesced slowly through the revision process, as Anzaldúa depersonalized part of her discussion and shifted her focus from la facultad first into "conciencia of the mestiza" and then into "new mestiza consciousness."

Anzaldúa returned to her theory of new mestiza consciousness after *Borderlands'* publication, both to clarify the definition and to explore its intersections with contemporary western theory. After the book's publication, she was frequently asked to discuss new mestiza consciousness and to specify who could (or could not) enact it. From 1988 to 1990 or so, during her graduate work at UCSC and her creation of *Making Face, Making Soul/ Haciendo Caras*, Anzaldúa put new mestiza consciousness into dialogue with other US women of colors' theories, including Chela Sandoval's differential consciousness, Alice Walker's womanism, and Audre Lorde's house of difference. (See for instance drafts of her table of contents for this edited collection in 108.9). In part, this engagement was stimulated through her coursework and dissertation writing, as she grappled with poststructuralist and postmodernist analyses of subjectivity. While in many ways these poststructuralist subjectivities resonated with Anzaldúa's own experiences of lifelong multiplicity and fragmentation, mainstream postmodern scholars rarely, if ever, acknowledged women-of-colors theories and instead presented postmodern subjectivities as innovative and new. Anzaldúa critiqued this oversight in her dissertation chapters and elsewhere. In "Poet as Critic," for instance, she explored women-of-colors theorists' development of "a new kind of oppositional space" based on the oscillation between their "outsider position" and their access to (conventional theoretical) perspectives, describing it as "a poststructural terrain": "The theories of women of color point out a new kind of oppositional space of an outsider position that has access to perspectives and provides a new basis for coalition because of its oppositional practice (i.e., Sandoval's 'differential consciousness'). This new discursive space is a poststructural terrain (of overlapping spaces or Borderlands, house of difference, mestiza consciousness), a space the mestiza subject with her ability to cross borders and travel from one world to another can inhabit while at the same time be both inside and outside simultaneously occupying multiple sites, operating in multiple tracks while code switching." During this time Anzaldúa also began working with Shelley Fisher Fishkin to co-edit a collection of writings on new mestiza consciousness. (This project was never completed, perhaps due to Anzaldúa's struggles with diabetes.)

In the mid-1990s, as Anzaldúa delved more deeply into her exploration of border arte and expanded her theory of nepantla, she shifted her focus from new mestiza consciousness into more profound investigations of nepantla, nos/otras, and other theories. The term "mestiza consciousness" appears infrequently in Anzaldúa's copious writing notas from the 1990s, and it only appears twice in *Light in the Dark* (44, 141). However, this shift in names does not denote a shift away from the relational thought and holistic worldview that new mestiza consciousness represents but rather a deepening of it: By the mid-1990s, Anzaldúa seems to have incorporated new mestiza consciousness into nepantla. In both "Taller Nepantla" and "Nepantla: The Creative Process" (1995) she states that nepantla includes "a state of awareness, un conocimiento characterized by a sort of new mestiza consciousness"; in "Re-configuring Fronteras: New Navigations of Nepantla and the Cracks Between Worlds" (1996) she writes, "The future belongs to those who can not [*sic*] merely tolerate contradictions, cultural differences and ambiguity, but can use them to forge a new mestiza consciousness. Such a hybrid consciousness transcends the 'us' vs. 'them' mentality and carries us into a nos/otras position bridging different worlds and realities, of entering a place between the extremes of our cultures." By the end of her life, Anzaldúa had merged her theory of new mestiza consciousness into conocimiento and las nepantleras. She summarizes this shift in the final chapter of *Light in the Dark*:

> Tussling con remolinos (whirlwinds) of different belief systems builds the muscles of mestiza consciousness, enabling it to stretch. Being Chicana (indigenous, Mexican, Basque, Spanish, Berber Arab,

Gypsy) is no longer enough; being female, woman of color, patlache (queer) no longer suffices. Your resistance to identity boxes leads you to a different tribe, a different story (of mestizaje), enabling you to rethink yourself in more global-spiritual terms instead of conventional categories of color, class, career. It calls you to retribalize your identity to a more inclusive one, redefining what it means to be una mexicana de este lado, an American in the U.S., a citizen of the world, classifications reflecting an emerging planetary culture. In this narrative, national boundaries dividing us from the "others" (nos / otras) are porous, and the cracks between worlds serve as gateways. (141)

Given statements like this, it's uncertain that Anzaldúa would have returned to new mestiza consciousness had she lived longer—unless readers asked her questions about it, in which case she might have delved back into its implications.

RELATED THEORIES

- B/borderlands
- Coatlicue state
- conocimiento
- Coyolxauhqui process
- la facultad
- El Mundo Zurdo
- nepantla
- nepantlera
- new mestiza
- new tribalism
- nos/otras

FUTURE DIRECTIONS

- What can an analysis of Anzaldúa's early autohistorias teach us about new mestiza consciousness?
- How might Anzaldúa's interest in esoteric knowledge and practices have shaped her theory of new mestiza consciousness?
- What can an analysis of the drafts of *Borderlands* tell us about the evolution of new mestiza consciousness from la facultad?
- What's the relationship between Anzaldúa's theories of the borderlands and new mestiza consciousness?

- How might scholars' reception of new mestiza consciousness have impacted Anzaldúa's later work on the theory?
- What does an analysis of Anzaldúa's UCSC Lloronas dissertation chapters tell us about shifts in her definition of new mestiza consciousness in the late 1980s and early 1990s?
- What's the relationship between Anzaldúa's theories of nepantla and new mestiza consciousness? In what ways, if any, does her theorization of new mestiza consciousness change as she deepens her theory of nepantla?
- In what ways, if any, do Anzaldúa's theories of las nepantleras, nos/otras, and new tribalism impact her work with new mestiza consciousness?
- What can analysis of the many drafts of "now let us shift" tell us about the relationship between new mestiza consciousness and conocimiento?

USEFUL TEXTS
- *Borderlands* drafts
- "Esperando la serpiente con plumas"
- *Interviews/Entrevistas*
- *Light in the Dark/Luz en lo Oscuro*
- "Nepantla: The Creative Process"
- "Notes on El Mundo Surdo Essay"
- "Poet as Critic"
- "Re-conocimientos and Producing Knowledge: The Postmodern Llorona"
- "Reimaging Identities: The Geography of Nos/otras"
- "Taller Nepantla"
- "Writing outside the Story"
- Writing Notas I, N

New Tribalism

You hear la Llorona wail and the urge to do something about your condition takes you over. You realize that change is easier to go through if you stop resisting, let go, and sway with the shifting ground. You begin a regime of meditation, reflection, exercise, and writing, practices [with] which you call the scattered pieces of your soul back to your body. You start the arduous task of rebuilding yourself and of creating a story to match your new identity. You seek out allies, and together, create spiritual, political communities that struggle for personal growth and social justice. By compartiendo stories and ideas, you and your allies encourage reflective dialogue among people in various communities. You create a new tribalism.—"now let us shift. . . . the path of conocimiento. . . . inner work, public acts" (2000)[16]

Our goal is not to use differences to separate us from others, but neither is it to gloss over them. Many of us identify with groups and social positions not limited to our ethnic, racial, religious, class, gender, or national classifications. Though most people self-define by what they exclude, we define who we are by what we include—what I call the new tribalism. Though most of us live entremundos, between and among worlds, we are frustrated by those who step over the line, by hybridities and ambiguities, and by what does not fit our expectations of "race" and sex.—"(un)natural bridges" (2002)

DEFINITION

A post-*Borderlands* theory, new tribalism offers an innovative approach to individual and collective identity formation, identity shifts, and alliance-making. Typically, identity categories are based on oppositions: we define who we are by asserting who we are not, but in order to do so, we create inflexible boundaries between "us" and "them." With new tribalism, Anzaldúa replaces this binary-oppositional approach with an affinity-based, relational framework that acknowledges the boundaries between "us" and "them" but makes these boundaries permeable. New tribalism gives us a lens with which to view identities relationally—as influenced, shaped, and altered by both inner and outer people, environments, and events. Like her theory of the new mestiza, new tribalism replaces either/or modes of identity formation with a transformational both-and approach, as seen in Anzaldúa's assertion in *Light in the Dark*: "The new tribalism is about being part of but never subsumed by a group, never losing individuality to the group nor losing the group to the individual" (85). With new tribalism, Anzaldúa takes this holistic, transformational approach even further, moving beyond the human to offer expansive identity constellations. As with other identity-related theories like the new mestiza, nos/otras, and El Mundo Zurdo, new tribalism relies on relational definitions of difference. Here, Anzaldúa applies this relationality to questions of nationalism and other forms of separatism, exploring how we can acknowledge the value of ancestry (traditions, family, etc.) without reifying these cultural roots or in other ways using them like rigid barricades that impede our ability to connect with others. In part, new tribalism does this work by offering a more complicated understanding of identity "devoid of any kind of romantic illusions" ("New Mestiza Nation") or the conventional anthropocentric lens we typically use when exploring identity-related concerns.

As discussed below, new tribalism grows at least in part from Anzaldúa's desire to offer an alternative to assimilationism, on the one hand, and nationalism, on the other. Whereas assimilationist approaches to identity ignore differences and boundaries in an attempt to impose a single dominant standard and identity on everyone, new tribalism acknowledges the importance of identity-related differences and strives to create commonalities that honor these differences. The goal is not assimilation but careful transformation, where identities change relationally, based on experiences, encounters, and lessons learned. And, whereas separatist approaches to identity erect rigid boundaries around a specific identity, sharply demarcating insiders from outsiders and thus greatly inhibiting the possibility of developing alliances, new tribalism redefines these boundaries as permeable, allowing for interchange and allegiance among groups. New tribalism offers a porous nationalism—or what, in conversation with Inés Hernández-Ávila, Anzaldúa calls "nationalism . . . with a twist" (*Interviews* 185). Unlike conservative nationalisms that reify and revere the nation's or group's history and origins, new tribalism affirms history, origins, and roots while also embracing change, growth, and shifts. As Anzaldúa explains,

> Periods of being forced to assimilate, encouraged to forget all about the indigenous roots, alternate with periods of resistance—especially during the Chicano Movimiento, a nationalistic movement of claiming Chicanohood as central to our lives. It was followed by the movement dying down and un movimiento macha surging up. Chicana feminists, artists, activistas, and intellectuals, many of us dykes. We looked for something beyond just nationalism while continuing to connect to our roots. If we don't find the roots we need we invent them, which is fine because culture is invented anyway. We have returned to the tribe, but our nationalism is one with a twist. It's no longer the old kind of "I'm separated from this other group because I'm a Chicana so I therefore don't have anything to do with blacks or with Asians or whatever." It's saying "Yes I belong. I come from this particular tribe, but I'm open to interacting with these other people." I call this the New Tribalism. It's a kind of mestizaje that allows for connecting with other ethnic groups and interacting with other cultures and ideas. (*Interviews* 185)

New tribalism's synergistic both-and approach to individual and collective identity has important implications for alliance-making and community-building. As Anzaldúa asserts in *Light in the Dark*, "The new tribalism is about being part of but never subsumed by a group, never losing individuality to the group nor losing the group to the individual. The new tribalism is about working together to create new stories of identity and culture, to envision diverse futures. It's about rethinking our narratives of history, ancestry, and even of reality itself" (85). As this passage indicates, new tribalism acknowledges both the personal and the collective dimensions of selfhood and community in ways that can facilitate development of sustainable, radically inclusive communities.

Anzaldúa offers the most detailed discussion of new tribalism in "Geographies of Selves—Reimagining Identity: Nos/otras (Us/Other), las Nepantleras, and the New Tribalism," the fourth chapter of *Light in the Dark*, in which she applies it both to debates among Chicanx and Latinx and to other individual, cultural, and planetary identity-related issues. She uses the analogy of a huge tree (el árbol de la vida) with deep roots, a thick trunk, and many branches to illustrate her theory: "Roots represent ancestral/racial origins and biological attributes; branches and leaves represent the characteristics, communities, and cultures that surround us, that we've adopted, and that we're in intimate conversation with. Onto the trunk de mi árbol de la vida I graft a new tribalism. This new tribalism, like other new Chicano/Latino narratives, recognizes that we are responsible participants in the ecosystems (complete set of interrelationships between a network of living organisms and their physical habitats) in whose web we're individual strands" (67). New tribalism here serves as a mechanism with which one can reevaluate one's identity and more intentionally move through the world. More specifically, and to work with Anzaldúa's analogy, when we enact new tribalism we embrace our roots (which include ancestral traditions, genetics, environment, lineage, and much more) that shaped us as we grow—expanding our trunk and allowing new branches and leaves to unfurl. Here, new tribalism could also be described as a relational autonomy that exceeds the human, linking us with the beyond-human world.

Anzaldúa explores ways to foster new tribalism in *Light in the Dark*, in which she associates its emergence with soul loss and shadow work (89–90). She suggests that we can develop new tribalism by approaching each situation with self-reflection and flexibility: sometimes our boundaries are porous, but other times they are not; as she explains in an early draft of "now let us shift," "The new tribalism asks that you step outside your biological and cultural tribe, but keep your root identity and your tribe of origin and make changes to it, and you add other tribes to the trunk of your tree of life, like you would graft other types of trees." Importantly, new tribalism's self-reflection does not occur in isolation but, rather, the "self" who reflects does so in community, with others: "The new tribalism is about working together to create new 'stories' of identity and culture, to envision diverse futures. It's about rethinking our narratives of history, ancestry, and even of reality itself" (*Light* 85). This rethinking is deeply relational and expansive, exceeding consensual reality. At its most innovative, new tribalism represents an approach to identity that includes both the human and the more-than-human.

Despite the theory's visionary, forward-looking components and its origins in Anzaldúa's desire to disrupt oppressive power dynamics, the term itself (particularly the word "tribalism") can prevent readers from investigating its innovative dimensions and radical potential. However, as a reading of "Speaking across the Divide" suggests, Anzaldúa works carefully to distinguish her reference to mestizaje and Indigeneity from romanticized appropriations of the concept and term.

NEW TRIBALISM'S STORY (ORIGINS AND DEVELOPMENT)

Although Anzaldúa did not mention new tribalism until 1991, it has a precursor of sorts in her late 1970s and early 1980s calls to "gather the tribe," which she discussed in interviews and early manuscripts. This "tribe" consisted of like-minded souls, people who—regardless of cultural/racial/gender/sexual identity—would work together to heal and in other ways transform the planet. As she writes in "La serpiente que se come su cola,"

> We journey alone, in pairs, groups, nations. La camarada. La Palomilla. Reunión de las tribus. The red race, la raza cosmica (Chicanos), the black raze [*sic*], the yellow race, the white race
> a tribalism of choice.
> a new kind of tribe.

This gathering was composed of "kindred spirits" who shared a similar holistic consciousness and desire for planetary healing, a "cooperation between all species of life, a symbiosis." New tribalism also emerged, at least in part, from personal experiences: the many years that Anzaldúa wrestled with her competing urges to claim, shape, and assert her own mestizaje tejana identity; her realization that this identity—as well as other socially invented and inscribed identities—were too limited to completely represent us; scholars' (mis)reading of Indigeneity in *Borderlands*; and the boundary-policing and other limitations in Chicano and Chicana nationalism. Anzaldúa especially uses new tribalism in dialogue with nationalist movements' restrictive approaches to identity. As she explains in her interview with Debra Blake and Carmen Abrego, her involvement with various anticolonial movements during the 1970s felt too narrow. It was

> an important nationalistic movement for Chicanos, . . . but it didn't address the oppression of women. Our struggle focused on securing the culture, securing the race, but to me it felt like the movement was trying to secure the *male* part of the culture, the male ideology. I was critical of this nationalistic movement but I didn't quite know why. As I came into feminism and began reading—when I became a lesbian, when I had a little more time to grow—I realized it wasn't enough to fight, to struggle for one's nationality; one also had to struggle for one's gender, for one's sexual preference, for one's class and for those of all people. These issues weren't addressed in any of the nationalist movements because they struggled for ethnic survival and, because the male leaders felt threatened by these challenges women presented, they ignored them. (*Interviews* 214–15)

It was not until 1991 and in direct conversation with a misinterpretation of *Borderlands* that Anzaldúa arrived at the term "new tribalism." In "Professional Aztecs and Popular Culture," David Rieff criticized Anzaldúa as a "professional Aztec," implying that she romanticized Indigeneity to elevate her career, enacting what he called a "new tribalism." Rather than angrily protest his misinterpretation and point out the irony (e.g., that what Rieff names a "new tribalism" is actually the *old* nationalist tribalism that Anzaldúa herself had rejected years ago and critiqued in *Borderlands*), Anzaldúa adopted Rieff's term but expanded it. As she explains in her 1999 talk at the University of Illinois, Urbana-Champaign, "Nos/otros: 'Us' vs. 'Them,' (Des)Conocimientos y compromisos," "I've taken over the term, and I've used it as something more inclusive. The old tribe is the Mexicano here, the Puerto Rican there. The new tribe is all of us together. But we can't lose site [*sic*] of where we came from, so how can you maintain your borders, but still open them up. And if you find out, then tell me, because I sure would like to know." As this bluntly honest final sentence suggests, in 1999 Anzaldúa was still formulating this theory by living the questions it evoked: How do we maintain connections and allegiance with our home communities but also expand outward, creating porous, permeable boundaries and networks of connections?

The 9/11 terrorist attacks, Anzaldúa's work co-editing *this bridge we call home*, and her theorizing of conocimiento and nepantleras gave her ample opportunities to continue exploring these and related questions. What began as an effort to articulate a nonromanticized understanding of Indigeneity, origins, and ancestral ties expanded into a theory of inclusive identity formation and alliance-building, as Anzaldúa drew on her experiences with diverse groups to theorize identities and coalitions that address differences relationally in ways that neither create dichotomous divisions nor blur everything into homogeneity. During the final years of her life she expanded new tribalism in several ways. First, she intentionally included white-raced people. As she states in her preface to the 2002 edition of *This Bridge Called My Back*, "The new tribalism includes white and non white. Not to do so invites separatism and hostilities. It's a tribalization that includes everyone. To exclude is to close the bridge." Second, she moved beyond race to encompass additional social identity categories as well (*Light* 156). Third, she went beyond *social* identity categories to include a spiritual component. And fourth, she investigated how we might create a new tribalism through mindfully, selectively examining individual and collective self-definitions (*Light*, 65–94). Had she lived longer, it's possible that Anzaldúa would have continued exploring innovative forms of new tribalism. However, given twenty-first-century associations of "tribe" and "tribalism" with Indigenous groups and Indigenous organizing, as well as the desconocimientos often indicated by recent non-Indigenous uses of the term, it's questionable whether Anzaldúa would have developed it further *as* "new tribalism" or whether she would have invented another way to name this theory.

RELATED THEORIES

- B/borderlands
- conocimiento
- geographies of selves
- El Mundo Zurdo

- nepantla
- nepantlera
- new mestiza
- new mestiza consciousness
- nos/otras

FUTURE DIRECTIONS

- What can an analysis of Anzaldúa's early autohistorias teach us about her theory of new tribalism?
- What's the relationship between Anzaldúa's theories of new tribalism and new mestiza?[17]
- What's the relationship between new tribalism and conocimiento?
- How does Anzaldúa's development of new tribalism illustrate a post-oppositional approach to academic critiques?
- What can an analysis of the many drafts of "Geographies of Selves" teach us about this theory?
- In what ways might new tribalism be related to Anzaldúa's discussions of retribalization (cf. *Light* 151–52)?
- Where might Anzaldúa have taken this concept, had she lived longer? How might she have addressed the ways some scholars used her theory against her, to accuse her of appropriation?
- In her analogy of new tribalism as el árbol de la vida, Anzaldúa grafts new tribalism onto the trunk, rather than a branch (*Light* 66). What are the implications of this location?
- What can new tribalism teach us about twenty-first-century identity politics?
- How might the approach to identity put forward in new tribalism be used to formulate and enact planetary citizenship?
- Should the term "tribalism" be retired, given its problematic associations when applied to non-Indigenous peoples?

USEFUL TEXTS

- "(Des)Conocimientos: Resisting New Forms of Domination/Oppression"
- "Esperando la serpiente con plumas"
- "Foreword: lessons from the firing"
- *Interviews/Entrevistas*

- *Light in the Dark/Luz en lo Oscuro*
- "Nepantla: The Creative Process"
- "The New Mestiza Nation"
- "Nos/otras: Theorizing Mestisaje"
- "Nos/otros: 'Us' vs. 'Them,' (Des)Conocimientos y compromisos"
- "Notes on El Mundo Surdo Essay"
- "now let us shift. . . . the path of conocimiento. . . . inner work, public acts"
- "Proving Ground: La artista y su comunidad"
- "Queers of Color"
- "La serpiente que se come su cola"
- "Speaking across the Divide"
- Writing Notas 107.3, 107.12, 108.3
- Writing Notas K, N

Nos/Otras

The Spanish word "nosotras" means "us." In theorizing insider/outsider I write the word with a slash between nos (us) and otras (others). Today the division between the majority of "us" and "them" is still intact. . . . Hopefully, sometime in the future we may become nosotras without the slash.—*Interviews/Entrevistas* (1996)

Nos/otras is my narrative of self and others, an imaginary map/topography of Otherness, a story of alterity. Nos/otras is my symbol for this divide (and future bridge), and for the hope that someday we will have removed completely the slash between "nos" and "otras." The slash can be a chasm whose origin is ignorance, lack of awareness and knowledge—in other words desconocimientos. Or it can be the bridge between the two. . . . The concept of nos/otras claims an identity beyond that of other—neither black or white but racially mixed. It disrupts binary oppositions that reinforce relations of subordination/dominance, other/subject, them/us. In nos/otras the boundaries are blurred, subjectivity is fluid and mobile.—"Geography of Selves" (2003)

DEFINITION

A visionary, post-*Borderlands* theory, nos/otras offers an inclusive framework to explore identity, community, and alliance-building in ways that acknowledge commonalities, complicity, and differences. "Nosotras," the Spanish word for the feminine "we," implies a collective identity or consciousness—a community of sorts. By partially dividing "nosotras" into two, Anzaldúa affirms this collective while also acknowledging the differences among people (*nos* implies *us*, while *otras* implies *others*). Joined together, nos + otras holds the promise of healing: we contain the others, and the others contain us. Significantly, nos/otras does not represent assimilation or sameness; the differences among us still exist, but they function dialogically, enabling us to also recognize previously hidden commonalities and, ideally, create new connections. Nos/otras offers an alternative to binary self/other constellations, a philosophy and praxis with which to acknowledge, bridge, and sometimes transform the distances between self and other.

As with some of her other later theories (especially new tribalism and geographies of selves), nos/otras also represents Anzaldúa's attempt to offer alternative "identity narratives"—ways to conceive identity that don't simply adopt existing social scripts but instead simultaneously critique and transform them. Here, she creates an alternative to dichotomous self/other configurations in which we shore up our personal identities by "othering" those who are not "like" us. As Anzaldúa asserts in *Light in the Dark*, "As an identity narrative, nos/otras has the potential to overturn definitions of otherness. When we examine the us/them binary deeply, we find that otra-ness may be deceptive, merely a cage we assign to others" (81). By redefining self/other in less binary terms, Anzaldúa's theory opens points of connection among diverse groups, including those typically othered. Nos/otras thus functions as an invitation to reflect more deeply on our assumptions about identity and group formation. As Anzaldúa explains in *Light in the Dark*, "According to Buddhism, the primal distinction between self and other is illusory because the existence of self is, itself, an illusion. This distinction is responsible for all evil and sorrow. There is no wrong, no vice, no evil in this world, except what flows from the assertion of entirely independent selfhood. There are no 'otras'—we all emerge from humanity's basic shared, communal ground, an emotional-spiritual ground of being. Nos/otras (as the slash becomes increasingly permeable) puede ser el nuevo nombre de seres que escapan de jaulas" (81). Nos/otras erodes the belief in pure otherness without denying or ignoring the experiences of being othered or the unjust power dynamics that reify otherness in many areas of life.

Nos/otras serves several interrelated functions: First, it redefines the "other" in less dichotomous terms. In western identity configurations, self and other are defined oppositionally: I define who I am (my "self") by what and who I am not (the other). In this binary frame, self and other are entirely distinct; there is no overlap, no merger, no shared commonality. Nos/otras blurs this division by locating the other in the self, and the self in the other. Second, nos/otras offers a nuanced approach to issues of complicity, as explained below in more detail. And third, nos/otras facilitates coalition-building. As Anzaldúa asserts in "Us/Them . . . The Commitment and the New Tribalism," "Nos/otros is my attempt to change the story of who we are, rewrite cultural inscriptions, and facilitate our forging alliances with other groups."

NOS/OTRAS' STORY (ORIGINS AND DEVELOPMENT)

Although the theory of nos/otras did not emerge until the 1990s, it could be described as a continuation of Anzaldúa's attempts to disentangle questions of otherness, complicity, community-building, and transformation that she worked on throughout her career. The terms "nos/otras" and "nos/otros" (which at times Anzaldúa seems to have used almost interchangeably) grew from her engagement with postcolonial theory during her graduate studies at the University of California, Santa Cruz, as she explored and, eventually, critiqued the self/other configurations that developed during colonialism. In her 1991 draft, "Mujeres que tienen lengua: Living under the Shadow of Silence—A Response to Columbus' Re/Discovery," she accuses Columbus of inventing the language of otherness and imposing it on herself and her mestiza sisters, justifying the conquest and uneven power dynamics while creating a profound sense of alienation and otherness that they internalized:

> Esa es una de tus legacias, Colón. Hemos interiorizado las falsas es-
> teriotipos, estamos enjauladas en ellos, hechas siempre "otras." Tu
> en tus cartas nos inventates como "otros" y "otras" tan diferentes de
> ustedes para excusar, desculpar, y racionalizar la conquista.
> [That is one of your legacies, Columbus. We have internalized the
> false stereotypes, we are caged in them, always made "others." You in
> your letters invented us as "others" and "others" so different from you
> to excuse, denounce, and rationalize the conquest.]

However, unlike many postcolonial and marginalized theorists of that time, Anzaldúa did not simply adopt this label of otherness and speak as the other. Instead, she questioned this stance as overly tainted by the colonial frameworks that they were trying to critique. As she notes in a later version of the same essay, when postcolonial theorists adopt the voice of "the other," they unintentionally adopt the colonizer's worldview; they use dichotomous thinking and remain trapped in the discourse they aspire to overturn. Moreover, this stark division between colonized and colonizer oversimplifies: "There is *No real Other*. The voice of the Other is contaminated and mediated by colonialism. No 'pure' Other can exist in a hybrid, multicultural society" (59.6). This statement reflects Anzaldúa's profound recognition that monolithic concepts of purity reflect falsehoods used by those in power to impose hierarchical structures like the self/other division. As she asserts in a late draft of her "Geographies of Selves" chapter, "The traditional assigning of the 'nos' to the good guys and 'otras' to the bad guys doesn't work (and has never worked). Though the divide has always been racialized to favor 'whites,' at one time or another all of us are on both sides of the divide."

In her search for a term that troubled but did not erase these self/other configurations, Anzaldúa arrived at "nos/otras." She explains its origins in the Q&A following her 1992 lecture, "Talk on Multiculturalism":

> Do you know what nosotras means? Otras means others. Nos means us. . . . It was the Europeans who started using the term and theory of "other" and "otherness." . . . [S]o we became "others" and we have taken that term and used it but it is not a good term. Not any more. So what I have taken is nos/otras. Put it together with a slash. . . . I am trying to come up with concepts and theories that get us out of the binary them/us, subject/object because that is a trap. You get sort of trapped between the binary, the dichotomy. It is not two.

Here we see an important part of Anzaldúa's motivation: the desire to avoid and move beyond binary identity categories and dichotomous thinking without simplistically positing sameness. She sought fresh alternatives.

In the mid-1990s, as she interacted with ongoing debates in the United States concerning the culture wars and identity politics, Anzaldúa expanded her theory of nos/otras to explore how twentieth-century colonialism had blurred the boundary between self and other. As she explains in an interview with Andrea Lunsford, by virtue of our immersion in the dominant culture's worldview (education, media, etc.), the sharp division has been eroded:

> It used to be that there was a "them" and an "us." We were over here; we were the "other" with other lives, and the "nos" was the subject,

the white man. There was a very clear distinction. But as the decades have gone by, we—the colonized, the Chicanos, the blacks, the Natives in this country—have been reared in this frame of reference, in this field. So all of our education, all of our ideas come from this frame of reference. We are complicitous for being in such close proximity and intimacy with the other. Now "us" and "them" are interchangeable. Now there is no such thing as an "other." The other is in you; the other is in me. This white culture has been internalized in my head. I have a white man and woman in here, and they have me in their heads, even if it's just a guilty little nudge sometimes. (*Interviews* 254)

These blurred boundaries have important implications for social justice work: without mindful attention, unacknowledged complicity in the dominant epistemology drives our critiques, thus undermining our attempts to effect progressive structural change. Similarly, in "(Des)Conocimientos: Resisting New Forms of Domination/Oppression" she explores "The Complicity of Nos/Otras," suggesting that as we innovate our identities we must be wary of importing western and masculinist assumptions.

With her theory of nos/otras, Anzaldúa mindfully approached this challenge by recognizing, exploring, and in other ways working intentionally with self/other divisions: "I try to articulate ideas from that place of occupying both territories: the territory of my past and my ethnic community—my home community, the Chicano Spanish, the Spanglish—and the territory of the formal education, the philosophical, educational, and political ideas I've internalized just by being alive. Both of these traditions are inherent in me. I cannot disown the white tradition, the Euro-American tradition, any more than I can the Mexican, the Latino, or the Native, because they are all in me" (*Interviews* 254). By acknowledging (rather than disavowing) these contradictory territories and traditions, she attains "the nos/otras position of being simultaneously both insider/outsider." This liminality energizes her relational epistemology: "The future belongs to those who can not merely tolerate contradictions, cultural differences and ambiguity, but can use them to forge a new mestiza consciousness. Such a hybrid consciousness transcends the 'us' vs. 'them' mentality and carries us into a nos/otras position bridging different worlds and realities, of entering a place between the extremes of our cultures" ("Navigating Nepantla").

By the late 1990s Anzaldúa had further deepened her theory of nos/otras. Invited to speak at the "Territories and Boundaries: Geographies of

Latinidad" conference at the University of Illinois, Urbana-Champaign, she put nos/otras into dialogue with other theories she was developing at that time (desconocimientos, new tribalism, and conocimiento) to explore identity politics debates. In her keynote, "Nos/otros: 'Us' vs. 'Them' . . . (Des) Conocimientos y compromisos," she presented this theory as a vehicle to assist in identity reconstruction and alliance-building: "not an alternative to identity politics but in conjunction"—an approach to alliance-building among differently situated groups. When we work from a nos/otras position, we don't just work with those from our specific identity group. Nor do we view those outside our group in oppositional terms; instead, we use compassion and imagination, exploring events and situations from their perspectives. As her keynote suggests, although Anzaldúa almost always referred to this theory as "nos/otras," she occasionally used the terms "nos/otros" and "nos/otras" almost interchangeably while discussing it. Even as late as 2004, she asserts that she "alternate[s] between nos/otras and nos/otros."[18] Although Anzaldúa does not explain why she shifts between the two, her fluid terminology points to this theory's inclusiveness; while it has gender-related implications, it goes beyond gender to include other forms of identity as well. (*Had she lived longer, it's likely that she might have replaced both terms with "nos/otrxs."*)

Importantly, Anzaldúa does not use her theory of nos/otras simply for critique but instead to intervene in and offer alternative perspectives. We see this interventionist approach in the close association Anzaldúa draws between nos/otras and desconocimientos—defined in her Urbana keynote as the willed ignorance and/or reluctance to learn about those we consider to be our others, which can lead to divisions. Desconocimientos functions as both the problem and the potential solution: it's the division between self and other but also a map toward healing. As Anzaldúa revised the lecture transcript, converting it into a dissertation/book chapter for *Light in the Dark*, she focused on the slash between "nos" and "otras," describing it as "the divides, chasms, and clashes between us originating from los desconocimientos." Rather than ignore, erase, or in any way diminish this gap, she dives into it and suggests that "[t]he slash (la rajadura) gives us a third point of view, a perspective from the cracks and a way of re-configuring ourselves as subjects outside binary opposition, outside existing domination relations." By focusing on (*by excavating, exploring, and working to transform*) our desconocimientos, we can redefine ourselves (our nos/otras) in increasingly complicated terms. In later drafts Anzaldúa underscores this point: "Our identity is complex; it consists of irreconcilable positions such as the 'us' and the 'not us.' As nos/otras our identity blurs the boundary between us and them. We are both subject and object, self and other, have's and have-not's, conqueror and conquered, and oppressor and oppressed. The clash of cultures is enacted within our psyches, resulting in an uncertain position. We can't lock-down our identities [into] tidy and simple categories. Many of us defy binaries—gender, race, class, sexuality. Many of us reside in multiple realities" ("Nos/otros: Us/Them"). With nos/otras, Anzaldúa embraces the contradictions, locating them within herself and others who "reside in multiple realities." She does so not by romanticizing this embrace but by acknowledging the challenges that nos/otras experience.

Near the end of her life Anzaldúa extended nos/otras into "the nos/otras imperative": the drive to address and heal the division between us and them. Had she lived longer, she might have explored this imperative, investigating the effort required to create new forms of identity and community by "removing the slash" between self and other (*Light* 85). To do so requires innovative identity narratives, like her geographies of selves, coupled with the willingness to forge new communities (or what she called new tribalisms). It's likely that Anzaldúa would have continued exploring nos/otras, especially in dialogue with the metaphysics of spirit, nepantla, and nepantleras. In 1999 she added a metaphysical dimension, describing nos/otras as the "[s]plit between the physical self and spiritual self, between humans and the environment where the body is punished and undervalued, and the spirit is elevated" (Writing Notas J). In a March 2003 draft of *Light in the Dark*'s fourth chapter, she associates the slash between self and other with nepantla and suggests that diving into the division offers a way through it.

RELATED THEORIES

- conocimiento
- desconocimiento
- geographies of selves
- nepantla
- nepantleras
- new mestiza
- new mestiza consciousness
- new tribalism
- spiritual activism

- What does an analysis of nos/otras' development from 1991 until Anzaldúa's death tell us about the theory and about Anzaldúa's theorizing method?
- What does an analysis of Anzaldúa's UCSC Lloronas dissertation drafts teach us about nos/otras?
- What is the relationship between nos/otras and new tribalism?
- How does desconocimientos function in nos/otras? What can we learn about both theories by reading them in dialogue?
- What is the relationship between nos/otras and geographies of selves? In what ways, if any, does nos/otras energize or function in geographies of selves?
- How might nos/otras enable us to develop additional forms of identity politics?
- What shapes and motivates the nos/otras imperative; is it internally driven, externally imposed, or some combination of the two?
- How can we expand Anzaldúa's explorations of the nos/otras imperative?
- How might we apply Anzaldúa's critique of postcolonial theory to twenty-first-century versions of decoloniality?

USEFUL TEXTS

- *"Carta a Colón: Surpassing the Tongue—Lloronas que tienen manos, 500 Years of Resistance"*
- "counsels from the firing . . . past, present, future"
- "(Des)Conocimientos: Resisting New Forms of Domination/ Oppression"
- "Geographies of Selves—Reimagining Identities: Nos/Otras (Us/ Other), las Nepantleras and the New Tribalism"
- *Interviews/Entrevistas*
- *Light in the Dark/Luz en lo Oscuro*
- "Mujeres que tienen lengua: Living under the Shadow of Silence—A Response to Columbus' Re/Discovery"
- "Navigating Nepantla and the Cracks between the Worlds"
- "New Mestiza Nation"
- "Nos/otras: The Split and How to Bridge It"
- "Nos/otros: 'Us' vs. 'Them,' (Des)Conocimientos y compromisos"

- "Notes—CONOCIMIENTO"
- "Notes for Reimagining Identities"
- "Reimaging Identities: The Geography of Our Many Selves"
- "Subject to Changes: Mestiza Identities and Positionings"
- "Talk on Multiculturalism"
- Writing Notas J, L, M

Spiritual Activism

Spiritual work is a feminist political and spiritual issue. Become a spiritual activist, not only to cope with the stresses and traumas of daily life, with external and internal oppression but to connect with other people, other aware species like animals and trees, with the living organism that is the Earth.—"Spiritual Mestisaje Drafts" (1996)

The inner/outer work makes bridges between the life of the mind, the life of the body, and the life of the spirit, the life of the collective. In the moments of connection between the inner and outer worlds the soul and the physical world come together, intersect. Spiritual activism stitches the two fabrics together. It advocates direct communication, not direct confrontation.—"Nepantla: Creative Acts of Vision" (2002)

DEFINITION

One of Anzaldúa's signature theories, spiritual activism is a politics of spirit that offers a holistic approach to social change with metaphysical/onto-logical, epistemological, ethical, and aesthetic components. Anzaldúa's oft-quoted statement, "I change myself, I change the world," could be spiritual activism's slogan. Although Anzaldúa did not coin the term "spiritual activism," she was instrumental in bringing it into academic feminist discourse. She began developing the philosophy and ethics it represents early in her career and used the term frequently in her twenty-first-century writings to describe her politics of spirit—a visionary, experientially based ontology, epistemology, and ethics grounded in and based on a metaphysics of radical interconnectedness. At the ontological level, spiritual activism ensures (and explains) our ability to interact with and transform both inner and outer realities. Anzaldúa associates spiritual activism's ontology with Indigenous philosophies, esoteric teachings, and her own nonwestern mestizaje cultural traditions, describing spiritual activism as an inheritance from her cultures (*Light* 10). At the epistemological level, spiritual activism incorporates relational modes of thinking that engage body, soul, spirit, and mind. This holistic epistemology embraces contradiction; questions and "sees through" the status quo (or what Anzaldúa calls "consensual reality"); accesses additional dimensions of reality; and makes meaning through dialogic engagement with inner and outer worlds. At the ethical level, spiritual activism requires concrete actions designed to intervene in and transform existing social conditions.

Spiritual activism is distinct from organized (institutional) religion, commodified "New Age" spiritualities, and spiritual bypassing. Unlike organized religions, which typically rely on some type of hierarchical framework that imposes authority on individuals through external teachings, texts, standards, and/or leaders, Anzaldúa's spiritual activism is nonhierarchical. It locates authority within each individual who, through careful self-reflection and the use of spiritual technologies, listens closely for inner guidance while also reading the outer world for insights, messages, information, and other forms of alignment.[19] As Anzaldúa asserts, "Our spirituality does not come from outside ourselves. It emerges when we listen to the 'small still voice' (Teish) within us which can empower us to create actual change in the world" ("El Mundo Zurdo: The Vision" 195). Unlike "New Age" belief systems that focus almost, if not entirely, on the personal and thus leave the existing oppressive social structures in place, spiritual activism—by definition—associates the personal with the collective in order to "create actual change in the world" by exposing, challenging, and transforming unjust social structures. Indeed, by making "activism" the noun (and the key topic) and "spiritual" the adjective modifying the noun, Anzaldúa foregrounds the world-changing component. The term itself reminds us that spiritual activism is not passive. And unlike spiritual bypassing, which uses spirituality as a way to avoid acknowledging—let alone addressing—social injustice, spiritual activism insists that we must work to transform the outer world. There is no room in spiritual activism for what Anzaldúa calls "Pollyanna-like sentiments disconnected from the grounded realities of people's lives and struggles" (Light 39). Indeed, as the closely related theories of the Coatlicue state and the Coyolxauhqui process suggest, spiritual activism includes shadow work; it encourages us to dive into, rather than avoid, the painful, wounding dimensions of our lives and the external worlds in which we live.

Anzaldúa describes those who adopt and/or enact spiritual activism as nepantleras and spiritual activists. Spiritual activism empowers these practitioners in many ways: it offers a mechanism to foster self-knowledge, self-love, and self-confidence; provides tools (spiritual technologies) to create innovative insights and produce transformational knowledge; and facilitates the development of new strategies and tactics for social change. Spiritual activism also fosters resilience in social activists in several ways: First, spiritual activism includes self-care as part of political practice. Second, spiritual activism offers new modes of connection enabling spiritual activists to create alliances and communities that replenish and support them. And third, spiritual activism inspires them to keep working toward transformation. By positing a spirit-infused world, spiritual activists can sustain a hopeful yet realistic outlook. Spiritual activism is spirituality for social change, spirituality that recognizes the many differences among us yet insists on our commonalities and uses these commonalities as catalysts for transformation.

Despite spirit's foundational role in spiritual activism (*and its ubiquity in the theory itself*), Anzaldúa does not define the term. It is, in fact, almost the reverse. Throughout her explorations of spiritual activism, she moves among various spirit-inflected words like "body," "mind," "spirituality," "vibration," "energy," and "soul," confounding readers' attempts to pin down her definition. In *Light in the Dark*, for example, she describes nature as "alive and conscious" and the entire world as "ensouled," attributing this sentience to "spirit, a presence, force, power, and energy within and without." This spirit/presence/power/force is ubiquitous: "Spirit infuses all that exists—organic and inorganic—transcending the categories and concepts that govern your perception of material reality. Spirit speaks through your mouth, listens through your ears, sees through your eyes, touches with your hands" (136–37). As this passage implies, spirit is all around (and within) us; however, it exceeds human definition. Moreover, for Anzaldúa the specific words we use to describe this ubiquitous force are much less important than the creative, sustaining, and potentially transformative work it does in the world.

SPIRITUAL ACTIVISM'S STORY (ORIGINS AND DEVELOPMENT)

Although Anzaldúa did not use the term "spiritual activism" in her work until 1996, its roots run much deeper—anchored in her childhood psychic experiences, nurtured through family stories and ancestral guidance, and developed in her writings from the late 1970s and early 1980s. Indeed, one could argue that she steadily developed this theory-praxis throughout her career. Early in her activist work Anzaldúa was dissatisfied with conventional progressive politics and determined to create a politics of spirit, or what she sometimes referred to as "El Mundo Surdo," that could embolden the individual, create new coalitions, and effect social change. In early book-length manuscripts like "Poetry & Magick: A Practicum for Developing Literary+Psychic Skills," "Esperando la serpiente con plumas," "La serpiente que se come su cola," and "Notes on El Mundo Surdo Essay," she explored key traits that later make their way into her formulation of spiritual activism: The entwinement of spirit and politics into a "sacred politica" and "spirit warrior"; the synthesis of mind, body, spirit, and soul into a "new Heresy, a politics of body-mind-and-spirit"; and the belief that change begins with the individual but moves outward ("one begins at ground zero, with the masses, with the individual. The change has to take place there first")—to name a few. During the early 1980s Anzaldúa drew on an array of esoteric teachings and occult wisdom traditions to support her political metaphysics.[20] She believed that occult practices offer access into alternate realities and wisdom traditions with information that can empower contemporary social justice activists: "[W]e can access these realities, pull knowledge & power, & use it to make change" ("La serpiente"). In "La Oya," a 1982 talk for Salsa Soul Sisters, she asserts that we each have a "divine spark" and a calling: "Everyone has a task in life, a destiny. The reason why they incarnated into this lifetime was to perform this task and thereby grow, evolve."

Prior to using the term "spiritual activism," Anzaldúa referred to herself as a "spiritual activist" in 1996 drafts of "Spiritual Mestizaje," the foreword to Randy Conner, David Hatfield Sparks, and Mariya Sparks's book, *Cassell's Encyclopedia of Queer Myth, Symbol and Spirit: Gay, Lesbian, Bisexual and Transgender Lore.* Associating spiritual activism with personal survival and collective coalition work, she explained that she became a spiritual activist in order to "cope with" microaggressions and small wounds (the "stresses and traumas of daily life"), as well as the larger wounds caused by external and internalized oppression. She used the term "spiritual activism" two years later, in a 1998 conversation with me, as she elaborated on her philosophy of conocimiento: "The work of conocimiento—consciousness work—connects the inner life of the mind and spirit to the outer worlds of action" (*Interviews* 178). During the late 1990s, as Anzaldúa developed conocimiento's seven stages, she explored it in terms that would later overlap with her discussions of spiritual activism.

Around 1999 or so, Anzaldúa developed spiritual activism *as* a theory—rather than simply a useful description (for herself and her work). We see this intentionality in two pre-drafts, both titled "Spiritual Activism." As discussed in chapter 2, pre-drafts functioned as the ground of thought and theory development for Anzaldúa. When she set out to invent a new theory or write a new piece, she amassed material that she might include. Although neither pre-draft references "spiritual activism" by name, they both consist of material related to the topic: excerpts from other manuscripts, including the earlier material mentioned previously, as well as personal experiences illustrating spiritual activism's unique combinations of social change politics and self-inquiry. Around this time Anzaldúa also associated spiritual activism with her early 1980s work on altar-making in "Spiritual Activism: Making Altares, Making Connections."

Anzaldúa brought the term "spiritual activism" into the world (though not in a big way) in her 1999 talk, "Nos/otros 'Us' vs. 'Them,' (Des)Conocimientos y compromisos," delivered at the Geographies of Latinidad conference. Describing spiritual activism as a component of conocimiento, she associated it with activists' self-care—that is, with the spiritual technologies and mindfulness practices required to prevent burnout and foster resilience:

> [C]onocimiento, to me, has a spiritual component. I call it spiritual activism. Politics are fine, we are all in a political struggle. But most of the people who accompanied me in my struggle, way back in the 60's, 70's, 80's, some of them have died, have fallen by the wayside, have burned out, have been disillusioned by the movement, have dropped out. I don't want you guys doing the same thing. I want you to take care of yourself. Which means, getting in touch with something in you that will nurture you. Self development has to go hand-in-hand with social transformation, social development. It has to be both the inner and the outer.

Once again, we see a foundational tenet of spiritual activism: the necessity of simultaneous inward- and outward-directed action, but at this point spiritual activism functions primarily as a component of conocimiento.

Around 2000, Anzaldúa began more fully articulating spiritual activism as a theory and praxis. She did so in dialogue with conocimiento and nepantleras—two other theories she was developing at that time. In part this focus was inspired through her work co-editing *this bridge we call home* and preparing her contributions for this book. Because Anzaldúa and I intentionally envisioned the book's final section to focus on and thus foster spiritual activism, Anzaldúa's own attention to this theory is unsurprising. By 2001, Anzaldúa had made spiritual activism a large part of her dissertation project, describing the dissertation's theme as ". . . Towards Spiritual Activism" (Writing Notas L). The final chapter of *Light in the Dark* contains Anzaldúa's most extensive published exploration of this theory. In it, she draws from earlier manuscripts, her experiences, and her fiction to unfold spiritual activism as part of (or perhaps *as*) conocimiento. Had she lived longer, it's likely that Anzaldúa would have continued developing this theory. Three possible directions would be putting spiritual activism into dialogue with her emergent theory of queer conocimiento; exploring spiritual activism's embodied dimensions (including those in spiritual activists' physical bodies); and/or articulating spiritual activism's ethics and aesthetics.

RELATED THEORIES

- Coatlicue state
- conocimiento
- Coyolxauhqui process
- la facultad
- El Mundo Zurdo
- nepantla
- nepantlera
- nos/otras

FUTURE DIRECTIONS

- What can analysis of Anzaldúa's early autohistorias teach us about spiritual activism and about Anzaldúa's politics of spirit, more generally?
- In "Esperando la serpiente con plumas," Anzaldúa calls for "guerrilleras divinas, divine warrior women and men"; in what ways do her spiritual activists answer this call?
- What can Anzaldúa's two pre-drafts titled "Spiritual Activism" teach us about her formulation of this theory?
- What's the relationship between new mestiza consciousness and spiritual activism?

- How can we use new mestiza consciousness as we enact spiritual activism?
- What is the relationship between spiritual activism and conocimiento?
- In Writing Notas K Anzaldúa offers a quick list of instructions to enact conocimiento (as she defined it at that time); what might these instructions teach us about how we can enact spiritual activism?
- In one of her many drafts of "now let us shift," Anzaldúa states that "la tarea of spiritual activism begins with the body." What are the implications of this statement? How might scholar-activists develop it further? How might Anzaldúa have developed it further, especially as she struggled with her physical health?
- What does it look like when we put identity politics and spiritual activism into dialogue? How might spiritual activism enable us to innovate contemporary identity politics?
- Given Anzaldúa's final writing notas, which explore and expand spiritual activism, where might she have taken the theory, had she lived longer?
- What roles can visionary thinking and optimism (à la José Esteban Muñoz) play in enacting Anzaldúan spiritual activism, especially considering statements like this, from an early draft of "now let us shift": "You begin to trust that there is enough of everything for each human being on the planet and that each person is equally responsible for shaping the future."
- Anzaldúa's "+notes-b" includes a section titled "how to train a spiritual activist," but unfortunately she did not live long enough to develop this training manual. Drawing on Anzaldúa's work (especially her discussions of nepantleras), what might an intentional training for spiritual activists look like? What would we include? What would we aspire to instill in our trainees?

USEFUL TEXTS
- "+notes-b"
- "Altares: On the Process of Feminist Image Making"
- "Esperando la serpiente con plumas"

- "En estilo mestisaje—In the Writing I Cross Genres, I Cross Borders"
- "Conocimientos: Creative Acts of Vision, Inner Works, Public Acts"
- "Conocimientos, Now Let Us Shift: Inner Work and Public Acts"
- "Holding Together"
- *Light in the Dark/Luz en lo Oscuro*
- "Nepantla: Creative Acts of Vision"
- "Nos/otros 'Us' vs. 'Them,' (Des)Conocimientos y compromisos"
- "Notes on El Mundo Surdo Essay"
- "On the Process of Feminine/Feminist Image-Making"
- "On the Process of Feminist Image Making"
- "Poetry & Magick: A Practicum for Developing Literary + Psychic Skills"
- "La Prieta"
- "Speaking across the Divide"
- "Spiritual Activism: Making Altares, Making Connections"
- "Spiritual Mestisaje, an Other Way"
- Writing Notas 108.7
- Writing Notas H, J, L

PART III

EXCAVATING
THE FUTURE:
THE ARCHIVES
AND BEYOND

5. THE GLORIA EVANGELINA ANZALDÚA PAPERS

Creation Story, Treasure Map, and More

What about our collective sense of community, our collective understanding of how we form and practice "community," how we create a sense of cultural place and belonging, how we develop "virtual" space and how that transforms our understanding of "actual" places, artifacts, and cultural practices of ethnically and culturally diverse communities, our sense of civic and community identity, what our projected future for "community" is. . . . How can we contribute to a public dialogue of these issues? What role do archives, collections, monuments and cultural practices (through lectures, symposia, exhibitions, and public forums at gatherings or conferences) [play] as vehicles through which diverse communities and individuals from the past and present speak to us? What role do they play in the transmission of cultural values?—Anzaldúa, "Gigs"

Gloria Anzaldúa's archive, officially known as the Gloria Evangelina Anzaldúa Papers, is enormous. Located in Austin, Texas, at the Nettie Lee Benson Latin American Collection, it consists of more than two hundred boxes and includes a wide range of materials spanning Anzaldúa's entire life, from birth certificates to obituaries and beyond. Each box is 3 feet long, filled with folders containing manuscripts and other material. Were these boxes laid out in a straight line, they would cover more than 128 feet. (*It's an overwhelming amount of material!*) The archive has already grown

20 feet since its introduction to the public in 2006, and it will continue growing as Anzaldúa's colleagues and friends donate relevant materials to the collection.

From the 1960s until her death in 2004, Anzaldúa saved just about everything related to her intellectual, creative, artistic, and daily life. The archive contains fiction, poetry, and essay manuscripts; an entire play in poetic verse; multiple versions of her pre-*Borderlands* autobiographies with intriguing titles like "La serpiente que se come su cola: The Death Rites of Passage of a Chicana Lesbian"; early drafts of *Borderlands* with unexpected, highly significant authorial and editorial revisions; thousands of pages of writing notes; letters, emails, memos, and other correspondence with friends, publishers, scholars, fans, and lovers; and all sorts of magical paraphernalia and tools that she used for her oracular research (*candle affirmations, Tarot, I Ching, channeled recordings and writings, astrology readings, etc.*). In addition to the manuscripts themselves, the Anzaldúa Papers includes Anzaldúa's personal books with handwritten marginalia; notebooks of drawings, glifos, and doodles; audio and video recordings of writing workshops, meditations, and speaking engagements; over twenty journals; photographs; and much more. For a (*readerly*) bird's-eye view on the collection's enormity, take a look at the online finding aid: https://legacy.lib.utexas.edu/taro/utlac/00189/lac00189.html.

As even a quick look through this finding aid reveals, the archive can be daunting. (*It IS daunting.*) Even scholars who have visited the Anzaldúa Papers numerous times can feel overwhelmed. (*Despite my role in assembling it and my many visits to the Benson, I STILL experience a heart-stopping combination of intimidation and awe every time I step into the reading room.*) In chapters 5 and 6, I aspire to make archival research less daunting and more manageable for researchers. In this chapter, I offer an archival origin story of sorts, a summary of what you'll find should you visit the Benson, and suggestions for how to work effectively (*and less stressfully*) in the archive. My goal is threefold: (1) to demystify Anzaldúa's archives and thus increase their usefulness; (2) to deepen our appreciation both for Anzaldúa's prescience in preserving the artifacts of her writing process and for the archives' contributions to Anzaldúan thought; (3) to underscore Anzaldúa's brilliance by presenting the Gloria Evangelina Anzaldúa Papers as her final, most complex literary and philosophical production. As Suzanne Bost has suggested, the archives invite us into never-ending conversations in which we co-create with Anzaldúa herself. This chapter also sets the stage for the next: a list of many archival manuscripts along with key points about them.

The archives' enormity and relevance to Anzaldúan studies is directly related to Anzaldúa's writing process, which (as explained in chapter 2) was recursive, overly perfectionistic, excessive, intuitive (*nonlinearly intuitive*), and only partially within her conscious control. Regardless of the genres in which she worked, Anzaldúa enacted a multi-stage writing process, created numerous projects simultaneously, revised most pieces many (*many, many, many*) times, and produced multiple drafts for each piece. Given this complex process, the drafts for each project range widely in terms of (in) completion: some drafts are better described as pre-drafts, while others expand greatly in length, sometimes becoming bloated with additional ideas which Anzaldúa later deleted or moved to other projects (*or both*).

This process produced an expansive set of artifacts that Anzaldúa preserved for us: books with marginalia; scrapbooks and folders with memorabilia, magazine clippings, and more; Post-its and other handwritten notes on scraps of paper tucked into folders, journals, and books; thousands of pages of writing notes (most handwritten, some typed); academic course papers; dissertation chapter drafts; interview transcripts; lecture transcripts; typed manuscripts, many with handwritten edits; peer critiques from writing comadres; drawings, artwork, family photographs, phone logs, receipts, calendars, diabetes logs, altar items, and more.

At the Birth of Anzaldúa's Creations

Having worked with Anzaldúa for over ten years, I was very aware of her interest in preserving and creating her own archives. When I interviewed her in 1991, she asked me for copies of the recording, the written transcript, and all communication related to the project; when I began working more closely with her, she instructed me to document and preserve every aspect of our work together. When I edited *Interviews/Entrevistas*, I learned that she had saved the transcripts and tapes from most (if not all) interviews, talks, and recorded conversations from the early 1980s onward.[1] When we developed *this bridge we call home* and other projects, she instructed me to save everything: our notes on work-related conversations, emails, contributor communication, table of contents drafts, and so on. And we talked about her archives, especially during the final years of her life as she worked to manage the type 1 diabetes. (*She needed good health* insurance, which was expensive, and to generate funds she considered selling her papers to a university archive.)

And yet, despite my great familiarity with Anzaldúa's writing proclivities and her intentional efforts to preserve her work, I was stunned by the vast amount of material that Anzaldúa had carefully saved. Going to her house in Santa Cruz, California, and working with her executor and another close friend to collect her materials for an archive after her unexpected death in 2004 was one of the most bittersweet yet amazing experiences of my life. Even now, years later, I'm filled with gratitude and astonishment as I reflect on the huge amount of material that Anzaldúa produced, collected, and preserved—for us (*and for her literary reputation*). Her foresight gives us the opportunity (*and invitation*) to nurture and in other ways foster her theories and literary-intellectual work—potentially for centuries after her death. In this section, I retrace a few steps from my initial encounter with what has become the Anzaldúa Papers. I do so to underscore the care with which Anzaldúa documented and preserved her work and the range of work she produced and preserved.

As I began making my way through Anzaldúa's house, I found an amazing wealth of materials carefully packed into every nook, cranny, shelf, box, and room—from the coat closet located immediately to the right of the front door, to the bookshelves in her back study. Even the garage (*especially the garage!!!*) was a treasure trove (*but more on this later*).

Each room, each filing cabinet, shocked me with its hidden contents. Take for example one of the cabinets that stood at the end of Anzaldúa's hallway: I'd walked past these cabinets many times during my visits with Gloria. There they stood, serving primarily (*or so I thought at the time!*) as informal altaritas. But when I opened the drawers, I was shocked by the amazing array of documents, including many previously unknown projects. The top drawer contained a dazzling collection of poetry manuscripts (*most never published*): multiple drafts of handwritten, typed, and revised poems and poem cycles, including large projects: "La Chingada" (a book-length drama in verse, dated 6 noviembre 1979); "Tres lenguas del fuego" (a complete manuscript of poems written in the late 1970s and apparently completed by February 1980); and "Night Face" (a poetry collection submitted for the Walt Whitman Award); many poems that Anzaldúa had never mentioned, and early versions of poems and prose that, in very revised form, had made their way into *Borderlands*. The middle drawer contained interview transcripts. And the bottom drawer held documents related to Anzaldúa's editing projects—primarily *Making Face, Making Soul/ Haciendo Caras: Creative and Critical Perspectives by Women of Color*: various tables of contents, her letter soliciting material, a project outline, contributor biographies and permissions/agreements, page proofs, correspondence with contributors, and many drafts (*including handwritten notes*) of "haciendo caras," Anzaldúa's introduction; course materials from the 1988 UCSC course that Anzaldúa taught and refers to in her introduction; reviews of *This Bridge Called My Back*, *Borderlands*, and *Making Face, Making Soul/Haciendo Caras*; and dozens of interview transcripts. Another filing cabinet (this one in Anzaldúa's study) contained materials related to her graduate work at both the University of Texas, Austin, and the University of California, Santa Cruz: her master's thesis, term papers, qualifying exam for the doctoral degree, and an abundance of dissertation chapters. Elsewhere, Anzaldúa had preserved several anthology projects, including one on mestiza consciousness and another on Chicana/o lesbians and gays (tentatively titled "de las otras"). Tucked away elsewhere throughout the house, the treasures continued, all carefully grouped: a bound collection of early, autobiographical/fictional pieces, a bound copy of her pre-*Borderlands* autobiography titled "La serpiente que se come su cola: The Death Rites of Passage of a Chicana Lesbian," a large envelope with "La serpiente" discards, a shorter essay titled "La serpiente," another early autobiography, many drawings and sketches, numerous boxes of research and writing notas on a wide range of topics, and closet shelves lined with bound journals—each journal filled with memories, self-reflection, writing notas, and more.

The garage held its secrets, too (*amazing secrets*). Covered in plastic and sitting on pallets next to Anzaldúa's car, I found a row of boxes all marked "Drafts of Borderlands." Carefully labeled and preserved, these boxes contained the various iterations of Anzaldúa's iconic book, from the 1985 poetry collection (simply titled "Borderlands" and submitted to Spinsters Aunt Lute in 1985) to the hybrid genre text (*Borderlands/La Frontera: The New Mestiza*) that launched Anzaldúa into lasting fame. She had carefully organized the manuscripts: One box held the earliest versions of the prose section, a single essay divided into several parts; other boxes held revised drafts of each chapter—the versions meticulously arranged to document chronological development, from handwritten notes to copyedited manuscript. Another box held the endnotes and the poetry sections; another box, "Leftovers from *Borderlands*," contained bits and pieces that didn't make it into the published book; and still another box contained publisher proofs, galleys, and other materials related to the publication process. Elsewhere I found a scrapbook called "Borderland Reviews."

I learned so much about Anzaldúa and her work as I looked through these materials. Although I'd assumed that she conceived and wrote *Borderlands'* prose section as seven distinct chapters (almost like separate essays), the drafts told a different story, showing me that she originally wrote a single essay, divided into four parts. And although in conversations and interviews she sometimes implied that she wrote the prose *after* writing the poetry, those boxes in the garage (*and elsewhere in Anzaldúa's home*) offered a more complex, nonlinear chronology. Perhaps, for me, the most startling insight I gained from my work retrieving and compiling Anzaldúa's archives is that Anzaldúa was working out key theories (*like the Coatlicue state and la facultad*) years prior to *Borderlands*. The modesty and quiet confidence of it all still stuns me: the enormity of Anzaldúa's efforts and accomplishments, the proof of her hard work, the promise of her contributions, and the care with which she organized and preserved her work.

Even now, so many years later, I still grasp for the words to sufficiently convey my amazement upon first encountering Anzaldúa's unpublished treasures. I'm still filled with awe as I consider the depth, range, and extent of the materials that Anzaldúa preserved for us and what these materials—with so many drafts and so many previously unseen essays—might mean for her literary reputation. These additional, previously unknown manuscripts invite (*and permit*) us to dive deeply into Anzaldúa's creative process, investigate her writing practice through its many recursive stages, and appreciate the artistry of her work. (*Indeed, their existence calls out to us, demanding that we do these excavations.*)

My point in narrating this discovery story is to emphasize that Anzaldúa began thinking about her archives very early in her career and developed them throughout her adult life with great intentionality. Everything you find in the Gloria Evangelina Anzaldúa Papers is there because Anzaldúa preserved it for future readers—for you and for me. (*I make this point because the material can be so intimate at times that a researcher might feel as if they're violating Anzaldúa's privacy. And maybe we are; however, we must also remember that Anzaldúa invited us into this intimate space—she created it, at least in part, for us. She anticipated future readers. She called us into being, so to speak. But more on this topic later.*)

In addition to this enormous stash of physical manuscripts, Anzaldúa bequeathed us her laptop, filled with additional projects. This material has been printed and included in the archive (*although it's not really marked as such; you need to examine the documents to ascertain which material was printed after her death and which she printed out herself*).

Archival Challenges

Not surprisingly, given this vast array of material, the Anzaldúa Papers presents a few challenges (*to say the least!*). Some challenges emerge from Anzaldúa's writing proclivities (*the repetition, the cutting and pasting of material, the endless revisions, the peer review feedback*), while others emerge from archival logistics (*organization, labels, and previous researchers*). In what follows, I briefly discuss these challenges.

Anzaldúa's multi-stage recursive writing process confounds any attempt to organize her material in linear chronological order. Indeed, ascertaining the specific dates for when Anzaldúa composed and/or revised a piece is quite challenging (*if not impossible*). Often, though not always, she included handwritten dates on the first page (*top right-hand corner*) of a piece. But what do the dates refer to: When she originally wrote it? When she revised it? (*And if the latter, did her revisions always happen only on the single date indicated on the draft?*) Given Anzaldúa's habit of returning (*years later*) to earlier projects and drafts, this distinction is vital: if scholars just assume that the handwritten date refers to Anzaldúa's actual creation of a piece, they can misidentify manuscripts from the early 1990s as part of her twenty-first-century work and thus fail to appreciate significant shifts in her thinking over the years.

Although Anzaldúa dated some drafts, she left others undated. Moreover, she regularly pulled pages from one draft, inserted them into another (either a later version of the same piece or a different piece entirely), and renumbered the pages accordingly. Prior to the advent of computers, Anzaldúa used a mechanical cut, copy, and insert procedure in which she'd sometimes remove pages from one manuscript and insert them into another; rearrange an existing manuscript, scratching out the original page numbers and inserting others; or cut a page into several strips and insert the parts into other manuscripts—possibly even different projects. (*"La Prieta" and "Speaking in Tongues" illustrate this cut-and-paste process, where Anzaldúa would use scissors to cut paragraphs from one draft, tape them onto another piece of paper, and insert the page[s] into another project.*) These revision strategies can make accurate dating of material a challenge. (*And sometimes it leads to gaps in a manuscript—the early Serpiente manuscripts are a case in point.*) While working on projects near the end of her life, Anzaldúa often returned to earlier material (*essay drafts, writing notas, interviews, journals*) for inspiration. As part of this process, she'd pull up drafts from her hard drive, read them over, possibly move them into a new folder, and resave them. When this material was printed after her death, we indicated the date that it was last saved on the print-out. However, these dates can be confusing, if interpreted to indicate that she wrote (or even revised) it on that date, because at times it seems that she made no alterations in the material. (*"Border Arte: Nepantla, el lugar de la frontera" [58.4] is a case in point.*)

Many drafts include substantial handwritten edits and revisions (title changes, insertions, material crossed out, notes that Anzaldúa wrote to herself); linkages among various pieces; and peer critiques from her "writing comadres," editors, and others. Look for instance at "*Autohistorias-teorías— Mujeres que cuentan vidas*: Personal & Collective Narratives That Challenge Genre Conventions." This essay, a chapter in Anzaldúa's Lloronas dissertation, exists in numerous drafts (*well over two hundred pages of material*) with a wide variety of titles, including "Ethnic Autohistorias-teorías: Writing the History of the Subject," "*En mujer que cuenta vida*: Writing the Personal & Collective Histories of Subject & Problematizing Assumptions about Autorepresentation in Contemporary Racial Ethnic/Other *Autohistorias-teorías*," and "*Mujeres que cuentan vidas:* Writing the Personal & Collective Histories of Subject & Problematizing Assumptions About Autorepresentation in Contemporary Racial Ethnic/Other *Autohistorias-teorías*"—to name only a few. Although Anzaldúa last saved it in 2002, she drafted it much earlier—from 1989 to 1991, as part of her UCSC doctoral studies and dissertation project. She returned to it in the early twenty-first century and considered including it in *Light in the Dark* but decided that the draft needed too much work to be revised by her deadline. Or, for another example of the complexities that stem from Anzaldúa's multiyear revision process, see the many versions of "Border Arte," which you'll find, under various titles, in Boxes 45, 58, and 96.[2]

These challenges are further complicated by the archival collection and research process. Like Anzaldúa herself, her manuscripts resist facile categorization and boundaries. While the Benson finding aid is invaluable, the folder descriptions don't always correlate with their contents. Each box holds many folders. While some folders are devoted to a single draft of one essay (*or book or dissertation chapter*), many are not. Some folders contain several drafts of different distinct essays; other folders contain multiple drafts of the same essay; and some folders hold both. The finding aid cannot offer these nuanced distinctions, but instead these observations must be made by researchers. There's no way to know for sure exactly how many different essays or drafts of the same piece a folder contains until you open it and start reading. Moreover, because other readers have looked through the folders, flipped through and read the pages, and the pages themselves are all loose, there's no guarantee that the order in which an essay or series of essays sits in a folder is accurate. (*And because we can request several folders at a time, researchers might accidentally place pages from one folder into another.*) As if to complicate your research even further, Anzaldúa often revised the titles; at times, it can take a bit of reading and sleuth work to determine whether you're reading a different essay or another iteration of the same essay.

How to Work with the Anzaldúa Papers without Becoming Overwhelmed

When you arrive at the Special Collections room of the Benson Library, you're confronted with the daunting task of figuring out what to look at and how to maximize your time. Be prepared! Prior to your visit, look through the finding aid and the annotated bibliography (*located in the next chapter!*); decide what you hope to learn; figure out your plan of action; and prioritize the work.

- Ask yourself questions like these: What do I hope to discover? What are my research questions? Are my questions and aspirations related to a specific point in Anzaldúa's career?
- Use these questions to structure and focus your precious time. (*For instance, if I'm investigating conocimiento, I'll start with materials from the late 1990s, but if I'm researching la facultad, I'll begin with pre-Borderlands work, like the unpublished Serpiente autohistorias.*)
- Look through the online finding aid and make a list of manuscripts you'd like to examine. Be sure to include the box and folder number for each piece, and rank your list so that you begin with the documents you're most interested in reading. (*Time*

moves differently in the archive; chances are, you won't explore as much material as you're hoping to.)

- Consider the approach you'll take for examining the manuscripts: Will you read quickly, and hope to get through as much material as possible? Do less reading and more picture-taking? (That is: take lots and lots of pictures and read them later?) (*But this, of course, is tricky: What if some of the images are unclear or for some other reason you need to go back through the material?*) Or perhaps do a combination of both methods?
- Arrive at the Benson with your ranked list of manuscripts, by box and folder number, so that you can get started right away.

Regardless of your preparations, the actual experience at the archive can feel overwhelming. Do what you can, trust the process, and intentionally breathe. (*If you, like Anzaldúa, include oracular research in your process, you might meditate, set intentions, offer prayers, or do other rituals to strengthen your intuition and guidance.*)

With her archives, Anzaldúa played a leading role in shaping (*and inviting us to foster*) her literary reputation for years (*centuries!*) to come. She collected her material with thoughtfulness. She documented and preserved her work for other readers—for you and me. The Anzaldúa Papers' existence is an invitation to readers. The manuscripts beckon, inviting us to engage in further conversations with Anzaldúa.

Like far too many other women-of-colors and queer authors, Anzaldúa has not been adequately appreciated for her intellectual contributions or her artistry. However, as researchers delve into her archival materials, closely examine her complex meaning-making process, and produce scholarship inspired by these investigations, they will more fully recognize and demonstrate that Anzaldúa was a theorist, artist, philosopher, and author of the highest caliber. And here's what I find really exciting: Anzaldúa reserved some of her most innovative, provocative, and potentially transformative ideas in prepublication drafts and unpublished writings. As we make our way through her vast holdings, the archive will continue to reveal its hidden treasures, one startling discovery at a time.

To whet your appetite, I share a few of my random archival discoveries and speculations about Anzaldúa and her work. I hope that these preliminary insights will pique your interest. You'll find more information about the manuscripts I refer to in the following chapter.

- Anzaldúa had planned to further revise "La Prieta" prior to its publication in *This Bridge Called My Back*; however, her hysterectomy slowed her down, and she was a few days late in submitting her revisions. See her message to Persephone Press and Cherríe Moraga [45.11], in which she indicates the additional changes she planned to make (which include a section titled "The Birth of Healing Woman") and the message she received informing her that she'd missed the deadline.
- Anzaldúa associated her early menstruation with her relationship to language. See for instance "Autohistoria de la artista as a Young Girl" (57.12), in which she writes, "This precocious puberty [Roz Spafford's term] is connected to words or rather the absence of language with which to talk about a woman's body. It is connected to the unnameable, the sense of difference or distance that allowed me to see clearly."
- "Metaphors in the Tradition of the Shaman" was originally part of a much longer paper and a dissertation chapter. The version located in "The Writing Subject: Racial Ethnic/Others Inside Enemy Territory" (95.20) is particularly fascinating.
- Following a project through Anzaldúa's many drafts gave me new insights into the subtle (*and sometimes not-so-subtle*) shifts in her thought. Take, for example, her Lloronas dissertation (1988–92). Prior to examining the manuscripts, I had not realized the amount of time, energy, and paper Anzaldúa had poured into this project. She produced hundreds, if not thousands, of pages and enough material for several books. At its most expansive, the projected dissertation consisted of seventeen chapters, divided into two volumes: "Volume One—Writing and Representation" and "Volume Two—Llorona: Noche y su nidada."
- Space is a key concept and motivator in the Lloronas dissertation, as evidenced especially (but not exclusively) in the chapter drafts titled "Chicana Space, Ground of Being: Theories of Self, Sex, Psyche and Writing (A Chicana Writer Explores Cultural, Self and Sexual Identities from the Perspective of Space)." (*Note that "drafts" is plural here: as you'll see in the following chapter, Anzaldúa produced more than one draft of this chapter—as typically was her wont.*) In these drafts and others Anzaldúa explores inner space, territorial space, imaginal space, and more. I attribute her

growing interest in nepantla at least partially to this process: as she tried to make "space" do such extensive work, she realized the limitations in western spatial metaphors and theories. Importantly (*and surprisingly*), "nepantla" does not appear in the dissertation itself. (*Students of Anzaldúa's work could make many discoveries here.*)

- Although Anzaldúa abandoned her Lloronas dissertation project, the time she spent researching and drafting it increased her self-confidence *as* a theorist-philosopher and inspired her own theory creation. This impact is especially evident in "Poet is Critic"; even the title changes point to this shift, seen for instance in the shift from "Poet as Critic" to "Poet *is* Critic" (my emphasis).

This list is short and brief. An astounding, unpredictably large number of possibilities lay hidden within the Gloria Evangelina Anzaldúa Papers, just waiting for us to encounter and create them. Potential research projects and undreamt of insights beckon.

6. ANZALDÚA'S ARCHIVAL MANUSCRIPTS
Overview, Insights, Annotations

"I have a book," I tell myself. "And I need to work on what I have and stop adding new material. . . . I will deal with the new material at a future time, in a future book. Everything is in process—including my life. No finis. There are no ends. After the end comes after the end. Type what you have," I tell myself.—Anzaldúa, "Esperando la serpiente con plumas"

This unconventional chapter called itself into being; it emerged from my research notes rather than from the original book proposal. Shortly after I began working with Anzaldúa's archival material, I realized that I would become completely overwhelmed if I didn't develop a system to document and organize the manuscripts I'd read. While the Benson's finding aid was extremely useful, Anzaldúa's writing proclivities—especially her nuanced title changes, numerous drafts, and cut-and-move revisions—demanded additional strategies to track a project through its many stages and iterations. And so, I began keeping an informal annotated bibliography for this project: each entry included title, archive location, (*tentative*) date, summary notes, interesting insights gleaned, connections with other manuscripts, and key topics. In typical Anzaldúan fashion, this document began small and grew (*as if with a will of its own*) until, by September 2019, it was over 23,000 words in length. What follows is a trimmed version of this longer document, revised to be outward-facing (*with other readers, rather than just myself, in mind*). I removed some of my speculations, questions, and personal notes for future research projects. I also replaced my unwieldy entries on Anzaldúa's writing notas (*both the notas that Anzaldúa labeled as such, as well as other folders of notes*) with a much more succinct summary (see "Writing Notas," below). I did so because each writing nota contains approximately one hundred pages of material on a huge range of topics; there was no way to adequately summarize the contents, and any summary I prepared would be far too influenced by my personal interests.

I've organized the entries alphabetically rather than by date, due to the lengthy, multiyear revision chronologies for some pieces. (*Indeed, given the fact that Anzaldúa sometimes worked sporadically on a piece for a decade or more, arranging the material chronologically would have been impossible.*) Each entry includes, in this order, the following: title, location (box and folder number), date, brief description/summary, and key topics. Because most manuscripts have multiple titles, I typically use the most recent title for the entry and include previous titles in the entry itself. (At times, Anzaldúa produced multiple drafts of a single manuscript with slight variations in title capitalization; each variation reflects a somewhat different manuscript draft with different edits.) For location, I've borrowed the numbering system developed by Ricardo F. Vivancos-Pérez: box number followed by folder number (*so, for instance, Box 38, Folder 3 becomes 38.3*). Chronology matters, and I've tried to date each piece, drawing on Anzaldúa's various notes to do so.[1] Those entries with a range of dates indicate essay constellations revised over multiple years. A "ca." in front of a date indicates that I have intuited it based on the context and other hints in the documents themselves. When referring to manuscripts printed from Anzaldúa's hard drive after her death, the dates indicate when the draft was last saved, which might or might not indicate when Anzaldúa actually last worked on a piece.[2] (*Often it does not.*)

Each entry concludes with an alphabetized list of topics explored in the manuscript drafts. These lists are not exhaustive but represent my best effort to capture the breadth and depth of Anzaldúa's thought. I developed the topics somewhat nonliterally, focusing on what might be useful to readers (*including researchers*). So, for instance, if a piece includes extensive discussion of self-writing, I've indicated "autohistoria" and/or "autohistoria-teoría" in the list (cf. "Rampas de salida"); if a manuscript includes Anzaldúa's notes for a lecture, I've indicated "gigs."

What follows is not a complete list of everything Anzaldúa wrote. Although I aspired to read and analyze all of her prose drafts, including all writing notes (both those she formally labeled as such as well as the many other randomly titled notes), it's likely that I overlooked some material. Anzaldúa's archives are far too nonlinear and complex, much too filled with surprises, to presume that one could ever be truly exhaustive. (*The material in Boxes 103 through 111 might be particularly enticing to those readers wondering what might have been overlooked.*)

For most readers, this chapter is not one to be read in conventional linear fashion but rather something to dip into for specific projects or research trips to the archives. (*For those of you fascinated by all things Anzaldúa, and/or those scholars who have dedicated much of your lives to her work, you might enjoy reading through what follows from beginning to end. If so, let me know because, quite possibly, you'll develop some interesting, amazing insights through an immersive reading.*) Regardless, I hope you find this chapter to be enjoyable, useful, and inspiring.

The Entries

"+ART" (98.14) ca. 2001. Three pages of single-spaced, typed notes last saved on Anzaldúa's hard drive on August 4, 2001, and printed after her death. Its location indicates that Anzaldúa planned to use it as part of her book, to be published after the dissertation, in a chapter on the self in community. Includes notes that resonate with "Queer Conocimiento" and "Nepantla: Creative Acts of Vision."

> Topics: art, connection, consciousness, Coyolxauhqui, literature, love, meaning, metaphor, mind, naguala, Prieta, reality, transformation, unconscious

"+NOTES-B" (98.14) ca. 2001. Fifty-five pages of single-spaced, typed notes last saved on Anzaldúa's hard drive on June 11, 2002, and printed after her death. Located in a folder titled "4-plus for diss," it's likely that Anzaldúa planned to use these notes as she developed a chapter for her book, to be published after the dissertation. Some material resonates with *Light in the*

Dark, suggesting that this material could include earlier drafts or material from writing notes. Also includes notes for her Prieta stories and material from various listservs that indicate Anzaldúa's interests in environmental issues, peace studies, astrology, etc.

> Topics: activism, altar-making, anger, awakening, bearing witness, beliefs, body, change, communication, community, compassion, conocimiento, consciousness, Coyolxauhqui, creativity, desconocimiento, difference, energy, epistemology, eroticism, ethics, evil, feminism, geography of self, God, healing, identity, images, information, knowledge, leadership, love, meditation, mind, mindfulness, naguala, nature, near death experiences, nepantla, nepantleras, nos/otras, nos/otros, pain, passion, path of conocimiento, peace, prayer, Prieta stories, queering reality, reality, ritual, science, self-awareness, self-reflection, shaman, shame, soul, spirit, spiritual activism, "spiritual cultivation," spirituality, stories, Tao, thresholds, time, vibration, wisdom, wounds, writing, "yoga of the mind," zen

"ACTING OUT THE VISION, SPIRITUAL ACTIVISM, ACTIVISTAS" (49.6) 2000. A five-page, single-spaced, typed manuscript composed primarily of notes on spiritual activism that Anzaldúa used in September 2000 as she drafted "now let us shift." The final page includes a section titled "How to train a spiritual activist." (She has handwritten the date "9/13/00" in the upper right-hand corner.)

> Topics: academia, activism, art, bridging, conflict, conocimiento, energy, facultad, meditation, El Mundo Zurdo, naguala, shamans, spirit, spiritual activism, writing

"ADD BRIDGE" (49.2) 2000. Eight single-spaced typed pages of notes culled from other sources and one additional handwritten page as part of Anzaldúa's brainstorming for "now let us shift." (She has handwritten the date "8/30/00" in the upper right-hand corner.)

> Topics: activism, alignment, cenote, change, Chicana artists, Chicano studies, community, conocimiento, energy, happiness, healing, Latino studies, mindfulness, myth, nature, objectivity, ontology, paradigms, reading, ritual, spirit, spiritual activism, spirituality, stress, susto, tradition, women's studies, writing

"ALTARES: ON THE PROCESS OF FEMINIST IMAGE MAKING" (57.2, 57.3, 57.4) 1982–90. This piece exists in several iterations and titles, with the earliest handwritten version dated April 14, 1982, and the latest dated January 1, 1999; it includes both handwritten and word-processed drafts. Anzaldúa revised the title several times: "On the Process of Feminine/Feminist Image-Making," "On the Process of Feminist Image Making" (57.2 and 57.4), and, most recently, "Altares: On the Process of Feminist Image Making" (57.3), printed after Anzaldúa's death from her hard drive, where it was last saved on January 1, 1990, as "doc 2:08 drafts: dupli_altars"; this draft is a compilation of the earlier drafts. For two other, more recent versions of this piece, see also "Spiritual Activism: Making Altares, Making Connections."

Topics: altars, astrology, body, candles, cenote, Coatlicue, curanderas, hope, I Ching, image-making, imaging, intention-setting, meditation, nagual, occult knowledge, ontology, pendulum, ritual, serpent, spirit, spiritual activism, stress, Tarot, tree, unconscious, visualization, writing process

"ART OF SELF-EDITING, RE-READING, RE-VISION, RE-WRITING" (57.5) 1985. Eight pages of handwritten notes and typed untitled poems that Anzaldúa used for poetry readings and workshops. The date "10 marzo 85" is handwritten in the corner of one page ("Part I Internal Goings On: A Reading Plus"); other titles are "Alchemical Changes: A Reading and a Talk," "Writing Workshop: Creative Prose, Poems, and Stories," "Part II Internal Goings On: A Writing Workshop Plus," and "An Image is Worth a Thousand Words: A Writing Workshop." This material offers insight into Anzaldúa's poetry readings: she organizes her talks by first reading a poem and then discussing how she wrote the poem. Includes background (initial idea/inspiration) of "Immaculate, Inviolate" and "Sea of Cabbages" (later published in *Borderlands*).

Topics: alchemy, *Borderlands*, creative process, gigs, metaphor, poetry, reading, relationship between writer and reader, transformation, writing process

"AUTOBIOGRAPHY" (57.6, 57.7, 57.8) 1983–85. Anzaldúa stored this material as "Autobiography"; contents include material related to *Borderlands* and earlier work:

- 57.6: Two short drafts of what eventually became the preface to *Borderlands*. The first, handwritten and dated "5 marzo 85," is titled "Autobiography"; and the second, typed with handwritten edits, is titled "Gloria Anzaldúa." Anzaldúa positions herself as a "border woman" and Chicana author, offering an overview of key aspects of her life.
- 57.7: Drafts and discards from short stories, interviews, and early autohistorias, including material, like "Cervicide," that eventually made its way, in revised form, into *Borderlands*.
- 57.8: Over one hundred pages of material, including multiple versions of "Her First Fuck," many with handwritten edits, and several drafts of "People Should Not Die in South Texas."

Topics: adversity, astrology, autohistoria, body, border, la Chingada, consciousness, crisis, death, drugs, education, facultad, feminism, gigs, Guadalupe, hieros gamos, hysterectomy, images, lesbian, Llorona, meditation, mestiza, midlife crisis, out-of-body experience, power, Prieta, reading, sex, Shakti, soul, spirit, spirituality, survival, teaching, Texas, *This Bridge*, transformation, whiteness, writing

"AUTOHISTORIA DE LA ARTISTA AS A YOUNG GIRL" (57.9, 57.10, 57.11, 57.12) 1991–93. Drafted in 1991, this project represents Anzaldúa's most sustained bildungsroman—a narrative of her life and thought, focusing on childhood events that shaped her identity and vocation as a writer. First titled "*Autoretratos de la artista: de la autora como niña*," it was written for a collection edited by Christian McEwan, who invited Anzaldúa to contribute an essay about her "early years and what being Chicana, working class, 'spiritual,' and a girl had to do with [her] becoming an author" (57.12). In late 1991 McEwan handed the project over to Julia Penelope, who informed Anzaldúa of the change in a letter dated August 19, 1993 (57.9), and invited her to publish a shortened version of her piece, which Penelope edited for her (see 57.10). 57.11 consists of a typed draft of "*Autoretratos*" with handwritten comments by the editor or another reader; 57.12 includes the version prepared for McEwan. This folder also includes a letter from Anzaldúa describing the piece and explaining her use of first- and third-person perspectives; the draft also contains handwritten edits and commentary.

Topics: alchemy, art, artist, autohistoria, autohistoria-teoría, class, consciousness, creative process, death, depression, destiny, difference, education, embodiment, fear, gender, insomnia, language, meditation, memory, menstruation, mysticism, nagual, nepantla, pain, possession, religion, ritual, shadow, shamanistic writing, soul, spirituality, visualization, writing blocks, writing process

"AUTOHISTORIAS AS PROCESS WRITING" (55.8) mid-1990s. This thirteen-page, 1.5-spaced, typed document is a section from Anzaldúa's writing guide manuscript. It was printed after Anzaldúa's death from her hard drive, where it was last saved on January 29, 1994.

Topics: art, autohistoria, autohistoria-teoría, body, breath work, consciousness, creative process, creativity, defamiliarization, dream, energy, images, fantasy, fiction, flor y canto, meditation, memory, ontology, reading, representation, self-reflection, sensation, transformation, vibrations, visualization, writing process

"AUTOHISTORIAS-TEORÍAS—MUJERES QUE CUENTAN VIDAS: PERSONAL & COLLECTIVE NARRATIVES THAT CHALLENGE GENRE CONVENTIONS" (94.2, 94.3, 94.4, 94.5) 1989–91, 2002. This essay, a chapter in Anzaldúa's Lloronas dissertation, exists in numerous drafts with revisions, title edits, and questions for readers, as well as readers' comments. Although she last saved it in 2002, Anzaldúa drafted it much earlier—from 1989 to 1991, as part of her UCSC course work. She returned to it in the early twenty-first century and considered including it in *Light in the Dark* but determined that the drafts needed too much work and thus could not be revised in time for her deadline. Not surprisingly, and as Anzaldúa notes, this piece is one of the most conventionally academic of her papers: "its style is more academic than my other essays. i [sic] wrote it while i was doing course work & it shows" (email communication with Keating). Offering Anzaldúa's most sustained investigation of autohistoria and autohistoria-teoría, the manuscript's various iterations illustrate her development of the theory (*with the early drafts falling short because she had not yet fully grasped Coyolxauhqui's role in the writing process*). This essay exists in many versions and titles:

- "Ethnic Autohistorias-teorías: Writing the History of the Subject" (91.30, 92.16). See below for more on this version.
- "*En mujer que cuenta vida*: Writing the Personal & Collective Histories of Subject & Problematizing Assumptions about Autorepresentation in Contemporary Racial Ethnic/Other

Autohistorias-teorías" (94.4). This draft revises the title from single ("En mujer que cuenta") to plural ("Mujeres que cuentan").

- *"Mujeres que cuentan vidas:* Writing the Personal & Collective Histories of Subject & Problematizing Assumptions about Autorepresentation in Contemporary Racial Ethnic/Other *Autohistorias-teorías"* (91.20, 94.2, 94.3) 1990. The draft in 94.3 (dated September 30, 1990) includes Anzaldúa's description of chapter focus and origins in two previous papers; the draft in 94.2, dated November 6, 1990, is the version that Anzaldúa distributed to her feminist dissertation group and includes a useful memo summarizing her dissertation project as she envisioned it at the time, as well as copies with readers' comments.

See also "Remembering and Subverting in the 'Historias' of Chicanas and Women of Color" and "Self-Representation and Identity" (below).

Topics: aesthetics, appropriation, audience, autobiography, autohistoria, autohistoria-teoría, body, cenote, class, code-switching, colonialism, dreams, dualism, ego, estilo mestizaje as "writing strategy," fiction, gender, genres, history, identity (individual/collective, private/public), imagination, intersubjectivity, literary genres, Llorona, memoir, memory, mestiza consciousness, mind, narrative, ontology, origins, personal/collective identity, race, reader response theory, reading, reality, representation, sentimentality, spiritual confession, survival, theory, trauma, writing, writing process, writing reality

"AUTOHISTO-TEORÍAS: THEORIZING SELF-REPRESENTATIONS" (238.5) ca. 1989, 2003. Printed from Anzaldúa's hard drive after her death and last saved October 13, 2003, but written much earlier. This short manuscript (one page of notes and a fourteen-page bibliography) focuses on the 1990s UCSC qualifying exam and dissertation, "Lloronas—Women Who Wail."

Topics: autobiography, autohistoria, autohistoria-teoría, Chicana feminism, Chicana theory, Chicano/a subjectivity, fiction, haunting, hysteria, identity, Llorona, musa bruja, origins, subjectivity

"BARRED WITNESS: LITERARY/ARTISTIC CREATIONS AND CLASS IDENTITIES" (57.14, 57.15, 57.16, 57.17, 57.18, 57.19, 58.1). Written in 1990–91, this piece began as a Lloronas dissertation chapter, but Anzaldúa also planned to submit it for a special issue of *Cultural Studies*, edited by Henry A. Giroux and Peter McLaren. (See 57.14 for Giroux's letter and 57.19 for this version of the piece.) It is, arguably, Anzaldúa's most extensive critique of conventional western academic training. She draws on a variety of academic-related experiences (visiting professor and student at UCSC, speaker at conferences and universities, and her liminal academic status) as she explores the challenges women-of-color students and writers experience in formal education systems. Drafts exist in various titles with handwritten edits indicating Anzaldúa's thought process:

- "The Art of Bearing Witness: The Economies of Literary and Artistic Creations and Class Identities of Female Ethnic/Others" (57.17)
- "The Art of Bearing Witness: Artistic Creations and Class Identities of Female Ethnic/Others" (57.17)
- "The Art of Bearing Witness: Literary/Artistic Creations and Class Identities of Female Ethnic/Others" (57.18)
- "Barred Witness: Literary/Artistic Creations and Class Identities of Female Ethnic/Others" (57.18)

Topics: accountability, anger, appropriation, art, artist, audience, autohistoria, autohistoria-teoría, blank spots, Chicana/o nationalism, class, cosmopolitanism, deconstruction, difference, embodiment, ethnic studies, exile, graduate education, "intellectual oppression-repression," isolation, knowledge production, literary canon, Llorona, memory, mestiza, methodology, methods, musa bruja, passing, pedagogy, perfectionism, plagiarism, postcolonial theory, post-traumatic stress, power dynamics, privilege, public speaking, relationship between women-of-color and white feminists, representation, self-invention, silence, teaching, theory, time, voice, white academic feminism, women of color, writer, writing process, writing programs

"BEGGING TO DIFFER, DISSENTING DISCOURSES: A COMMENTARY" (58.2) 1990–96. This short piece (approximately nine typed pages) critiques three chapters in "Representations of the Chicana/o Subject: Race, Class, and Gender," a section of Héctor Calderón and José David Saldívar's *Criticism in the Borderlands: Studies in Chicano Literature, Culture, and Ideology*;

however, it was not included in the published volume. The manuscript exists in two drafts, one printed post-death and last saved March 20, 1996.

Topics: autobiography, Chicana feminism, class, gender, genres, identity, literary genres, mestiza, mestizaje, nagual, new mestiza, representation

"BOOKS I'VE READ" (103.9) 1997. Also titled "The Pleasures of Reading," this five-page, single-spaced document recounts Anzaldúa's reading experiences, focusing especially on novels that she has read (or aspires to read). Offers insights into her taste in fiction.

Topics: fiction, heterosexuality, mysteries, orgasm, reading, romance novels, sex scenes, writing

"BORDER ARTE: NEPANTLA, EL LUGAR DE LA FRONTERA" (45.5, 58.4, 58.5, 58.6, 58.7, 58.8, 58.9, 58.10, 58.11, 58.12, 58.13, 58.14, 58.15, 59.16, 96.4) 1991–92, 2002–2004. Based on Anzaldúa's attendance in 1992 at the special exhibit, "AZTEC: The World of Moctezuma," at the Denver Museum of Natural History (renamed in 2000 as the Denver Museum of Nature & Science), this essay investigates border art and border artists, with the border here defined as the US-Mexico dividing line and "border artists" primarily as Chicana/o. Anzaldúa worked on this essay from 1991 to 1993 and picked it up again in 2002. It exists in multiple drafts, including three different published forms: "Border Arte: Nepantla, el Lugar de la Frontera," published in *La Frontera/The Border: Art about the Mexico/United States Border Experience* (a catalog coordinated by Kathryn Kanjo, Centro Cultural de la Raza & Museum of Contemporary Art, San Diego); "Chicana Artists: Exploring Nepantla, *el Lugar de la Frontera*," published in NACLA *Report*, July–August 1993 (59.16); and "Border Arte: Nepantla, el lugar de la frontera," published in *Light in the Dark/Luz en lo Oscuro*. Title changes as follows (from earliest to latest):

- "*El arte de la frontera*: The Border as Place, People and Politics" (58.7, 58.8, 58.12)
- "El arte de la frontera: The Border as Place, *Pueblo* and Image" (58.8, 58.9, 58.14)
- "El arte de la frontera: The Border as Place, Pueblo, Image and Nepantla" (58.6, 58.11)

- *"El arte de la frontera:* The Border as *Nepantla*, Place and *Pueblo"* (58.6, 58.11)
- "Border Arte: Nepantla, el lugar de la frontera" (58.4, 58.5, 58.10 [this folder includes the contract], 58.13, 58.15, 96.4)
- "Border Arte: Nepantla, el Lugar de la Frontera" (45.5)—with edits dated "5/24/02."

Topics: activism, altars, ancestors, appropriation, art, artists, assimilation, Aztec, border, border art, border crossing, Borges, cenote, Chicanx, Chicanx artists, codices, colonization, consciousness, Coyolxauhqui, creativity, death, diversity, ethnocentrism, floricanto, gender, gender-blending, Guadalupe, identity, image, imagination, Indigeneity, jaguar, Llorona, Malinche, Mayan, mestiza, metaphor, Mexico, mundis imaginalis, museum studies, myth, Native Americans, nepantla, Olmec, pop culture, queer theory, Quincentennial, representation, ritual, sacrifice, shamanism, snake, space, trauma, Virgen de Guadalupe, wholeness

"BORDER WRITING" (58.16) 1988–89. Originally titled "Border Crossings," this thirteen-page, double-spaced essay is a revised version of a presentation that Anzaldúa delivered at Cornell University (Ithaca, NY) in fall 1988 and published in *Trivia.* See also "En estilo," below.

Topics: appropriation, audience, autohistoria-teoría, body, border crossing, *Borderlands,* canon, class, colonization, feminisms, fire, genres, historias, identity, imagination, isolation, land, language, literary canon, margins, meaning, memory, mestiza, mestizaje writing, oral tradition, point of view, racism, reading, representation, silence, Southwest, survival, theory, *This Bridge,* truth, white culture, women-of-color authors, world-traveling, writers, writing, writing blocks

"BORN UNDER THE SIGN OF THE FLOWER" (92.1, 92.2, 92.3, 92.4, 92.5, 92.6, 95.5) 1987–90. Drafts of what eventually became a dissertation chapter existing in multiple versions, from handwritten and typed notes (92.1, 95.5) to complete drafts. Explores the history of male homosexuality in preconquest Mexican Indigenous cultures, Anzaldúa's personal memories of gay male friends, the impact of AIDS, revisionist mythmaking and "queer sexual activity," gender dichotomies, stereotyped assumptions about sexuality, and intersections between queer sexuality and spirituality. An excellent demonstration of Anzaldúa's early contributions to queer theory. Exists in several titles and multiple drafts, some with handwritten edits and/or reader feedback:

- "Born under the Sign of the Flower: *Los jotos* in Ancient Mexico" (92.3): The first draft, dated November 25, 1987.
- "Born under the Sign of the Flower: *Los jotos* in Ancient Mexico and Modern Aztlan" (92.2, 92.4, 92.5): At least three labeled versions of this essay: "A," "B" (92.2), and "C" (92.6), each version with handwritten edits and variations; additional drafts, including one for José Limón (92.4); one with "the Mestizo Queer" inserted, as handwritten edit, into the essay title: "Born under the Sign of the Flower: *Los jotos* in Ancient Mexico and the Mestizo Queer in Modern Aztlan" (92.4); and a draft printed after Anzaldúa's death, last saved September 4, 2002, but dated "3/21/90" (92.5); this draft includes Anzaldúa's rationale for the essay: "My motivations? Why am I 'traveling' through the male homosexual world? For Randy and David's anthology. Because I couldn't find a Chicano to take on this task. Because I am close to the cultural landscape having just written Borderlands/La frontera [*sic*]. To set the background for the lesbian piece to follow."

Topics: AIDS, archetypes, Aztecs, Catholicism, Chicano, la Chingada, Coatlicue, codices, colonization, conflict, creativity, culture, curandera, death, depression, difference, embodiment, essentialism, Freud, gender, goddess, health, heterosexuals, history, homosexuality, immune system, isolation, language, lesbianism, Mayan, Mesoamerican myth, mystic, nature, obsidian mirrors, queer, queer theory, Quetzalcoatl, reality, religion, ritual, sexual difference, sexuality, shaman, social constructionism, sodomy, soul, spirits, spiritual energy, spirituality, subjectivity, supernatural, surveillance, survival, Tamoanchan, Tarot, Tezcatlipoca, Tlazolteotl, Toltecs, trans, underworld, Uranians, Xochiquetzal

"CARTA A COLÓN" (59.6, 59.7, 59.8, 59.9, 59.10, 59.11, 59.12, 59.13, 59.14, 59.15) 1991–93. Planned as a chapter for the Lloronas dissertation, this piece explores colonialism, postcolonialism, writing as resistance, language, and related issues. Anzaldúa also planned to include a version in Elaine Hedges and Shelley Fisher Fishkin's edited collection *Listening to Si-*

lences: New Essays in Feminist Criticism (90.1). This piece exists in multiple drafts and titles (listed chronologically from earliest to latest):

- "Mujeres que tienen lengua: Living under the Shadow of Silence—A Response to Columbus' Re/Discovery" (61.17) 1991: Printed from Anzaldúa's hard drive after her death, this forty-one-page, 1.5-spaced manuscript was last saved June 30, 1991, as "colon 2."
- "*Surpassing the Tongue—Lloronas que tienen lengua*, 500 Years of Resistance and Struggle to Reclaim America" (59.6): Twenty-page draft dated "10/10/91," with handwritten edits (including title edits).
- "*Carta a Colón: Surpassing the Tongue—Lloronas que tienen manos*, 500 Years of Resistance" (59.6, 59.7, 59.8, 59.9): 1991 and 1992 drafts. The draft in 59.7, printed after Anzaldúa's death from her hard drive, indicates that she viewed this version as the third. Some drafts have handwritten edits (59.8, 59.9).
- "Carta a Colón: Despierta la Tongue—Lloronas que tienen manos, 500 Years of nos/otras" (59.9, 59.10): Fourth version, as indicated by handwritten edits (including title insertions) on the draft in 59.9. The draft in 59.10, printed from Anzaldúa's hard drive after her death, was last saved April 6, 1992.
- "Carta a Colón-nialism: Surpassing *la lengua—Nos/otras tenemos manos*" (59.9, 59.11, 59.12, 59.14, 59.15): April, May, and June 1992 drafts with handwritten edits (59.9); the draft in 59.12 was printed after Anzaldúa's death from her hard drive but last saved March 18, 1993. 59.14–reader comments, 59.15–Anzaldúa edits.

Topics: academia, appropriation, autohistoria-teoría, body, *Borderlands'* reception, canon, Chicano literature, Christianity, code-switching, colonialism, colonization, consciousness, death, education, estilo mestizaje, ghosts, haunting, identity, internalized colonization, Jews, knowledge, language, literary conventions, Llorona, Malinche, marginalization, mestizas, muse, narrative, nature, neocolonization, nos/otras, oppression, pisar la sombra, political correctness, postcolonialism, reading, reality, representation, repression, serpents, silence, Sor Juana, space, subjectivity, susto, Texas, theory, trauma, white feminist ideology, whiteness, writing, writing process

"CHAPTER ANNOTATIONS" (96.2) 2004. These five pages of single-spaced notes printed from Anzaldúa's hard drive after her death and last saved April 13, 2004, take us into Anzaldúa's thinking as she completed her twenty-first-century dissertation and what would become *Light in the Dark*. Includes a to-do list for remaining dissertation-related tasks and her annotations for chapters 2 through 6.

> Topics: appropriation, archetype, artists, belief, body, borderlands, conflict, conocimiento, consciousness, cosmic tree, Coyolxauhqui, creativity, death, (des)conocimientos, diabetes, dreaming, elements, embodiment, enemies, epistemology, fiction, geographies of selves, hatred, identity, imaginal, imagination, intellect, journeying, memory, mental health, mestizaje, mind, nagual, nature spirituality, narrative, nepantla, "nonordinary" realities, nos/otras, ontology, queer, Raza studies, reading, remolinos, roots, shamanism, space, spirit, subjectivity, susto, transformation, writing process

"CHICANA FEMINIST THEORY" (91.6) n.d. Two pages of single-spaced typed notes describing Anzaldúa's plan for the three UCSC qualifying exam essays: (1) Chicana subjectivity and representation, "ethnic women's identity . . . using the figure of la Llorona as the ghostly body of Chicana racial/cultural and personal past"; (2) "'The Post-Modern Llorona: Sub-jected to Others' in which I explore the relationship between Chicana feminist theory [and] poststructuralism"; and (3) "'El desarrollo, the Economy of Self-Development,' on Chicana aesthetics and Chicana Mestiza artistic and intellectual identity."

> Topics: aesthetics, autohistoria-teoría, Chicana feminist theory, identity, Llorona, mestiza, postmodernism, representation, subjectivity

"CHICANA SPACE, GROUNDS OF BEING" (92.7, 92.8, 92.9, 92.10, 92.11, 92.12) 1988–90. An early paper in which Anzaldúa presents her Lloronas dissertation ideas: "In undertaking this research I will lay the foundation for QE [Qualifying Exam] topics and the dissertation. My research will focus on sexual, cultural, psychic and literary identities of Chicana/mestiza women of color from [a] spatial/temporal perspective. I will use the culture figure and metaphor of la llorona to link the three broad areas: the Chicana lesbian, the Chicano queer, and the mestiza writer. Ultimately I want to write and fuse personal narrative and theoretical discourse to present the consciousness and reality of the Chicana/mestiza's lived, imagined and artistic experience" (92.7). This manuscript demonstrates that Anzaldúa aspired to create a multigenre dissertation: "predominantly essays but including letter-essay, speech and fiction" (92.8). The manuscript exists in a variety of drafts with slightly different titles:

- "Theories of the Self and a Chicana Ground of Being" (92.10), written spring 1988 for a UCSC course. See below for more on this draft.
- "Chicana Space, Ground of Being: Theories of the Self" (92.9, 92.12)
- "Chicana Space, Grounds of Being: Theories of Self, Sex, & Writing" (92.11). This draft has many handwritten edits and was revised, according to Anzaldúa, on "3/11/89."
- "Chicana Space, Ground of Being: Theories of Self, Sex, Psyche and Writing (A Chicana Writer Explores Cultural, Self and Sexual Identities from the Perspective of Space)" (92.12)
- "Chicana Space, Ground of Being: Theories of Self, Sex, Psyche and Writing (A Chicana Writer Explores Cultural, Self and Sexual Identities from the Perspective of Space)" (92.7), printed post-death from Anzaldúa's hard drive, last saved February 6, 1990. Third outline of this chapter. Offers useful early (pre–Qualifying Exam) description of dissertation project.
- "Chicana Space, Ground of Being: Theories of the Self (A Chicana Writer Explores Spacio and (Self)Identities at the Junctures of Race, Class, Gender, Sex, Culture and Literature)" (92.8)
- "Chicana Space, Grounds of Being: Theories of Selves, Sexes and Writing" (92.11, 92.12)

Topics: autobiography, autohistoria, autohistoria-teoría, body, creativity, curanderismo, emotion, epistemology, exile, facultad, identity, identity formation and space, language, literature, Llorona, metaphor, method, myth, narrative, ontology, postmodernism, psyche, queer, separatism, sexuality, shamanism, silence, space, spirituality, subjectivity, theory, writing

"CHICANA WRITER GLORIA ANZALDUA: POLITICS OF A POET" (39.9) 1988. An interview with Anzaldúa published in *City on a Hill* (UC Santa

Cruz). The interview took place on March 19, 1988, and focuses primarily on *Borderlands*.

Topics: balance, border crossing, borderlands, *Borderlands*, El Mundo Zurdo, women of color, writing

"LA CHINGADA" (84.1, 84.2, 84.3, 84.4, 84.6) 1979–80. Handwritten and typed drafts of a dramatic piece that combines narrative with verse. Drafts indicate that Anzaldúa expanded the original poem into a scripted dramatic performance. Includes feedback from writing comadres and many edits. Anzaldúa revised the title several times: "La Chingada" (84.1); "La Chingada: A Poem-Play with Dance, Ritual, and Song" (84.3); "La Chingada: A Poem-Play with Music and Dance" (84.2)

Topics: Aztecs, La Chingada, colonialism, Cortes, gender, Llorona, love, Montezuma, Quetzacoatl, revisionist mythmaking, ritual

"CITIZEN OF THE UNIVERSE" (108.9) early 1980s. A three-page, double-spaced, typed essay draft.

Topics: borders, Chicano movement, citizenship, difference, gay men, identity, lesbians, nationalism, queers, spiritual activism

"COUNSELS FROM THE FIRING . . . PAST, PRESENT, FUTURE. FORE-WORD TO THE THIRD EDITION" (45.5, 45.6, 45.7, 45.8, 45.9, 45.10, 52.3) 2001. Foreword to the 2002 edition of *This Bridge Called My Back: Writings by Radical Women of Color*, this short manuscript exists in multiple versions with at least seven distinct drafts with handwritten notes, edits, and feedback from other readers. Titles vary:

- "Foreword" (45.5, 45.9)
- "Foreword: lessons from the firing" (45.5, 45.6)
- "Foreword: lessons from the firing . . . looking backward, looking forward" (45.5)
- "Foreword: counsels from the firing . . . past, present, future" (45.5, 45.7, 45.8)
- "Foreword: counsels from the firing . . . looking back, looking ahead" (45.5)
- "*counsels from the firing . . . past, present, future*: Foreword to the Third Edition" (45.5, 45.9, 45.10)

Topics: alienation, autobiographical information, autohistoria, bridges, bridging, change, conflicts, conocimiento, consciousness, desconocimiento, empowerment, energy, exile, geography of selves, healing, identity categories, imagination, inclusivity, love, new tribalism, nos/otras, ontology, privilege, race, social justice, spirit, *This Bridge*, threshold, women of color, wounds

"THE CRACKS AND HOLES BETWEEN THE WORLDS" (103.8, 112.5) 2000. Seven single-spaced pages, notes for a speech presented at the University of Michigan during the "Shades of a New Era: Pushing Intellectual Boundaries in Theory and Practice" conference (February 11–13, 2000). The title refers to outsiders, especially women-of-colors academics ("Trojan burras"), who refuse to assimilate and, instead, crack the walls: "What does cracking the wall do for both parties: the Trojan burras and those in power, the keepers of the gated city? It creates reflective dialogue, lets in new ideas of the way things are. What do you bring in through the holes you made? You bring your story, your frame of reference. You enter the story by challenging the dominant narratives and then by changing the official story." Anzaldúa drew on this material while writing her preface to *this bridge we call home*. She offers useful advice to graduate students and others interested in entering the academy's "wounding field." (The version in 112.5 was printed after her death from her hard drive.)

Topics: academia, activists, agency, assimilation, Chicanx/Latinx, community, compromise, conocimiento, contemplation, corazón con razón, cosmos, Coyolxauhqui, desire, education, empowerment, energy, exile, gigs, graduate school, healing, isolation, meaning, narrative, passion, political correctness, post-oppositionality, power, reflective dialogue, resistance, spiritual activism, spiritual practice, survival, Trojan burras, vision, wounds

"THE CRACKS BETWEEN THE WORLDS AND BRIDGES TO SPAN THEM" (112.5) 1999. Eight pages of single-spaced notes with handwritten edits for a talk delivered at Tufts University, February 22–24, 1999. Despite the title's similarity to the 2000 University of Michigan speech, the content is quite different with only slight overlap. In this piece, Anzaldúa worked out details concerning conocimiento. Includes conocimiento writing exercises "to help us talk across differences."

Topics: academia, activism, anger, árbol de la vida, attention, barran-cas, body, bridging, conflict, conocimiento, consciousness, descono-cimiento, difference, diversity, East Coast, emotional transformation, energy, environment, ethics, facultad, gigs, guided meditation, heal-ing, I Ching, knowledge, meditation, mind, El Mundo Zurdo, nep-antla, new tribalism, oppression, paradigm shift, passion, remolinos, ritual, soul-daemon, Southwest, spirit, spiritual activist, spirituality, spiritual work, Taoism, trauma, violence, vision, wounds, writing

"(DES)CONOCIMIENTOS: RESISTING NEW FORMS OF DOMINATION/OP-PRESSION" (60.3) April 1996. A midway-finished draft of approximately 3,300 words exploring conflict, identity politics, and other forms of op-positionality, in which Anzaldúa works to develop new forms of activism. This draft offers useful insights into Anzaldúa's thought as she began devel-oping her theory of conocimiento, which she describes as "The deep inner work of healing internalized sexism, racism, classism, homophobia, anti-semitism [sic], speciesism, ableism, sizeism, ageism, and other ism's [sic]; overcoming hindrances to our connections with each other; the process of enemy making; the process of making friends; honoring and celebrat-ing difference; renewing our commitment to reeducate ourselves out of cultural prejudices; the need to sacralize all life forms on earth; honoring the diversity of the global women's spiritual community; and the need to respect diversity in the process fo [sic] feminist community-building." In-terestingly, "conocimiento" is used only once in this draft (in relation to new tribalism and a call for new strategies and coalitions among different groups); Anzaldúa doesn't use "(des)conocimientos" except in the title.

Topics: activism, activist intellectuals, affirmative action, allies, as-similation, bridging, Chicanx/Latinx, civil disobedience, community, complicity, conflict, conocimiento, (des)conocimientos, difference, education, ethnic hostility, healing, identity, language, marginaliza-tion, masculinity, mestiza identity, mixed race, nationalism, new tribalism, nos/otras, oppression, post-oppositionality, power, Propo-sition 187, queer theory, remolinos, resistance, tension, Trojan mula/burra, white backlash, women-of-color academics

"EL DESARROLLO: THE ECONOMY OF SELF-DEVELOPMENT" (60.2, 92.14) 1988–89, 2001. Originally part of Anzaldúa's Lloronas dissertation project, this manuscript exists in two drafts: "El Desarrollo: The Economy of Self-Development" (92.14), dated "9/26/89," is five single-spaced pages; "El desarrollo and future of Chicana theory: The Economy of Self-Development" (60.2) is ten single-spaced pages (a five-page essay and five pages of notes) and was printed after Anzaldúa's death from her hard drive, where it was last saved December 25, 2001. These drafts offer insight into Anzaldúa's aspirational views of Chicana (and women-of-colors) literature:

> I'd like us to go beyond the limits, burst through the perimeters, romper barreras push ourselves into taboo, forbidden territories and yell boo in their faces, scattering nightmares. I want our literatures to take us places no other literature has. . . . I'd like to see visionary works that delve into the psychological and the mythical and that value the internal life, of dreams and spiritual life. Literature that illuminates sociopolitical realities and places in social context the distress people feel about the status quo. I want to see elements of the extraordinary and the fantastic/phantastic (un)real realistic irreal supra/supernatural celebration of the monstrous and the outcast because confronting these is ultimately enlightening.

Also includes recommendations for women-of-colors authors, discussion of the challenges of "[w]riting outside the mainstream," and exploration of the relationship between art and theory.

> Topics: aesthetics, Aztlán, borderlands, Chicana feminism, colonialism, creativity, darkness, embodiment, emotion, energy, epistemology, femininity, genres, healing, horror, imagination, knowledge production, literature, logocentrism, meditation, mestiza, method, new mestiza, power, reading, recovery, self-development, spirituality, stress, survival, television, theory, transformation, whiteness, writing blocks, writing process

"DOING GIGS" (60.4) 1991. Three-page double-spaced rough draft on Anzaldúa's experiences "doing gigs"—giving lectures for a living—with handwritten feedback from a writing comadre or assistant. Offers a brief glimpse into the challenges (*and toll*) Anzaldúa experienced as a lecturer, as well as her speculations about how audiences perceived her (and what they wanted from her) and her view of her gigs as a "political act."

Topics: body, epistemology, gigs, insomnia, patience, spirit, teaching, writing

"EMBODYING LA LLORONA: THE MESTIZA BORDER WRITER/ARTIST AND THE UNSPEAKABLE. THE WOMAN WHO WRITES, THE WOMAN WHO WRITES ME. MY LIFE AS A WRITER: *CUENTOS DE ESPANTO* (TALES OF TERROR)" (95.19) 1991. Twenty-seven-page, 1.5-spaced document with material from the Lloronas dissertation project. Notes, excerpts from previous writing, and material from an interview that Anzaldúa drew on while preparing her November 1991 talk for the Conference on College Composition and Communication. Includes Anzaldúa's visionary aspirations for future women-of-colors writing as well as information on her writing process and personal aspirations as a writer.

Topics: academia, art, astrology, autobiographical information, body, censorship, Chicana artist, consciousness, creativity, dark fantasy, death, detribalization, dreams, energy, experimental writing, facultad, genres, guilt, Jonah complex, knowledge, language, Llorona, maternal, mestisaje,[3] metaphysics, modernity, musa bruja, mysticism, myth, nepantla, Prieta, psychoanalytic theory, reading, religion, self-acceptance, soul, space, subjectivity, tension, transgression, Uranus, vision, women's writing, writer's block, writing, writing process

"EN ESTILO MESTISAJE—IN THE WRITING I CROSS GENRES, I CROSS BORDERS" (92.15, 121.4) 1989–90. A typed, 1.5-spaced, eleven-page transcript of a 1988 talk delivered at Cornell University that Anzaldúa planned to expand into an essay. Many handwritten edits and revisions. The talk was transcribed and published in *Trivia* as "Border Crossings."

Topics: aesthetics, autohistoria, autohistoria-teoría, body, borderlands, *Borderlands*, borders, class, colonization, emotion, estilo mestizaje, exile, feminisms, genres, ideology, isolation, Jews, knowledge, landscape, language, literary canon, literature, margins, mestiza, naming, poetics, representation, self-representation, spiritual activism, survival, symbols, whiteness, women-of-colors authors, world-traveling, writing

"ENTREGUERRAS, ENTREMUNDOS / CIVIL WARS AMONG THE WORLDS" (66.9, 66.10, 66.11, 66.12) 1980s, 1989–93. Handwritten and typed drafts and notes for a multigenre collection, composed of material from the 1970s through the early 1990s, that Anzaldúa planned to publish with Aunt Lute in the early 1990s. Includes typed table of contents with handwritten notations in various colors, indicating that Anzaldúa returned to this project several times.

Topics: aesthetics, angel, animism, anxiety, autohistoria, avatar, bardo, body, breath, consciousness, daimon, death, desire, drugs, fear, fiction, friendship, gods, hysterectomy, intersex, Joan of Arc, karma, leadership, lesbians, magic, meditation, mushrooms, ontology, orgasm, pain, psyche, reading, reality, ritual, sex, shadow, shaman, soul, spirit, spirit guide, Sri Aurbindo, stone, subtle body, *Twilight Zone*, violence, la Virgen, water, women of color, work, writing

"EN NEPANTLA" (70.12) 1991. Multiple drafts of a short story with handwritten annotations indicating that Anzaldúa revised this piece into the later short story "Puddles." Some drafts include feedback from writing comadres; other drafts include Anzaldúa's handwritten edits and revisions (including references to Joseph Campbell and Victor Turner). In this brief story, the protagonist undergoes a ritual crossing over with death, dismemberment, and transformation.

Topics: alienation, animism, border crossing, borders, chakras, embodiment, identity, imaginal, language, nepantla

"ESPERANDO LA SERPIENTE CON PLUMAS (WAITING FOR THE FEATHERED SERPENT)" (78.9) 1982. The first draft of Anzaldúa's early autobiography, consisting of 113 typed, double-spaced pages written between July 1981 and September 1982. Anzaldúa planned to fictionalize sections in her proposed novel, *Andrea*, and she cannibalized it for other projects as well. She describes this manuscript as "colors, threads, patterns and forms [that] trace my initiation in the Spirit and into the Body. And also into self-knowledge. They track my attempts to integrate intellect and intuition, trace and retrace my steps in the journey toward becoming a mujer íntegra." Written in first person, this draft seems more factually autobiographical than later versions. Anzaldúa's letter to "Prospective Publisher," included as part of the draft, indicates her intention to create a multigenre text with "poetry, prose, story, myth, song, litter [sic], dialogue, drama, journal entry"; by thus "combining different forms (genres), I hope to break through traditional fences." Scholars will find this manuscript useful as they consider how Anzaldúa incorporated the personal into autohistoria and autohistoria-teoría. This draft also represents an early, complex artic-ulation of Anzaldúa's philosophy, including her politics of spirit—the roots or seeds of what she later named spiritual activism.

> Topics: activism, ancestors, anger, art, attention, autohistoria, autohistoria-teoría, Aztec(s), Aztlán, body, breath, bruja, Buddhism, burnout, chakras, la Chingada, Christ, collective unconscious, con-sciousness, creativity, curandera, death, depression, destiny, divine, drugs, dualisms, epistemology, estrangement, evil, facultad, fear, flesh, guerrilleras divinas, Hinduism, hysterectomy, I Ching, iden-tity, images, imagination, Inanna, initiation, intuition, liberation, love, magic, Marx, Mayan, meditation, menstruation, El Mundo Zurdo, mysticism, myth, Native American, near death experiences, new paradigm, noosphere, OBE (out-of-body experience), occult, ontology, oppression, Plato, poets, politics, Prieta, psychic, queers, raza cosmica, reading, revolution, ritual, roots, sacred politica, ser-pents, sexuality, shaman, soul, spirit, spiritual activism, spirituality, survival, Tarot, Third World feminists, transformation, tree, Uranus, vastation, vibrations, visions, visualization, vocation, wounds, writ-ing, writing blocks, Xochiquetzal

"ETHNIC AUTOHISTORIAS-TEORÍAS: WRITING THE HISTORY OF THE SUBJECT" (91.30, 92.16, 92.18, 92.19) 1989–90. An early version of "*Autohistorias-teorías—Mujeres que cuentan vidas*: Personal & Collective Narratives That Challenge Genre Conventions," this paper exists in mul-tiple drafts and copies, including rough notes (92.16), handwritten inser-tions, and comments from other readers. Anzaldúa used part of this essay to develop "Metaphors in the Tradition of the Shaman." We see Anzaldúa incorporating psychoanalytic theory and other contemporary movements as she develops her methodology while exploring the writing process and identity formation (among other things). See also "Remembering and Subverting in the 'Historias' of Chicanas and Women of Color." Titles vary considerably:

- "Remembering and Subverting in the 'Historias' of Chicanas and Women of Color" (91.30), paper written for Donna Haraway's course, winter 1989 quarter. It includes handwritten edits and notes, as well as material that became "Metaphors in the Tradition of the Shaman."

- "Writing the Subject: Narrative and History in Ethnic *Autohistorias-teorías*" (92.17)
- "Writing the History of the Subject: Ethnic *Autohistorias-teorías*" (92.17)
- "Ethnic Autohistorias-teorías: Writing the History of the Subject" (92.17)
- "Ethnic Autohistorias-teorías: Writing the Personal & Collective History of the Subject" (92.17)
- "Ethnic *Autohistorias-teorías*: Writing the Personal & Collective Histories of the Subject" (92.20, 92.21)

Topics: aesthetics, autobiographical information, autobiography, autohistoria, autohistoria-teoría, autohistoteorías, body, Chicana cultural criticism, Chicana feminist critic, Chicana literature, Coatlicue states, colonization, depression, desire, embodiment, essentialism, facultad, fiction, flesh, geology, historia, history, identity, imagination, individual/collective, literature, Llorona, loss, memory, menstruation, metaphor, methodology, mother, myth, narrative, ontology, oral tradition, origins, power, process, psychoanalytic theory, race, reading, reality, religious discourse, resistance, revision, rhetoric, semiotics, source, storytelling, subjectivity, survival, testimonial, theory, trauma, women-of-color literary production, writing

"EXPLORING CULTURAL LEGACIES: USING MYTHS TO CONSTRUCT STORIES OF MODERN REALITIES" (112.12) 1999. Thirteen pages of single-spaced notes for Anzaldúa's March 1999 talk at Eastern New Mexico University in Portales, NM. Offers one of her most organized and expansive discussions of revisionist mythmaking (its functions, forms, epistemology, etc.). The notes on spirituality resonate with portions of *Light in the Dark*, chapter 2, as does the ontological framework.

Topics: aesthetics, árbol de la vida, archetypes, autohistoria, body, Buddhism, candle magic, cenote, Chicanas, Cihuacoatl, Coatlicue, collective unconscious, consciousness, Coyolxauhqui, curanderismo, deities, dreaming, emotion, entering the serpent, environment, epistemology, facultad, fear, ghosts, gigs, goddesses, grief, Guadalupe, guilt, horror, identity, jaguar, Jung, Llorona, meaning, musa bruja, mythology, naguala, nagualismo, narrative, nature, nepantla, ontology, remolinos of change, revisionist mythmaking, ritual, Serpent Woman, Shadow Beast, shamanism, spirit, spirituality, supernatural, susto, thought, time, tradition, transformation, visionary, wounds, Xochiquetzal, zombies

"FACULTY SELF-DESCRIPTION" (39.8) 1980s. One-page biographical statement written when Anzaldúa was living on the East Coast. Offers personal information, including her work and goals as an educator.

Topics: alchemy, archetypal psychology, astrology, autobiographical information, books, consciousness, curanderismo, dreams, education, I Ching, numerology, reading, spirituality, Sri Aurobindo, Tarot, Texas, writing practice

"FANTASY" (103.11) 1990. Printed after Anzaldúa's death and last saved January 12, 2004, these eight 1.5-spaced pages of notes, written when Anzaldúa was attending UCSC, combine summaries of psychoanalytic theory with discussion of her Lloronas dissertation.

Topics: aesthetics, autohistoria, body, daydreams, depression, emotion, epistemology, fact, facultad, fantasy, fiction, Freud, hysteria, intuition, knowledge production, language, Llorona, method, mourning, ontology, personal experience, psychoanalytic theory, realism, reality, representation, sexuality, sexual trauma, style, subconscious, time, void, writing

"FOREWORD TO THIS BRIDGE CALLED MY BACK" (45.4) 1982–83. Two double-spaced, typed drafts of Anzaldúa's short foreword to the Kitchen Table Press edition of This Bridge. Includes handwritten edits. One draft is three pages, and the other six.

Topics: accountability, agency, consciousness, gay men, gigs, homophobia, lesbianism, meditation, racism, soul, women of color

"FRA RESEARCH APPLICATION" (91.7) 1990. Two single-spaced pages of notes (with handwritten edits) for a research application in support of

Anzaldúa's research on Chicana art and representation. Closely connected with the Lloronas dissertation.

Topics: artists, autobiographical information, Chicana/Mexicana representation, critical theory, identity, space, writing

"GEN NOTES" (103.13) 2004. Last saved on April 30, 2004 (less than one month before Anzaldúa's death), these twenty-four single-spaced pages of notes offer entry into Anzaldúa's interests and mind near the end of her life, including her relationship to Indigeneity, creativity, and imagination. She's working out material for the preface and chapter 2 of *Light in the Dark*, as well as "Speaking across the Divide" and "SIC."

Topics: academic discourse, anxiety, body, boundaries, creativity, deconstruction, depression, difference, dreams, ecosystem, embodiment, epistemology, global warming, Guadalupe, health, horror films, horses, identity, imagination, Indigeneity, Jung, Kaballah, Llorona, Malinche, meditation, Medusa, metaphysics, miracles, nepantla, neoshamanism, ontology, otherness, peace, perception, physics, poetry, polarization, postcolonialism, Prieta, psychoanalytic theory, punctuation, racism, reality, sensory experience, sexuality, shamanism, space, time travel, transformation, truth, vision, water, writing

"GEOGRAPHIES OF SELVES—RE-IMAGINING IDENTITIES: NOS/OTRAS (US/OTHER), LAS NEPANTLERAS AND THE NEW TRIBALISM" (96.12, 96.14, 96.18, 96.21, 96.22, 97.1, 97.2, 97.3, 97.4, 97.5, 97.7, 97.8, 97.9, 97.10, 97.11, 97.12, 97.15, 97.17) 1999–2004. This essay, which became chapter 4 of *Light in the Dark*, exists in the form of a lecture transcript (96.12), an outline (96.12), conversations with writing comadres (96.21, 96.22), and an overwhelming number of drafts with a confusing variety of titles:

- "Nos/otros: Us vs. Them . . . El compromiso" (96.12) 1999
- "Nos/otros: 'Us' vs. 'Them,' (Des)Conocimientos y compromisos" (96.12, 96.14) 1999
- "Nos/otros: Us/Them. . . . The Commitment and the New Tribalism" (96.12) 2001
- "Nos/otros: Us/Them. . . . The New Tribalism and Recommitment to la Lucha" 2001

- "Nos/otras: Us/Them . . . Re-imagining Identity: The New Tribalism and Renewing our Commitment to la Lucha" (96.18) dated "11/22/02–1/22/03"
- "Geographies of the Self—Re-imagining Identity: Nos/otras (Us/Other) and the New Tribalism" (96.21: 2/18/03; 96.22: 3/3/03) February and March 2003
- "Geography of the Selves—Re-imagining Identity: Nos/otras (Us/Other) and the New Tribalism" (97.1) May 2003
- "Geography of Selves—Re-imagining Identity: Nos/otras (Us/Other) and the New Tribalism" (97.2, 97.3, 97.4, 97.5, 97.7, 97.8, 97.9) June 2003
- "Geography of Selves—Re-imagining Identity: Nos/otras (Us/Other), Las nepantleras, and the New Tribalism" (97.10, 97.11, 97.12) October 2003
- "Geographies of Selves—Re-imagining Identities: Nos/otras (Us/Other), Las nepantleras and the New Tribalism" (97.15, 97.17). 97.15: 1/21/04; 97.17: 4/30/04—printed from Anzaldúa's hard drive after her death.

Originally, Anzaldúa wrote this piece to be included in *Geographies of Latinidad,* an edited collection developed from the conference of the same name, but as the many drafts indicate, she had great difficulty in completing this piece for numerous reasons, including shifts in her identity-related theories. While the earliest versions foreground Anzaldúa's theory of (what would eventually become) nos/otras and have the word "nos/otros" in the title, the later versions (beginning February 2003) shift focus to her theory of the geographies of selves. See also "Nos/otros 'Us' vs. 'Them'" (below).

Topics: árbol de la vida, body, Chicana/o identity, Chicano movement, conflict, conocimiento, Coyolxauhqui, Coyolxauhqui imperative, Coyolxauhqui process, culture, decoloniality, ethnic studies, ethnocentrism, exile, feminism, gender, geographies of selves, healing, identity, imagination, immigration, loss, media, mestiza, mestizaje, multiculturalism, naguala, narrative, nationalism, nature/nurture, nepantla, nepantlera, new tribalism, nos/otras, othering, plane of identity, PTSD, rajadura (perspective from the cracks), Raza studies, representation, self-in-communities, shadow beast, spiritual activism, spirituality, subjectivity, susto, transformation, transgender, transnationalism, trauma, wounds

"GEO OF SELVES—OLD NOTES" (97.14) 1999–2004? Twenty-three pages of single-spaced notes that Anzaldúa drew on while writing and revising "Geographies of Selves." This manuscript, last saved January 15, 2004, was printed from her hard drive after her death; it focuses especially on social identity categories and spirituality.

> Topics: academia, assimilation, border, borderlands, community, conflict, culture, disidentification, epistemology, ethnic studies, fear, feminism, gender, geographies of selves, identity, identity politics, imagination, interconnectedness, intersex, narrative, nationalism, nepantla, nepantleras, new mestiza, new tribalism, nos/otras, Raza studies, self-recovery, spiritual activism, spirituality, theory, transformation, transgender, women of color

"THE HAUNTINGS OF LA LLORONA" (91.11, 93.1, 93.2, 93.21) 1989. An early version of a dissertation chapter indicating Anzaldúa's focus at that time, especially her work with Llorona ("Her ghostly body, wandering and wailing, is my vehicle for symbolic identity and for changing the concept of identity as well. For me as a writer, she is my 'necessary monster,' a *musa bruja* whose utterances decode, subvert and hopefully destroy, the denigrating cultural roles assigned us" [103.13]). For an even earlier version of this chapter, see "La Llorona y la víbora que se mete por allá." For notes Anzaldúa used while constructing this piece, see "notes—horrific" (93.3) and "notes—llorona" (93.4), both discussed below.

- 93.1: A one-page letter, dated "10/19/89," to José Limón, outlining the course paper, which even at this point Anzaldúa conceived to be part of her dissertation.
- 93.2: Multiple drafts, some with handwritten edits and reader feedback. The opening pages on the body are amazing. Under "Hauntings" is the introduction: "*Nomos*, the Feeding Place, the Dwelling Space."
- 93.21: Draft dated June 1989 and revised September 30, 1989. Handwritten revisions of title, changing it several times, from "La Llorona y la víbora que se mete por allá" to "Encounters with La Llorona" to "The Hauntings of La Llorona."
- 91.11: May 1990 draft sent to Norma Alarcón, opens with Anzaldúa's request for specific feedback.

Topics: anxiety, autobiographical information, autohistoria-teoría, bodies, la Chingada, class, colonization, Cortes, death, desire, discourse, embodiment, fantasy, feminine, fiction, folklore, folk tales, gender, history, hysteria, identity, imaginary, Llorona, Malinche, melancholy, memory, mother, mourning, myth, nagual, pain, patriarchy, perception, phenomenology, representation, resistance, sacrifice, semiotics, serpents, shape-shifting, space, spirits, storytelling, subjectivity, supernatural, survival, symbol, transgression, trauma, vampires, violence, Virgin Mary, wounds, writing

"HOLDING TOGETHER" (108.9) 1982. A short talk (approximately 2,500 words) delivered on May 22, 1982, possibly as the opening for an event related to the El Mundo Surdo Reading Series. Focuses on queers' leading role in effecting social-spiritual transformation and illustrates Anzaldúa's early innovations in queer theory.

Topics: attunement, clairvoyance, facultad, gay men, lesbians, masculinity, El Mundo Surdo, politics, queers, queer theory, release the four hands, spirit, spiritual activism, transformation, vocation

"HOW I GET MYSELF TO THE WRITING" (103.29) n.d. Slightly over two single-spaced pages of rough draft in which Anzaldúa reflects on her writing process and reasons for writing. Printed after Anzaldúa's death from her hard drive, this document was last saved on February 16, 1999; however, it was probably written much earlier (as evidenced by Anzaldúa's reference to her typewriter) and seems to have originated in an interview or transcribed conversation. The folder location and file name indicate that Anzaldúa viewed this manuscript as part of her larger explorations of writing and spirituality.

Topics: alchemy, altar-making, anger, autobiographical information, epistemology, feminism, habits, identity, images, imagination, meditation, ontology, rituals, visualization, writing, writing process

"HOW I'VE SURVIVED" (60.11) 1991. A four-page first-person narrative in which Anzaldúa discusses her coping strategies, how she manages her depression ("Coatlicue state"), and "writing as self-therapy" (which seems like a type of freewrite, where she would write whatever came into her mind); identity as multiple and somewhat within our control to change;

self-reflection, etc. This manuscript might have originated as a transcript from an interview; it includes handwritten comments.

Topics: autobiographical information, breath, candle magic, class, Coatlicue state, depression, gender, healing, identity, meditation, oppression, Prieta, self-reflection, solitude, survival, violence, writing process

"IDEOGRAPHS" (91.8) 1991. Nineteen pages of handwritten notes and drawings, developed at least partially in preparation for Anzaldúa's gig at the University of Arizona on October 14–18, 1991, and the "8ᵗʰ NAOO conf" in October 1992. The full-page drawings offer interesting insights into Anzaldúa's views of identity in the early 1990s.

Topics: activism, borderlands, la Chingada, colonialism/colonization, Columbus, conocimiento, ghost, haunting, identity, language, Llorona, mestiza consciousness, nepantla, nos/otras, nostalgia, pisar la sombra, resistance, silence and voice, Sor Juana, speaking in tongues, susto, Thich Nhat Hanh, "las tres madres," La Virgen, writing

"ID—SUBJECT TO CHANGES: MESTIZA IDENTITIES AND POSITIONINGS OF THE BODY" (93.6, 93.7, 93.8, 93.9, 93.10, 93.11, 93.12) 1989–92. This manuscript (which exists in multiple versions with various titles, handwritten edits, and reader feedback) began as a paper for a course Anzaldúa took during her doctoral work at UCSC, and is closely related to several dissertation chapters: "Noche y su nidada," "Llorona y la víbora," and "Subject to Changes: Mestiza Identities and Positionings." Titles include the following:

- "ID—Subject to Changes: Mestiza Identities and Positionings of the Body" (93.7)
- "ID—Subject to Shiftings: Mestiza Identities and Positionings of the Body" (93.7)
- "ID—Subject to Shiftings: Disturbing Identities & Representations" (93.8, 93.9)
- "ID—Subject to Shiftings: Disturbing Identities and Representations" (93.11, 93.12). The draft in 93.11 includes handwritten comments by Liz Grosz (the course professor), and the draft in 93.12 was the version Grosz read.

- "ID—Subject to Shiftings/Slippage: Disturbing Identities and Representations" (93.10)

Here we see Anzaldúa's unique spin on identity ("Who I present myself to be to the world, who I feel I really am and who my different worlds push me to be don't equal the same person. I am more Chicana or more lesbian or more water depending on whether I'm in, or distanced from, the Chicano community, in or separate from my lesbian feminist community, near or distanced from a body of water. I am all these identities all the time except that one or two take center stage in particular instances") and her desire "to uncover a different subjectivity, one that overcomes the opposition between individual and collectivity."

Topics: appropriation, assimilation, authenticity, autohistoria-teoría, body, Chicano culture, colonialism, consciousness, difference, ego, ethnic/Others, facultad, feminism, gender, history, humanism, identification, identity, language, lesbian, Llorona, memory, mestiza, nagual, nationalism, new mestiza, oppression, patterns, postcolonialism, poststructuralist theory, psychoanalytic theory, race, reality, representation, shape-shifting, space, subjectivity, symbol, transformation, water, way station, women of color, writing

"INSOMNIA" (93.13) early 1990s. Two copies of one page of typed notes, printed after Anzaldúa's death from two locations on her hard drive; although last saved January 1, 2002, these notes are from the early 1990s.

Topics: autobiographical, body, identity, insomnia, Llorona, sexuality

"INTRODUCTION: EN EL SILENCIO DE MI ESPACIO" (91.9) 1989. An early, thirteen-page version of the Lloronas dissertation prospectus, hand-dated "10/19/89," offering a useful overview of Anzaldúa's project as she envisioned it at the time.

Topics: autohistoria, autohistoria-teoría, Chicana, depth psychology, difference, domination, feminism, folklore, gender, guilt, humanism, identity, imaginal, individual/collective identity, intersectionality, isolation, Llorona, Marxism, method, New Criticism, new historicism, new mestiza, poststructuralism, race, ritual, sensory experience, sexuality, space, structuralism, subjectivity, survival, theory, time, Virgen, women of color, writing

"LECTURES ON THEMES AND THEORIES" (103.14) 1990. Ten 1.5-spaced pages of notes, printed from Anzaldúa's hard drive after her death but last saved on June 11, 1990. Based on their file location, it seems that Anzaldúa planned to use these notes, drawn from her time as a visiting professor at UCSC, in later essays. (The document was saved as "lectures-UCSC" in a folder titled "8d-beg essays.") In part, the notes are drawn from notes for the table of contents for *Making Face, Making Soul*.

> Topics: aesthetics, anxiety, class, coalitions, Coatlicue state, colonialism, creativity, feminism, feminist theory, identity, imaginal, imagination, internalized oppression, language, literature, myth, neocolonialism, pseudo-universality, psychoanalytic theory, racism, rationality, separatism, sexuality, theory, Third World feminism, white feminism, whiteness, womanism

"LLORONA/SPACE" (91.13) 1989. Thirty-seven pages of notes (some typed, some handwritten) with material for course papers, dissertation chapters ("Desarrollo" and "Writing Edge of Stress"), and gigs.

> Topics: alliance work, anger, blank spots, body, *Borderlands*, class, coalition, colonialism, communication, conflict, conocimiento, critique, difference, disabilities, emotions, entering into the serpent, entitlement, ethnocentrism, feminism, idealism, identity, internalized oppression, Llorona, men, mestiza, postmodernism, racism, reading, ritual, Santa Cruz, silence, sisterhood (including divisions between women-of-color and white feminists), solidarity, space, survival, whiteness, women of color, women's studies, writing

"LA LLORONA TELLS HER STORY" (93.18) 1995. A one-page typed first-person narrative of Llorona telling her own story in her own words.

> Topics: death, lesbian, Llorona, loss, wailing

"LLORONA, THE WOMAN WHO WAILS: CHICANA/MESTIZA TRANSGRESSIVE IDENTITIES" (93.15, 93.16) ca. 1990. Multiple copies of an essay on La Llorona that Anzaldúa either drew on for the early 1990s prospectus or used as part of a later book project. Includes earlier drafts titled "Llorona, the Woman Who Wails: Chicana/Mestiza Identities" (93.15, 93.16). Typed with handwritten edits. This essay focuses on Llorona "as a feminist subject, a sign for postmodernism." Anzaldúa viewed it as "a companion piece" to other essays from that time: "Postmodern Mestiza" and "ID: Mestiza Identity and Chicana/o Subjectivity."

> Topics: anxiety, archetype, body, Chicanas, la Chingada, depression, desire, embodiment, exile, folk tales, ghosts, grief, haunting, hysteria, identity, Llorona, "La Llorona complex," Malinche, melancholy, menstruation, mourning, myth, narrative, patriarchy, postmodernism, power, psychoanalytic theory, representation, resistance, serpents, Serpent Woman, supernatural, survival, victimization

"LA LLORONA Y LA VÍBORA QUE SE METE POR ALLÁ" (93.19, 93.20, 93.21, 93.22, 94.1) 1989–92. Multiple drafts of a paper for Teresa de Lauretis's UCSC course, including title edits (93.21) and de Lauretis's feedback (93.22), offering insight into Anzaldúa's intention for the dissertation, including her focus on Llorona: "I want to help *la llorona* by writing her story differently, by 'rewriting' it. Her ghostly body, wandering and wailing is my vehicle for carrying symbolic identity and for changing the concept of identity as well. For me as a writer she is my necessary monster, a *musa bruja* whose utterances decode, and hopefully destroy, the denigrating cultural roles assigned us." "In *la lorona* is contained the symbolic product or synthesis of the lived experiences of all mestizas. . . . La llorona is a scream that punctures a hole in space, a bloodcurdling wail that keeps alive the trauma of the past, a trauma frozen in time, eternal, a trauma of separation and death. The scream is followed by a slow prolonged moaning." Anzaldúa later worked this paper into "Chicana Space."

> Topics: autobiographical information, bodies, Chicanas, Chicana writers, la Chingada, Coatlicue state, colonialism, Cortes, depression, environment, exile, facultad, fantasy, folk tales, ghosts, haunting, history, hysteria, identity, isolation, Llorona, "La Llorona complex," Malinche, melancholy, memory, mestizas, mourning, myth, nagual, oppression, origin, phenomenology, postmodernism, psyche, psychoanalytic theory, resistance, shape-shifting, space, spirits, supernatural, symbol, trauma

"LLORONAS BOOK: REWRITING REALITY" (91.12) 1994. Three pages of single-spaced typed notes related to Anzaldúa's dissertation.

Topics: aesthetics, autohistoria-teoría, consciousness, identity, knowledge production, lesbian, Llorona, postcolonialism, time, writing

"LLORONAS NOTES FOR THE PROSPECTUS" (91.18, 93.17) 1990. Notes for the prospectus:

- 91.18: Ten pages of handwritten brainstorming notes (proposal and abstract) on the early 1990s UCSC dissertation. "Helene" at the top of page 3 indicates that Anzaldúa took these notes during a meeting with Helene Moglen, her dissertation chair. This material also includes perhaps the first outline of Anzaldúa's projected dissertation chapters, which at this time numbered ten.
- 93.17: Twenty-four pages of typed and handwritten miscellaneous notes (including reading notas on Llorona-related myths and Norma Alarcón's feedback) in which Anzaldúa worked out her theory of embodiment and Llorona through doodles, drawings, and other brainstorming. "La Llorona is a transgressive ethnic other"—this simple line says so much about the projected dissertation and Anzaldúa's connections with Llorona, or as she puts it "why I sympathize and identify so much with La Llorona."

Topics: autobiography, autohistoria, autohistoria-teoría, bodies, colonialism, Columbus, desire, discourse, embodiment, exile, gender, horror, identity formation, language, Llorona, loss, masturbation, mestiza consciousness, musa bruja, myth, narrative, new mestiza, postcolonial, postmodernity, psychoanalytic theory, rajadura, selfhood, semiotics, silence, space, subjectivity, suicide, transgression, voice, writing

LLORONAS PROSPECTUS (91.22, 91.24) ca. 1990, 2002. Two prospectus drafts for the Lloronas dissertation: "Description: Lloronas—Women Who Wail: (Self)Representation and the Production of Writing, Knowledge and Identity" (91.24). Both were printed after Anzaldúa's death from her hard drive, and were last saved May 20, 2002.

Topics: autohistoria-teoría, Chicana, colonialism, identity, knowledge production, language, Llorona, memory, mestiza consciousness, mestiza subjectivity, myth, narrative, Sor Juana, space, trauma, women of colors' writing process, writing production

"LLORONAS—WOMEN WHO WAIL: *AUTOHISTORIAS-TEORÍAS* AND THE PRODUCTION OF WRITING, KNOWLEDGE AND IDENTITY PROSPECTUS" (91.1, 91.20, 91.21, 91.28) 1990–92. Proposal for the Lloronas dissertation. Anzaldúa began thinking about her dissertation project early in her UCSC coursework and, throughout her studies, produced numerous drafts, notes, and tentative tables of contents for this project. Titles varied considerably:

- "Lloronas—Women Who Wail: Ethnic/Other Explorations of (Self)-Representation and Identity and the Production of Writing and Knowledge" (91.1). This folder contains several copies of abstract drafts with readers' feedback; it offers a helpful overview of Anzaldúa's intentions for the dissertation: "The work is an investigation of self-representation and the production of writing, knowledge, memory, imagination, consciousness, identities and the political resistance and agency of female postcolonial cultural Other (particularly the Chicana/mestiza)."
- "Lloronas—Women Who Wail: Ethnic/Other Explorations of Identity, (Self)-Representation & Writing" (91.1, 91.20)
- "Lloronas—Women Who Wail: Explorations of (Self)Representation and Identity and the Production of Writing and Knowledge" (91.21) 1991. The signed copy of the prospectus, dated "5/30/91." Dissertation adviser: Helene Moglen; Committee: José David Saldívar and Donna Haraway. The orals reading list is dated "10/15/90."
- "Lloronas—Women Who Wail: *Autohistorias-teorías* and the Production of Writing, Knowledge and Identity" (91.28) 1992. By this relatively late point, Anzaldúa planned to divide the dissertation into two "volumes": "Volume One—Writing and Representation" and "Volume Two—Llorona: *Noche y su nidada.*" Volume one has ten chapters; volume two has seven.

Topics: autohistoria-teoría, Cihualcoat, class, emotion, epistemology, feminist theory, gender, identity, identity formation, knowledge production, literary studies, Llorona, mestiza consciousness, methodology, myth, postcoloniality, queer, race, representation, self-representation, stress, subjectivity, theory, voice, writing

"LLORONAS—WRITING, READING, SPEAKING, DREAMING" (91.23, 91.28) ca. 1997. Printed after Anzaldúa's death and last saved October 21, 2001, this short annotated table of contents (less than six hundred words) is so distinct as to be, in many ways, a different project. Also includes a version titled "Rewriting Reality: Lloronas—Writing, Reading, Speaking, Dreaming" (91.28) and probably represents Anzaldúa's attempt to convert her early 1990s dissertation material into a book.

> Topics: activism, agency, altars, artist, Coyolxauhqui, depression, domination, facultad, knowledge production, multiculturalism, nepantla, planetary citizen, remolinos, resistance, spiritual mestisaje, theory, virtual community, writing

"METAPHORS IN THE TRADITION OF THE SHAMAN" (61.12, 61.13, 61.14, 107.1) ca. 1988. A short piece in which Anzaldúa reflects on *Borderlands'* publication and explores how metaphors function as a healing process for readers. Exists in various drafts and copies:

- "Sick Metaphors & the Shamán" (107.1) n.d.: The six-page handwritten version of what would become "Metaphors in the Tradition of the Shaman." Quite possibly this draft was written for a speaking engagement.
- "Sick Metaphors and the Shaman" (61.13) n.d.: Two-page single-spaced draft.
- "Metaphors in the Tradition of the Shaman" (61.12) last saved January 19, 1990, and printed from Anzaldúa's hard drive after her death.
- "Sick Metaphors and the Shaman" (61.14) last saved June 17, 2002, and printed from Anzaldúa's hard drive after her death.

See also the 1990s Lloronas dissertation, especially "Poet is Critic."

> Topics: belief, body, *Borderlands*, Chicanas, communication, consciousness, cultural identity, healing, images, imagination, Latinas, metaphors, misinformation, poet, reading, resistance, shamanism, transformation, writing

MISCELLANEOUS LECTURE NOTES (96.9) late 1990s. Nineteen pages of writing notas (most handwritten) for various speaking events: the 1999 University of Illinois Geographies of Latinidad conference, the preface for *this bridge we call home*, the foreword for *This Bridge Called My Back*, and the Cal State Dominguez Hills talk.

> Topics: academia, art, autobiographical information, awakening, balance, body, bridging, cenote, citizenship, Coatlicue, conflict, conocimiento, desconocimiento, dreaming, ecology, energy, epistemology, exile, feminism, feminist theory, gender, geography of selves, identity, oppression, out-of-body experience, queer, reality, Sor Juana, soul, transfiguration, women's studies, writing

"MISC. NOTES" (107.7) 1980s and 1990s. Fourteen pages of handwritten notas on a variety of topics, including material for the Prieta stories.

> Topics: alter/native, art, autobiographical information, body, cemetery, compostura, conferences, Coyolxauhqui, critique, death, depression, dreams, emotions, feminist theory, grief, guilt, heterotopia, hummingbirds, identity, initiation, language, Llorona, memory, El Mundo Zurdo, nature, Prieta, queer theory, ravens, shamanism, space, stories, Texas, vultures, writing

"NAVIGATING NEPANTLA AND THE CRACKS BETWEEN THE WORLDS" (61.19) 1996. This short manuscript (less than two thousand words) exists in three versions (all included in 61.19) with handwritten revisions and comments, as well as a page of notes titled "Re-Configuring Frontiers." These drafts allow us to chart Anzaldúa's shifting perspectives on bridging, borderlands, and nepantla. Earlier version titles:

- "Nepantla: The Crack between Worlds"
- "Re-Configuring Fronteras: New Navigations of Nepantla and the Cracks between the Worlds"

As in "Border Arte," in these manuscripts we see Anzaldúa's theoretical shift from frontera and border to nepantla; the manuscripts offer useful clues in how to navigate and in other ways work with nepantla.

> Topics: activism, agency, appropriation, artist, autobiographical information, borderlands, bridge, Chicana culture, Columbus, complicity, conocimiento, consciousness, creativity, critique, dream state, epistemology, fiction, frontier, geography of selves, identity, knowledge production, language, literary studies, mestiza, mestiza

consciousness, myth, nepantla, nos/otras, ontology, postcolonialism, postmodernism, reading, reconocimiento, remolinos, resistance, re-visioning, survival, theory, Trojan mula/burra, writing

"NEPANTLA: THE CRACK BETWEEN WORLDS" See "Navigating Nepantla"

"NEPANTLA, CREATIVE ACTS OF VISION" (49.5, 112.20) 2000–2002. Drafts of the talk that Anzaldúa prepared for Psychology at the Threshold, the International Archetypal Symposium hosted by the Pacifica Graduate Institute in Santa Barbara, California (August 31–September 5, 2000). 49.5 includes three drafts: two with dates (August 26, August 31) and the third undated. This material was drawn from "Conocimientos, Now Let Us Shift: Inner Works, Public Acts," a draft of the essay she was developing for *this bridge we call home*. In "Nepantla," Anzaldúa focuses primarily on two of conocimiento's seven aspects: (1) nepantla and (2) spiritual activism, especially as they relate to identity (re)formation and social justice work. As she states near the beginning, "I am interested in how nepantla and spiritual activism are connected to the inner life of the mind and spirit [and] to the outer world of social action. I want to bring a psycho-mythological dimension to this work of identity formation, cultural transformation and spiritual practice through willed creative acts. // I will begin with an offering and end with a prayer, an artist, activist prayer" (49.5). The eleven-page, double-spaced draft in 112.20 was printed after Anzaldúa's death and last saved on July 28, 2002, in the electronic folder for chapter 10 ("self-in-community") of the book Anzaldúa planned to publish after her dissertation. Portions of this material made its way into chapter 2 of *Light in the Dark*.

Topics: activism, agency, alienation, anxiety, art, artist, body, bridge, chamanería, Coatlicue, conocimiento, consciousness, corazón con razón, Coyolxauhqui, creative process, creativity, death, epistemology, facultad, identity, illness, imaginal, imagination, Indigeneity, inner-and-outer work, kindness, Llorona, mestisaje, myth, nagual, nagualism, "neocolonization of the spirit," nepantla, nonordinary reality, ontology, oppression, passion, path of conocimiento, perception, personal and social change, prayer, remolino, self-awareness, self-esteem, shadow, shamanism, shape-shifting, social justice, Sor Juana, spirit, spiritual activism, "spiritual imperialism," spirituality, struggle, teaching, time, Toltec, transformation, transitions, unconscious, writing

"NEPANTLA AND THE CREATIVE PROCESS" (55.17) ca. 1995. Twenty 1.5-spaced typed pages of material on the writing process. Includes both Anzaldúa's explorations of creativity and the writing/art-making process as well as "[c]oncentration, visualization, and meditation exercises" for art-making and writing. Titles of exercises include "Processing the Writing/Art Making"; "Overwhelmed? How to Make Order out of the Mess"; "Writing Take-Offs from Phrases, Photos and Visual Images"; "Coming Face to Face with Yourself / Enfrentandote a tí misma"; "Discover Your Personal Story or Myth"; "Self and Territory and Influences"; "Information about You and Ideas for Your Art Work from the Astrology Houses"; "Using a Series of Writing Semillitas (Little Seeds)"; "Grounding Meditation"; "Running Energy"; "Memory Traces"; "Breath Awareness"; and "How to See Images." This piece brings insight into how we might work with (and in) nepantla as we create.

> Topics: ancestors, art, artist, astrology, autohistoria, body, breath work, class, conocimiento, consciousness, consensus reality, daydreaming, death, dreams, energy, ethnicity, experience, facultad, feelings, flor y canto, gender, healing, identity, image, imagination, meditation, memory, mirrors, narrative, nepantla states, ontology, perception, process, reader, realities, representation, self-reflection, sensory perceptions, sexuality, transformation, vibration, visualization, water, writing

"NEPANTLA: THE CREATIVE PROCESS" (55.17) 1995. Last saved in October 1995 on Anzaldúa's hard drive in her folder with material for her planned writing guide, this six-page, 1.5-spaced draft consists of notes compiled during or from the Montalvo artists' workshop proposal.

> Topics: alchemy, altar, árbol de la vida, arrebato, art, artists, autohistoria, body, cenote, Coatlicue state, community, compostura, conocimiento, consciousness, Coyolxauhqui, creativity, death, desconocimiento, entering into the serpent, exile, identity, imaginal, immigration, jaguar, language, llamada, Llorona, metaphor, myth, mythopoesis, nagualismo, nepantla, new tribalism, nos/otras, on-

tology, rationality, reconocimiento, shaman, symbol, tree, writing process

"NEPANTLA: IN/BETWEEN AND SHIFTING: THEORIES OF COMPOSITION AND ART" (55.18) 1997. Printed after Anzaldúa's death from her hard drive, but last saved on October 31, 1997, with material for her planned writing guide, this thirty-two-page, typed, single-spaced manuscript offers one of Anzaldúa's most substantial discussions of nepantla, in which she brings forward and builds on ideas developed in previous manuscripts as she focuses on the artist's creative journey. This piece offers extensive insight into the internal and external constraints—including anxiety, insecurities, loneliness, and frustration—Anzaldúa experienced as a self-employed writer, as well as some goals for her writing; because it's a draft rather than a polished piece, she openly expresses her anxiety, insecurities, loneliness, and frustration. This manuscript was built, in part, with pieces from "Nepantla: The Theory & Manifesto."

Topics: agency, anxiety, arrebato, art, artists (especially Chicana/ Latina feminist artists), assimilation, autobiography, autohistoria, borderlands, cenote, censorship, Coatlicue, community, complicity, conocimiento, consciousness, Coyolxauhqui, creativity, curandera, desire, dislocation, dreaming, dreaming body, exile, fantasy, fear, First Amendment, geography of selves, guilt, healing, identity, image, imagination, Kali, knowledge, language, Llorona, memory, mestiza, monster, musa bruja, myth, narrative, nepantla, nepantla body, nepantlera, new tribalism, nos/otras representation, ontology, pleasure, reading, resistance, risk-taking, serpent, silence, subjectivity, susto, transgression, trauma, water, writing, writing process

"NEPANTLA: THEORIES OF COMPOSITION AND ART" (61.20) ca. 1993. Fifty-three typed pages, composed of several previous documents, with handwritten comments, edits, and highlighting. In a handwritten insertion, Anzaldúa includes this phrase in the title: "An Imaginary/Reading Body That Dwells Within," implying, perhaps, a tentative connection with her developing theory of naguala. The handwritten comments seem to indicate that Anzaldúa took sections from this draft and used them in "Nepantla: In/Between." Even later, it's possible that she used material from this manuscript as she drafted "Putting Coyolxauhqui Together."

Topics: activism, anger, arrebato, art, artists, autohistoria, body, borderlands, cenote, Chicanas, Coatlicue, colonialism, colonization, composition, consciousness, Coyolxauhqui, creative process, death, desire, dismemberment, dreams/dream world, embodiment, emotion, environment, fantasy, fiction, geography of selves, guilt, haunting, identity, identity formation, images, imaginary, imagination, language, Llorona, memory, mestiza, myth, naguala, narrative, nepantla, nepantla body, ontology, queer, reader, reading, reality, reconocimientos, sacrifice, spirit, spirituality, supernatural, susto, trance, transformation, women of color, writing, writing process

"NEPANTLA: THE THEORY & MANIFESTO" (61.21) ca. 1995. Forty-five typed pages focusing closely on nepantla, with much duplication. As her use of "nepantlero" (masculine) rather than "nepantlera" (feminine) indicates, this document also offers clues into Anzaldúa's theorization of la nepantlera. Possibly Anzaldúa envisioned this manuscript as an extended poem and/or a short book; it has a beautiful poetic quality.

Topics: autohistoria, cenote, Chicana/Latina, Coyolxauhqui, dreams, exile, identity, identity formation, imagination, Llorona, myth, nepantla, nepantlero, ontology, reconocimientos, remolinos, theory

"NEW MESTIZA NATION: A MULTICULTURAL MOVEMENT" (61.22) ca. 1992. Based on a talk Anzaldúa delivered at St. Olaf's College on March 7, 1992, this piece exists in handwritten notes and multiple drafts spanning about a decade. Other titles include "The New Mestiza Nation: Multicultural Education/Values, Colonialism, and the New Tribalism" (early September 1992). Anzaldúa offers both a summary of her position in *Borderlands* and an important extension into the next phase of her theoretical development. She unpacks her theory of the "new mestiza," emphasizing that, as she defines it, "mestizaje" can take multiple forms, including some that go beyond biological/racial identity categories to include the intellectual, spiritual, aesthetic, and more. Anzaldúa also draws on her own experiences to discuss some of the difficulties women of colors and other racial/ethnic, intellectual, and/or emotional mestizas might experience in the academy. See also "Talk on Multiculturalism."

Topics: academia, activism, age, ageism, appropriation, assimilation, body, borderlands, boundaries, bridge work, Chicanx/Latinx, colonialism, communication, community, complicity, conocimiento, creativity, disciplinary boundaries, education, hate tactics, history, identity, Llorona, mestizaje, mestizas, multiculturalism, nationalism, new mestiza, new tribalism, origins, poststructuralism, shame, silence, stress, survival, Trojan mulas, whiteness, women of color, working-class people

"NIGHT FACE" (84.5, 84.9, 84.10) 1978–91. Notes, poetry drafts, and related material for a poetry collection. Includes early poems from the late 1970s, the table of contents to the version submitted to the Walt Whitman poetry contest in 1984 (84.9), and numerous poems printed from her hard drive after her death, as well as notes titled "En Buscas del Mit Moderno" (84.5) that offer insight into Anzaldúa's aesthetic interests during this time.

Topics: anger, daimon, death, depression, desire, dragons, Earth, feminism, fire, friendship, gigs, health, illumination, insomnia, karma, love, menstruation, mental illness, mysticism, process, queers, reality, reincarnation, sanctions, serpent, soul, spirits, symbols, Texas, transformation, vampires, war, writing, Yemaya

"NOCHE Y SU NIDADA/NIGHT AND HER NEST" (94.6, 94.7, 94.8, 94.9, 94.10, 94.11, 94.12, 94.13) 1989–90. This manuscript began as a paper in a UCSC graduate course (taught by Teresa de Lauretis), and Anzaldúa planned to include it in the dissertation, describing it as "the fifth of a probable seven" chapters (94.7). The essay exists in multiple versions with significant revisions, expansions, and deletions. It focuses on identity-related issues: how our identities form and are impacted by gender, sex, race, racism, etc. The paper has four sections: "Identity: Waystations of Consciousness," "Necessary Monsters," "The Dream's Navel," "Patlaches/De las otras: The Chicana/ mexicana Lesbian." Anzaldúa's June 1989 letter to de Lauretis (93.19) indicates that de Lauretis introduced Anzaldúa to psychoanalytic theory, which Anzaldúa planned to use in her dissertation. "*Nomos* (from the Greek word for 'custom,' 'law,' 'convention') means a feeding place, the abode assigned to one, a dwelling place (*Dictionary of Philosophy* 189). My dwelling place is my body, this *lugarcito*, this little space *en donde yo* where I place myself before my self in full presence of my self" (94.6). Anzaldúa also draws on Merleau-Ponty and phenomenology. Anzaldúa first titled this piece "*De las otras, Noche y su nidada* (Night and Her Nest)" (94.8) but later deleted "*De las otras*" from the title and expanded the subtitle, which she revised several more times:

- "The Feeding Place, the Dwelling Place (*Nomos*) and the Wandering Place: Identities and Positionings of Consciousness" (94.7, 94.8)
- "The Wandering Place, the Feeding Place and *Nomos*, the Dwelling Place: Mestiza Identities and Positionings of Consciousness" (94.8)
- "The Wandering Place and *Nomos*: The Feeding Place, the Dwelling Space: Mestiza Identities and Positionings of the Body Consciousness" (94.6, 94.8)

Anzaldúa later developed some sections into other dissertation chapters and projects (e.g., "Born under the Sign of the Flower," "Rampas de entrada y salida," "Metaphors in the Tradition of the Shaman").

Topics: anger, autobiography, autohistoria, autohistoria-teoría, body, cenote, Coatlicue state, colonialism, consciousness, desire, embodiment, ethnocentrism, facultad, fate, feminisms, identity, identity changes, identity formation, identity/subjectivity, imaginal, introjection, knowledge, language, lesbian, lesbian feminist, Llorona, Medusa, Mexican, mother, narrative, phenomenology, power, Prietita, psychoanalytic theory, queer, queer theory, representation, revisionist mythmaking, Sabian symbols, self-definitions, sexuality, subjectivity, susto, unconscious, "waystations of consciousness"

"NONFICTION DRAFTS" (103.18) ca. 1980–90. These two drafts, each approximately twenty-eight pages long and consisting of notes that Anzaldúa had culled from earlier manuscripts and writing notas, were printed after her death but last saved on her hard drive in 1990.

Topics: AIDS, alchemy, alienation, archetypes, astrology, autobiography, Aztec, body, borderlands, Catholicism, Chicano/as, la Chingada, Christianity, Coatlicue state, colonialism, consciousness, daimon, death, dreams, emotions, facultad, guilt, identity, Indigeneity, knowledge, language, Libra, Llorona, loneliness, magic, Malinche, Mayan, Medusa state, mirror, Native Americans, New England, nonhuman world, original sin, revisionist mythmaking, sacrifice, sexuality, shadow, soul, supernatural, symbols, Tlazolteotl, Uranus, white consciousness, whiteness, writing

"NOS/OTRAS: THE SPLIT AND HOW TO BRIDGE IT" (96.20) 2003. A six-page, double-spaced piece on nos/otras that Anzaldúa pulled from "Geography of Selves"; the draft includes handwritten edits and is dated October 15, 2003. Anzaldúa included sections of this piece, in revised form, in *Light in the Dark*.

> Topics: assimilation, bridging, desconocimiento, education, emotions, ethnic studies, geography of selves, identity, nepantla, nepantla brain, nepantleros, nos/otras, othering, perception, post-oppositionality, rajadura, Raza studies, women's studies, world citizens

"NOS/OTRAS: THEORIZING MESTISAJE" (96.10) 1998. Five pages of notes (four single-spaced typed pages and one handwritten page) for the talk delivered on January 23, 1998, in Boise, Idaho, in which Anzaldúa describes nos/otras as a "new emerging story."

> Topics: assimilation, borderlands, borders, change, Chicano/a, cognitive dissonance, community, compromise, conocimientos, courage, Coyolxauhqui, cracks between the worlds, culture, desconocimiento, difference, epistemology, freedom, identity, Llorona, mestisaje, multiculturalism, narrative, nationalism, nepantla, new tribalism, nos/otras, oppression, passion, queer raza, racism, storytelling, violence, vision

"NOS/OTROS 'US' VS. 'THEM,' (DES)CONOCIMIENTOS Y COMPROMISOS" (96.12, 96.14, 96.15, 96.16, 96.17) 1999–2001. A talk delivered at the University of Illinois, Urbana-Champaign, on October 29, 1999, as part of a conference titled "Territories and Boundaries: Geographies of Latinidad." It offers useful insight into Anzaldúa's later view of the academy ("The academy especially is a wounding field"), identity, and the debates and divisions within and among Latinx and Chicanx groups. This piece, in extremely revised and expanded form, became chapter 4 of *Light in the Dark*. It exists in multiple versions, from transcript of the talk to essay; many drafts have handwritten edits and modified titles:

- "Nos/otros: Us/Them. . . . The Commitment and the New Trib-alism" (96.12) ca. 2000. A relatively early version of the paper delivered at the conference at the University of Illinois, Urbana-Champaign, with feedback from writing comadre Irene Lara.
- "Nos/otros: Us/Them. . . . The New Tribalism and Re-commitment to la Lucha" (96.15, 96.16, 96.17). Draft 96.17 includes title revision.
- "Nos/otros: Us/Them. . . . Re-Imagining Identity: The New Trib-alism and Re-commitment to la Lucha" (96.17).

For later drafts, see "Geographies of Selves—Re-imagining Identities: Nos/otras (Us/Other), Las nepantleras and the New Tribalism" (above).

Topics: academics, adversity, age, agency, árbol de la vida, blame, border crosser, change, Chicanas/Latinas, compassion, conflict, con-ocimiento, contemplative practices, courage, Coyolxauhqui, cultural invention, desconocimiento, desire, difference, dualisms, ecopsy-chology, education, embodiment, empathy, energy, ethnic studies, fear, feminism, gender, geography of selves, healing, identity, identity politics, illness, imaginal, imagination, immigration, information/ knowledge, Latina/o studies, Latino/as, Llorona, machismo, mano zurda, media, mestisaje, mind/body, narrative, nationalism, new tribalism, nos/otras, nos/otros, oppression, passion, peace, postcolo-nialism, power, psychic numbing, racism, remolinos, science, self-care, sexism, social change, social movements, spiritual activism, spirituality, stories, survival, time, Trojan burro/a, violence, vision, women of color, women's studies, wounds, writing

"NOTES—1994" (107.6) 1994. Fifty pages of handwritten notes on a variety of topics; in part, Anzaldúa wrote and used these notes as she prepared for speaking engagements, drafted Prieta stories, and brainstormed for her "SIC" essay. These notes indicate that during the mid-1990s Anzaldúa sought new approaches to relational subjectivity, reflected on her identity as a writer, and grappled with the changes in her health as she processed the diabetes diagnosis. (The following list of topics does not do justice to the wide-ranging nature of Anzaldúa's explorations in these pages.)

Topics: academia, activism, aesthetics, aging, AIDS, appropriation, artist, authority, autohistoria-teoría, body, boundaries, class, colonialism, comedy, conferences, conocimiento, curandera, depression, desconocimiento, diabetes, embodiment, equality, feminism, gigs, identity, illness, Llorona, mestizas, Mexico, mind/body division, multiculturalism, nagual, narrative, nos/otras, ontology, oppression, pain, plagiarism, Prieta, queer, racism, readers, resistance, ritual, sexuality, spirituality, subjectivity, witch, writing

"NOTES-B FROM CONOCIMIENTO ESSAY" (49.3) 2001. Two sets of typed, single-spaced notes that Anzaldúa used when writing "now let us shift." One set (thirty pages, dated March 18) contains handwritten edits and material drawn from earlier writing notes; the other set (eight pages, last saved November 20, 2001) was printed from Anzaldúa's hard drive after her death.

Topics: activism, aging, anger, art, body, bridging, chakras, Coatlicue, communication, community, compassion, conflict, conocimiento, consciousness, courage, Coyolxauhqui, creativity, dreams, energy, erotic, facultad, feminism, geography of the body, identity, illness, imagination, Llorona, meditation, naguala, nagualismo, nature, nep-antla, nepantlera, new mestiza, ontology, paradigm, prayer, queering reality, reading, ritual, science, seasons, self-care, sensory experience, shaman, soul, spirit, spiritual activism, spiritual practice, spirituality, Tao, tonal, transformation, trauma, via negativa, wisdom, writing

"NOTES—HORRIFIC" (93.3) early 1980s to mid-1990s. Ten pages of typed, single-spaced notes printed from Anzaldúa's hard drive after her death. Al-though Anzaldúa last saved it on November 11, 1994, she wrote some of the material in the early 1980s; it includes, for example, a section titled "The Insomnia Diary 20 Julio 81," which seems to have been keyed in from her journals.

Topics: anger, anxiety, astrology, change, la Chingada, death, desar-rollo, desire, embodiment, emotion, fear, freedom, gender, ghosts, guilt, horror, insomnia, love, masturbation, meditation, mestiza, El Mundo Surdo, ontology, power, Sabian symbols, sacrifice, sexuality, spiritual mestisaje, spirituality, tarot

"NOTES—LLORONA" (93.4) early 1990s. Two copies of ten pages of typed notes about La Llorona, printed after Anzaldúa's death, last saved in 1999 but written in the early 1990s as part of Anzaldúa's dissertation work; this material especially resonates with the chapter titled "The Hauntings of Llorona."

> Topics: alienation, astrology, Chicana folklore, la Chingada, Cortes, displacement, estrangement, exile, identity, isolation, Llorona, Malinche, postcolonialism, sexuality, Tonantzin, wounding, writing

"NOTES—PREFACE" (52.9) 2001. Printed from Anzaldúa's hard drive where it was last saved on November 26, 2001. Eight pages of notes (most single-spaced) that Anzaldúa drew on as she drafted her preface to *this bridge we call home*, "(un)natural bridges."

> Topics: academia, bridges, bridging, conocimiento, consciousness, conversion, dreams, fear, Hermes, identity, imagination, inclusivity, interconnectedness, Latinidad, *Making Face, Making Soul*, meditation, myth, naguala, Native Americans, nature, nepantla, nepantlera, nos/otras, people of color, politics, religion, science, shaman, spirit, spiritual activism, *Star Trek Voyager*, *This Bridge Called My Back*, *this bridge we call home*, thresholds, tonglen, transformation, whites, writing

"NOTES FOR LLORONAS DISSERTATION" (91.10) 1989–90. Over one hundred pages of handwritten notes that Anzaldúa later typed up and used in the Lloronas prospectus and dissertation chapters ("Poet is Critic," "En silencio," "Stress-Writing Self," "Cuerpo," "Ethnic Autohistorias-teorías"). These notes also offer useful information on the sources Anzaldúa drew on during this time. (The following list of topics does not do justice to the wide-ranging nature of Anzaldúa's explorations in these pages.)

> Topics: academic disciplines, aesthetics, alienation, art, autobiographical information, autobiography, autohistoria, autohistoria-teoría, chamana, Chicana literature, Chicanos, class, colonialism, colonization, communication, culture, empiricism, epistemology, exile, fear, feminist theory, fiction, higher education, identity, imagination, literary studies, Llorona, mestiza subject, oppression, poetry, postmodernism, racism, reading, representation, self-representation, self-writing, sexual difference, shape-shifting, short story, sleep, spirituality, standpoint, stress, survival, theory, transmodern mestiza, vision, women of color, writing

"NOTES FOR REIMAGING IDENTITIES: THE GEOGRAPHY OF OUR
MANY SELVES—U OF S.F." (98.5) ca. 1996. The original material Anzaldúa
used while developing her Davies Forum lecture, "Reimaging Identities," to
be given at the University of San Francisco. The notes include handwritten
edits and highlights and are titled "U. Of S.F.—original notes for talk." Anzaldúa had moved this fourteen-page manuscript into the folders she used
while working on *Light in the Dark*.

> Topics: anger, arrogance, art, body, "border mestiza consciousness,"
> change, citizenship, community, conflict, conocimiento, Coyolxauh-
> qui, creativity, culture wars, desconocimiento, fiction, gender wars,
> geography of selves, global citizenship, grief, grounding, identity, im-
> ages, imagination, individual self, injustice, intelligence, intuition,
> Latinx, mindfulness, multicultural awareness, nation, national-
> ism, nepantla, nepantla brain, nepantleras, new mestiza, new trib-
> alism, nos/otras, psychoanalytic theory, remolinos, structuralism,
> subjectivity

"NOTES ON EL MUNDO SURDO ESSAY" (61.18) 1983–84. Over seventy
pages in length, this collection of handwritten notes, workshop outlines,
typed excerpts from interviews, and manuscript drafts was the preliminary
material that Anzaldúa saved in a folder titled "Notes on El Mundo Surdo
essay." See the end of "La Prieta," where she refers to this project. Anzaldúa
planned to write a lengthy essay on El Mundo Surdo and a follow-up piece
to "La Prieta," tentatively titled "La Prieta II." The outline, included in this
folder, is titled "El Mundo Zurdo (the Left-Handed World): A Political-
Spiritual Vision for the Third World and the Queer." This material offers
a useful overview of Anzaldúa's spiritual-political vision in the early 1980s.

> Topics: action, anger, archetype, astrology, bisexuality, body, breath,
> Brooklyn, burnout, ceremony, compassion, consciousness, contem-
> plation, decision-making, destiny, disease, divine, dreams, energy,
> evil, fear, feminine, guilt, harmony, hatred, healing, homophobia, I
> Ching, inspiration, intuition, Latinas, leadership, lesbianism, medi-
> tation, El Mundo Surdo, nature, people of color, perception, plane-
> tary citizenship, poetry, politics, Prieta, queer theory, racism, reli-
> gion, revolution, right/left brain, ritual, sacrifice, self-growth, soul,
> source, spirit, spirits, spiritual activism, spirituality, *Star Trek*, survival,

Taoism, tarot, Third World people, transformation, transpersonal, unity, womanists, women, workshops, writing

"NOW LET US SHIFT. . . . THE PATH OF CONOCIMIENTO. . . . INNER WORK, PUBLIC ACTS" (49.2, 49.3, 49.4, 49.6, 49.7, 49.8, 49.9, 49.10, 49.11, 49.12, 49.13; Box 50, Folders 1–17; Box 51, Folders 1–12) 1999–2001. First published in *this bridge we call home* but also used, in slightly revised form, in *Light in the Dark*, this piece exists in a dazzling array of versions. Box 49 contains collections of notes (49.2, 49.3, 49.4), outlines, extremely rough drafts in which Anzaldúa brainstorms and works out parts of the essay's trajectory (49.4, 49.6), drafts with different titles (see below), and more. The numerous drafts in 49.6 shed light on Anzaldúa's writing and revision process during fall 2000. These drafts offer the patient scholar a remarkable journey through Anzaldúa's mind as she pulls together her thoughts from decades, creating the path of conocimiento. Title revisions include:

- "Conocimientos, Now Let Us Shift: Inner Works, Public Acts" 1999
- "Conocimientos, Now let us shift: Inner work and public acts" (49.4) 1999–2000
- "Conocimientos: Creative Acts of Vision, Inner Works, Public Acts" (49.6) September 2000 drafts, both pre-drafts and early essay drafts
- "conocimientos: creative acts of vision, inner works, public acts" (49.6, 49.7, 51.10) September–October 2000
- "now let us shift . . . conocimientos: inner works, public acts" (49.8) October 2000
- "now let us shift . . . conocimientos . . . inner works, public acts" (49.9) October 2000
- "now let us shift . . . the path of conocimientos . . . inner work, public acts" (49.9, 49.10, 49.11, 49.12, 49.13; Box 50, Folders 1–17; Box 51, Folders 1–12)

Topics: activism, agency, art, artist, blank spots, body, capitalism, Christianity, Coatlicue, communication, conocimiento, consciousness, corazón con razón en la mano, Coyolxauhqui, creativity, death, decolonization, desconocimiento, diabetes, digital realities, epistemology, escapism, facultad, geography of selves, hope, I Ching, imagination, intuition, Llorona, love, mano zurda, mestiza consciousness, El Mundo Zurdo, naguala, nagualismo, narrative, neocolonialism, nepantla, new tribalism, ontology, oppression, path of conocimiento, postmodernism, post-oppositionality, queer, queer conocimiento, re-conocimiento, remolinos, ritual, seeing through, self-reflection, shape-shifting, soul-daemon, spiritual activism, spiritual identity crisis, spirituality, spiritual privilege, suffering, survival, trauma, wounding, writing, Xochiquetzal

"ON MY METHOD AND WAYS OF ORDERING AND STRUCTURING" (61.11) ca. 1987 or 1988. A two-page, single-spaced draft, derived from the transcript of a talk; Anzaldúa discusses her nonlinear dialogic method of writing and her expectation that readers will enter into her words, allow those words to enter into our bodies, and together produce meaning. She seems to have drawn on this material while writing "haciendo caras" and "Metaphors in the Tradition of the Shaman"; she included a version of it in her Lloronas dissertation chapter "THE POET IS CRITIC."

Topics: anger, autobiography, border crossing, *Borderlands*, code-switching, emotion, gigs, graduate school, interpretation, mestiza, "mestiza mind," method, rationality, reading, representation, self-trust, suicide, women of color, writing

"ON WRITING" (55.20) n.d. Last saved January 9, 2004, and printed from Anzaldúa's hard drive after her death. Nineteen single-spaced pages of notes about writing (writing exercises, definitions of terms, etc.) drawn from her personal experiences and research. Given that Anzaldúa saved this document on her laptop, rather than in a specific folder, it's likely that she was actively working with it in the last months of her life. Though consisting largely of quotations, it also includes material that she might have included in her writing guide.

Topics: aesthetics of cost, art, artist, belief system, characters, creativity, disease, dreaming, emotion, fiction, grief, literary agents, metaphor, novel, passion, perspective, plot, poetry, recipes, symbols, voice, writer's block, writing

"ORALS READING LIST" (91.14) ca. 1990. This ten-page document was printed after Anzaldúa's death from her hard drive, where it was last saved on October 21, 2001, though developed much earlier. A bibliography of books and articles for her UCSC qualifying exams, this document indicates her wide-ranging interests and influences. The bibliography is divided into two parts: "Narrative, Poetry, and Theory Focusing on the Americas 19th and 20th Centuries" and "Theory," and each part is divided into subsections.

> Topics: autobiography, Chicano studies, feminist theory, Lloronas dissertation, narrative, poststructuralism, psychoanalytic theory, sexuality, theory

"LA OYA" (108.9) 1982. A four-page typed manuscript with handwritten edits, consisting of remarks prepared for Salsa Soul Sisters and delivered on May 12, 1982. Offers unique insights into Anzaldúa's life philosophy, including her theory-praxis of conocimiento and spiritual activism.

> Topics: alchemy, autobiographical information, blame, cauldron, cooking, destiny, energy, fire, gig, I Ching, la oya, psyche, purification, sacrifice, spirit, spiritual activism, transformation, vocation, writing

"LAS PASIONES DE LA LLORONA: THE POLITICS OF EMOTIONS" (95.1) early 1980s. A short (eight single-spaced typed pages) manuscript in which Anzaldúa uses third-person voice to explore her profound anger (directed both internally and externally) and investigate alternative power sources for herself and other marginalized people. Although dated September 26, 1989, it includes material from Anzaldúa's early autohistorias.

> Topics: anger, animals, animism, autobiographical information, body, breath, la Chingada, Coatl, depression, dreams, embodiment, emotions, energy, environment, evil, fear, feminist movement, imaginal, Llorona, magic, menstruation, mugging, El Mundo Zurdo, nonhuman world, Prietita, ritual, serpent, solitude, spirit, spiritual activism, susto, terror, unconscious

"PATLACHES: CHICANA DYKES" (61.24) late 1980s. This undated short (three-page, 1.5-spaced) piece explores lesbian-of-color feminists, Chicana lesbians, sexuality, and naming. Anzaldúa planned to expand this document into a dissertation chapter, tentatively titled "Patlaches/De las otras: The Making of the Chicana/mejicana/mestiza Lesbian Feminist Self."

Topics: academia, activism, Chicana lesbians, Chicana queer literature, compartmentalization, identity, immigrants, language, lesbians, naming, oppression, Prieta, queer, racism, Sappho, sexuality, Sor
Juana, theory, *This Bridge*, whites

"PLUNGING INTO EL CENOTE: CREATIVE NONFICTION" (95.19) late
1980s. Six 1.5-spaced typed pages with handwritten edits and comadre
reader feedback. In this short rough draft, Anzaldúa works with ideas
and metaphors that make their way into her theories of autohistoria y
autohistoria-teoría and el cenote, as well as her later essay, "Putting Coyolxauhqui Together." Offers useful formative clues as to autohistoria's development and Anzaldúa's agonizing but intentional, multi-layered writing
process. Her discussion of writing blocks, "this winter place of the creative
act," resonates with her theory of the Coatlicue state.

Topics: alienation, archetypes, autobiography, autohistoria, bridging,
composition, consciousness, cenote, creation, creative process, deadlines, death, destiny, facultad, genre, images, imaginal world, imagination, intuition, letting go, Medusa, memoir, metaphysics, method,
musa bruja, orgasm, Prometheus, Quetzalcoatl, revision, sacrifice,
shaman, soul, spirit, survival, testimonial, tree, unconsciousness,
underworld, water, world-traveling, writing blocks, writing process

"THE POET IS CRITIC/THE POET IS THEORIST: SPEAKING IN TONGUES,
QUERIDAS MUJERES ESCRITORIAS DE COLOR CARTA TWO" (55.29, 55.30,
61.25, 61.27, 61.28, 62.1, 62.4, 62.5, 62.7, 62.9, 62.13, 63.1, 63.2, 94.13, 95.2,
95.3, 95.14, 95.15, 95.19) 1988–91. This dissertation chapter originated in
a course paper that Anzaldúa first drafted in 1988 and worked with at least
until 1991. From this seedling, it grew exponentially, morphing into several
additional chapters. Anzaldúa's statement of intent, from the essay's opening, offers a useful perspective: "In this letter I will attempt to describe the
space we are trying to push out, the literary place we are making for ourselves, a site or sites where I/we can pursue, continue my/our work of subject finding, subject recovery, subject formation while in the written presence of myself and you, mujeres de color." As this statement and the essay
subtitles suggest, Anzaldúa viewed this piece as a continuation of "Speaking in Tongues"; however, as is often the case with Anzaldúa, the drafts
expanded considerably, shifting beyond her original intentions. Anzaldúa

saved most, if not all, drafts—including drafts with extensive handwritten edits, readers' comments, notes from Anzaldúa to readers and readers' notes to her on the drafts, and drafts saved on her hard drive and printed out after her death. This material offers useful information on Anzaldúa's complicated relationship with writing (impostor syndrome, perfectionism, insomnia); the demands on her time and her psyche while in graduate school; her aesthetics; her method; her analysis of Chicana literature; and more. A small portion of one draft (95.14) was published as "Metaphors in the Tradition of the Shaman" in James McCorkle's book, *Conversant Essays: Contemporary Poets on Poetry*; however, her correspondence with McCorkle (61.26) indicates that Anzaldúa originally planned to contribute the entire essay. This piece exists in multiple versions with a wide range of titles:

- "The Woman Who Writes: Una carta para mestiza writers" (55.29) n.d.
- "The Woman Who Writes: *Una carta para mestizas* inside Enemy Territory" (55.30) n.d.
- "The Woman Who Writes: The Writing Subject: Racial Ethnic/ Others inside Enemy Territory" (55.29, 55.30, 95.14)
- "The Writing Subject: Racial/Ethnic/Others inside Enemy Territory [8L]" (55.30)
- "The Writing Subject: Racial/Ethnic/Others inside Enemy Territory, Speaking in Tongues, *Carta* Two." (95.14)
- "The Woman Who Writes: The Writing Subject—Plunges into El Cenote" (95.19) 1988–89?
- "The Poet as Critic, The Poet as Theorist" (63.2): This handwritten draft is the earliest version; it includes notes as well as partial draft.
- "THE POET AS CRITIC: Speaking in Tongues, Dear Women Writers of Color Letter Two" (62.1, 62.5, 62.9)
- "THE POET AS CRITIC/THE POET AS THEORIST: Speaking in Tongues, Dear Women Writers of Color Letter Two" (61.25, 61.26, 62.7)
- "THE POET AS CRITIC/THE POET AS THEORIST: Speaking in Tongues, Dear Women Writers of Color *Carta* Two" (61.27, 62.4, 62.7, 63.1, 95.3)
- "THE POET IS CRITIC/THE POET IS THEORIST: Speaking in Tongues, *Carta* Three" (95.2)

- "POET IS CRITIC/THE POET IS THEORIST" (62.2, 62.13),
  "THE POET IS CRITIC/THE POET IS THEORIST" (62.3)

Of these many drafts, scholars might find those located in 62.4 especially interesting for their revisions, including the important title shift from "The Poet *as* Critic and Theorist" to "The Poet *is* Critic and Theorist" (my emphasis), which might suggest a change in Anzaldúa's relationship to theory and knowledge creation. Other drafts with extensive revisions include those in 62.5, 62.7, and 62.9. And see also "Writing the Selves: Chicana/Colored Creativities inside Enemy Territory" (below). The time stamp on Anzaldúa's computer files indicates that she reexamined this essay in 1999 and 2000 as she drafted her final dissertation/book.

> Topics: academia, aesthetics, appropriation, autobiography, autohistoria, autohistoria-teoría, blank spots, body, California, cenote, Chicana/mestiza writer, colonialism, consciousness, creativity, desconocimiento, energy, exile, fact, facultad, fantasy, femininity, feminist theory, fiction, graduate school, "high" theory, identity, imaginal, imagination, insomnia, isolation, language, lesbian/feminists of color, literary studies, new mestiza, ontology, oppositionality, origins, privilege, reading, representation, seeing through, self-writing, silence, space, stress, subjectivity, theorizing, women of color in the academy, women-of-color writers, writing process

"POETRY & MAGICK: A PRACTICUM FOR DEVELOPING LITERARY + PSYCHIC SKILLS" (63.3) 1976–81. Described as "Book in Progress," this manuscript is over 150 pages in length and consists of an assorted collection of handwritten notes on varied topics, spiritual technologies, guided meditations, writing practices and prompts, research notes (on literature, critical theory, etc.), and visualizations that Anzaldúa planned to develop into a book on writing as ritual and transformation, based on her belief that "[t]he tools of writing are the same as those for making magic." This document indicates that Anzaldúa posited an animist, spirit-inflected, relational approach to reading, writing, and aesthetics: "Poetry + Magick: the search for connections, the science of connections // Bridge between physical + psychic or imaginative."

> Topics: aesthetics, alchemy, art, astral projection, astrology, audience, body, breath, chakras, Christianity, clairvoyance, community,

connection, consciousness, correspondence, creativity, criticism, crossroads, dance, dream work, emotions, energy, eroticism, feminism, fiction, food, goddess, grounding, healing, I Ching, imagination, instinct, intuition, language, lesbian, light, literary skills, literature, love, lunar phases, magic, making soul, manifesting, mantras, meditation, mindfulness, miracles, moon, El Mundo Surdo workshop, myth, mudras, muse, nagual, obstacles, occult, ontology, organic writing, personal power, poet, poetry, politics, power, probabilities, psychic skills, psychology, reading, relationships, revolution, rhythm, ritual, self-confidence, self-making, self-trust, sexuality, shaman, soul-making, spider, spirit guide, spiritual activism, survival, symbols, Tarot, theories of poetry, tree, "Tres lenguas," truth, unconscious, universals, vibrations, visualization, women's writing, workshops, writing, Yemaya, yoga

"PREFACE: GENIUS LOCI, THE SPIRIT OF THE PLACE" (91.17) 1996. Dated July 13, 1996, this short manuscript (three double-spaced pages with handwritten edits) was written while Anzaldúa was on a writing retreat at Norcroft. More notes than a cohesive essay, it's an early version of the preface to her short story cycle/novel, tentatively titled "La Prieta is Dreaming."

Topics: autobiography, Chicana art, Coyolxauhqui, decoloniality, exile, fear, genres, imagination, immigration, interpretation, Llorona, nagualismo, nature, pain, personal/collective memory, poetry, Prieta, reading, Texas, writing

"PRE-WRITING JOURNAL" (103.23) 1994, 1999, 2000. Titled by Anzaldúa, these five single-spaced, typed pages of journal-esque notes offer insights into her thought process, daily life, changing health, and relationship to writing.

Topics: addiction, agency, anxiety, body, change, Chicanas, chronic illness, commitment, consensual reality, deadlines, desconocimiento, diabetes, energy, fear, gigs, hardships, health, illness, income taxes, intuition, loss, meditation, nature, ontology, procrastination, remolinos, rituals, shadow beast, spiritual crisis, spirituality, symbols, Texas, willpower, writing, writing process

"LA PRIETA" (44.14, 44.15, 44.16, 44.17, 44.18, 45.11) 1979–81. Anzaldúa's first published autohistoria, this manuscript exists in multiple drafts, from early notes (44.18) and discards (44.15, 44.16) to the Spanish translation (44.17) and to the final edits and additions that Anzaldúa made to the copy-edited draft which arrived at the publisher too late to be included in the published version (45.11). These folders include fascinating material that didn't make its way into the published version, as suggested by early section titles like "Queer Baiting," "The Wall," "The Cultural Fuck," "Energies and Powers," and "Meditaciones sobre el mundo surdo." Folders 14, 15, and 16 include philosophical and autobiographical details that Anzaldúa used to germinate the essay, stripping away intimate factual material as she revised. For instance, she recalls *Bridge's* origins at Merlin Stone's February 1979 "retreat at Willow, a women's retreat north of San Francisco" in which Stone protested the staff's treatment of Anzaldúa. Anzaldúa also recounts various pivotal times in her life (her hysterectomy, falling off a hill, being mugged, working as an educator in South Texas and Indiana) and how these events functioned like messages calling her to create better balance in her life. This material deepens our understanding of Anzaldúa's self-image and response to hardship.

Topics: alchemy, anger, assimilation, blame, bridging, complicity, consciousness, cultural bias, dark nights of the soul, depression, difference, education, empathy, energy, epistemology, fear, Feminist Writers' Guild, heterosexuality, homophobia, hysterectomy, I Ching, identity, interconnectedness, intimacy, karma, labels, lesbianism, Lilith, love, Marxism, menstruation, mugging, nationalism, numerology, oppression, perception, queer theory, racism, sexism, sexuality, shame, silence, sorrow, spiritual activism, stereotypes, survival, Tarot, tokenism, transformation, trickster, visualization

"LA PRIETA IS DREAMING/GENIUS LOCI, THE SPIRIT OF THE PLACE" (108.1) 1996. Draft of a poem written at Norcroft and dated "1/13/96," with revisions "10/9/96." We see Anzaldúa working out many of her ontological and spiritual beliefs, especially those concerning the relationship between spirit, politics, and magick, as well as the relationship between spiritual and political change.

Topics: animism, body, conocimiento, dreams, epistemology, fear, history, imaginal, memory, metaphysics, nature, ontology, spirits, spiritual activism, stress, Taoism, tradition and transformation, writing

"LA PRIETA'S ENCOUNTER WITH SUPERNATURALS" (108.1) 1996. Handwritten draft consisting of a one-page poem and two pages of notes, written while Anzaldúa was in residence at Norcroft.

Topics: dreams, imaginal, journeying, nonordinary, ontology, Prieta, shamanism, spirits, supernatural

"PROVING GROUND: LA ARTISTA Y SU COMUNIDAD" (63.4, 63.5) 1994. Dated October 1, 1994, this fourteen-page, 1.5-spaced, typed manuscript with handwritten edits explores the relationship between an artist/writer of color (especially Chicana/mestiza/dyke) and her culture, focusing on aesthetic, ethical, political, and representational issues that culminate, in later work, in Anzaldúa's theory of autohistoria-teoría: "Ours is the problem of stepping outside our culture to get a perspective on it while we sit in the middle of it. We develop a meta-consciousness—awareness of being part of a pattern—while trying to change that pattern (culture)." Anzaldúa's handwritten outline suggests that she viewed this piece as a companion to her essays on "Border Arte" and nepantla ("Nepantla: The Creative Struggle"); it exists in an earlier form as "Proving Ground: Theorizing Ethnic Artmaking" (63.5).

Topics: aesthetics, árbol de la vida, art-activism, artists of color, audience, autobiographical information, autohistoria, Chicana artists/writers, colonization, community, consensual reality, creativity, difference, emotions, ethics, feminism, guilt, healing, identity, imagination, Llorona, mestiza, metaphor, metatext, nationalism, new tribalism, patronage, psychoanalysis, quality, queer communities, revolutions, self-reflection, sexuality, space, standpoint, storytelling, subjectivity, survival, symbols, tokenization, writer's block, writing

"PUTTING COYOLXAUHQUI TOGETHER: A CREATIVE PROCESS" (63.6, 63.7, 63.8, 63.9, 63.10, 63.11, 63.12, 63.13, 63.14, 63.15, 63.16, 63.17, 64.1, 64.2, 64.3, 64.4, 64.5, 64.6, 64.7, 64.8, 64.9, 64.10, 98.12, 98.13) 1997–2004. Anzaldúa's most sustained and in-depth exploration of her writing process, this piece exists in at least seventeen drafts, thus illustrating (*by enacting!*) her writing process from the original invitation (63.6) to the 1998 version published in *How We Work* (63.10) to the *Light in the Dark* draft that she worked on in 2004. Anzaldúa produced many drafts, changing the title numerous times:

- "How I Work" (63.7)
- "The Writing Habit: How I Work—Process and Stages" (63.7)
- "Dreaming the Story: My Writing Habits, Process, and Stages" (63.7)
- "Embodying the Story: Writing Process and Habits" (63.8, 63.9, 63.11, 63.12, 63.13, 63.14)
- "Embodying the Story: How I Write" (63.15, 63.16, 63.17, 64.1, 64.8)
- "Embodying the Story: How I Write / Embodying the Story: My Process of Writing" (63.17)
- "Embodying la historia: How I Write/My Process of Writing" (64.2)
- "Embodying la historia: How I Write" (64.3)
- "Working the Story: Como escribes, How You Write" (64.4, 64.6, 64.7)
- "The Dance of Nepantla: Dreaming Naguala, Re-membering the Bones, Putting Coyolxauhqui Together" (64.5)
- "Becoming naguala, Writing between Realities: Como escribes: How You Write, Writing in the Dark" (64.6)
- "Putting Coyolxauhqui Together: A Creative Process" (98.12, 98.13)

Topics: animism, art, artist, audience, autobiographical information, body, "bodymind," cenote, cognition, community, concentration, Coyolxauhqui, creation, creativity, diabetes, dreaming, facultad, fear, fiction, genre, gigs, guilt, I Ching, imaginal, "imaginal mind," imagination, internet, isolation, llamada/the call, Llorona, meditation, memoir, metaphors, metastory, meta-writing, musa bruja, naguala, nepantla, "nepantla consciousness," ontology, perfectionism, poem, readers, reading, reconocimiento, revision, risks, ritual, sacrifice, self-reflection, "soul work," stress, tokenization, trees, vulnerabilities, writing blocks, writing comadres, writing process

"QUEER CONOCIMIENTO" (49.2) 2000. A ten-page, 1.5-spaced document consisting primarily of notes composed at least in part of material Anzaldúa culled from earlier sources—including *Interviews/Entrevistas* and her writing notes, which Anzaldúa used for a talk at UCSC and while drafting "now let us shift." Anzaldúa saved this manuscript in a folder with other material she drew on while drafting "now let us shift" and editing *this bridge*. The exploration of ontology (in the section titled "constructions of reality") is one of Anzaldúa's most sustained discussions of this topic outside *Light in the Dark*.

> Topics: art, autohistoria, chakra, composition, conocimiento, consciousness, corazón con razón, Coyolxauhqui process, desconocimiento, dreambody, education, emotion, epistemology, geography of self, Indigeneity, Llorona, meaning, meditation, mindfulness, naguala, nature, nepantla, nepantlera, new tribalism, nos/otras, ontology, perception, reading, ritual, self-development, shamanism, shadow, spirit, spiritual activism, spirituality, storytelling, Taoism, transformation, wounds, writing, writing exercises

"QUEERS OF COLOR" (112.26) 1999. A five-page, single-spaced draft of a short talk delivered at UCSC on June 3, 1999, and printed after Anzaldúa's death from her hard drive, where it was last saved on June 3, 1999. In it, Anzaldúa offers a visionary perspective on queers of colors' vital contributions, as well as encouragement to live out queerness in new ways. Some of this material made its way, in revised form, into two published pieces: "(un)natural bridges" and "now let us shift." This piece offers tantalizing clues into the directions Anzaldúa might have taken her emergent theory of queer conocimiento, had she lived longer: "Living with queerness is a choice. Living in a queer way contributes to community, nation, planet. Such a way of life has the power to change the world. Living queerly is political, it is spiritual, it is an immensely conscious way of life. We can contribute a queer conocimiento, a perspective on life different from that of other people."

> Topics: biology, brujería, citizenship, commonality, communication, conflict, conocimiento, consciousness, curanderas, difference, diversity, epistemology, geography of selves, identity, liberalism, mano zurda, media, mind, multiculturalism, mysticism, mythopoetic, nature, ontology, otherness, paradigms, queer conocimiento, queer theory, reality, shamanism, shape-shifting, solidarity, spirit, spiritual

activism, spirituality, *This Bridge Called My Back*, *this bridge we call home*, transgender

"RAMPAS DE ENTRADA, AN INTRODUCTION" (95.6) ca. 1990. Typed, 1.5-spaced, twenty-two-page early draft of the introduction to the Lloronas dissertation, previously part of the chapter titled "Noche y su nidada" (as a section titled "Rampas de entrada y salida"); it contains handwritten comments by another reader. This draft offers a fascinating interpretation of Llorona's ghostly body and psychic body, as well as a discussion of autohistoria-teoría's origins and evidence of Anzaldúa's engagement with contemporary twentieth-century theories.

> Topics: alienation, archetypes, autobiographical information, autohistoria-teoría, body, Chicana feminism, colonization and conquest, decoloniality, difference, embodiment, epistemology, femininity, gender, haunting, identity, Indigeneity, literature, Llorona, loss, memory, mestiza, metaphysics, musa bruja, myth, nagual, ontology, personhood, psyche, psychoanalytic theory, reality, sexuality, shadow, shape-shifting, space, symbolic, symptom, theory, time, trauma, wounds, writing process

"RAMPAS DE SALIDA" (55.25) ca. 1990. A four-page, single-spaced, typed early draft of the conclusion to the Lloronas dissertation printed after Anzaldúa's death from her hard drive, last saved on October 31, 1997, but written earlier. In it, Anzaldúa draws on her writing process to offer writing-related suggestions for writers interested in transformational writing (for selves and others).

> Topics: agency, autohistoria-teoría, borderlands, breath, children, consciousness, Coyolxauhqui imperative, Creative Life Force, creativity, ego, energy, facultad, ghosts, hierarchy, humor, identity, images, imagination, language, liberation, meditation, mestiza consciousness, mestiza feminist, El Mundo Zurdo, oppression, postmodern mestiza, psyche, psychic protection, revision process, risking the personal, sexuality, soul, spirituality, transformation, visualization, writing process, writing with the left hand, writing workshops

"RE-CONFIGURING FRONTERAS: NEW NAVIGATIONS OF NEPANTLA AND THE CRACKS BETWEEN THE WORLDS" See "Navigating Nepantla"

"RE-CONOCIMIENTOS AND PRODUCING KNOWLEDGE: THE POSTMOD-
ERN LLORONA" (95.8) 1990s. Seventeen-page, single-spaced draft printed
after Anzaldúa's death from her hard drive, where it was last saved on
December 20, 1997. Originally written for UCSC coursework, this essay
focuses on the "postmodern mestiza" and her literary interventions; the
relationship between women of color, "minority discourse," and poststructuralist theory; and Chicana literature stages. Outline: "I. Movidas of the
Mestiza: Teorías to Save Our Lives"; "II. Theorizing New Knowledges";
"III. Critical Stages: Aesthetics, Strategies for Building a Literary Culture."
Despite the title, "Re-conocimientos" does not actually discuss Anzaldúa's
theory of conocimiento and was probably written prior to its development.
It does, however, usefully illuminate a key dimension of Anzaldúa's goal
as knowledge creator as well as her relationship to late-twentieth-century
theory.

> Topics: body, Chicana literature, colonialism, conocimiento, cre-
> ativity, cultural imperialism, difference, discourse, epistemology,
> feminism, gender, Guadalupe, identity, literary criticism, Llorona,
> mestiza critic, metacriticism, modernism, oppositionality, othering,
> postmodern mestiza, poststructuralism, representation, sexuality,
> silencing, *Star Trek*, subjectivity, surveillance, survival, theorizing,
> tokenism, white feminist critics, women of color

"REIMAGING IDENTITIES" (96.8, 96.11) 1996–98. An essay originating
from the transcript of a talk (delivered as the Davies Forum lecture at the
University of San Francisco on May 9, 1996) focusing on citizenship and
social justice. The transcript (96.8) contains handwritten edits, insertions,
and other notes indicating that Anzaldúa planned to further develop it.
Although this piece precedes the development of her philosophy of conocimiento, here we see part of its foundation. And again, we see that conocimiento grows from Anzaldúa's investigations of desconocimientos and
the sleepwalkers among us (that is, most people). It exists in three drafts
(approximately thirteen single-spaced pages) with handwritten edits and
two titles: "Reimaging Identities: The Geography of Our Many Selves"
(96.8), from 1996; and "Reimaging Identities: The Geography of Nos/
otras" (96.11), with edits dated February 25, 1998. These drafts can be read
for how Anzaldúa viewed the stages of her writing process. See also "Notes

for Reimaging Identities" and "Nos/otras: Reimaging Identity—A Chicana Notion of a Nation."

Topics: affirmative action, anger, artist, binary oppositions, bodies, change, citizenship, colonialism, complicity, conocimiento, Coyolxauhqui, culture, desconocimiento, displacement, dominant culture, facultad, fear, geographies of selves, geography of selves, hope, ideas, identity, imagination, interdependence, manifest destiny, mestisaje, mestiza, mindfulness, narrative, neocolonialism, nepantla, new tribalism, nos/otras, nos/otras imperative, occupational stress, ontology, othering, personhood, progress, queer theory, racism, remolinos, segregation, shadows, space, survival, vocation, whiteness, writing

"REMOLINOS Y CONOCIMIENTOS—IMAGINATION AND GLOBAL COMMUNITY" (64.15, 64.16) 2000–2002. Twelve single-spaced pages of notes on various topics related to conocimiento, imagination, and community-building. It exists in two very similar documents, both printed after Anzaldúa's death from her hard drive; Folder 15 was last saved February 9, 2000, and Folder 16 was last saved December 24, 2001.

Topics: academia, activism, affirmative action, agency, ambiguity, borderlands consciousness, borders, bridging, Chicanx, citizenship, community, conocimiento, culture wars, death, desconocimiento, difference, dreaming, empowerment, healing, history, ideas, identity, identity politics, imagination, individualism, labels, language, malaise, mestisaje, neoconservatism, nostalgia, power, race, racism, resistance, tension, white backlash

"RE-READING, RE-VISION, RE-WRITING: THE ART OF SELF-EDITING" (57.5) 1985. Five handwritten pages for a piece on writing and/or writing workshops that focuses on Anzaldúa's writing process. It contains a shorter draft of comments to present at a poetry reading; a brief discussion of her writing process for "Immaculate, Inviolate" and "Sea of Cabbages"; and a description of a writing workshop titled "An Image Is Worth a Thousand Words: A Writing Workshop." Also includes three typed poems (or partial poems). The assortment of material offers insight into an early stage of Anzaldúa's writing process.

Topics: alchemy, autobiographical information, energy, friendship, gender relationships, love, poetry, reading, writers, writing process

"RIDING THE BACK OF DANGER: HOW TO GET THRU THESE PERILOUS TIMES" (108.9) 1982. Consisting of two typed pages with handwritten edits and notes, this manuscript is a draft of a talk delivered at Yale on April 22, 1982, in which Anzaldúa critiques consensual reality (especially racism and heterosexism), claiming that "[o]ur system of life is fucked up." She encourages her audience to "act with integrity and confidence" and to "remain true to only that part of our nature, our culture, which is good to us."

Topics: autobiographical information, Chicano/a, Collective Force, colonialism, decoloniality, gig, habits, heart, heterosexuality, I Ching, Latinas/os, oppression, reason, soul, spiritual activism, survival, Taoism, transformation, water

"THE SECOND NIGHT HOME FROM THE HOSPITAL" (78.5) mid-1980s to 1991. An autohistoria based on Anzaldúa's experiences shortly after her hysterectomy. Includes various edited drafts and handwritten notes by Anzaldúa and at least one other reader. This story exists in two drafts, both located in 78.5. The later draft was last saved in 1991 and printed after Anzaldúa's death from her hard drive.

Topics: alchemy, autobiographical information, body, Coatlicue, death, disease, hysterectomy, Kundalini, nature, pain, Prieta, sacrifice, serpents, terror, transformation

"SELF-IN-COMMUNITY" (98.14) ca. 2003. Nine pages of single-spaced, typed notes last saved on Anzaldúa's hard drive on June 6, 2003, and printed after her death. Its location indicates that Anzaldúa planned to use it as part of a post-dissertation book, in a chapter on the self in community. Anzaldúa seems also to have used some of this material, which represents some of her later thinking on the topics, to develop a theory of identity formation and shadow work.

Topics: body, bridge, cenote, collective self, community, conocimiento, desconocimiento, empathy, energy, exile, horrific, identity, kabbalah, knowledge, memory, mind, nature, nepantlero, ontology, realities, remolinos, selfhood, shadow work, solitude, soul, spiritual activism, trees, unconscious, watcher, wounded healer

"SELF-REPRESENTATION AND IDENTITY IN CONTEMPORARY ETHNIC/ OTHER AUTOBIOGRAPHY" (95.9, 95.10, 95.11, 100.12) 1990. Early drafts of the Lloronas dissertation chapter on autohistoria-teoría, including the original course paper (which Anzaldúa also used as part of her qualifying exams), handwritten edits, comments by other readers, Anzaldúa's letter of June 16, 1990, to her dissertation committee stating that she'd like this paper and the topics it explores as her qualifying exam (QE) paper (95.9), and a note to her writing group ("los escritorastes") describing this piece as a very rough draft in which she "took two separate papers and combined them—the merging is not smooth yet." In fall 1990, Anzaldúa revised the essay's title: "Self-Representation and Identity in Contemporary Racial Ethnic/Other *Autohistorias-teorías*: Writing the Personal & Collective Histories of the Subject and Problematizing Assumptions about Autorepresentation" (95.10). These drafts document the development of Anzaldúa's ontology, especially the blurring of fact, fiction, imagery, memory, and "actual" events.

Topics: aesthetics, alienation, authenticity, autobiography, autohistoria, autohistoria-teoría, body, censorship, desire, difference, ego, epistemology, estilo mestisaje, ethnic/Other, fantasy, fiction, gender, gender and autobiography, genre-crossing, genres, historia, home, idealism, identity, individual/collective, Llorona, memoir, memory, mestiza, narrative, narrator, ontology, origins, readers, reading, reality, recovery, religious confession, representation, repression, revision, self-knowledge, self-reflection, self-representation, social inscriptions, space, subjectivity, theory, transformation, trauma, women-of-color writing, writing process, "*yo-ísmo*"

"LA SERPIENTE QUE SE COME SU COLA: THE DEATH RITES OF PASSAGE OF A CHICANA LESBIAN" (78.10–78.11) 1982–83. This manuscript is 215 typed, double-spaced pages; the first half is located in Folder 10 and the second half in Folder 11. This version includes handwritten edits and insertions, poems (like "Cervicide") that made their way into *Borderlands*, and Prieta short stories (including "El segundo orazon" and "People Should Not Die in South Texas"). Edits indicate that Anzaldúa originally subtitled this manuscript "The Deaths and Rites of Passage of a Chicana Lesbian." This draft shifts from the first-person narrative of "Esperando" into third person, suggesting that Anzaldúa worked to transform her personal experiences into what she would later (almost twenty years later) describe as enacting autohistoria-teoría. It includes her three encounters with death, the origins of her spiritual activism, and much more. See Box 68 for fragments and revisions of this material, which Anzaldúa used as she converted portions of this manuscript into shorter publications.

> Topics: alchemy, animism, astrology, autobiographical information, autohistoria, autohistoria-teoría, bisexuality, body, Buddha, Catholicism, la Chingada, Christ, Coatlicue, death, drugs, evil, facultad, fate, fire meditation, Gnosticism, homosexuality, hunger, hysterectomy, I Ching, imagination, individualism, initiation, Kundalini, language, loneliness, meditation, menstruation, monotheism, El Mundo Zurdo, musa bruja, mushrooms, naguala, naming, new mestiza, out-of-body experiences, pain, queer, Quetzalcoatl, religion, ritual, safety, self-control, serpent, sexuality, spirit, spiritual activism, spiritual/political division, spiritual technologies, Taoism, Tarot, transformation, Vietnam War, writing

"SIC: SPIRITUAL IDENTITY CRISIS: A SERIES OF VIGNETTES" (64.22, 64.23, 64.24, 64.25) ca. 1993–2002. A series of multigenre vignettes in which Anzaldúa explores the relationship between her embodiment and spirituality during the years she struggled and learned to live with diabetes. She seems to have started this piece when she received her diabetes diagnosis; she wrote these vignettes at random intervals, charting her internal struggles and diabetes' impact in nonlinear form. Had she lived longer, it's likely that Anzaldúa would have included this piece in a book chapter. The essay exists in several drafts with various subtitles:

- "S.I.C.: Spiritual Identity Crisis: A Series of Vignettes" (64.22): This thirty-three-page, single-spaced document was printed after Anzaldúa's death from her hard drive, where it was last saved on February 27, 1999. An essay-in-progress, this draft offers the most detailed lens into Anzaldúa's attempts to understand and cope with diabetes' physical, emotional, metaphysical, and ethical implications. This document contains reflections, poems, a recipe, and notes.

- "SIC" (64.23): Seven typed, single-spaced pages of notes that Anzaldúa planned to include in "SIC: Spiritual Identity Crisis." This draft was printed after Anzaldúa's death from her hard drive, where it was last saved on April 27, 1999.
- "SIC: The Geography of Illness" (64.24): Three single-spaced pages of notes printed after Anzaldúa's death from her hard drive, where the file was last saved on July 7, 2002.
- "SIC: MAL DE SER" (64.25): Fourteen pages of single-spaced notes printed after Anzaldúa's death from her hard drive, where it was last saved on October 13, 2003. This draft is probably the most intimate.

This material offers some of Anzaldúa's most sustained reflections on living with diabetes.

Topics: academia, addiction, aging, art, astrology, autobiographical information, blame, body, chronic illness, consciousness, coping, curanderismo, death, depression, desconocimiento, diabetes, disease, dreams, elements, emotion, energy, food, healing, homosexuality, hypothyroidism, images, imagination, indigestion, intuition, language, Llorona, love, mal ojo, medicine, meditation, metaphysics, nature, ontology, remolinos, self-reflection, shadows, shock, spirituality, stress, suffering, supernatural, transformation, trauma, women and stress, writing, writing blocks

"SONOMA STATE UNIVERSITY LECTURE NOTES" (112.3) 2003. Last saved on May 12, 2003, this one-page, single-spaced document consists of notes for Anzaldúa's Heritage Month lecture at Sonoma State University. The location where it was saved indicates that Anzaldúa drew on it as she wrote *Light in the Dark*.

Topics: activist, artist, border crossing, borders, boundaries, conocimiento, culture, home, identity, nepantla, nepantleras, new mestiza consciousness, safety, seeing through, *this bridge*

"SPACE AND IDENTITY OF PLACE/ESPACIO" (64.18) ca. 1989–91. This twenty-one-page, 1.5-spaced document exploring interrelationships among space, place, identity, time, and power as it applies to "how each of us inhabits space" was part of Anzaldúa's Lloronas dissertation but printed after her death. The section titles offer useful insight into Anzaldúa's intentions for this piece: "*En el silencio de mi espacio*"; "The Body Speaks, Identity Defines Space"; "Imaginative, Protective Space"; "On Time and the Ethnic/Racial Other."

> Topics: altars, autobiographical information, autohistoria, autohistoria-teoría, body, Chicana literary representation, class, community, coping, differences, domination, embodiment, emotions, environmental issues, ethnicity, exile, femininity, gendered space, history, home/house, identity, imagination, intuition, land, landscape, margins, nature, navigation, phobias, place, power, private/public, reading, safety, selfhood, silence, space, spirit, survival, time, trees, tribal land, women and space, women of color, writing

"SPEAKING IN TONGUES: A LETTER TO THIRD WORLD WOMEN WRITERS" (44.19, 44.20, 44.21, 45.1, 45.2, 45.3) 1979–81. One of Anzaldúa's earliest published pieces, this epistolary essay was first published in the Feminist Writers' Guild's writing guide, *Words in Our Pockets*, and was republished, with edits, in *This Bridge Called My Back*. The drafts beautifully illustrate Anzaldúa's early cut-and-paste revision process (44.19, 44.20). In addition to the material that made its way into the published essay, these drafts include material that Anzaldúa used in "La Prieta" and the short introduction to section VI ("Speaking in Tongues") in *This Bridge* (44.19, 44.20). This material also includes later drafts with what are probably the copyeditor's insertions, as well as page proofs.

> Topics: academia, alchemy, assimilation, body, censorship, la Chingada, class, colonialism, complicity, courage, eating, energy, fear, homophobia, imagination, inspiration, language, madness, making soul, El Mundo Surdo, muse, nuclear destruction, oppression, pain, poverty, race, racism, reading, reality, self-esteem, silence, soul, stereotypes, survival, tokenism, transformation, voice, white feminists, whiteness, women of color, wounds, writing, writing practice

"SPEECH—CAL STATE U, DOMINGUEZ HILLS" (96.9) 1999. Eleven pages of handwritten notes (including one page that refers to the lecture Anzaldúa had recently given at the University of Illinois, Urbana-Champaign) and eight pages of typed notes for a talk on feminism delivered at California State University, Dominguez Hills, during Anzaldúa's visit (September 12–14, 1999). The notes offer useful clues into Anzaldúa's thinking and interests at this time, as well as one of Anzaldúa's most sustained discussions of feminism.

> Topics: activism, belief, body, change, Chicanas, collaboration, compassion, con el corazón en la mano, conocimiento, consciousness, cosmic self, death, ecology, energy, epistemology, ethnicity, fear, feminism, feminist activism, feminist epistemology, feminist theory, freedom, gender, immigration, information, internet, intuition, language, law, memes, mestiza consciousness, nos/otras, oppression, power, queer theory, rape, remolinos, respect, Sor Juana, speaking engagements, spiritual activism, susto, theory, tradition, transformation, transgender, trauma, violence, voice, women and knowledge production, women of color, women's studies

"SPIRIT NOTES" (103.29) 1980s–90s? Eleven single-spaced pages of notes on spirituality and autobiographical self-reflection printed from Anzaldúa's hard drive after her death. Although last saved on November 22, 2001, the material was primarily if not entirely written in the 1980s. It includes material culled from interviews, journals, reading, and elsewhere.

> Topics: alchemy, altars, anger, archetypes, astrology, body, breath, candle magic, cenote, consciousness, death, healing, I Ching, illness, intuition, journeying, mantras, moon, El Mundo Zurdo, mushrooms (niñitos), ontology, power, reincarnation, ritual, Sedna, self-esteem, serpents, shamanism, shape-shifting, spiral, spirit, spirit helpers, spiritual activism, spirituality, spiritual mestisaje, symbolism, Tao, Tarot, Texas, trancing, transformation, trees, visualizations, writing

"SPIRITUAL ACTIVISM" (103.27) 1980s–2000. Two sets of notes on spiritual activism (one set is eight single-spaced pages, and the other is seven single-spaced pages), both titled "Spiritual Activism," that Anzaldúa collected in 1999 and planned to develop into an essay on the topic.

> Topics: activism, altar-making, art, autobiographical information, body, conflict resolution, conocimiento, creativity, depression, dreambody, emotion, energy, facultad, fiction, Indigeneity, mind, El Mundo Zurdo, naguala, nagualismo, nature, ontology, oppression, pendulum, science, soul, spirit, spiritual activism, spirituality, spiritual

technologies, supernatural, transcendence, transformation, unconscious, wisdom, women's spirituality movement, writing

"SPIRITUAL ACTIVISM: MAKING ALTARES, MAKING CONNECTIONS"
(64.19, 64.20, 64.21) ca. 1996–99. Later drafts of "Altares: On the Process
of Feminist Image Making" (see above). This essay exists in two ten-page,
single-spaced versions, including one with highlighted passages (64.21).
Here Anzaldúa has expanded her focus from altar-making to the spiritual
activism that altar-making can represent; she includes ontological discussion and additional spiritual technologies as she discusses how various en-
actments of and connections with spirit foster resiliency.

> Topics: altars, astrology, blank spots, body, bridging, Buddhism, ce-
> note, Chicana queerness, Coatlicue, colonialism, curanderas, energy,
> Guadalupe, I Ching, image-making, imaging, meditation, mestisaje,
> mestiza, El Mundo Zurdo, nagual, nepantla, ontology, la oya, pendu-
> lum, psychic, ritual, serpent, shamanism, spirit, spiritual activism,
> supernatural, survival, Taoism, Tarot, tree, unconscious, visualiza-
> tion, Wicca, women's spirituality, writing

"SPIRITUAL MESTISAJE, AN *OTHER* WAY" (64.26, 64.27, 64.28, 64.29) ca.
1991–96. This piece exists in multiple drafts charting the origins and development of Anzaldúa's foreword for Randy Conner, David Hatfield Sparks,
and Mariya Sparks's edited book, *Cassell's Encyclopedia of Queer Myth, Symbol and Spirit: Gay, Lesbian, Bisexual and Transgender Lore*. Drafts range from
the fourteen-page typed transcript of a talk or interview on spirituality and
spiritual practices, simply titled "Spiritual Mestisaje," that Anzaldúa used
as the basis for the preface (64.26), to a rough first draft developed from
this transcript (64.27), to drafts with handwritten edits, reader feedback,
etc. (64.29). This material offers a fairly intimate gaze into Anzaldúa's spirituality and ontology (magic, shamanism, animism, consciousness in the
beyond-human world, etc.). Anzaldúa speaks very frankly (and comfortably) about her belief in multiple realities and magic, as well as shape-
shifting's relationship to identity formation, world-traveling, and more.

> Topics: academia, affirmations, altars, animism, autobiographical
> information, blank spots, candles, Catholicism, colonialism, connec-
> tions, curanderismo, devil, dreaming, energy, enlightenment, ghosts,
> grounding, Guadalupe, history, I Ching, identity labels, imagina-

tion, Indigeneity, land, magic, Mayan, meditation, metamorphosis, El Mundo Zurdo, myth, nagualas, nature, near death experiences, ontology, perception, postcolonial mestiza, queer conocimiento, queer facultad, queer theory, religion, ritual, the sacred, self-image, shamanism, shape-shifter, Siddha Yoga, spirit, spiritual activism, spirituality, spirit world, subliminal tapes, supernatural, survival, symbology, symbols, Taoism, Tarot, transformation, trauma, Virgen de Guadalupe, Wicca

"SUBJECTED TO/BY OTHERS: THE POST MODERN MESTIZA SUB-JECT" (64.30, 95.4, 95.12, 95.13) 1989 to early 1990s. This Lloronas dissertation chapter exists in multiple drafts in various stages of development and revision. In it, Anzaldúa puts mestizas, women of color, and other marginalized people into dialogue with theory creation, postmodernist thought, subjectivity, oppressive power dynamics, and literary theory. She explores the mestiza as a postmodern subject centuries before postmodernism itself was invented and challenges conventional assumptions about marginalized people's (non)relationship to academic "high" theory. She interrogates recent poststructuralists' interest in and appropriation of women-of-color theory. Drafts and notes are located in various boxes and folders, as indicated below, with titles organized chronologically, from earliest to latest:

- "Subjected to Others: The Post Modern Mestiza Sub-Ject" (95.4): Nineteen typed, single-spaced pages of notes with handwritten edits that Anzaldúa dated September 26, 1989. She envisioned this draft with three sections titled as follows: "I. *Movidas* of the Mestiza: *Teorías* to Save Our Lives"; "II. "Theorizing New Knowledges"; "III. Critical Stages: Aesthetics, Strategies for Building a Literary Culture." Seems like a paper written for a course.
- "Subjected to/by Others: The Extra Modern Mestiza Sub-Ject" (95.13): Twenty-six typed, double-spaced pages with handwritten edits, including the word "by" inserted into the title.
- "Subjected to/by Others: The Post Modern Mestiz[a] Sub-Ject" (95.12): Printed after Anzaldúa's death from her hard drive, where it was last saved on May 12, 1990. Twenty-four typed, double-spaced pages.
- "Subjected to/by Others: The Extramodern Mestiza" (64.30) 1990s: An eleven-page, typed, 1.5-spaced draft with some handwritten comments.

Topics: aesthetics, Chicana literary criticism, class, difference, discourse, feminist theory, gender, identity, ideology, knowledge, language, literary representations of the Other, literary studies, literature, mestiza/Chicana feminist critic, mestiza subject, mestiza writer, modernism, oppression, postmodernism, postmodern mestiza, poststructuralist theory, power, representation, silence, *Star Trek*, subjectivity, survival, theory, tokenism, women of color, writing

"SURVEY ON LA LLORONA" (91.26) late 1980s to early 1990s. Produced during Anzaldúa's UCSC graduate studies, this eight-page Scantron survey with fifty multiple choice questions and instructions to prospective participants indicates that Anzaldúa planned to use the data "in a paper presented for Multicultural Approaches to Literature at the University of Texas at Austin." Anzaldúa seems to be assessing people's knowledge of Llorona—what they know (about Llorona's appearance and story) and where they acquired their knowledge (family?).

Topics: gender, Llorona, race/ethnicity, Southwest, storytelling

"TALK ON MULTICULTURALISM" (123.3) 1992. Twenty-eight-page, double-spaced transcript of a talk given at St. Olaf College on March 7, 1992, and transcribed in April of the same year; Anzaldúa developed this transcript into "New Mestiza Nation." In it, she discusses her experiences as a graduate student (at UTA and UCSC), her shifts in economic/class status, how she survived as a student and teacher, and more. The Q&A following the talk offers insights into Anzaldúa's thinking at that time.

Topics: academia, autobiographical information, backlash, border crossing, breath, bridging, Chicanx, class, colonialism, communication, conocimiento, dichotomies, education, ethnic studies, exile, feminist theory, graduate school, identity, "lesbian," Mayan philosophy, mestizaje, multiculturalism, El Mundo Zurdo, music, naming, new mestiza, new mestiza nation, nos/otras, origin stories, people of color in the academy, pisando la sombra, political correctness, poststructuralism, power, privilege, racism, resistance, self-care, sexuality, Texas, *This Bridge*, Trojan mula, violence, women's studies, whiteness

"TALLER NEPANTLA: LETTER OF PROPOSAL FOR THE *NEPANTLA* PROJECT" (127.3) ca. 1995. Printed from Anzaldúa's hard drive, where it was last saved on November 5, 1997, this draft of Anzaldúa's proposal for the five-week residency/retreat at Villa Montalvo, California, offers insight into the development of nepantla as Anzaldúa puts it into dialogue with creativity and the creative process, helping to shape what later becomes the path of conocimiento. This unpublished manuscript should be especially useful for readers interested in exploring how conocimiento developed, at least in part, from other theories.

Topics: alchemy, art, artist, autobiography, body, border, *Borderlands*, Chicana art, Coatlicue state, colonialism, community, conocimiento, consciousness, Coyolxauhqui, crafts, creativity, death, decoloniality, entering into the serpent, exile, healing, history, identity, imaginal, immigration, meditation, monster, myth, narrative, narrative art, new mestiza consciousness, nepantla, poetry, ritual, shaman, space, tree, uncanny, visual narrative

"THEORIES OF THE SELF AND A CHICANA GROUND OF BEING: CHICANA SPACE, CHICANA TIME" (91.19, 92.10, 92.11) 1988. A paper Anzaldúa wrote for a course she was taking at UCSC during spring 1988, which she viewed as "lay[ing] the foundation for QE [Qualifying Exam] and the dissertation." Here's how Anzaldúa described her project in the course paper:

My research will focus on the axes of identity/survival for the Chicana/mestiza women of color from the perspective of spatial/temporal (emotions are places) dimensions of identity. I will draw from multiple disciplines in order to formulate a theory of the construction of the Chicana self and her positionings. Using psychoanlaysis [*sic*] to examine the construction of gender and female representation, psychology of self-hood, cultural anthropology and cultural criticism, history and folklore in Chicano literature, everyday life and politics. I have divided the areas of exploration into roughly three areas: The Mexican, The Queer, and The Writer. Ultimately I want to put into personal narrative and theoretical form the consciousness and reality of the Chicana/mestiza's lived, imagined and artistic experience.

Like most of Anzaldúa's work, this paper underwent numerous revisions with many handwritten insertions and edits. See especially 92.10 for multiple versions, many early, charting the development of her Lloronas dissertation ideas and her theorizing more generally.

Topics: AIDS, autobiography, autohistoria-teoría, body, Chicana, la Chingada, colonialism, colonization, consciousness, curanderismo, depression, difference, dreaming, emotions, estrangement, feminist, gender, genres, guilt, identity, imagination, lesbian, literary studies, Llorona, mestiza feminist lesbian, ontology, out-of-body experiences, personhood, psyche, psychoanalytic theory, queer Chicano, queer theory, representation, self-reflection, sexuality, shame, silence, space, spirituality, subjectivity, survival, temporality, territory, third sex, unconscious, women of color, writing

"TO(O) QUEER THE WRITER—READING, WRITING, AND IDENTITY" (65.1, 65.2, 65.3, 65.4, 65.5, 65.6, 65.7, 65.8, 65.9, 65.10, 65.11, 65.12, 65.13, 65.14, 65.15) 1990–2002. This essay exists in multiple versions and drafts, and Anzaldúa seems to have saved them all, as well as correspondence, handwritten insertions and edits, and feedback from other readers on both the 1990s version and the 2000s version, copies of which were printed from Anzaldúa's hard drive after her death. It was first published as "To(o) Queer the Writer—*Loca, escritora y chicana*" in Betsy Warland's 1991 edited collection, *InVersions: Writing by Dykes, Queers, and Lesbians* (65.15). When Warland invited Anzaldúa to contribute to the project, Anzaldúa explained that because of time constraints she couldn't write a formal essay but could begin with a recorded conversation and convert the transcript "into a prose piece" (65.1). Later, she considered revising and using this piece in both the Lloronas dissertation and her twenty-first-century dissertation. (65.3 includes the 2002 versions of the piece). In a note to her writing comadres (at the end of her 2002 draft), she states, "In this draft I want to bring identity issues up to date, also my ideas on reading & reader response. I welcome any ideas you may have on these issues" (65.3). She also wondered if she should "dwell more on la facultad" and "elaborate on the decolonization of reading/writing & identity construction." Ultimately, however, Anzaldúa believed the piece needed too much work to fit the dissertation timeline, and she postponed further revisions until after completing her degree. As with "La Prieta" and other early texts, this piece illustrates the formative role Anzaldúa played in queer theory.

Topics: academia, aesthetics, assimilation, audience, autohistoria, Chicana, class, coming-out stories, community, decoloniality, difference, (dis)identification, education, facultad, formula writing, genre, homophobia, identity, imaginal, knowledge production, labels, language, lesbian, mestiza, nepantla, ontologies, otherness, positionality, queer facultad, queer theory, racism, reading, reality, theory, whiteness, writing

"TRES LENGUAS DEL FUEGO" (85.3, 85.4) 1979–95. Described as a "cycle of poems and prose pieces" in which Anzaldúa "tried to reinterpret the history and myth of Spanish women living during the transition period between the medieval and Renaissance periods. To show that they, indeed, played roles other than the traditional feminine ones." The material in Folder 3 includes multiple drafts (typed, handwritten, and edited), research notes, and freewrites; the material in Folder 4 contains poems last saved in 1995 and printed from Anzaldúa's hard drive after her death.

> Topics: alchemy, artist, the Black Virgin, Crowley, death, fascism, fire, gender, goddess, Guernica, gypsies, Inquisition, intuition, Islamic art, lust, moon, mysticism, numerology, nuns, priests, Pyrenees, religion, revisionist myth, scribes, self-hypnosis, Sor Juana, soul, Spain, spirit, stress, Sufis, Tarot, Teresa Avila, thought, water, witches, women, wounds

"LA TROJAN BURRA Y LA LUCHA INTELLECTUAL." (96.19) ca. 2003. Printed from Anzaldúa's hard drive after her death, where it was last saved on March 19, 2003, this eight-page, single-spaced draft is part of a draft of the fourth chapter of *Light in the Dark*, which Anzaldúa had removed.

> Topics: academia, activism, artist/activist, Chicanas/Latinas, colonialism, conocimiento, diabetes, facultades, feminist, healing, identity, intellectual struggle, knowledge, Llorona, media, mentoring, mestiza, nepantleras, queers, racism, Raza studies, representation, self-recovery, survival, Trojan burra, women of color in the academy, wounds

"(UN)NATURAL BRIDGES" (52.3, 52.4, 52.5, 52.6, 52.7, 52.8) 2001. Pre-drafts and drafts for Anzaldúa's preface to *this bridge we call home*; also includes material for her preface to the 2002 edition of *This Bridge Called My Back* and "now let us shift." This draft offers some of Anzaldúa's final thinking on racial categories and whiteness, as well as her efforts to grapple with the 9/11 terrorist attacks shortly after they took place.

Topics: 9/11, activism, AIDS, bridges, bridging, capitalism, Coatlicue state, community, compassion, conocimiento, consciousness, conversion, Coyolxauhqui, desconocimiento, difference, dreaming, empathy, empowerment, exclusion, feminist theory, future, healing, Hermes, identity, images, imagination, inclusivity, intolerance, knowledge, meditation, multiculturalism, myth, nepantla, nepantlera, new tribalism, nos/otras, ontology, political correctness, prayer, privilege, progress, race, racism, reading, risk, ritual, self-reflection, shaman, silence, social change, social identities, spirit, spiritual activism, *Star Trek*, storytelling, *this bridge*, *This Bridge*, thought, tradition, transformation, whites, women of color

"VIOLENT SPACE, *NEPANTLA* STAGE" (65.17) ca. 1996. Printed after Anzaldúa's death from her hard drive, where it was last saved on March 20, 1996, this five-page typed document (more notes than an essay draft) offers insights into Anzaldúa's development of her theory of nepantla, including (as the title might suggest) an exploration of nepantla as pain—as a type of limbo with concrete psychic and physical effects.

Topics: academia, autobiographical information, body, conflict, depression, extinction, identity, labels, Llorona, loneliness, marginalization, muggings, nepantla, personal narrative, reality, resistance, shame, survival, terrorism, theory, victimization, violence, women of color, wounds, writer's block, writing

WRITING NOTAS (Boxes 101–110). As discussed previously, writing notas were instrumental to Anzaldúa's creative process. She took copious notes and developed many pages of freewrites which she carefully preserved. The notas cover most of her career, but beginning in November 1996 she slightly formalized her process, labeling the notes alphabetically. (See Boxes 101 and 102.) Many notas are handwritten; some have been "keyed in" (transcribed); and others were composed entirely on the laptop. The topics are far too diverse, multiplicitous, and far-ranging to be summarized here; however, they are well worth your investigations.

"WRITING OUTSIDE THE STORY" (82.9, 107.8) 1995–2002. As the title hints, in this short piece, Anzaldúa writes about her Prieta stories from *outside* the stories, summarizing key points and aspirations. As such, this piece offers useful insights into Anzaldúa's fiction and her writing process more generally. As evidenced by the drafts, had she lived longer, she would have revised this piece into the preface to her short story collection. It exists in several distinct drafts, with slightly different titles:

- "Writing Outside the Story" (107.8) 1995: The first draft, dated January 15, 1995, consisting of two handwritten pages, is part of Anzaldúa's writing notas.
- "Writing outside Other Stories" (82.9): Last saved on September 10, 1998, 6.25 single-spaced typed pages.
- "Outside Other Stories" (82.9): Dated October 9, 1998, consisting of seven single-spaced typed pages.
- "Writing outside the Story" (82.9): Dated June 17, 2002, this manuscript is the most complete. These seventeen single-spaced pages are a draft of the preface Anzaldúa planned to include with her Prieta stories.

Topics: aging, art, autobiographical narrative, autonomy, bodies, borderlands, brujería, change, Coatlicue, consciousness, Coyolxauhqui, divine, embodiment, gender, imagery, intimacy, language, liminality, magic, nepantla, perspective, Prieta, psychic, reality, representation, ritual, soul, storytelling, transgender, trauma, violence, water, writing

"WRITING THE SELVES: CHICANA/COLORED CREATIVITIES INSIDE ENEMY TERRITORY" (65.21, 95.16, 95.17, 95.18, 95.19, 19.20) ca. 1988–1990? Early drafts of what eventually became several Lloronas dissertation chapters. This material includes handwritten notes and edits, Anzaldúa's brainstorming about the dissertation topic, title, and contents, and communication with her dissertation chair. An early version indicates that Anzaldúa anticipated dividing this piece into six sections: "Writing, Riding, Righting the *yo*, the Self"; "Writing on the Edge of Stress"; "Intrapsychic Defenses of Writers"; "The Reader as Voyeur, the Writer as Exhibitionist"; "In Psychic Exile, the Writer"; and "Metaphors in the Tradition of the Shaman." In a handwritten message to Helene Moglen (Anzaldúa's dissertation committee chair) located at the bottom of the outline, Anzaldúa states that the essay "developed out of the piece I did for the Race, Class, & Gender seminar" (95.16). Other titles and drafts are listed below.

- "Writing the Selves: Chicana/Colored Creativities Inside Enemy Territory Speaking in Tongues, *Carta* Two"; "The Writing Subject Writing the Subjects, Writing the Selves: Chicana/Colored Creativities Inside Enemy Territory" (95.18): Dated April 15, 1989.
- "The Writing Subject: Racial Ethnic/Others Inside Enemy Territory" (95.20) n.d.; "Chicana/Colored Creativity Inside Enemy Territory"; "Chicana/Colored Creativities Inside Enemy Territory: Speaking in Tongues, *Carta* Two" (95.17)
- "Writing the Selves: Chicana/Colored Creativity Inside Enemy Territory" (95.20): Printed from Anzaldúa's hard drive and last saved May 19, 1999.
- "Writing the Selves: Ethnoracial/Other Writer/Artists Within Enemy Territory, Speaking in Tongues, *Carta* Two" (65.21): This seventy-one-page, double-spaced draft was printed from Anzaldúa's hard drive, where it was last saved on November 30, 1990.
- "Ethnoracial/Other Self-Writing Subjects Inside Chicana/Colored Creativities inside Enemy Territory, Speaking in Tongues, *Carta* Two" (95.17): Dated May 28, 1990. Sixty typed, double-spaced pages. This draft seems to have had two original and two revised titles. The outline (page 1) was originally titled "Writing the Selves: Chicana/Colored Creativities Inside Enemy Territory"; Anzaldúa crossed out portions of this title and made handwritten insertions, so that it read, "The Writing Subject: Racial Ethnic/Others Inside Enemy Territory." The draft itself was originally titled "Writing the Selves: Ethnoracial/Other Writer/Artist Within Enemy Territory, *Carta* Two"; Anzaldúa revised this title to read, "Ethnoracial/Others, Writing Subjects Inside Enemy Territory, *Carta* Two" (page 2).

Because Anzaldúa did not date all drafts, titles are not organized chronologically. Anzaldúa later used portions of this piece in other dissertation chapters, including "THE POET IS CRITIC."

Topics: academia, aesthetics, anxiety, archetype, autobiography, autohistoria-teoría, bearing witness, Chicana writers, Coatlicue state, consciousness, creativity, death, depression, ego, energy, exile, facultad, fantasies, fiction, genres, healing, identity, imagination, intellect, literary production, masochism, metaphors, musa bruja, mythologizing, nagual, new mestiza, paradigms, perception, post-modern mestiza, rationality, reader, reality, representation, resistance, rites, self/other binary oppositions, self-reading, self-writing, shadow, shamanism, silence, soul, space, spirit, stress, survival, theorizing, time, transformation, transgression, voice, women of color, writer, writing, writing blocks, writing process

"YO VIVO NEPANTLA: IN-BETWEEN STATES AND PROCESSES OF CREATING IDENTITIES AND OTHER REALITIES" (96.10) 1990s. A thirteen-page, single-spaced, very rough draft/collection of notes with handwritten edits and highlights. In it, Anzaldúa explores issues related to identity (individual and collective, relational identity formation, and much more) as an ongoing process. Anzaldúa stored this draft in a folder with a page of handwritten notes on nos/otras and notes for her 1998 talk in Boise, Idaho, "Nos/otras: Theorizing Mestisaje."

Topics: academia, alienation, altered states of consciousness, anger, assimilation, belief, border crossers, change, Chicana identity, colonialism, community, complicity, composition, conocimiento, core identity, cracks between worlds, desconocimiento, desires, energy, environment, fear, feminism, gender, geography of selves, grief, identity, illness, jaguar, Latinos, masculinity, mestisaje, naming, nationalism, nepantla, nos/otras, purpose, queer mestisaje, queer raza, remolino, representation, sacrifice, selfhood, self-knowledge, shifting, Sor Juana, spiritual practices, stories, tension, theory, Trojan burras, values, women of color

POSTSCRIPT

Working with Anzaldúa and Her Theories

Mine is a discontinued, interrupted discourse, mine is a fragmented discourse, an incomplete one. you [*sic*] the listener, you the reader are forced into participating in making meaning. My perspective shifts, I shift topics, or so you think. You are forced to connect the dots, to connect the fragments. You have to put it together and in putting it together you participate in the discourse, that is you help me make meaning, but it's your meaning, not the one I shoveled into your open mouths.—Anzaldúa, "On My Method and Ways of Ordering and Structuring"

Gloria Anzaldúa never assumed her words would enter us with her exact meaning intact, nor did she want them to. (*And, in fact, "exact meaning" is an inaccurate term when applied to Anzaldúa's work, given its generative, recursive, agentic meaning-making process.*) She did not view her texts as the passive conveyor of her ideas. Nor did she presume that meaning could be fully distilled, pinned down, and deposited into the written word—fixed in print. As the above epigraph drawn from an unpublished early-stage manuscript suggests, Anzaldúa experienced writing and reading as an interrelated, never-ending meaning-making process. Indeed, she worked intentionally to invite readers into her texts as co-creators. To enhance this invitational, participatory approach, she eschewed linear organization and logical argument. As she states later in the same piece, "I don't trust rational order and rational modes. I do not offer you a synthetic reduction of the readings nor a summation. The readings are to be experienced, to be felt, they are to be assimilated by your emotional body, and to be processed by it first before allowing the intellect to work on it. I also don't believe in interpreting the material and opening up your skulls and feeding it to you. I want you to interpret and translate the material for yourself using your experiences." Here we see Anzaldúa's confidence in her readers (*in you, in me, and in those to come*). She invites us to soak up her words, to engage with them deeply and creatively, to interact with them using our emotion, intuition, and (*last on the list!*) rational thought. (*And, as her reference to our "emotional body" suggests, it seems likely that Anzaldúa wrote with subtle energies in mind, that she worked to engage with us on multiple embodied and psychic levels. But that's an exploration for another day.*)

Again, in her 1992 talk at St. Olaf College, Anzaldúa emphasizes our role as co-creators and the permeable boundary between writer, readers, and texts. After asserting that she wants her theories to be "not assimilable" but "accessible," she explains,

> [I]f you are reading *Borderlands*, you can access that book but hopefully [it] won't get consumed out of existence, or tokenized or assimilated. It is original. The original impulse I have for writing it. I know that those ideas, they are in the text and you will recreate them as you read them, you will reinterpret them. You will read them at home and do what ever you want with them. So it is not like I am trying to say the ideas are mine and don't do anything with them. You can access them and sort of take them in but maybe not melt them. ("Talk on Multiculturalism")

Here we see Anzaldúa's pride in her work, her desire to share her theories with others, her acknowledgment that we will "recreate them as [we] read," and her plea that we don't distort them so much that we violate the theories themselves. (*I have seen these violations when scholars use Anzaldúa to build walls rather than bridges, to exclude rather than create radical inclusion.*) Anzaldúa does not hoard her ideas or prevent others from using them; she does not insist on solitary ownership over them. She is generous: "You can access them and sort of take them in but maybe not melt them." I appreciate her tentative language: as "sort of" and "maybe" indicate, she presumes the partiality of readers' comprehension and acknowledges the possibility that the theories could be assimilated—their uniqueness lost, written over by the readers' needs and views. She knows the risks involved in sharing her theories (*theories which in many ways were her Self, her embodied experiences, her desires, aspirations, and more*). She willingly (*willfully*) takes those risks, trusting us and our inner wisdom. Generous to a fault.

Gloria Evangelina Anzaldúa was one of the most generous thinkers I have known—in person and/or in print. I could share so many anecdotes about her—anecdotes drawn from her own life, from my years working with her, and from my discoveries in the archives—to illustrate this generosity. While she very much saw herself as a creator—as a poet, writer, artist, philosopher, and so on—she typically did not insist on extreme ownership over her ideas and theories. She did not try to control them or fully shape them into fixed forms. She wanted her theories and philosophy out in the world—doing their work, making change, helping others.

A decade later, near the end of her life, Anzaldúa again reiterates her view of readers as, potentially, co-creators. As she states in an email to the students in my Gloria Anzaldúa graduate seminar, "Any of you estudiantes, please feel free to unravel these concepts (or any other of 'my' concepts)—once they go out into the world they cease to 'belong' to me" ("Disability & Identity" 300). (*And I know from observations over the years that this generous view of readers was not an anomaly but rather how Anzaldúa moved through the world: she believed in our inner wisdom, our ability to interpret and build on her words. Note also how the use of quotation marks around "my" and "belong" underscores Anzaldúa's generosity.*)

Given this gracious invitation (and the expectation that we'll co-create with Anzaldúa), how do we work with Anzaldúan theories respectfully? How do we interpret them without imposing *our* will and our views on them? How do we nurture them (and ourselves), allowing both to grow? Answering these questions thoroughly would require an entire book of its own. Here, I offer a few insights gleaned from my decades-long experiences working with Anzaldúa and with Anzaldúan theories, students, and scholars.

Be in Relationship

Be in relationship with the writings and with Anzaldúa herself. As I've emphasized (*repeatedly!*) throughout this book, Anzaldúa fostered and enacted a participatory relationship with the world. She was in conversation with herself, the spirits, her surroundings, her readers, her previous ideas and theories, and much more. She used ritual, intention, imagination, writing, and other spiritual technologies to foster this relational worldview. She built the conversations through self-reflection: she assessed her emotional, intellectual, and energetic needs and considered how these needs helped to shape her encounters with the various worlds through which she traveled and about which she wrote. She looked for patterns and messages; she opened herself to el cenote, and she took the necessary risks to dive in, doing the shadow work that Coatlicue demanded.

You can learn from Anzaldúa and her practices; you can create your own Anzaldúan rituals. You can summon her energies, and possibly her spirit, through self-reflection, through your intentions, and through small practices (freewrites, contemplative walks, journaling, and much more). I want to especially emphasize the importance of honest self-reflection: because Anzaldúa and her work can function like a mirror, inviting us to see ourselves in her words, it's important to be discerning and to ask difficult questions about where we've imposed our meaning on hers, rather than co-creating together.

Be Respectful Yet Bold

There's no need to be a sycophant or aspire for literal interpretations and usage. Open yourself to the theories—put yourself into conversation with them. Listen and learn, with the willingness to be surprised and startled out of your current perspectives. Apply Anzaldúa's theories to your interests, your situations, your lives. You have permission to do so from Anzaldúa herself! But don't abuse Anzaldúa's generosity. When working with her theories, it's imperative to do so with integrity and respect. Here, I use "integrity" to represent bringing one's self (*your whole self*) into alignment with the Anzaldúan principles of inclusivity, open-mindedness, and radical interconnectedness, as seen in her overarching, generous philosophical frameworks of conocimiento, El Mundo Zurdo, and spiritual activism.

We show respect by learning the theories and their contexts deeply, by honoring each theory's situational engines, by understanding their original connections with Anzaldúa's life, and by acknowledging (not erasing) these connections even as we expand upon them. So, for example, if you discuss and apply her theory of new mestiza consciousness, you should acknowledge both its roots in Anzaldúa's geographic, embodied location (*her personal experiences as well as the geographic and historic Mexico-US border)* and the nuanced ways she expanded these roots. And then, as you work with new mestiza consciousness, note the points where your interpretation and application overlap with Anzaldúa's, and where they diverge. By thus respecting the theories and their origins, scholars will be less likely to appropriate and distort the theories themselves. (*We can also show respect by trying to spell and pronounce the theories—whether Nahuatl, Spanish, or English—correctly. And note that I say "trying"—the effort itself indicates respect.*)

Adopt an Attitude of Intellectual Humility and Balanced Self-Confidence

Approach the theories (*as, of course, we should approach everything and everyone we encounter*) with the reminder that, as humans, our knowledge is always partial and, thus, open to change. The world is too huge for us to know it in its entirety. Truth is too complex, too ample, too multivalent for our human minds to entirely grasp, to articulate, or to distill into sound bites or sentences on a page or a computer screen. Remain open-minded throughout your work with Anzaldúa's theories. No matter how long you've been investigating them and/or how deeply you've dived into her work, do not assume that you have fully grasped their meaning or that you precisely know Anzaldúa's intentions. (*In fact, Anzaldúa herself did not entirely grasp her theories' meaning or her own intentions; the theories are agentic, with an autonomy, or semi-autonomy, that exceeds their creators.*) Acknowledge (always) the possibility for expansion, reinterpretation, and growth. No matter how long you've been working with a specific theory or text and no matter how much you've already learned, there's still opportunity for new perspectives. It's as if her theories (or possibly Anzaldúa herself) are time travelers, surprising us with new insights as the years pass and we continue reading and working with her words. (*I can attest to this ongoing experience of surprise: each time I tried to wrap up this book project, I encountered something new—a sentence, idea, or manuscript that seemingly appeared out of the blue. Even as I read through the copyedited pages, I am gleaning additional insights and discovering previously overlooked archival information.*)

Balance this intellectual humility with self-confidence in your ability to receive and create insights about the work. If you're drawn to Anzaldúa's writings (*or even a select theory or two*), assume that the writings and theories are drawn to you—are drawing *you* to *them*. If it feels as if Anzaldúa and/or her words are calling out to you, trust that they are: her words invite you into dialogue and encourage you to respond.

Yes. Although it might seem like a contradiction, I'm suggesting that you approach and enact Anzaldúan theory with self-confident intellectual humility. Be both humble and bold. How, though, do we live out this contradiction? Here, too, Anzaldúa is instructive. Throughout her career, she self-confidently insists on her intellectual power, her inspired wisdom, and her ability to develop innovative work but also remains open-minded, asks questions, and acknowledges the limitations in her knowledge. By so doing, she makes space for the unknown. See the final section of "La Prieta" for a beautifully instructive example of this balanced intellectual humility. Anzaldúa boldly asserts her worldview and her vision for the future while also acknowledging that she is uncertain and confused about how to achieve it. She leans into the questions and lives them out in the following years. (*As I explain elsewhere, she can do so through her process of alignment, a process she invites us to enact.*)

Assume that you'll learn more. Be open to new insights. This openness is always important for scholars, but with a shape-shifting, time-traveling author like Anzaldúa, it's even more crucial. Many readers have had the experience of returning to Anzaldúan texts read previously and discovering what seem like completely new insights. (*I've had this experience many times, even with* Light in the Dark—*which is truly weird, given that I edited the volume and had read all of the manuscript drafts multiple times.*)

Perhaps most importantly, then, remain open to being surprised.

Notes

Introduction

1. Anzaldúa has achieved extensive international recognition. See Norma Elia Cantú's "Doing Work That Matters: The Impact of Gloria Anzaldúa's *Borderlands/La Frontera: The New Mestiza*"; the contributions in Keating and Gloria González-López's *Bridging: How and Why Gloria Anzaldúa's Life and Work Transformed Our Own*; and the El Mundo Zurdo conference proceedings for details on her international impact. Anzaldúa's writings have been included in highly influential, canon-building anthologies in the fields of literature, feminist theory, Chicana writing, and composition—to mention only a few: *Border Texts*; *The Chicano Studies Reader: An Anthology of Aztlán, 1970–2010*; *Feminism and "Race"*; *The Heath Anthology of American Literature*; *Infinite Divisions: An Anthology of Chicana Literature*; *The Latino/a Condition*; *Living Chicana Theory*; *The Norton Anthology of American Literature*; *The Norton Anthology of Literature by Women*; *The Norton Anthology of Theory and Criticism*.

2. I follow Anzaldúa's practice of not italicizing non-English words. She believed (and I agree) that to italicize non-English words denormalizes them. While in her earliest writings Anzaldúa sometimes italicized Spanish, Latin, and so on, she was inconsistent in doing so. I interpret her inconsistencies as a somewhat half-hearted attempt to adhere to English language writing conventions of the time, which dictated that non-English words be italicized. That said, I do keep the italics when quoting from Anzaldúa's early writings.

3. "Writing notas" was Anzaldúa's term for her incredibly extensive journaling/note-taking. I discuss these notas in more detail in chapters 2 and 6.

4. El cenote is one of the Anzaldúan theories explored in part II.

5. Anzaldúa's perfectionism, coupled with her organic aesthetics and prolific writing habits, creates unique challenges. Because she cared greatly about *how* her words were conveyed, Anzaldúa often made intentional decisions about capitalization, punctuation, paragraph breaks, spelling, etc., that defied conventional rules. And yet, like most of us, Anzaldúa made typographical errors, changed her preferences along the way, and occasionally deferred to publishers and professors. I've done my best to respect her intentional choices, but issues around capitalization have been especially tricky. At

times, she capitalized words and phrases that at other times she did not (e.g., "Creative Force," "Soul"). And often (especially in her later years), she made her titles lowercase.

6. I use "women-of-colors," rather than "women-of-color," to underscore the complex diversity within this category. Thanks to Indigo Violet for introducing me to this term in her essay, "Linkages."

7. For a metaphoric example of this heart-ripping gesture, see Caren Neile's "The 1,001-Piece Nights of Gloria Anzaldúa: Autohistoria-teoría at Florida Atlantic University."

1. Risking the Personal, Redux

1. Anzaldúa retells this event frequently in interviews and includes it in "Autohistoria de la artista" and her Prieta stories.

2. For more on this topic, see Anzaldúa's discussion with Christine Weiland in *Interviews/Entrevistas* (94–100).

3. Anzaldúa probably learned the word "daemon" (more commonly spelled "daimon") from James Hillman, and used it to describe a wise inner guide. As she writes in an early draft of "Conocimientos" (49.3), "The lacunae of consciousness, the missing parts, those blank spots, those blind spots in my consciousness, something I've missed. So again and again I'm thrown in repeat performances of certain experiences that cause me discomfort, mental anguish and despair. My soul-daemon throws these happenings at me so I can look for the lessons and cultivate the skills to handle them in a new way, to look at the problems from a new perspective and to learn to enjoy the process and create a form, a pattern or a ritual that gives these activities meaning."

4. Anzaldúa experienced intersectional racism/sexism throughout her education; from kindergarten through to grade 12 she excelled in schoolwork, regularly achieving high grades. The teachers, all Anglo, were consistently surprised that she did so well because they assumed that their Mexican American students were intellectually inferior. The young Gloria challenged this stereotype, though the teachers refused to acknowledge their limited views and instead treated her as an oddity—unusual in her intelligence. This treatment did not give Anzaldúa additional benefits but became a burden, marking her as different from her (Mexican American) classmates.

5. Thanks to Becky Thompson for noting the significance of this quotation and encouraging me to elaborate.

6. This scholarly interest in Mesoamerican philosophy represents a continuation of Anzaldúa's earlier interest, as indicated by her June 1974 journal entries in which she references the Olmecs, Aztec mythology, and Colin Wilson's *The Philosopher's Stone*.

7. Anzaldúa describes these experiences in "Autohistoria," interviews, and writing notas, interpreting them in various ways. Late in life, in "Conocimientos," she writes, "Alter state of consciousness, change channels, not for escapism but [to] get a more accurate reading of the nature of reality. I would like to think that that was my purpose in taking mushrooms, peyote and LSD but I'm not sure that my curiosity about the

nature of reality was not tinged with the urge to flee my particular and lonely reality of the mid 1970s: Through the cracks of reality I sought a way into the numinous universe behind the material world of sensory. But what I lacked was a deeper cultural context. I was ingesting these psychoactives in a vacuum—no ceremonies, no prayers."

8. Anzaldúa's desire to cultivate nonordinary practices preceded her Austin years; as she noted in June 24, 1974, "I am interested in parapsychology and would like to have an astral projection and explore the other dimensions." She read Jane Roberts' Seth books and other similar material, taking pages of notes and highlighting information in the books. Anzaldúa held on to these books throughout her life, placing them on the bookshelves next to her bed. (*And I assume that, like many of us, she kept her dearest books near to her as she slept.*)

9. "Vastation" is the term philosopher William James used to describe a paralyzing encounter he experienced with another realm. Although Anzaldúa herself doesn't use this term, the parallels between their experiences are uncanny (*pun intended*).

10. Although Anzaldúa moved away from Austin, she did not abandon her doctoral studies.

11. Book projects included her "Serpiente" autohistoria and several poetry collections; for more on the El Mundo Surdo Reading Series and workshop, see the entry on El Mundo Zurdo in chapter 4.

12. Conversation with Anzaldúa, early 2000s. For additional details on *This Bridge's* origins and evolution, see *Interviews* and Anzaldúa's drafts of "(un)natural bridges" and "counsels from the firing."

13. Anzaldúa did not use the phrase "spiritual activism" itself until later in her career. See the entry on spiritual activism in chapter 3 for more on this topic.

14. Although Anzaldúa's family might have questioned her in many ways, they were extremely supportive. (*Readers who know Anzaldúa's family primarily through the eyes of* Borderlands *and/or* "La Prieta" *might be surprised by the family's staunch support.*)

15. Anzaldúa often used the word "gigs" to describe her speaking engagements, and so I use it as well. (She used it frequently in conversation, but see also emails and the essay draft "Doing Gigs.")

16. Although Anzaldúa had not yet developed her theories of autohistoria and autohistoria-teoría, I believe that she is enacting them in some of her earlier work; indeed, it's possible that her writing practice called the theories themselves into being. (*Thanks to Becky Thompson for asking me to address Anzaldúa's use of third person in this manuscript. I've become so used to Anzaldúa's very personal third person voice that I'd normalized it to myself.*)

17. Coined by John Welwood, "spiritual bypassing" refers to the use of spirit and spirituality to escape from social injustice and other dimensions of everyday physical-material reality.

18. From her journal entry of December 31, 1983.

19. Anzaldúa bought the house with a friend; she had the funds to do so, at least in part, because she had been awarded a National Endowment for the Arts award. The house figures significantly in her later work; it was both a haven and a time drain.

20. Pinkvoss had encouraged Anzaldúa to submit her poetry to the press.

21. For a thorough, extremely insightful discussion of the book's evolution, see Ricardo Vivancos-Pérez's "On the Process of Writing *Borderlands/La Frontera* and Gloria E. Anzaldúa's Thought."

22. I'm referring specifically to Anzaldúa's discussions of El Mundo Zurdo; for more on this manifesto, see the entry on it in chapter 4 of this book.

23. Anzaldúa, of course, used the term "women of color" (a term which she helped to bring into the academy); as mentioned in the introduction, I have pluralized the term to underscore the complex diversity within this category. Thanks to Indigo Violet for introducing me to this term.

24. I use "pragmatic" in the Jamesian philosophical sense and in dialogue with Patricia Hill Collins's theory of visionary pragmatism.

25. In "SIC" Anzaldúa recalls her decision like this: "Language. I've resisted academic language but then felt that there was a language I'd turn away from and that I should return to grad. sch. [*sic*] and learn that language."

26. See for instance "Autohistoria de la artista," in which she describes herself as "translating these morsels of personal history into 'authentic' autobiography or 'fictionalized' narrative forms" and suggests that this translational work "calls on traditional genre techniques as well as newer techniques, as yet unnamed, techniques we are still in the process of inventing."

27. Anzaldúa's theory and method for this dissertation included revisionist mythmaking: an approach to knowledge production that views myth and mythic figures as containing profound (*sacred*) truths that have been lost, suppressed, distorted, or in other ways hidden. As I argue in *Women Reading*, by revising the dominant culture's version of these myths (and by recovering mythic stories and figures that had been erased), revisionist mythmaking offers alternative, potentially transformative ontologies, epistemologies, ethics, and more.

28. For more on Anzaldúa's engagement with Coyolxauhqui, see chapter 4 of this book.

29. Key titles: "Lloronas—Women Who Wail: Ethnic/Other Explorations of (Self)-Representation and Identity and the Production of Writing and Knowledge"; "Lloronas—Women Who Wail: Ethnic/Other Explorations of Identity, (Self)-Representation & Writing"; "Lloronas—Women Who Wail: Explorations of (Self)Representation and Identity and the Production of Writing and Knowledge"; "Lloronas—Women Who Wail: *Autohistorias-teorías* and the Production of Writing, Knowledge and Identity." (See chapter 6 for more on this dissertation project.)

30. See chapter 6 for a list of the many drafts and title revisions.

31. "Ditched" is the word Anzaldúa uses in an email to me when describing her relationship to the Lloronas dissertation. (*We could have an entire conversation exploring Anzaldúa's use of this verb and its implications.*) Concerning Anzaldúa's growing self-confidence, see the many drafts of the dissertation chapter (finally) titled "THE POET IS CRITIC/THE POET IS THEORIST: Speaking in Tongues, Queridas mujeres escritorias de color Carta Two." Even the title change, from "The Poet *as* Critic, The Poet *as* Theorist" to "The Poet *is* Critic, The Poet *is* Theorist" (my emphasis) points to her

growing confidence in her theorizing power and her identity as a theorist (as well as creative artist).

32. Because Anzaldúa was self-employed, obtaining adequate, reasonably priced insurance was an ongoing challenge. She talked to me often about health insurance (in)decisions and (bad) options, and her writing notas contain additional documentation of this struggle.

33. Concerning this depression, Anzaldúa writes in "SIC," "Depression. I fall into despair so dark it's as though I've plunged into a bottomless chasm, wounded so deep it will take years for a scar to cap it. Depression dims the light, shuts the door, silences the soul." This document offers a heart-wrenching, detailed depiction of Anzaldúa's experiences living with diabetes.

34. She also received income by renting out the upstairs portion of her Santa Cruz house. For a glimpse of Anzaldúa the landlord and friend, see Irene Reti's "Living in the House of Nepantla."

35. During the early 1990s Anzaldúa worked on several fiction projects, including a multigenre collection, "Entreguerras, entremundos / Civil Wars Among the Worlds"; her Prieta stories; and her children's books: *Friends from the Other Side/Amigos del otro lado* (1993) and *Prietita and the Ghost Woman/Prietita y la Llorona* (1995).

36. For example, in Writing Notas K she asks, "Does the personality create the body? Is the size of a person voluntary?"; and in Writing Notas E, "What feeling am I blanking? Am I afraid of something? What am I afraid of? Something awful, protect myself from knowing what it is." See part III, especially chapter 6, for more on the notas.

37. The group was composed of Anzaldúa and another writer (Isabel Juárez Espinosa), as well as three visual artists (Santa Barraza, Liliana Wilson, and Cristina Luna). See "Crack in the World" by Ann Elliot Sherman for a short summary of this project.

38. See chapter 4 for more on nepantla and Coyolxauhqui.

39. For a longer discussion of this essay's development, see appendix 5 in *Light in the Dark* and the entry on it in chapter 6 of this volume.

40. By "dissertation/book" I refer to *Light in the Dark*: as I explain in "Re-envisioning Coyolxauhqui," *Light in the Dark* was dissertation in name only. Though while drafting it, Anzaldúa called it her dissertation and indicated that she would transform it into a book, she wrote the entire manuscript without feedback from a dissertation chair or committee. She planned and wrote it *as* a book.

41. As the house aged, it required repairs (such as a new roof); Anzaldúa rented out the top half of the house, and when her long-time tenant and good friend, Irene Reti, moved out, Anzaldúa had to take care of the many responsibilities involved in finding and working with a new tenant.

42. See chapter 4 for a discussion of spiritual activism.

43. See chapter 4 for more on conocimiento.

44. "Descono**151**cimientos.": Anzaldúa here is reminding herself that she drew from a section of Writing Notas I that explores desconocimientos. If needed, she can go to that section for more material.

45. I define "nature" broadly to include all reality; Anzaldúa's metaphysics are a pluralistic monist animism.

46. Our book was published a year after our planned deadline, primarily because Anzaldúa felt it necessary to continue revising "now let us shift." At the time, because I was fielding impatient inquiries from contributors, I was very frustrated with her; however, in retrospect, the extensive time paid off. She produced a philosophy—not just the essay itself. See our email communication, located in her archive.

47. For a brief history of her dissertation process, see my introduction to *Light in the Dark*.

48. See my introduction to *Light in the Dark* for a more extensive history of Anzaldúa's dissertation/book.

49. The interview, eventually titled "Speaking across the Divides," was initiated by her good friend Inés Hernández-Ávila. At the time, I thought Anzaldúa was taking on too much and further jeopardizing her health; however, given her premature death, we're fortunate that she had this opportunity to reflect on Indigeneity and directly address critiques made of her work.

50. Almost all of these documents exist in multiple drafts. See chapter 6 for additional details about the manuscripts, including their dates and archival locations.

2. Writing as Ritual, Habit, Mission, Partner, and Joy

1. This quotation is from "Barred Witness," in which Anzaldúa also notes, "There is an unconscious conspiracy to convince us that we are much less than we think we are. We're not supposed to be good at certain things, to go beyond a certain point in efficiency or knowledge or power. We are not supposed to produce meaning." I have drawn heavily on this manuscript in what follows.

2. "We are not supposed to 'represent,' only to be 'represented'" ("Barred Witness").

3. "How do we find mentors, how do we form support groups and make alliances, find places to read our work, create anthologies and quarterlies to publish our work? How do we deal with agents and editors and publishing houses? How do we get teaching jobs? Why do we write or make art? Do we write for money, for fame, for power, to gain knowledge, to give others pleasure?" ("Barred Witness" [57.19]).

4. Anzaldúa discussed the impact of diabetes on her schedule in interviews and in her later writings. As she explains in the interview with Andrea Lunsford, "My illness has changed the way I work. I have diabetes, so I need to eat more often—every two and a half to three hours to keep my blood sugars balanced. I need to rest more and to exercise. I can't be a workaholic anymore" (*Interviews* 258).

5. Anzaldúa wrote often, in writing notas and unpublished drafts, about this perfectionism and its impact on her health. See for instance this statement from "Barred Witness": "I push myself to a point of agony with excessive demands on myself. At what costs? Episodes of severe depression; near panic states may result from measuring personal worth and self-esteem by success and productivity. Being time-pressured coupled with the mental habit called perfectionism makes for an incredible block." I experienced this perfectionism firsthand when working with her. I was astonished by how in-depth her revisions were for "now let us shift"; long after I thought the piece

was finished (*and I'm quite the perfectionist, too!*), she continued revising it in ways both large and small. See her archive for copies of these many drafts and our communication about them.

6. I make this suggestion inspired by "Barred Witness," in which Anzaldúa pairs each writing challenge with innovative tactics to resist, overcome, and transform.

7. An earlier version of this section can be found in my introduction to *Light in the Dark*.

8. Prior to meeting Anzaldúa "in the flesh," I'd communicated with her, sending her a draft of my book chapter that explored her work.

9. See Betsy Dahms's discussion of Anzaldúa's revision process. The drafts to "La Prieta" can be found at the archive, Box 14, Folders 14 through 18; "Speaking in Tongues" drafts can be found in Box 14, Folders 19 through 21, and Box 15, Folders 1 through 3.

10. Examples of projects initiated through these outer calls: "Speaking in Tongues"; "Autohistoria de la artista as a Young Girl"; the Lloronas dissertation; "haciendo caras, una entrada"; "Border Arte"; "Putting Coyolxauhqui Together"; "now let us shift"; "(un)natural bridges."

11. Anzaldúa's interest in metaphysical technologies and right-/left-brain thinking spans the majority of her life and merits a much larger study.

12. See Henri Corbin's "Mundus Imaginalis, or the Imaginary and the Imaginal."

13. For more on how Anzaldúa considered audience as she drafted, see *Interviews*, in which she repeatedly frames her discussions of writing in the context of readers; see also her "To(o) Queer the Writer."

14. Email dated February 20, 2003, on file with the author. Anzaldúa was telling me about her work on "Geographies of Selves" (chapter 4 in *Light in the Dark*), which was unending at that time.

15. See for instance "Border Arte" and "Puddles." I recall when I first met Anzaldúa, watching her edit the poems in her published copy of *Borderlands*! For examples of what Anzaldúa's complex revision process looks like, see the appendices to *Borderlands/ La Frontera: The New Mestiza, The Critical Edition*, which reproduce images of the early manuscript pages.

3. How the Theories Emerged

1. Anzaldúa offers a quick, speculative genealogy of the term "high theory" in "Poet is Critic" which, as I explain in what follows, she associated with classism and other disparities: "I do not know who originated the terms 'high' and 'low' theory. I do know that Edward Said used 'high' to designate a privileged, literate, human, and normal Eurocentric cultural model and 'low' for non-literate, non-human and non-European cultures. I think his terms can also be loosely applied to 'high' and 'low' theory."

2. For more on Anzaldúa's visionary approach, see "Re-conocimientos and Producing Knowledge," especially the section titled "Movidas of the Mestiza—Teorías to Save Our Lives," in which Anzaldúa contrasts women-of-color theorizing with mainstream academics' work.

3. See my book, *Transformation Now!*, in which I discuss status-quo stories, defining them as "worldviews that normalize and naturalize the existing social system, values, and standards so entirely that they prevent us from imagining the possibility of change. Status-quo stories contain 'core beliefs' about reality—beliefs that shape our world, though we rarely (if ever) acknowledge this creative role" (35).

4. See, for instance, "Exploring Cultural Legacies."

5. See Boxes 116 through 119. While some of the material was collected after her death, much was collected by Anzaldúa herself.

4. Eighteen Anzaldúan Theories

1. I define oracular research in chapter 3.

2. As explained in chapter 1, Anzaldúa shifts from first person in the earlier version to third.

3. Anzaldúa discussed this question with me at length in the early 2000s. She was really torn but decided that the revisions would take too long to complete within the dissertation timeline.

4. Thanks to anonymous reviewer #3 for asking about possible connections between Anzaldúa's theory and testimonio ("How did Anzaldúa adapt Latin America's 'testimonio' genre (if at all)? How are they similar and different?").

5. From the transcript of her 1993 interview with *DisClosure* (113.11). See also this comment in *Interviews*: "Borderlands with a small b is the actual southwest borderlands or any borderlands between two cultures, but when I use the capital B it's a metaphor for processes of many things: psychological, physical, mental" (176).

6. Anzaldúa uses third person but is describing herself.

7. See especially the dissertation chapter drafts titled "Carta a Colón."

8. Thanks to anonymous reviewer #1, whose comments on an earlier draft allowed me to recognize that I had not made this point clear.

9. The archive contains three *boxes* of drafts, constituting well over one thousand pages.

10. Thanks to anonymous reviewer #1 for suggesting that I say more about the relationship between the two.

11. This and the following two bullets were inspired by anonymous reviewer #3, who I thank for the useful suggestions.

12. Given her familiarity with and appreciation of James Hillman, it's quite likely that Anzaldúa was alluding to Hillman's transpersonal psychology here.

13. Anzaldúa intentionally used "blank spots" rather than the more commonly used "blind spots" to avoid ableist language.

14. See the entry on new mestiza consciousness.

15. This point gets lost in critiques of Anzaldúa's references to Indigeneity.

16. This passage is different from the version found in *Light in the Dark*.

17. Thanks to anonymous reviewer #1 for asking me to expand on the relationship between these two theories.

18. See footnote 3 in the eighth draft of "Geographies of Selves." Thanks to anonymous reviewer #1 for asking about Anzaldúa's shifts between "nos/otras" and "nos/otros."

19. "Spiritual technologies" is my term; I use it to describe an array of spiritual/esoteric/occult practices, including those Anzaldúa herself employed: Tarot, I Ching, candle magic, meditation, visualization, contemplative walking, imaginal journeys, etc. See chapter 1 for further discussion of the term and Anzaldúa's early autohistorias and the other manuscripts listed below for examples.

20. "Occult" here means hidden.

5. The Gloria Evangelina Anzaldúa Papers

1. Although I didn't distinguish between interview and conversation while editing *Interviews*, I would do so now, describing (for instance) the Weiland piece as a conversation, rather than an interview. An Anzaldúan conversation has a level of comfort and ease; it's a dialogue between friends, while the latter, typically, has a more formal question-and-answer format in which the interviewer approaches Anzaldúa as an expert (*whether revered author, iconic theorist, representative Chicana lesbian, etc.*), and Anzaldúa talks from her role as author-theorist.

2. See the entry for "Border Arte: Nepantla, el lugar de la frontera" in chapter 6 for more on the title shifts and nonchronological archival organization of this piece.

6. Anzaldúa's Archival Manuscripts

1. Anzaldúa often inserted dates in the top right-hand corner of the first page or sometimes within the draft itself.

2. As she worked to complete her twenty-first-century dissertation, Anzaldúa looked through many computer files, searching for material to borrow and update.

3. Here and elsewhere in this document, I follow Anzaldúa's spelling.

Primary Sources: Publications

Note: For unpublished references, see chapter 6. All sources in this section are authored by Anzaldúa unless specified otherwise.

Borderlands/La Frontera: The New Mestiza. Spinsters/Aunt Lute, 1987.

Borderlands/La Frontera: The New Mestiza, The Critical Edition, edited by Ricardo F. Vivancos-Pérez and Norma Cantú, Aunt Lute, 2021.

"The coming of el mundo surdo." 1977. *The Gloria Anzaldúa Reader*, edited by AnaLouise Keating, Duke UP, 2009, pp. 36–37.

"Disability & Identity: An E-mail Exchange & a Few Additional Thoughts." *The Gloria Anzaldúa Reader*, edited by AnaLouise Keating, Duke UP, 2009, pp. 298–302.

"Foreword, 2001: counsels from the firing . . . past, present, future." *This Bridge Called My Back: Writings by Radical Women of Color*, edited by Cherríe Moraga and Gloria Anzaldúa, 3rd ed., Third Woman Press, 2002, pp. xxxiv–xxxix.

Friends from the Other Side/Amigos del otro lado. Children's Book Press, 1993.

The Gloria Anzaldúa Reader, edited by AnaLouise Keating, Duke UP, 2009.

"haciendo caras, una entrada." *Making Face, Making Soul/Haciendo Caras: Creative and Critical Perspectives by Women of Color*, edited by Gloria Anzaldúa, Aunt Lute Foundation, 1990, pp. xv–xxviii.

Interviews/Entrevistas, edited by AnaLouise Keating, Routledge, 2000.

Light in the Dark/Luz en lo Oscuro: Rewriting Identity, Spirituality, Reality, edited by AnaLouise Keating, Duke UP, 2015.

Making Face, Making Soul/Haciendo Caras: Creative and Critical Perspectives by Women of Color. Aunt Lute, 1990.

"Metaphors in the Tradition of the Shaman." *Conversant Essays: Contemporary Poets on Poetry*, edited by James McCorkle, Wayne State UP, 1990, pp. 99–100.

"El Mundo Zurdo: The Vision." 1981. *This Bridge Called My Back: Writings by Radical Women of Color*, edited by Cherríe Moraga and Gloria Anzaldúa, 2nd ed., Kitchen Table: Women of Color Press, 1983, pp. 195–96.

"New Mestiza Nation." 1992. *The Gloria Anzaldúa Reader*, edited by AnaLouise Keating, Duke UP, 2009, pp. 203–16.

"On the Process of Writing *Borderlands/La Frontera*." 1991. *The Gloria Anzaldúa Reader*, edited by AnaLouise Keating, Duke UP, 2009, pp. 187–97.

"La Prieta." 1981. *This Bridge Called My Back: Writings by Radical Women of Color*, edited by Cherríe Moraga and Gloria Anzaldúa, 2nd ed., Kitchen Table: Women of Color Press, 1983, pp. 198–209.

Prietita and the Ghost Woman/Prietita y la Llorona. Children's Book Press, 1995.

"Speaking across the Divide." 2003. *The Gloria Anzaldúa Reader*, edited by AnaLouise Keating, Duke UP, 2009, pp. 282–94.

"Speaking in Tongues: A Letter to Third World Women Writers." 1981. *This Bridge Called My Back: Writings by Radical Women of Color*, edited by Cherríe Moraga and Gloria Anzaldúa, 2nd ed., Kitchen Table: Women of Color Press, 1983, pp. 165–74.

"To(o) Queer the Writer—*Loca, escritora y chicana*." *Inversions: Writing by Dykes, Queers, and Lesbians*, edited by Betsy Warland, Press Gang, 1991, pp. 249–64.

"(un)natural bridges, (un)safe spaces." *this bridge we call home: radical visions for transformation*, edited by Gloria Anzaldúa and AnaLouise Keating, Routledge, 2002, pp. 1–5.

Anzaldúa, Gloria, and AnaLouise Keating, eds. *this bridge we call home: radical visions for transformation*, Routledge, 2002.

Moraga, Cherríe, and Gloria Anzaldúa, eds. *This Bridge Called My Back: Writings by Radical Women of Color*, 4th ed., SUNY, 2015.

Secondary Sources

Baldwin, Elizabeth. "Gloria Anzaldúa: Bridge at the Crossroads." *Matrix*, May 1988, pp. 3, 13. Box 38, Folder 9.

Bost, Suzanne. *Encarnación: Illness and Body Politics in Chicana Literature*. Fordham UP, 2010.

Bost, Suzanne. "Messy Archives and Materials that Matter: Making Knowledge with the Gloria Evangelina Anzaldúa Papers." PMLA, vol. 130, no. 3, 2015, pp. 615–30.

Calderón, Héctor, and José David Saldívar, eds. *Criticism in the Borderlands: Studies in Chicano Literature, Culture, and Ideology*. Duke UP, 1991.

Cantú, Norma Elia. "Doing Work That Matters: The Impact of Gloria Anzaldúa's *Borderlands/La Frontera: The New Mestiza*." *Borderlands/La Frontera: The New Mestiza, The Critical Edition*, edited by Ricardo F. Vivancos-Pérez and Norma Cantú, Aunt Lute, 2021, pp. 7–15.

Cantú, Norma Elia, et al., eds. *El Mundo Zurdo: Selected Works from the Meetings of the Society for the Study of Gloria Anzaldúa 2007 & 2009*, Aunt Lute, 2010.

Conner, Randy P., David Sparks, and Mariya Sparks, eds. *Cassell's Encyclopedia of Queer Myth, Symbol and Spirit: Gay, Lesbian, Bisexual and Transgender Lore*, Cassell, 1997.

Corbin, Henri. "Mundus Imaginalis, or the Imaginary and the Imaginal." 1964. *Swedenborg and Esoteric Islam*. Translated by Leonard Fox, Swedenborg Foundation, 1995.

Cuevas, Jackie, et al., eds. *El Mundo Zurdo 4: Selected Works from the 2012 Meeting of the Society for the Study of Gloria Anzaldúa*, Aunt Lute, 2015.

Dahms, Betsy. "Shamanic Urgency and Two-Way Movement as Writing Style in the Works of Gloria Anzaldúa." *Letras Femeninas*, vol. 38, no. 2, 2012, pp. 9–26.

Elliott Sherman, Ann. "Crack in the World." *Metroactive*, 1995, http://www.metroactive.com/papers/metro/11.02.95/art-9544.html.

Hedges, Elaine, and Shirley Fisher Fishkin, eds. *Listening to Silences: New Essays in Feminist Criticism*, Oxford UP, 1994.

Irving, Kim. "From the Borderland: An Interview with Gloria Anzaldua [sic]." *Coming Up!*, September 1987, pp. 42–44.

Keating, AnaLouise. "Re-envisioning Coyolxauhqui, 'Decolonizing Reality': Anzaldúa's Twenty-First-Century Imperative." *Light in the Dark/Luz en lo Oscuro: Rewriting Identity, Spirituality, Reality* by Gloria Anzaldúa, Duke UP, 2015, pp. ix–xxxviii.

Keating, AnaLouise. "Risking the Personal: An Introduction." *Interviews/Entrevistas* by Gloria E. Anzaldúa, edited by AnaLouise Keating, Routledge, 2000, pp. 1–15.

Keating, AnaLouise. *Transformation Now! Toward a Post-Oppositional Politics of Change.* University of Illinois Press, 2013.

Keating, AnaLouise. *Women Reading Women Writing: Self-Invention in Paula Gunn Allen, Gloria Anzaldúa, and Audre Lorde.* Temple UP, 1996.

Keating, AnaLouise, and Gloria González-López, eds. *Bridging: How and Why Gloria Anzaldúa's Life and Work Transformed Our Own*, U of Texas P, 2011.

Mercado-López, Larissa M., et al., eds. *El Mundo Zurdo 3: Selected Works from the 2012 Meeting of the Society for the Study of Gloria Anzaldúa*, Aunt Lute, 2013.

Neile, Caren S. "The 1,001-Piece Nights of Gloria Anzaldúa: Autohistoria-teoría at Florida Atlantic University." *EntreMundos/AmongWorlds: New Perspectives on Gloria Anzaldúa*, edited by AnaLouise Keating, Palgrave Macmillan, 2005, pp. 17–27.

Reti, Irene. "Living in the House of Nepantla." *EntreMundos/AmongWorlds: New Perspectives on Gloria Anzaldúa*, edited by AnaLouise Keating, Palgrave Macmillan, 2005, pp. 57–59.

Reuman, Ann E. "Coming into Play: An Interview with Gloria Anzaldúa." *MELUS*, vol. 25, no. 2, Summer 2000, pp. 3–45.

Rhudyar, Dane. *An Astrological Mandala: The Cycle of Transformations and Its 360 Symbolic Phases.* Vintage, 1974.

Violet, Indigo. "Linkages: A Personal-Political Journey with Feminist of Color Politics." *this bridge we call home: radical visions for transformation*, edited by Gloria E. Anzaldúa and AnaLouise Keating, Routledge, 2002, pp. 486–94.

Vivancos-Pérez, Ricardo F. "On the Process of Writing *Borderlands/La Frontera* and Gloria E. Anzaldúa's Thought." *Borderlands/La Frontera: The New Mestiza, The Critical Edition*, edited by Ricardo F. Vivancos-Pérez and Norma Cantú, Aunt Lute, 2021, pp. 7–15.

Welwood, John. "Principles of Inner Work: Psychological and Spiritual." *Journal of Transpersonal Psychology*, vol. 16, no. 1, 1984, pp. 63–73.

Index

Anzaldúa, Gloria (continued)
  relational worldview, 305–6; self-
  confidence, 21, 23, 33; self-descriptions,
  230; spiritual-political vision, 145; as
  university educator, 26, 28–29; theoretical
  aspirations, 73; tokenization, 24, 29, 50.
  See also diabetes; risking the personal;
  speaking engagements; writing process;
  and under individual titles
Anzaldúan studies, 7, 11, 215
Anzaldúan theories, 23, 71; challenges to their
  exploration, 74–75, 78–79; healing and, 77;
  as invitational, 73–74; as living entities, 79,
  80, 307–8; social justice and, 82. *See also
  individual theories*
appropriation, 66, 153, 181, 191, 194, 293
árbol de la vida, 91, 190, 194
archetype(s), 153; el cenote and, 57, 100;
  knowledge and, 54, 135; Medusa, 105. *See
  also* Pacifica Graduate Institute
archival research method, 7, 10–11, 303–8
archives, 213. *See also* Gloria Evangelina
  Anzaldúa Papers
arrebato, el, 109–10, 135
art, 37, 89, 243; borderlands and, 95; conocimiento and, 109; nepantlera and, 170;
  transformation and, 38. *See also* artist(s);
  border arte; cenote, el
artist(s), 2, 18, 37–33, 263; border, 234;
  Chicanx, 234, 280; la facultad and, 135; as
  naguala, 160; nepantla and, 162; as nepantleras, 165, 168–69; as shaman, 121. *See
  also* "Autohistoria de la artista as a Young
  Girl"; Villa Montalvo Workshop
artist-activist, 38
art-making, 165, 262; El Mundo Zurdo and,
  145–46
assimilation, 169, 188, 196
astral travel, 21, 311n8
astrology, 11, 21, 39, 146–47, 214, 228, 262; el
  cenote and, 100; la facultad and, 135. *See
  also* Sabian symbols
Aunt Lute, 28, 217, 245
Aurobindo, Sri, 144
Austin, TX, 311n10
autobiography, difference from autohistoria, 82–83. *See also* autohistoria(s);
  autohistoria-teoría(s); genre

autohistoria(s), 4, 7, 81–91, 246–47, 274,
  311n16; Anzaldúa's, 45; examples of,
  230–31, 286; la facultad and, 135; El
  Mundo Zurdo and, 148; as new genre, 81;
  new mestiza and, 177. *See also* autohistoria-
  teoría(s); fiction
"Autohistoria de la artista as a Young Girl"
  (Anzaldúa), 18, 45, 47, 230–31, 310n1,
  312n25, 315n10
"*Autohistorias-teorías—Mujeres que cuentan
  vidas*" (Anzaldúa), 47, 75, 83, 84, 88, 89,
  220, 231–32, 246
autohistoria-teoría, 4, 81–91, 99, 246–47, 274,
  311n16; el cenote and, 27, 100; Coyolxauhqui process and, 123, 124; creativity and, 80;
  as method, 75, 85–86, 88; new mestiza and,
  177; origins of, 31, 78, 280, 283, 287–88; the
  personal and, 7, 27. *See also* autohistoria(s);
  "*Autohistorias-teorías—Mujeres que cuentan
  vidas*"; Borderlands/La Frontera
Aztec(s), 234; myth, 118, 310n6 (chap. 1);
  teachings, 103, 175. *See also* Coatlicue;
  Coyolxauhqui; Indigenous; nagualismo

Barraza, Santa, 313n37
B/borderlands, 316n5 (chap. 4); el cenote
  and, 101; geographies of selves and, 140;
  El Mundo Zurdo and, 147; nepantla and,
  156, 162; new mestiza and, 174, 177; new
  mestiza consciousness and, 185; new
  tribalism and, 193
beyond-human world. *See* more-than-human
  world
blank spots, 69, 129, 316n13; defined, 128; as
  desconocimientos, 127
body, 150, 152, 160, 251; el cenote and, 100;
  Coatlicue state and, 102–3; descono-
  cimiento(s) and, 126; identity and, 138;
  imaginal, 162; knowledge and, 110, 132–33;
  spirit and, 27; spiritual activism and,
  203–4, 206, 208, 209. *See also* diabetes;
  epistemology; nepantla; spirit(s); writing
border, 91–92; difference from borderland,
  92; Mexico-U.S, 140
border arte, 37, 95, 185, 234; nepantla and,
  159–60. *See also* border artists
"Border Arte" (Anzaldúa), 163, 185, 234, 280,
  315n10, 315n15

border artists, 159, 234

"Borderlands" (Anzaldúa), 93, 229

borderlands (theory of), 3, 73, 78, 91–96, 260; geographies of selves and, 137; nepantla and, 158. See also *Borderlands/La Frontera*; border(s)

borderlands, U.S.-Mexico, 33, 158, 306–7

Borderlands/La Frontera: The New Mestiza (Anzaldúa), 11, 27, 51, 91, 103–4, 315n13; Anzaldúa's view of, 40; creation of, 28; desconocimiento(s) and, 127; la facultad in, 184; later theories and, 74; manuscript drafts, 105, 132, 184, 214, 217–18, 229–30; nepantla and, 158; new mestiza in, 172, 174; theorizing in, 65

Borges, Jorge Luis, 89, 91

Bost, Suzanne, 4, 214

brain, 34, 50, 55, 115, 131; nepantla, 158, 160, 161, 164. See also epistemology

bridge(s), 26–27, 110, 277, 304; Anzaldúa and, 6, 27, 31, 36, 112, 125, 126; body as, 27, 69; la facultad and, 135; ideas, 92, 93; la naguala and, 150, 153; nepantlera and, 165, 167; nos/otras and, 195, 196; people, 92

Buddhism, 174, 196

butterfly, 133–34

Calderón, Héctor, 233–34

Campbell, Joseph, 245

Cartesian worldview, 23, 104, 107, 150

cenote, el, 5, 21, 88, 96–102, 165, 275, 306; defined, 57, 91; Coatlicue state and, 106; conocimiento and, 116; Coyolxauhqui process and, 123; desconocimiento(s) and, 130, 131–32; journeys into, 27; la naguala and, 154; nepantla and, 161, 162, 170; writing and, 56, 59

El Cenote Writing Workshop, 98, 99

chakras, 115, 146

change. See transformation

Chicana/o studies, 2

Chicano Movement, 22, 188

Chicanx, 44, 138, 171, 295; and Latinx, 190, 267–68; and new mestizas, 175–76

children's books, 1, 37, 313n35

"La Chingada" (Anzaldúa), 52, 216, 240

citizenship, 284

clairsentience, 129

clairvoyance, 132, 134

classism, 183, 242, 315n1

coalition(s), 185, 193, 206, 242; -building, 80, 111, 127, 165; desconocimientos and, 128; nos/otras and, 197

Coatlicue, xv, xxi, 103, 105, 118, 306. See also Coatlicue state; Coyolxauhqui

Coatlicue state, 38, 88, 102–8, 158, 218, 252; el cenote and, 101; Coyolxauhqui process and, 119, 123; desconocimientos and, 106; nepantla and, 156, 158, 162; new mestiza consciousness and, 185; spiritual activism and, 204, 208; writing blocks and, 274. See also conocimiento

Collins, Patricia Hill, 312n24

colonialism, 197, 198, 236; Coyolxauhqui process, 118

Columbus, Christopher, 197, 236–7

commonalities, 142–43, 166; new tribalism and, 188; nos/otras and, 195–96. See also El Mundo Zurdo; nepantlera(s); nos/otras; spiritual activism

community, 17, 146, 167, 201, 286; archives and, 213; -building, 165; new tribalism and, 190; nos/otras and, 195–96; writing and, 48. See also coalition

compassion, 122, 200

complicity, 128–29; nos/otras and, 195, 199

composition studies, 2

conflict, 42, 140, 156, 177; desconocimientos and, 125–26, 242; geographies of selves and, 140; psychic, 104, 110; resolution, 129

connectionist thinking, 108, 166

Conner, Randy, 21, 144, 145, 183, 206, 236, 292

conocimiento, 3, 21, 71, 78, 99, 108–18, 274, 285; autohistoria-teoría and, 88, 90; borderlands and, 95; el cenote and, 97, 101; Coatlicue state and, 106; Coyolxauh-qui process and, 123; creativity and, 73; desconocimiento(s) and, 130; development of, 41–42, 241, 242, 284, 294–95; la fac-ultad and, 135; El Mundo Zurdo and, 143, 147; la naguala and, 154; nepantla and, 158, 160, 161, 162; nepantleras and, 165, 170; new mestiza consciousness and, 185; new tribalism and, 193; nos/otras and, 200, 201; queer theory and, 116;

conocimiento (continued)
 seven stages of, 109–10, 116, 129; spiritual
 activism and, 206, 207–8; as systemic
 philosophy of change, 42. *See also* arrebato,
 el; desconocimiento(s); nepantla
conocimientos, 90, 125, 126; defined, 111
consciousness, 96; embodied, 139; panpsychic, 114. *See also* arrebato; conocimiento;
 desconocimiento(s); dreaming; mestiza
 consciousness
consensual reality, 38, 50, 67–68, 111, 147,
 286; artists' challenges to, 113, 168;
 defined, 21; desconocimiento(s) and,
 126, 130; difference and, 166; la faculta
 and, 132; nepantla and, 155, 156–57;
 nepantleras and, 165, 166; new mestiza
 and, 173, 174; new mestiza consciousness
 and, 182; new tribalism and, 191; theory
 creation and, 71
contemplation, 153
contemplative walking, 317n19
contradictions, 171, 173; nepantla and, 157; new
 mestiza consciousness and, 180; nos/otras
 and, 201; spiritual activism and, 203–4
Corbin, Henry, 88, 141, 315n12
Cortázar, Julio, 20
cosmos, 7, 23, 56, 100; la naguala and, 150, 153
Coyolxauhqui, 32, 38, 39, 106, 121; Coatlicue
 and, 107, 120, 121–22; conocimiento and,
 110, 114; consciousness, 123, 124; nepantla
 and, 162; new mestiza consciousness and,
 185; writing and, 121. *See also* conocimiento; Coyolxauhqui process
Coyolxauhqui imperative, 77, 118–19; defined,
 119; and nepantla, 161. *See also* writing
Coyolxauhqui principle, 118–19
Coyolxauhqui process, 38, 88, 99, 103,
 118–24; Coatlicue state and, 106, 120;
 conocimiento and, 114, 115; descono-
 cimiento(s) and, 130; development of, 41;
 geographies of selves and, 140; la naguala
 and, 154; nepantla and, 159; spiritual activism and, 204, 208. *See also* writing
creative life force, 40, 99, 309–10n5
creative process, 113; conocimiento and, 111;
 la facultad and, 134; naguala and, 149;
 nepantla and, 159, 160, 163, 294–95. *See
 also* el cenote; writing process

creativity, 249; desconocimiento(s) and,
 131–32; El Mundo Zurdo and, 145–45
critical whiteness studies, 131
cultural studies, 2

daimon/daemon, 19, 149, 154, 310n3; desconocimientos and, 127. *See also* nagual
Dahms, Betsy, 315n9
decoloniality, 84; Coyolxauhqui and, 124
decolonial wisdom traditions, 3
decolonization, 296; el cenote and, 101. *See
 also* border arte; knowledge; Coyolxauhqui
Denver Museum of Natural History, 159, 234
depression, 103; Anzaldúa's, 33, 43, 105, 252,
 313n33; Coyolxauhqui process and, 118,
 124. *See also* Coatlicue state
desconocimiento(s), 42–53, 125–31, 193, 284;
 autohistoria-teoría and, 88; conocimiento
 and, 109, 110, 116, 126; difference, 127, 129;
 nepantla and, 162; nos/otras and, 195, 201,
 202. *See also* Coatlicue state
diabetes, 10, 34–35, 39, 42, 106, 288–89,
 313n33, 314n4; Coatlicue state and, 106;
 conocimiento's creation and, 113. *See also*
 Anzaldúa, Gloria
difference(s), 142; la facultad and, 132; El
 Mundo Zurdo and, 142–44; new mestiza
 consciousness and, 182; new tribalism and,
 188; as relational, 148, 166. *See also* commonalities; nos/otras; *This Bridge Called My
 Back*; *this bridge we call home*
disability, 44
disability studies, 2
dismemberment, 118, 121, 158, 245
divine, 183, 206. *See also* Coatlicue;
 Coyolxauhqui
divine guerillas, 133, 170, 206, 208
Doll, Mary Aswell, 40
dreaming, 55, 56, 259; awake, 54; nepantla,
 161; writing process and, 54, 60. *See also*
 shamanism
dykes, 133, 182; Chicana, 189, 274–75

education, 23, 198–99; discrimination in, 16,
 50, 310n4; la naguala, 154; social change
 and, 16. *See also* academia; Anzaldúa, Gloria
emotion(s), 6, 19, 37, 274, 304; autohistoria/
 autohistoria-teoría and, 83, 85; Coatlicue

state and, 104; conocimiento and, 110; nos/otras and, 196; theory creation and, 69. *See also* body

energetics, 115, 117

energy, 49; conocimiento and, 117; Coyolxauhqui, 41, 124; El Mundo Zurdo and, 144; new mestiza consciousness and, 181; spiritual activism and, 205; subtle, 304; of transformation, 38, 157, 181

entering into the serpent, 38, 160

"Entreguerras, Entremundos" (Anzaldúa), 244–45, 313n35

environment, 113, 165; geographies of selves and, 137, 138, 139; new tribalism and, 188, 190; theory creation and, 9, 70

epistemology, 39, 80; Cartesian, 104, 107, 151, 179; dialogic, 113; of ignorance, 131; and El Mundo Zurdo, 143; and nepantla, 156; nonrational, 27, 56, 57, 69, 85, 143, 168; right- and left-brain thinking, 144, 315n11. *See also* conocimiento; la facultad; new mestiza consciousness; "seeing through"

esoteric, 8, 317n19; new mestiza consciousness and, 186; spiritual activism and, 203, 206; studies, 2; traditions, 21–22, 26, 156, 183

"Esperando la serpiente con plumas" (Anzaldúa), 55, 245–46; autohistoria/autohistoria-teoría and, 86; as *Borderlands'* precursor, 79; Coyolxauhqui process and, 121; la naguala and, 154

Espinosa, Isabel Juárez, 313n37

ethics, 39, 312n27; Anzaldúa's, 80; conocimiento and, 108, 117; nepantla and, 156, 157; new mestiza and, 175; new mestiza consciousness and, 179; spiritual activism and, 80, 203, 208; writing notas, 37. *See also* conocimiento; new tribalism; nos/otras; spiritual activism

ethnic studies, 2, 3, 36

Evans, Jamie Lee, 128

extrasensory perception (ESP), 132

facultad, la, 21, 70, 131–36, 151, 218, 296; as alternative to rational thought, 71; Anzaldúa's conflicting origin stories for, 79; borderlands and, 95; el cenote and, 101; Coyolxauhqui process and, 123; desconocimiento(s) and, 130; the imaginal and,

57; El Mundo Zurdo and, 147; la naguala and, 154; nepantla and, 163; new mestiza consciousness and, 185; spiritual activism and, 208. *See also* conocimiento

feminism, 2, 21, 28, 68, 192, 291; international, 144

feminist theory, 2, 21, 25; Anzaldúa's, 25, 28–29

Feminist Writers' Guild, 24

fiction, 23, 38, 39, 67, 89, 234, 287; Anzaldúa's, 1, 11, 33, 214, 245, 298–99, 313n35; autohistoria/autohistoria-teoría and, 82–83, 85, 87, 312n26; la facultad and, 134, 135, 136; la naguala in, 151–52, 153, 155; nepantla and, 33, 155, 163; speculative, 88, 158–59; spiritual activism and, 208; transformation and, 38, 39. *See also* Prieta stories

Fishkin, Shelley Fisher, 185, 236–37

folklore, 23, 32, 295

freewrite(s), 37, 53, 55, 58–59, 63. *See also* writing process

genre, 31, 47, 83. *See also* autohistoria/autohistoria-teoría

Geographies of Latinidad Conference, 140, 67, 199–200, 207, 250, 259, 267

geographies of selves, 4, 137–42, 196, 250; borderlands and, 95; identity formation in, 72–73; nepantla and, 163; nepantleras and, 170; new mestiza and, 177; new tribalism and, 193; nos/otras and, 201. *See also* árbol de la vida

geography, 98–99

ghost(s). *See* La Llorona

Giroux, Henry A., 233

glifo, 11, 214

Gloria Evangelina Anzaldúa Papers, 11, 213–14; challenges for researchers, 219–21; origins of, 215–17; suggestions for researchers, 221–22

goddesses. *See* Coatlicue; Coyolxauhqui; La Llorona; myth(s); Virgen de Guadalupe

grief, 32. *See also* La Llorona

Grosz, Elizabeth, 253

"haciendo caras, una entrada" (Anzaldúa), 64–65, 215

Haraway, Donna, 30, 246, 258

hauntings, 251, 269–70. *See also* La Llorona

healing, 39, 77; autohistoria and, 86; Coyolxauhqui process and, 118–19, 120–21, 123; creativity and, 130–31; desconocimientos and, 200; metaphors and, 259; la naguala and, 149, 153; nepantla and, 162; nos/otras and, 195–96; planetary, 191–92; trauma, 124

heart: epistemology of, 70, 115; conocimiento and, 117; El Mundo Zurdo and, 142, 145, 148

Hedgebrook, 39

Hedges, Elaine, 236–37

Hernández-Ávila, Inés, 111, 188, 314n49

Hillman, James, 105, 310n3, 316n12

History of Consciousness Program (UCSC), 29

homosexuality, 235–36. *See also* queer(s)

Huitzilopochtli, 118, 121

I Ching, 11, 26, 55–56, 146–47, 174, 214, 317n19

identity, 122, 251, 252, 253–54, 284–85, 296, 301; categories and, 251; desconocimientos and, 127; embodiment and, 33; geographies of selves and, 137; inclusive, 25; El Mundo Zurdo and, 143; la naguala and, 152; as process, 138; shifts, 158; writing notas, 37. *See also* identity formation; nepantla; new tribalism; nos/otras; way station(s)

identity formation, 73, 138, 156, 261, 286; collective, 80; naguala and, 150; nepantla and, 157, 158; new tribalism, 188, 193. *See also* árbol de la vida; autohistoria-teoría

identity politics, 146, 194, 195, 242; nos/otras and, 202

image(s), 52, 58, 59, 74, 85; as agentic, 57, 81–82; emotions and, 69; el cenote and, 97, 98, 99; la facultad and, 131–32; writing process, 61

imaginal, 38, 94; autohistoria/autohistoria-teoría and, 83–84; defined, 56; la facultad and, 135; journeys, 55; knowledge and, 85; El Mundo Zurdo and, 147; writing and, 51. *See also* el cenote; image(s)

imagination, 2, 3, 23, 37, 249, 285, 306; autohistoria/autohistoria-teoría and, 84, 88; geographies of selves and, 140; la naguala and, 149, 153, 154; nonrational, 146; nos/

otras and, 200; transformation and, 18, 31, 38; writing and, 58, 60. *See also* el cenote; la naguala

immigration, 141

imposter syndrom, 276

inclusivity, 306. *See also* commonalities; new tribalism; nos/otras; spiritual activism

Indiana University, 20, 47

Indigeneity, 191, 192, 193, 249, 314n49; Anzaldúa's relation to, 100, 174–75, 316n15. *See also* Indigeneity

Indigenous: identity, 172, 173, 186–87; nepantla and, 156; new tribalism and, 193, 194; philosophies, 55, 153, 156, 183, 203

individualism, 107, 153

instinct(s), 69

integrity, 306

intellectual humility, 8, 307–8; Anzaldúa's, 78, 305

intention(s), 58, 306

intentionality, 126

intersectionality, 25

Interviews/Entrevistas (Anzaldúa), 41, 282, 317n1 (chap. 5)

intuition, 56, 79, 304; autohistoria/autohistoria-teoría, 84; El Mundo Zurdo and, 143; la naguala and, 150. *See also* la facultad

James, William, 311n9

Jane Eyre, 18

Joysmith, Claire, 43

Jung, Carl, 129

Keating, AnaLouise, 315n8, 316n3 (chap. 3)

knowledge(s), 56, 163; Anzaldúa's love of, 18, 30, 48; autohistoria-teoría and, 85; esoteric, 28, 156, 183; spiritual, 73; theory and, 67; transformative, 47, 61. *See also* conocimiento; epistemology; imagination; new mestiza consciousness; spiritual activism

knowledge creation, 6–7, 32, 39, 51, 69, 70–74, 161. *See also* el cenote; Coatlicue state

language(s), 15, 48, 62, 69, 109, 179, 236; ableist, 316n13; academic, 312n24; auto-

historia/autohistoria-teoría and, 75; conocimiento and, 113; English, 109, 309n2; of
images, 57, 58–59; magical, 17; menstruation and, 223; nepantleras and, 166; new
mestiza and, 166, 181; of otherness, 197; secret, 57; Spanish, 4, 6, 16, 50; theoretical,
8, 31, 65, 312n25; theory creation and, 69;
transformational, 18, 61. *See also* writing
Lara, Irene, 268
"La serpiente que se come su cola" (Anzaldúa), 26, 144–45, 152, 187–88; archives,
217; autohistoria/autohistoria-teoría, 86; as
Borderlands' precursor, 79
Latinx, identity formation, 72. *See also* geographies of selves; new tribalism; nos/otras
de Lauretis, Teresa, 30, 32, 256, 265
left hand, 147, 179. *See also* El Mundo Zurdo
lesbian(s), 25, 87, 139, 184, 217, 274. *See also*
queer(s); sexuality
LGBTQ. *See* queer(s)
LGBTQ studies, 2
Light in the Dark (Anzaldúa), 22, 28, 40–41,
44, 62, 70, 100, 153, 249, 308; borderlands
and, 94–95; chapter drafts, 238, 261; nepantla and, 162; nepantleras and, 170; spiritual activism, 208; status-quo stories, 71
Limón, José, 236, 251
listening, 112, 132
literary studies, 2
literature, Chicana, 242–43, 276, 284; and El
Mundo Zurdo, 145–46. *See also* writing
La Llorona, 17, 187, 255, 270–71, 294; Coatlicue and, 107; ghostly body, 32, 152, 238,
251, 256, 283; identity and, 32; la naguala
and, 154; as symbolic body, 152. *See also*
Lloronas dissertation
Lloronas dissertation (Anzaldúa), 33, 43, 238–
39, 249–50, 270, 295–96; chapter drafts,
220, 231–32, 232–33, 236–37, 243–44, 251,
253, 265, 287, 299–300; conclusion, 283;
new mestiza consciousness and, 187; nos/
otras and, 202; prospectus, 254, 255–56,
256–57, 258
Loma Prieta earthquake, 72
Lomas, Clara, 43
Lorde, Audre, 184
Luna, Cristina, 313n37
Lunsford, Andrea, 122, 195, 314n4

magic, 98–99, 277, 279, 292; la facultad and,
135; El Mundo Zurdo and, 142
Making Face, Making Soul/Haciendo Caras
(Anzaldúa), 28–29, 64–65, 255
making soul, 49, 103
Marxism, 21
Maya, 97, 98–99
McEwan, Christian, 230
McLaren, Peter, 233
meditation, 21, 27, 146–47, 187, 262, 317n19;
el cenote and, 98; conocimiento's creation
and, 113; guided, 99, 276; writing and, 55,
58–59, 146
Medusa, 105, 106
Medusa state, 7, 105–6
melancholia, 106
memoir, 100. *See also* autohistoria/
autohistoria-teoría
memory, 97, 100; body's, 124
Merleau-Ponty, Maurice, 265
mestiza, 139–40, 171. *See also* mestiza consciousness; mestizaje; new mestiza; new
tribalism
mestiza consciousness. *See* new mestiza
consciousness
mestizaje, 173, 174, 186, 191. *See also* new
mestiza; new tribalism
metaphor(s), 62, 69; and la facultad, 132
"Metaphors in the Tradition of the Shaman"
(Anzaldúa), 223, 246–47, 254, 273, 276
metaphysics, 17, 39, 40, 50, 201, 206,
313n45; and nepantla, 156. *See also*
conocimiento
metaphysics of radical interconnectedness,
6, 9, 23, 203, 306
method: autohistoria-teoría as, 86; conocimiento, 111, 116; dialogic, 4, 42, 53,
70–74; El Mundo Zurdo as, 143, 148; la naguala, 154; new tribalism, 193; nonrational,
62. *See also* writing process
mind, 104, 150; spiritual activism and, 203–4,
206. *See also* epistemology
mind/body division, 104
mindfulness, 153, 181, 207. *See also* meditation; self-reflection
Moglen, Helene, 257, 258, 299
monte, el, 17
Moraga, Cherríe, 25, 146

more-than-human world, 6, 10, 16, 22–23, 26–27, 43, 70, 292; conocimiento and, 114; spiritual activism and, 203. *See also* animism

Morris, Marla, 40

Movimiento de Arte y Cultura Latino Americana (MACLA), 37–38

multiculturalism, 2, 173

El Mundo Surdo, 143, 144, 206

El Mundo Surdo Reading Series, 24, 146, 148, 252

El Mundo Zurdo, 4, 16, 41, 99, 142–49, 306; borderlands theory and, 73, 92; conocimiento and, 108, 111, 116; la facultad and, 135; la naguala and, 154; nepantleras and, 170; new mestiza and, 177; new mestiza consciousness and, 185; new tribalism and, 188; spiritual activism and, 208. *See also* nepantlera(s)

musa bruja, 32, 34, 49–50, 62, 256

mushrooms, 21, 310–11n7

music, 58, 122

mysticism, 183

mythology, 54, 120, 310n6 (chap. 1)

myth(s), 32, 40; el cenote and, 98; Mesoamerican, 159. *See also* Coatlicue; Coyolxauhqui; Medusa

nagual, 17; Anzaldúa's, 19, 48, 149, 150. *See also* daimon/daemon; la naguala

naguala, 12, 149–55, 263; el cenote and, 100, 101; conocimiento and, 116; la facultad and, 135, 136; El Mundo Zurdo and, 147; nepantla and, 163; nepantlera and, 170; new mestiza and, 177

nagualismo: Aztec, 53, 150–51; nepantla and, 161, 163

nationalism, 95, 96, 140, 169; Chicanx, 192; desconocimiento(s) and, 130; geographies of selves and, 141; new tribalism and, 188, 189

National Women's Studies Association (NWSA), 167, 169

nature, 43, 55, 100, 153, 205, 313n45. *See also* animism; beyond-human world

near-death experiences, 24, 50

Neil, Caren, 310n7 (intro.)

nepantla, 3, 78, 99, 155–64, 260, 264; borders and, 91; el cenote and, 101; Coatlicue state and, 102, 106, 107; Coyolxauhqui process and, 123; creativity and, 73, 262; development of, 39, 41, 294–95, 298; geographies of selves and, 140; mind, 41; El Mundo Zurdo and, 147; la naguala and, 154; new mestiza and, 177; new mestiza consciousness and, 185, 186, 187; new tribalism and, 194; nos/otras and, 201; origin of, 33, 37–38; as shift from borderlands, 93, 94–95; spiritual activism and, 208; spirit world and, 93; states, 43. *See also* conocimiento; nepantlera(s)

"En Nepantla" (Anzaldúa), 155, 246

nepantla body, 158, 160, 163, 164

nepantla brain, 41, 158, 160, 164

nepantlera(s), 16, 71, 165–71, 264; borderlands and, 95; el cenote and, 101; Coyolxauhqui process and, 123; conocimiento and, 116; la facultad and, 133; geographies of selves and, 140; El Mundo Zurdo and, 143, 147; la naguala and, 154; nepantla and, 158, 163; new mestiza and, 177; new mestiza consciousness and, 185, 186, 187; new tribalism and, 193, 194; nos/otras and, 201; in spiritual activism, 204–5, 207–8, 209. *See also* la facultad

Nettie Lee Benson Latin American Collection, 11, 213. *See also* Gloria Evangelina Anzaldúa Papers

New Age: movement, 145; spiritualities, 204

new mestiza, 3, 171–79, 263; borderlands and, 95; geographies of selves and, 140; nepantlera and, 170; new tribalism and, 188, 194. *See also* new mestiza consciousness

new mestiza consciousness, 3, 38, 70, 78, 179–87, 306–7; alternative to rational thought, 71; borderlands and, 95; Coatlicue state and, 106; Coyolxauhqui process and, 123; la facultad and, 134, 135; geographies of selves and, 137–38; nepantla and, 156, 158, 185; nepantlera and, 170; new mestiza and, 177; new tribalism and, 194; nos/otras and, 199; spiritual activism and, 208, 209. *See also* conocimiento; mestizaje

"New Mestiza Nation" (Anzaldúa), 172–73, 263

new tribalism, 4, 71, 187–95, 196, 200; conocimiento and, 111, 116, 242; desconocimiento(s) and, 130; geographies of selves

queer theory, 25, 28, 115; Anzaldúa's contributions, 2, 235–36, 252, 296. *See also* El Mundo Zurdo; queer conocimiento

race, 1, 25, 48, 94, 143, 177; nepantla and, 157; nepantlera and, 165; new mestiza, 172; new mestiza consciousness and, 182. *See also* mestizaje

racism, 104, 169, 183; autohistoria and, 85–86; conocimiento and, 242; desconocimiento(s) and, 127, 129; in Texas, 20; in universities, 30

racism/sexism, 310n4

rational thought, 57, 69, 84, 179–80, 304; el cenote and, 98, 99; la facultad and, 132; nepantla and, 157. *See also* epistemology

Raza, 140, 170

reader(s), 52; Anzaldúa's, 2–3, 6–7, 12, 34, 60–61, 315n13; as co-creators, 302–3, 305; theory creation and, 73–74. *See also* Anzaldúa, Gloria

reality, 22–23, 42–43; multidimensional, 150, 152, 165; nonordinary, 98, 108–9, 132–33, 147; theory and, 67. *See also* consensual reality

religion, 18–19, 25; difference from spiritual activism, 204; in identity, 177; in mestisaje, 174

representation, 31, 33, 88; autohistoria/autohistoria-teoría and, 84, 85, 88; individual/collective, 50, 68; literary, 84, 87

resilience, 205, 207, 292

respect, 56, 306–7

Reti, Irene, 313n34, 313n41

Reuman, Ann, 176

revisionist mythmaking, 105, 235, 247–48; defined, 312n26

revision process, Anzaldúa's, 52, 53–54, 315n9, 315n15. *See also* writing

Rich, Adrienne, 139, 140

Rieff, David, 192

risking the personal, 4–7, 8; la naguala and, 150

ritual, 42, 70, 306, 310n3, 310–11n7; el cenote and, 97, 98; transformation, 158; writing, 58–59, 79, 122

Roberts, Jane, 311n8

Rudhyar, Dane, 134, 135

Sabian symbols, 55–56

sacrifice(s), 121–22; el cenote and, 98, 101; desconocimiento(s), 126; human, 27. *See also* Coyolxauhqui; writing

Said, Edward, 315n1

Saldívar, José Davíd, 233–34, 258

Salsa Soul Sisters, 274

Sandoval, Chela, 184, 185

Sankofa, 10–11

Santa Cruz, 26, 28, 45. *See also* Anzaldúa, Gloria

"seeing through," 102, 111–12, 132; spiritual activism and, 203–4. *See also* naguala

self-care: Anzaldúa's, 35; and spiritual activism, 205, 207

self-inquiry, 23, 207, 252–53

self-reflection, 23, 252–53, 306; in autohistoria/autohistoria-teoría, 83–84; el cenote and, 98; as method, 42; la naguala and, 152; new tribalism and, 190–91; spiritual activism and, 204; writing notas and, 37

separatism, 188; desconocimientos and, 128. *See also* new tribalism

sexism, 25, 140, 183; conocimiento and, 242; desconocimiento(s) and, 127. *See also* oppression

sexuality, 74; and knowledge production; and spirituality, 235. *See also* identity

shadow beast, 86. *See also* Coatlicue state; desconocimiento(s)

shadow work, 27, 32, 42, 286; in the Coatlicue state, 103; conocimiento and, 114; desconocimientos and, 127; Jungian, 98–99, 129; new tribalism and, 190; spiritual activism and, 204; in writing notas, 37

shamanic journey(s), 84, 105; la facultad and, 134

shamanism, 53, 150–51, 174, 292; el cenote and, 100. *See also* Coyolxauhqui process

shame, 104, 105

shape-shifting. *See* nagualismo; shamanism

shifting, 38. *See also* transformation

"SIC: Spiritual Identity Crisis" (Anzaldúa), 34, 249, 268, 288–89

situational engines, 45, 69, 306–7

sixth sense, 132

social change, 182; and Anzaldúa, 18, 19, 20; el cenote and, 100; El Mundo Zurdo and,

148; new mestiza and, 175; spiritual activism and, 203, 204–5, 206, 207; writing and, 48

social justice, 284; movements, 22, 145. *See also* conocimiento; social change

Society for the Study of Gloria Anzaldúa, 2

Sonoma State University, 162, 169, 289

soul, 24, 149, 162, 203; la facultad and, 133; la naguala and, 150; spiritual activism and, 203–4, 206. *See also* spirit(s); susto(s)

space, 33, 223, 289; as topic for theory, 73. *See also* nepantla

Spafford, Roz, 223

Sparks, David Hatfield, 146, 206, 236, 292

Sparks, Mariya, 206, 292

speaking engagements, 2, 26, 35–36, 243–44, 268, 284, 289, 311n15; and theory-creation, 72

"Speaking in Tongues" (Anzaldúa), 47, 52, 167, 210, 275, 290

speculative realism, 88

spirit(s), 3, 17, 130, 149–50, 205, 305–6; spiritual activism and, 203–4, 206; theory-creation and, 69. *See also* nepantla; spiritual activism; spirituality; tree(s)

spiritual activism, 3, 7, 100, 143, 203–10, 274, 306, 311n13; el cenote and, 100; conocimiento and, 109–10, 115, 116–17, 261; Coyolxauhqui process and, 123; creativity and, 73; development of, 41, 72, 228, 246–47, 287–88, 291–92; and ethics, 80; and El Mundo Zurdo, 146, 147, 148; nepantla and, 156, 161; nepantleras and, 165, 170; nos/otras and, 201; transformation, 25

spiritual bypassing, 27, 204; defined, 311n17

spirituality, 40, 121, 153, 291; embodiment, 44, 288–89; identity, 25, 251; nepantla and, 162, 165; politics and, 27, 204, 279. *See also* spiritual activism

spiritual technologies, 27, 146, 229, 277, 292, 306; defined, 317n19; in spiritual activism, 204–5, 207; in writing, 56. *See also* I Ching; meditation; Tarot

status-quo stories, 142, 157–58, 166; defined, 71, 315n1

Stone, Merlin, 24, 279

storytelling, 32. *See also* autohistoria/autohistoria-teoría

stress, 29–30, 33–35, 50, 126, 133; desconocimiento(s) and, 126; spiritual activism and, 203, 206

subjectivity, 71, 254; Chicana, 238; and writing notas, 37. *See also* identity

supernatural, 156–57. *See also* paranormal

survival: Anzaldúa's, 17; and la facultad, 132; and theory, 67

susto(s), 118, 187–88, 190; and Coyolxauhqui process, 118

synchronicity, 57

Taoism, 174

Tarot, 11, 26, 55–56, 146–47, 214, 317n19

testimonio, 89, 316n4 (chap. 4)

Texas, 16–17; public school system, 19–20. *See also* Anzaldúa, Gloria; *Borderlands/La Frontera*

theory: academic ("high theory"), 8, 30, 64–66, 73, 203, 293, 315n1; Anzaldúan, 4, 9–10, 12, 65, 71, 79, 80; as democratic and ordinary, 65; postcolonial, 197, 198, 202; postmodernist, 32; poststructuralist, 284; psychoanalytic, 32, 106, 176, 248, 265, 295; and transformation, 31; women of colors and, 66, 293, 315n2; writing process and, 69. *See also individual theories*

This Bridge Called My Back, 43, 145, 146; El Mundo Zurdo and, 73, 147; origins, 24–25, 26, 41, 279, 311n12; third edition, 56, 167

this bridge we call home, 41–42, 49, 128–29, 167, 215, 314n46; El Mundo Zurdo and, 147; new tribalism and, 193; spiritual activism and, 207–8

Thompson, Becky, 310n5, 311n16

transformation, 37, 41, 245; Anzaldúan theory and, 65; la facultad and, 136; identity and, 188; metaphysical, 21; nepantla and, 160; obstacles, 42; as topic for theory, 73; writing and, 283. *See also* conocimiento; nepantla; spiritual activism

transnationalism, 140

transpersonal psychology, 42

trauma(s), 106; autohistoria/autohistoria-teoría and, 85–86; Coyolxauhqui process and, 118, 124

tree(s), 10, 17, 23, 57, 190–91

"Tres lenguas del fuego" (Anzaldúa), 216, 297

Trojan burra(s), 241, 297
Turner, Victor, 245

unconscious, 56–57; el cenote and, 97, 98; la
naguala and, 149, 154. *See also* psyche
Unihipili, 55, 149
University of California, Santa Cruz (UCSC),
26, 28, 64–65, 197, 217
University of Texas, Austin (UTA), 11, 20–21,
144, 217, 294
"(un)natural bridges" (Anzaldúa), 43, 53, 282,
315n10

vastation, 22, 311n9
vibrations, 22, 205
Villa Montalvo Workshop, 72, 113, 160, 167,
168, 262
violence, 34, 132; intellectual, 66, 128
Violet, Indigo, 310n6 (intro.), 312n23
Virgen de Guadalupe, 58, 174
visionary pragmatism, 312n24
visualization(s), 55, 262, 277, 317n19
Vivancos-Peréz, Ricardo, 226, 312n21

Walker, Alice, 184
Warland, Betsy, 296
watcher, the, 100, 151
water, 10, 46, 121, 254. *See also* el cenote
waystation(s), 103, 139, 158, 254, 265
Weiland, Christine, 121, 132, 310n2, 317n1
(chap. 5)
well, 99, 101
Welwood, John, 311n17
West Cliff Drive (Santa Cruz), 28
Wilson, Colin, 310n6 (chap. 1)
Wilson, Liliana, 313n37
wisdom, embodied, 59

women of colors, 25, 293, 312n23; and
academic experiences, 233, 241, 264,
314nn1–3; artists, 280; authors, 243;
defined, 310n6 (intro.); literature, 244;
theorists, 28. *See also* Chicanx
women's and gender studies, 2, 36. *See also*
National Women's Studies Association
world-traveling, 160, 169, 292, 306
wounding, 39
writing, 8, 48; as activism, 112; blocks, 34,
103, 105, 274; Coyolxauhqui and, 122; as
knowledge production, 51; as making soul,
49; la naguala and, 151; nepantla and, 160,
161; as ontological, 31; organic, 58; as participatory, 48, 303–4; as political, 17, 61;
prompts, 277; as vocation, 46–47. *See also*
Anzaldúa, Gloria; el cenote; Coyolxauhqui
process
writing comadres, 41, 44, 52, 53, 61–62;
defined, 51. *See also* writing process
writing notas, 4, 47–48, 56, 63, 298, 313n36;
defined, 309n3; development of, 37; and
spiritual activism, 209
writing process, 273; Anzaldúa's, 48, 52–53,
128, 215, 219, 244, 274, 280–81, 283, 284,
285; desconocimientos, 127; drafting
phase, 59–62; la facultad and, 134, 135; la
naguala and, 153, 154; nepantla and, 162;
pre-drafts, 58–59, 207; revision phase,
61–62; spirituality and, 252; writing notas,
19. *See also* Coatlicue state; daimon/dae-
mon; freewrite(s); la naguala
writing workshops, 24, 61, 146

yoga, 26, 174
"yoga of the body," 117
Yucatán, 97